The People's President

The People's President

THE ELECTORAL COLLEGE IN AMERICAN HISTORY AND THE DIRECT VOTE ALTERNATIVE

Revised edition

Neal R. Peirce and Lawrence D. Longley

New Haven and London
Yale University Press

Published with assistance from the foundation
established in memory of Amasa Stone Mather
of the Class of 1907, Yale College.

Designed by Nancy Ovedovitz
and set in VIP Optima type.
Printed in the United States of America by
Murray Printing Company, Westford, Massachusetts.

Library of Congress Cataloging in Publication Data
Peirce, Neal R
The people's President.

Bibliography: p.
Includes index.
1. Presidents—United States—Election. I. Longley,
Lawrence D., joint author. II. Title.
JK529.P4 1981   324.6'3'0973   80-24260
ISBN 0-300-02612-9

LK 11-2-84

10   9   8   7   6   5   4   3   2   1

Contents

Preface

Some years ago, political columnist and sage Arthur Krock wrote, "the road to reform in the method of choosing the Presidents and Vice Presidents of the United States is littered with the wrecks of previous attempts."

The cause of electoral reform has always suffered from two handicaps—the unwillingness of reformers to agree on a single system and the insistence of some on reforming the system for their own partisan advantage.

Immutable laws seem to dictate that partisan motivation will always rear its head; it cannot be banished, though with luck it may be controlled. But the time may be ripe in American history to put aside the various halfway proposals for reform of the electoral college—all to be described later in this book—in favor of a simple direct vote of the people for their chief executive.

The history of past reform attempts, Tom Wicker suggested in a foreword to the first edition of this book in 1968, is a chronicle of one proposed reform after another gaining some popular favor but being defeated for lack of sufficient support. "One by one, the district system, proportional electoral votes, automatic electors, have come out of the pack like challenging horses only to fall back on the homestretch." Wicker suggested, however, that with the formidable support the direct vote had received in the late 1960s, it might have a better chance than earlier reform efforts:

> The time of this particular idea has come. Can it any longer be pretended that this great people needs the electors to choose wisely for it? Of course not. Yet that was the original theory. The President is the only American official who represents the American people entire—the whole constituency, every one of us, from Maine to California, Dixiecrat and New Left, white and black, man and woman—and what real reason is there that we should not vote directly for him and have our votes counted directly for him? We may be 50 states in Congress but we are one people in the White House—or should be—and the President ought to be ours to choose.

These arguments were not without their effect in the strong push after the 1968 election to abolish the electoral college and institute the direct vote. The 1968 election featured a near-reversal in the electoral college of the popular vote and a blatant attempt, by independent presidential candidate George Wallace, to prevent any majority in the electoral vote, so that he might play the role of bargainer-kingmaker. Indeed, a constitutional amendment providing for direct election of the president was adopted by the House of Representatives in 1969 by an overwhelming vote of 338–70. It enjoyed enormous support from diverse groups in the society, from the organized bar and conservative business circles to many liberal-leaning labor and good government groups. But it was narrowly defeated in the Senate in 1970, not by a substantive vote on its merits but by an undeclared yet effective filibuster.

A decade later, in 1979, yet another, and ultimately unsuccessful, attempt was made by congressional sponsors to win approval of the direct vote amendment. Senator Birch Bayh of Indiana again proved himself a worthy inheritor of the mantle of reform, passed down since the first decades of the republic from men who have labored tirelessly for true reform of our presidential election system without regard to personal or partisan advantage. In his efforts, Bayh built upon the work of such senators as Thomas Hart Benton of Missouri and Oliver P. Morton of Indiana in the past century and Henry Cabot Lodge of Massachusetts and Estes Kefauver of Tennessee in ours. The final vindication of these efforts will come one day in a simple, undiluted, unencumbered vote of the American people for their president. The only question is whether the nation must first undergo a cruel crisis, undermining popular faith in the Constitution and our system of government, before this eminently fair and logical reform is instituted.

For their advice and counsel in the preparation of the original edition of this book (written by Neal Peirce alone), a special debt of thanks is expressed to collaborator-advisers James C. Kirby, Jr., John D. Feerick, Robert G. Dixon, Jr., Charles W. Bischoff, and Roan Conrad.

The revised edition has benefited greatly from the analysis and reflections of Alan G. Braun and John H. Yunker, who were responsible for valuable research on which we drew heavily. We are also indebted for assistance and counsel to Professor William Crotty of Northwestern University, Professor Richard G. Smolka of American University, Warren Mitofsky of CBS News, and Nels Ackerson and his colleagues of the staff of the U.S. Senate Subcommittee on the Constitution. Special appreciation is due Marian Ash of the Yale University Press for her encouragement and intelligence regarding the revision. Above all, our wives, Barbara and Judith, provided greatly appreciated encouragement and support, both to the project and to their husbands, throughout our labors. We thank them.

Washington, D.C.   Neal R. Peirce
Appleton, Wisconsin   Lawrence D. Longley

The People's President

ELECTION NIGHT, NOVEMBER 4, 1980

It is the quintessence of what Americans call a "landslide" election, an echo of years like 1932 and 1936 (Franklin D. Roosevelt's greatest triumphs), 1952 and 1956 (Dwight D. Eisenhower's massive wins), and 1972 (the reelection of Richard M. Nixon over a Democratic opposition in total disarray).

Although most published national opinion surveys have suggested a 1980 election "too close to call" between Republican challenger Ronald Reagan and incumbent President Jimmy Carter, the suspense in the contest has drained away by late afternoon. "Exit polls" of voters leaving the polls across the nation, conducted by the CBS, NBC, and ABC television networks, are already showing a huge Reagan lead. As NBC signs on with its election night coverage at 7 P.M. (E.S.T.), commentator John Chancellor confidently predicts "Ronald Reagan will win a very substantial victory tonight, very substantial." And he is right. Over the course of the next hour, television election maps become awash in "Reagan blue" as state after state is called for the Republican.

Just an hour and a quarter into its election night programming, NBC at 8:15:21 (E.S.T.) flashes REAGAN WINS on the nation's screens, followed by ABC at 9:52 and CBS at 10:33. President Carter himself appears before his election workers (and the nation's television viewers) to concede the election before 10 P.M.—indeed hours before the polls have closed in the West. The shortest election night of the television era is over. The final returns will show Reagan winning 51 percent of the popular vote, Carter 41 percent, and independent candidate John B. Anderson 7 percent. In electoral votes, it will be an overwhelming 489 votes for Reagan, only 49 for Carter.

But the history of U.S. elections demonstrates clearly that it is not always so easy, that the electoral college which performs with so much apparent smoothness in a decisive election is a faltering and potentially dangerous mechanism when the contest is close.

Indeed, in the election immediately preceding the 1980 landslide, the United States had experienced a contest underscoring the system's vagaries and unreliability.

ELECTION NIGHT, NOVEMBER 2, 1976

Its polling completed, a curious nation waits to see whether Jimmy Carter will become president or whether Gerald Ford, who succeeded Richard Nixon to the nation's highest post, will be able to retain the job he first won by luck of appointment to the vice presidency. In most Americans' minds, the real race is in the popular votes. Since early evening, Carter has led by a rather comfortable margin; when the final returns are reported a few weeks later, the election night trend will be confirmed, and Jimmy Carter will enjoy a popular vote margin of 1,683,040 votes. It is not a stupendous plurality; in fact it is a pale shadow of the margin for Carter suggested in polls just after the two parties' nominating conventions. But it is an unambiguous, clear, unchallengeable margin. The people have spoken. Jimmy Carter is to be their next president.

But will he? Even as November 2 fades at midnight into November 3 on the East Coast, a sliver of doubt lingers in the minds of the professional politicians, the political aficionados, the political journalists. Regardless of that substantial popular vote margin, they know there is still a doubt, perhaps mostly theoretical but still not to be entirely dismissed, that Jimmy Carter will become president. The reason, of course, is that hoary eighteenth-century institution still chugging into the last quarter of the twentieth: the electoral college. In any close election, there is a chance the electoral college may choose a candidate the people have rejected. In this election, Carter's heavy vote is in his native South; his popular vote is not well distributed throughout other regions. Indeed, political commentators have already reported on the possibility of a 1976 misfire. Among them was one of the coauthors of this book, who wrote in a syndicated column on October 10, 1976: "the nation may face the greatest threat in this century that the antiquated electoral college system will elect the President who lost the popular vote." According to Peirce, campaign strategists on both sides were aware "that Jimmy Carter, bolstered by strong majorities in his native South, could lead by as much as 1.0 to 2.5 million votes in the national popular vote, but still lose in the electoral college because of narrow margins for President Ford in big Northern states with heavy electoral vote blocs."

The scorekeepers everyone is watching as this election night rolls along are a group of totally self-appointed persons, occupying positions beyond the farthest stretch of the imagination when the electoral college was first conceived. They are the staffs of the three national television networks, each with millions of dollars invested in the election coverage, reporting from their studios in New York City. An army of thousands of poll watchers has been phoning in election returns from selected precincts across the nation, permitting the networks to declare on the basis of clear trends from representative voting areas, even when the computed vote is quite incomplete, just which candidate will carry each state. They use complex formulas involving several cross-checking computations to decide whether a state can be "called" for one candidate or the other. There have been known instances of "goofs"—when a network has called a state and then had to withdraw its projection. But these cases are rare. And it is virtually unthinkable that a network would risk calling the entire presidential election for a candidate without being convinced, beyond reasonable doubt, that it was right.

At midnight, Carter is comfortably ahead in every network's electoral vote calls. If one is watching CBS News, Carter's score over Ford is 208–62. NBC viewers see a 156–76 score, those viewing ABC 224–113. Carter has won his electoral vote lead by sweeping most of the South and New England and winning a good share of the Mid-Atlantic regions plus Minnesota and Wisconsin. Two of the three networks have already credited Pennsylvania, with a hefty 27-vote bloc of electoral votes, to Carter; as early as 9:31 P.M., taking a flyer on the basis of what must have been quite fragmentary reports, ABC has credited New York, with its 41 electoral votes, to Carter.

But at midnight it is still not impossible to construct a scenario for a Ford win. CBS and NBC still consider New York too close to call; Ford has won Connecticut, Vermont, and New Hampshire and seems on his way to winning the lion's share of the Midwest and virtually all of the Mountain West. If the Pacific Coast and a handful of doubtful southern states all went for him, Ford might still be elected, Carter's popular vote plurality notwithstanding.

Within 43 minutes after midnight, Carter has added New York to his total in both the CBS and NBC projections. CBS also credits Carter with Missouri (12 electoral votes) and Oregon (6 votes) in the hour after midnight, for a total of 267—only 3 votes short of the 270 required for election. But then, for almost two hours—until 2:58 A.M.—Carter remains frozen at 267 in the CBS count. And it is not a firm 267: at 2:58 CBS rescinds its Oregon call, bringing Carter back down to 261 electoral votes. At the same hour NBC decides that Hawaii will be a Carter state (the Hawaiian call has taken so long because none of the networks had thought it worthwhile to establish sample precincts in the island state, so they had only raw vote returns to go on). At 3:28 A.M. CBS also decides to call Hawaii for Carter; now both CBS and NBC counts stand at 265 Carter electoral votes—5 short of the magic number.

In earlier decades, there would have been no doubt about the vote of Mississippi: for a century it had been one of the states in which the Democratic nomination was tantamount to election. But now, hours after the closing of the last polls, Mississippi has moved to center stage. It is the only uncertain state at that moment that (1) clearly leans toward Carter, and (2) has enough electoral votes (7) to put him over the top. ABC had called Mississippi for Carter at 1:37 A.M., but both CBS and NBC are extremely leary—and with good reason. For one thing, the vote is reported as exceptionally close. Secondly, Mississippi election law incorporates a provision one could well consider a relic in modern America—separate votes for the individual candidates for elector. (The only other states with similar provisions are Louisiana and South Carolina.) This feature means that in a close race it would be possible for the elector slate to split, some electors of one party being elected, some of another. The News Election Service, which the networks and wire services depend on for raw vote returns, is counting in Mississippi only the vote for the frontrunning Carter and Ford elector candidates, county by county. There is no way to look behind these returns to determine whether there is a major differential in the vote for various electors.

Finally, at 3:31 A.M., NBC decides to call Mississippi's 7 electoral votes for Carter. With that, the Carter vote is 2 over the 270 required for election, and the network declares him president-elect. ABC moves simultaneously to make a late call of Hawaii, also putting Carter over the top with 272 electoral votes. And fifteen minutes later, finally convinced of the soundness of the Mississippi returns, CBS follows suit. Most of America has already gone to sleep. Yet it is only now, hours after Carter's popular vote lead had been unequivocally established, that the networks dare confirm that the electoral college will follow the lead of the people.

And in fact 1976 went down in the history books as another election in which the college barely did its work. After most TV sets had gone dark, enough returns came in to confirm that several more states—California, Alaska, Maine, Illinois, Oregon, and South Dakota—had gone for Ford. Days later, it was confirmed that Carter had won Ohio by a razor-thin margin of 11,116 votes out of 4,111,873 cast. The final electoral vote count was 297 for Carter, 241 for Ford (actually reduced to 240 because of one "faithless" Ford elector in Washington state). Had an exceedingly small number of votes shifted from Carter to Ford—5,559 in Ohio, 3,687 in Hawaii—Ford would have had 270 electoral votes to Carter's 268 and won the election. But if the same faithless elector had then withheld his support from Ford, the Ford total would have been only 269—one fewer than the constitutionally required majority of the 538-member electoral college.[1] The issue would finally have been decided either in informal bargaining among or breaking of pledges by electors or, in a cumbersome contingent election procedure, by the U.S. House of Representatives. But at what cost to the stability of the American government and the legitimacy of the presidency, no one can know.

OUR ODD ELECTION MACHINERY

What is this odd election machinery, this strange method of choosing a president we call the "electoral college?"[2] In the annals of American history, one can find few outright supporters. An early analyst of the system called it "an abortive organism."[3] A latter-day political scientist depicts it as "a hoary and outworn relic of the stagecoach era."[4] One of the founding fathers believed it "the most pleasing feature of the Constitution,"[5] but only a few years later, one of the great reform advocates of the nineteenth century—Senator Thomas Hart Benton of Missouri—declared the system's operation "wholly incompatible with the safety of the people."[6] In our own times, the Supreme Court has declared that "the conception of political equality" behind the electoral college "belongs to a bygone day,"[7] and a blue-ribbon study commission of the American Bar Association characterized the electoral college method of electing the president as "archaic, undemocratic, complex, ambiguous, indirect, and dangerous."[8]

The electoral college is a double-election system for the American presidency. Instead of voting directly for their president, Americans vote for presidential "electors" equal in number to the representatives each state has in Congress plus each state's two senators. The winning slate of electors in each state—Republican or Democratic—meets in the state capitol the first Monday after the second Wednesday of December in a presidential election year to cast its votes. The results are forwarded to Washington, where they are opened in the joint session of Congress on January 6. If a candidate has a majority of the votes, he is declared elected. If there is no majority, the choice is thrown into the House of Representatives, where each state has a single vote. If there is no majority for vice president, the Senate makes that choice.

Once the people have selected the electors, they have nothing further to say about the election of the president. Three times in the last century—1824, 1876, and 1888—their will was frustrated, and the man who lost in the national popular vote was elevated to the presidency. Five times in this century—1916, 1948, 1960, 1968, and 1976—we came perilously close to another miscarriage of the popular will. Despite these experiences, we continue to rely, in the words of a foremost constitutional scholar, "on the intervention of that Providence which is said to have fools and the American people in its special care."[9]

But as illogical as the electoral college may appear for the United States in the second half of the twentieth century, it *did* seem to make sense in 1787 when the founding fathers devised it at the Constitutional Convention in Philadelphia. Consider the differences between the country for which the Constitution was written and the America we know today.[10]

Then, the nation—if one could call it that—consisted of thirteen contentious semisovereign states spread thinly along 1,300 miles of the eastern seaboard, from Massachusetts and its province of Maine in the north to Georgia in the south. *Now*, the federal union comprises fifty states, spanning the breadth of an entire continent and reaching into the Pacific to encompass Hawaii and Alaska.

Then, our frontier extended scarcely beyond the Appalachian Mountains; Pittsburgh was little more than a military post; Kentucky, just receiving its first great wave of migration; Cincinnati, a tiny village. Beyond these outposts there was little more than wilderness and solitude; no white man had yet beheld the source of the Mississippi River, and only a few men had seen the great western plains. *Now,* our continental frontiers long since tamed, outer space is the only physical frontier that remains before us.

Then, communications and travel were torturously slow throughout the land; Philadelphia was two or three days by stagecoach from New York; from Boston to Philadelphia the traveler was obliged to disembark and ride crude ferries across no less than seven rivers and could well spend ten days on the road, dusty in summer, mired with ruts in spring, limited to twenty-five miles in a day by winter's snows. The postal service was slow and unsure; the nation's eighty newspapers, avidly read in every hamlet they reached, were the strongest link between the people and their nation. *Now,* jet air transportation has reduced travel time to a few hours between virtually any two points in the United States. We have an unparalleled system of rail, air, and road transport; we complain when the mail takes more than a couple of days, even between distant points; our newspapers, television, and telephones form constant, almost instantaneous communications links between our people.

Then, we were an almost exclusively rural nation: 95 percent of the people lived independently on isolated farms or in villages of less than 2,500 persons, and eight in ten Americans took their living from the land. "At this time," wrote a not untypical farmer in 1787, "my farm gave me and my whole family a good living on the produce of it, and left me, one year with another, 150 silver dollars, for I never spent more than ten dollars a year, which was for salt, nails and the like. Nothing to wear, eat or drink was purchased, as my farm provided all."[11] *Now,* roughly three-quarters of our people live in great cities or towns of 2,500 or more. Six American cities have more than a million inhabitants; thirty-seven metropolitan areas have passed the million mark. Our economy is totally interdependent.

Then, the land could boast but a handful of colleges, and public schooling was haphazard at best. In New York and Pennsylvania a schoolhouse was never seen outside a village or town; in New England the little red schoolhouses were open but two months in winter for boys and two months in summer for girls. Illiteracy was a critical problem, especially on the frontier. *Now,* free public education carries most American children through high school, we have a great network of universities, and illiteracy has been practically stamped out. The American electorate is immeasurably better informed than in the first years of the republic.

Then, a clear class structure was apparent in America—less rigid than Europe's but still evident. It ranged from the distinct aristocracy of education and wealth from which the Constitution's framers sprang—landowners, merchants, lawyers—down through the great group known as the "middling sort" (farmers, shopkeepers, independent artisans)—to a "meaner sort" of laborers, servants, and hardscrabble farmers. And below all these, there were indentured servants and more than 600,000 black slaves. *Now,* we still find extremes of wealth and poverty, but the great mass of Americans form a dominant middle class in a land of pervasive affluence and extraordinary social mobility. Slavery is a century gone, though its scars remain.

Then, a myriad of property and tax qualifications imposed severe limitations on the right to vote. *Now*, we are approaching universal adult suffrage.

Then, the president of the United States was once removed from the people of the land; men's primary loyalty was still expected to remain with their states. The federal government was not expected to play a major role in taxation, education, or economic affairs of most immediate import to the people; a national communications system did not exist; the franchise was limited; we still lacked a party system to popularize American leaders. *Now*, the president is no longer removed but immediate—on our television screens, on the front page of every daily newspaper, in our consciousnesses because we relate to him directly, not as New Yorkers or Nevadans, Vermonters, or Oregonians but as Americans. As we do a member of the family, we may like him or dislike him, we may praise him or curse him, we may support him or oppose him. But when all is said and done, he *is* our president until the next quadrennial election.

If we would measure further the president's importance to us, we need only review the manifold functions he fulfills in modern American society. No one has summarized it better than the American historian Clinton Rossiter, who pointed to no less than ten major roles of the president:

He is *chief of state*, a "one man distillation of the American people just as surely as the Queen is of the British people."

He is *chief executive*, manager of the gigantic federal apparatus, with powers of appointment and removal and charged with the duty of seeing that the laws "be faithfully executed."

He is *commander in chief* of our military forces.

He is *chief diplomat*, with paramount responsibility for conducting the nation's foreign affairs.

He is *chief legislator*, proposing laws to Congress and devising the strategy to get them passed.

He is *chief of party*, the controlling figure behind national political party machinery, the inspirer of his partisans, his party's chief fund raiser.

He is *protector of the peace*, guarding the nation from internal revolt, moving swiftly to help when natural calamity strikes.

He is *leader of a coalition of free nations*, the newest responsibility, resulting from our emergence as the leading power of the Western world in the era since the Second World War.

He is *manager of the prosperity*, responsible under the Employment Act of 1946 and other statutes for maintaining a growing, stable economy.

He is the *voice of the people*, "the leading formulator and expounder of public opinion in the United States."[12]

Out of the Vietnam war era and the Watergate scandal of the early 1970s came a realization that it was altogether possible to accord too much power to a president and that reasonable constitutional limits—on every front from war powers to control of intelligence agencies to ownership of the papers a chief executive assembles in his conduct of official business—were necessary. In Richard Nixon the country was faced with the untenable assertion that a president might act above the law, indeed in violation of it, for "the national interest."

Despite the more circumscribed view of the presidency that emerged from those years, however, the office retained the essence of its national and global power, limited by the Constitution and by bureaucracy and incalcitrant foreign power blocs but still an immense force to be reckoned with. And there remained a belief in the president as a man of all the people, a vision the Englishman John Bright formulated more than a century ago:

We know what an election is in the United States for President of the Republic. . . . Every four years there springs from the vote created by the whole people a President over that great nation. I think the whole world offers no finer spectacle than this; it offers no higher dignity; and there is no greater object of ambition on the political stage on which men are permitted to move. You may point, if you will, to hereditary rulers, to crowns coming down through successive generations of the same family, to thrones based on prescription and conquest, to sceptres wielded over veteran legions and subject realms,—but to my mind there is nothing more worthy of reverence and obedience, and nothing more sacred, than the authority of the freely chosen magistrate of a great and free people; and if there be on earth and amongst men any divine right to govern, surely it rests with a ruler so chosen and so appointed.[13]

Few Americans could have put it better. But we must ask ourselves: to what world does our presidential election system really correspond? Is it adapted to a modern technological society in a politically mature nation, where every American considers the ballot his birthright? Or is it more a vestige of the world of two centuries past, when voting was haphazard, the secret ballot scarcely known, the society disjointed and spread over a vast frontier? Have we adequately assured the sanctity of the franchise of all Americans? In short, have we placed within the body of our Constitution a foolproof system that will give the person whom most of us have chosen to be our president a universally understood, unequivocal mandate to govern and to lead?

As long as the antiquated electoral college system remains imbedded in our basic law, the answer must be "no." In any election the electoral college can misfire, with tragic consequences. It can frustrate the will of the people, sending someone to the White House whom a majority has specifically rejected by its votes on election day. It can cause prolonged chaos and uncertainty by throwing an election into the House of Representatives. A malfunction of this awkward and outdated mechanism could undermine our prestige abroad. Just as serious, it could undermine the confidence of our own citizens in their Constitution and raise serious questions about the sincerity of our democratic ideals. If the system went awry in a time of peace and domestic tranquillity, it would be a monstrous embarrassment to us as a nation. If it misfired in a time of tension, in a time when we were close to open conflict with hostile powers, or when social divisions rent our nation, the consequences could be tragic. It would be foolhardy to expect that the goodwill and understanding of the American people would be so great that such a travesty would be tolerated. The electoral count "winner" could be placed under heavy pressures from press and people alike, to step aside. If he actually took office, his authority could be undercut at any moment by an opposition that honestly believed it had been cheated of the presidency. The nation and the presidency might survive such an ordeal, but we would all be the losers for it.

Throughout history a variety of proposals for electoral college reform has been brought forward. Some would divide the nation into small electoral districts that would vote separately for president. Others would divide each state's electoral vote proportionately, in the hope of a least approximating the popular will. But only one solution has ever been advanced that would assure the election of the person most Americans wanted: a direct popular vote of the people, with no institutional obstacle between them and their choice.

It may seem paradoxical that we assert the desirability of national majoritarian rule in selecting our president at a time when there is greater emphasis on state and local and even neighborhood-based innovation to re-create mutually supportive bonds between people and government at the level at which citizens lead their daily lives, on the capacity of states to act as "laboratories of democracy" as Louis Brandeis admonished, on the rich fabric of variegated federalism and its barriers to "megasolutions" imposed from afar. We suggest that one may support both developments, as we do.

The search for grass-roots community and trust can be thwarted if there is doubt about the legitimacy of the highest levels of government. Thus it is imperative to amend our Constitution to implement the direct vote, so that in fact as well as in theory, in constitutional guarantee as well as by happenstance in the electoral college, the person we choose may truly be the people's president. This is not a new idea; it was advanced first in the Constitutional Convention and then in Congress as early as 1816. When we have finally amended our Constitution to assure direct choice of the president by the people, future generations will surely look back with amused tolerance and wonder whatever took us so long.

2

The Birth of
the Electoral College

The American presidency and the electoral college method of choosing our chief executive were first defined in the federal Constitution, written by the Constitutional Convention, which met in Philadelphia between May 25 and September 17, 1787. The fifty-five delegates from twelve states (Rhode Island refused to participate) had won their liberty—and their first sense of nationhood—in the crucible of revolution. Many had affixed their signatures to the Declaration of Independence with its ringing assertion that governments derive "their just power from the consent of the governed." But the founding fathers were also preoccupied with order and were determined to end the governmental chaos that had reigned under the Articles of Confederation.

This desire for order was nowhere more apparent than in article II of the Constitution, starting with the words: "The executive power shall be vested in a President of the United States of America." The article spells out a wide range of presidential powers: to be commander in chief of the army and navy, to appoint federal officers and require reports of the heads of executive departments, to make treaties, to appoint ambassadors, to report to Congress on the State of the Union, and to "take care that the laws be faithfully executed." Proclaimed in an era when the legislative branches dominated the executive in almost every state, this grant of clear and independent executive authority was almost revolutionary in its impact. But the Constitution's framers took care to guarantee liberty as well, by circumscribing the power of each branch of the new federal government—executive, legislative, and judicial—to prevent a tyrannical exercise of power by any one of them. The delicate system of checks and balances written into the Constitution applied to the president as well as to Congress and the courts. The president could execute the laws but not make them. He could spend the federal government's money, but the specific appropriations would come from Congress. He could appoint federal officials and ambassadors, and he could make treaties, but only with the approval of the Senate.

In the course of our history as a nation, each of the branches of the federal government has come to exercise a degree of power scarcely dreamed of by the founders. There have been times when one of the branches seemed to dominate the others, when presidential power seemed to eclipse that of Congress and the judiciary, or when Congress assumed such a dominant role that the presidency faded in comparison, or when the judiciary made the vital national decisions. But the basic system of checks and balances has operated time and again to preserve this "balanced Constitution" and to make it safe and viable for a nation bearing little resemblance to the eighteenth-century union of newborn states.

More than a quarter of the Constitution's article on the presidency is occupied with spelling out the complex mode by which he is to be chosen. From start to finish, the Convention had great difficulty agreeing on this. Delegate James Wilson of Pennsylvania commented on the convention floor on September 4: "This subject has greatly divided the house and will also divide the people out of doors. It is in truth the most difficult on which we have to decide."[1]

BASIC ISSUES

One reason that the convention encountered such difficulty was that no plan could be considered neatly on its own merits. A host of tangential issues, some of them crucial to the basic nature of the Constitution, presented themselves at every turn. The result, as one commentator put it, was to transform the debates into something resembling a game of "three-dimensional chess."[2]

The Scope of Executive Power

How much authority would it be desirable—or safe—to lodge in the executive branch of a strengthened federal union? Should the national executive be one person or many? Should the executive be subservient to the legislative branch or equal in power to it? These questions were unsettled in the minds of most of the delegates when they arrived in Philadelphia.

Under British rule, the citizens of the colonies utilized every means to wring concessions from the executive authority, then embodied in each colony's royal governor. The legislatures provided the best means the colonials had to advance their own interests, and they used the opportunity to the fullest extent possible. When the revolution came and the control of the British crown evaporated, most states shifted to the state legislatures the power the royal governors had exercised. As the newly independent states drafted their charters of government, they placed stringent limitations on the power of their executives. Governors were generally chosen by the legislatures rather than the people, were elected for terms of just a single year (except for two years in South Carolina and three years in Delaware), and were hemmed in by executive councils that shared their power. Governor Edmund Randolph of Virginia said in 1786 that he was only "a member of the executive."[3] Most Americans seemed to share the sentiments of Tom Paine that the executive was "either a political superfluity or a chaos of unknown things" and should be "considered in [no] other light than as inferior to the legislative."[4]

Yet, by the time the Constitutional Convention was called, the shortcomings of exclusive legislative rule were becoming painfully apparent. Many legislative enactments were arbitrary or proscriptive in character, and the legislatures proved impotent or unwilling to deal with the financial crises that came in the wake of the revolution, culminating in the debtors' revolt under Daniel Shays in Massachusetts in the autumn of 1786. Viewing the radical uprising in the Bay State, James Madison wrote of the rebels: "They profess to aim only at a reform of their Constitution, and of certain abuses in public administration; but an abolition of debts, public and private, and new division of property, are strongly suspected to be in contemplation."[5] The delegates gathering at Philadelphia were acutely aware of the need for some stronger executive authority to protect the interests of property and order. As Madison himself would comment on the convention floor: "Experience has proved a tendency in our governments to throw all power into the legislative vortex. The executives of the states are in general little more than cyphers; the legislatures omnipotent. If no effective check can be devised for restraining the instability and encroachment of the [legislatures], a revolution of some kind or other would be inevitable."[6]

The nation's experience under the Articles of Confederation, which provided for no executive department whatever and rested on the principle of equal voting power for all states, large or small, had tended to confirm the delegates' misgivings about leaving all authority in the hands of a legislature. Under the Articles, Congress had shown serious inability to deal with crucial issues like taxation, western lands, the regulation of commerce, paper money, and Indian affairs. The problem was not only in getting effective legislation passed but in implementing it once it was approved. With no executive to entrust with implementation of laws, the Congress itself had to attempt the job. "Nothing is so embarrassing as the details of execution," Thomas Jefferson wrote. "The smallest trifle of that kind occupies as long as the most important action of legislation, and takes place of everything else. . . . The most important propositions hang over from week to week and month to month, till the occasion have past them and the thing never done." Jefferson said he hoped the Constitutional Convention would take care to separate the executive and legislative powers.[7]

Thus, many delegates to the Philadelphia convention began their deliberations predisposed to the idea that the nation needed a strong, albeit safe, executive power. As a model, they could look to the constitution New York State had adopted in 1777, which provided for a popularly elected governor in whom was vested "the supreme power and authority of the state." The New York governor was freed from the burden of a privy council, enjoyed powers of convening and adjourning the legislature, and was given a qualified right of appointment and veto of legislative enactments.[8] Interestingly, New York's ability to act as a model for the entire Union was an early example—even before the Constitution's adoption—of the creative role that states were to play as testing grounds for new concepts under a federal system of government.

The convention's first and most effective advocate of a strong executive was Pennsylvania's James Wilson. He took the floor early in June to urge that the chief magistracy be possessed by one man, "as giving the most energy, dispatch and responsibility" to the office. Wilson opposed hemming the president in with an executive council, "which oftener serves to cover than prevent malpractices." To place the executive on the same plane of power as the legislature, Wilson urged that both be chosen directly by the people, with similar short terms. The case was ably advanced by Gouverneur Morris, who declared that "we must either . . . renounce the blessings of the Union, or provide an executive with sufficient vigor to pervade every part of it."[9]

The convention had a strong minority, however, with quite different ideas. Roger Sherman of Connecticut told his fellow delegates that he "considered the executive as nothing more than an institution for carrying the will of the legislature into effect" and that the legislature "should have the power to remove the executive at pleasure." Elbridge Gerry of Massachusetts thought that an executive council, like those then prevalent in the states, should be appended to the executive. Randolph of Virginia, who had presented the Virginia Plan for a relatively powerful national government early in the convention's proceedings, believed that the executive should be composed of more than one person and appointed by the legislature. A single executive, he warned, would be "the foetus of monarchy."[10] The New Jersey Plan, constituting the small states' rejoinder to the Virginia Plan, provided specifically for a plural executive designated by Congress.

In the end, however, Wilson and the other advocates of a strong executive—including James Madison, who became a convert to their cause—would get most of what they wanted. On June 4 and again on July 17, the convention voted for a single executive.[11] Later in July, as a member of the convention's Committee of Detail, Wilson was able to write his concept of a strong and independent executive into the Constitution. In language that would be subjected to only stylistic improvement in the final days of the convention, Wilson wrote: "The executive power of the United States shall be vested in a single person. His title shall be 'The President of the United States of America.'" Wilson's language excluded any executive council and spelled out presidential powers in substantial detail.[12] The historian Charles Thach suggests that "when Wilson wrote into the report of the Committee of Detail the sentence, 'the executive power of the United States shall be vested in a single person,' it marked the final abandonment of the concept of the omnipotence of the legislature, and the substitution therefor of the characteristically American doctrine of coordinate departments."[13]

Wilson, Morris, and Madison failed to get their way in the direct election of the president (see page 21), but they did succeed in scuttling the proposal for electing the president in the national legislature. In its place, a system of intermediate electors was substituted—a system they hoped would approximate a choice by the people.

Reeligibility and Length of Term

The delegates had generally agreed that if the president were to be chosen by the legislature, he ought to be ineligible for a second term. Barring this limitation, George Mason of Virginia warned, there would be "a temptation on the side of the executive to intrigue with the legislature for a reappointment." The Virginia and New Jersey plans, both stipulating election by the legislature, made the chief executive ineligible for reappointment.

Major objections arose, however, to a one-term limitation. Sherman warned that such a policy would result in "throwing out of office the man best qualified to execute its duties" and insisted that "he who has proved himself to be most fit for an office, ought not to be excluded by the Constitution from holding it."[14] Fears were also expressed that a man barred from running again might resort to unconstitutional maneuvers to prolong his hold on the presidency.

To a degree, the possibility of a long term for the executive—the most common proposal was for seven years—seemed to reduce the disadvantages in limiting a chief executive to a single term. But even this alternative raised problems. Gunning Bedford of Delaware asked his fellow delegates "to consider what the situation in the country would be, in case the first magistrate should be saddled on it for such a period and it should be found on trial that he did not possess the qualifications ascribed to him. . . . An impeachment," Bedford said, "would be no cure for this evil, for an impeachment would reach misfeasance only, not incapacity." Gouverneur Morris said he favored making the executive reeligible lest one "destroy the great motive to good behaviour, the hope of being rewarded with a reappointment."[15]

In a speech to the convention on June 18, Alexander Hamilton of New York suggested that the executive authority be vested in a governor who would "serve during good behaviour." But when the convention actually debated a similar resolution on July 17, Mason of Virginia said he considered "an executive during good behaviour as a softer name for an executive for life. And that would be an easy step to hereditary monarchy."[16] The motion for an executive term on good behavior was rejected July 17 by a vote of 4 states in favor, 6 opposed.[17] When rumors began to circulate outside the convention that a monarchy might be established under a royal European family—there had even been rumors that George Washington might be made a crowned head—a firm denial was issued. "Tho we cannot, affirmatively, tell you what we are doing; we can, negatively, tell you what we are not doing—we never once thought of a King," read the key part of a message "leaked" to the press by an unidentified delegate in mid-August.[18] This would be the only break in the policy of strict secrecy maintained during the four months that the convention met.

The final presidential election plan adopted was reported by a special committee on September 4. It was immediately apparent that the proposals for legislative election, long terms, and ineligibility for reelection had been defeated. The president would serve for a period of four years, and he would be eligible for reelection indefinitely. This remained the basic law of the land until ratification in 1951 of the 22nd amendment, limiting the president to two four-year terms.

Large versus Small States

There were enormous disparities in population and power between the states at the Constitutional Convention. Each state was jealous of its own prerogatives; each had existed for generations as a separate colony and, for better or worse, as a near-sovereign state under the Articles of Confederation. Small states, like the Carolinas, Delaware, and Connecticut, were naturally the most apprehensive about a strong federal union, fearing that their lordly neighbors—states such as New York, Pennsylvania, and Virginia—might swallow them up.

The convention's initial decisions in the area of large- versus small-state power did not relate to the presidency but to representation in Congress. The Virginia Plan, presented early in the convention by Randolph though its chief author was Madison, was based on the assumption that an entirely new Constitution was required—not just a rewriting of the Articles of Confederation—and that a strong national government ought to be established. Representation in both houses of Congress would be based chiefly on population. Little basic objection was raised to the principle of a powerful national government, but small-state delegates did resent the apportionment scheme obviously written with the interests of the populous larger states in mind. "You see the consequences of pushing things too far," John Dickinson of Delaware told Madison on the convention floor. "Some of the members of the small states wish for two branches of the general legislature and are friends to a good national government; but we would sooner submit to a foreign power than . . . be deprived of an equality of suffrage in both branches of the legislature, and thereby be thrown under the domination of the big states."[19]

The stage was then set for the presentation on June 15 by William Patterson of the so-called New Jersey Plan, based on the principle of equal representation for all the states in Congress with a significant strengthening of the Articles of Confederation. At this point the convention appeared to be in real deadlock as the large states insisted on population-based apportionment and the small states held firm for equal representation. In a vote on June 19, seven states were in favor of continuing with the Virginia rather than the New Jersey Plan for the new government.[20] But the small states had made their case. As John Roche points out in an essay on the convention, "from that day onward, it could never be forgotten that the state governments loomed ominously in the background and that no verbal incantations could exorcise their power."[21]

As early as June 20 the first glimmerings of compromise appeared when Sherman suggested that the national legislature "have two branches, and a proportional representation in one of them, provided each state had an equal voice in the other." But the "nationalists," led by Madison and Wilson, were reluctant to give ground. Madison tried to allay small-state fears by saying that the large states had no common economic and religious beliefs that would unite them against the smaller ones. Wilson asked the delegates, "Can we forget for whom we are forming a government? Is it for *men*, or for imaginary beings called *states*?"[22]

Political realities militated against a nationalist victory, however, since it was clear that ratification of a constitution lacking strong guarantees for representation of the states *as states* would be difficult, if not impossible. By July 2 the earlier majority for population-based apportionment had been reduced to a dead tie, and a special committee of one delegate from each state was appointed to work out a compromise. The result was the famed "Connecticut Compromise," reported to the convention on July 5. The compromise provided population-based apportionment in the first branch of the legislature, which would have the authority to originate money bills. In the second branch of the legislature each state would have an equal vote. After many more days of debate, the Connecticut Compromise was finally approved on July 16 by the narrow margin of 5 states to 4.[23] The Convention had faced and survived its most serious crisis.

The problem of large- versus small-state power appeared again in the convention's debates on how the president should be elected. But the bulk of these debates took place *after* the Connecticut Compromise had been adopted, and they lacked the crisis atmosphere of the discussion and vote on congressional representation. The alignments, though, were similar. The "nationalist" group favored a direct vote or some other system accurately reflecting population distribution. Small-state delegations feared that they would have no significant vote, under these circumstances, in the choice of a chief executive. "The most populous states by combining in favor of the same individual will be able to carry their points," Charles Pinckney of South Carolina warned. Ellsworth and Sherman of Connecticut voiced the same fears, and on August 24 Sherman opposed the plan for election by the national legislature (as reported by the Committee of Detail) because it would deprive "the states represented in the Senate of the negative intended them in that house." Madison defended the use of a joint ballot of members of both houses of Congress in choosing a president, saying that the rule of voting would "give to the largest state, compared with the smallest, an influence as four to one only, although the population is ten to one."[24]

The small states were not mollified by Madison's argument, however. Four of them opposed the proposal to have the presidential election by joint ballot in Congress, and a motion by Jonathan Dayton of New Jersey to give each state one vote in the joint session to elect the president was barely defeated—5 states in favor, 6 opposed.[25] These votes made it clear that some further steps to appease small-state interests would have to be taken.

Concessions were apparent when on September 4 the Committee of Eleven reported to the convention the details of its intermediate elector plan, the plan that would become part of the Constitution. First, each state would have as many presidential electoral votes as it had representatives and senators combined. This carried the Connecticut Compromise over into the presidential election and gave the small states some relative advantage because of the two extra electoral votes corresponding to the number of senators, regardless of how small a state's population might be. But it must be noted that this compromise was *not* considered crucial at the time. It had not been sufficient to mollify the small states when attached to a proposal for election of the President in Congress. At no time after the Committee of Eleven reported was any mention made on the convention floor of the supposed advantage to small states of the senatorial "counterpart" votes. Nor was this apparent concession mentioned in the subsequent ratifying conventions.

What *was* considered a major concession to the small states was the provision of the intermediate elector plan, which stipulated that in the event there was no majority in the electoral college, the choice of the president would be transferred to the Senate, where each state would have equal voting power. (The convention subsequently voted to shift the contingent election responsibility to the House of Representatives, but the provision for equality of state voting power was preserved.) The delegates apparently believed that many of the presidential electors would vote for men from their own state and region, making a final choice in the electoral college unlikely and throwing most elections into Congress. The small states were expected to benefit further from the provision that the Senate (or later the House), when called upon to choose the president, would be required to choose from among the *five* persons who received the largest number of electoral votes. There was a good chance that one or more of the five would be small-state candidates. Sherman of Connecticut, who had been a member of the Committee of Eleven, told the convention that if the small states "had the advantage in the Senate's deciding among the five highest candidates, the large states would have in fact the nomination of these candidates."[26] Madison subsequently wrote that the presidential election provisions were "the result of compromise between the larger and smaller states, giving to the latter the advantage of selecting a President from the candidates, in consideration of the former in selecting the candidates from the people."[27]

Suffrage

A variety of complex voting qualifications existed in the states when the Constitutional Convention met. The revolutionary period had resulted in some loosening of the restrictive suffrage requirements of the colonial period, but most states still restricted the franchise to "freeholders"—men who possessed a specified amount of real property, with certain net value or annual yield. The stringency with which these requirements were enforced varied substantially from state to state. Some states were shifting to a simpler requirement that voters pay a certain amount of taxes. Vermont, entering the Union in 1791, would be the first state to permit all adult males to vote.

The major debate on suffrage at the convention centered on qualifications to vote for representatives. (The Senate was not a problem, since it was agreed that its members should be selected directly by the state legislatures.) Gouverneur Morris proposed a national freeholder qualification, warning that if votes were given to the propertyless, they would sell them to the rich. John Dickinson of Delaware supported Morris, saying it was necessary to restrict the suffrage to freeholders "as a necessary defense against the dangerous influence of those multitudes without property and without principle." Madison predicted that "in future times a great majority of the people will not only be without land, but any other sort of property. . . . The freeholders of the country would be the safest depositories of republican liberty."[28]

The proposal to write property qualifications into the Constitution stirred spirited opposition, however. Ellsworth of Connecticut argued that "the right of suffrage was a tender point, and strongly guarded by most of the state constitutions. The people will not readily subscribe to the national Constitution if it should subject them to be disfranchised. The states are the best judges of the circumstances and temper of their own people." In one of his rare speeches at the convention, Benjamin Franklin of Pennsylvania also opposed national freeholder qualifications: "It is of consequence that we should not depress the virtue and public spirit of our common people," said Franklin. "This class possess hardy virtues and great integrity."[29]

Morris's motion for a national freeholder qualification was defeated August 7 by a vote of 1 to 7, and the convention decided to leave the matter in the hands of the states by approving the recommendation of its Committee of Detail that the voting qualifications in House elections should be the same as those for the most numerous branch of the state legislature in each state.[30] Even if they were personally disposed toward a freeholder qualification, the delegates feared that an effort to impose a national standard on the states could result in disapproval of the Constitution.

The suffrage problem in presidential elections was circumvented by failure to guarantee any popular vote whatever for the chief executive. The final language of article II provided simply that "Each state shall appoint, in such manner as the legislature thereof may direct, a number of electors." The failure to guarantee any popular vote for president was doubtless a conscious act, since two plans for intermediate electors presented earlier in the summer had specifically stated that the presidential electors should be chosen by the qualified voters in the various states.[31] This proposal for direct vote had failed to specify just who were considered the "people" or "citizens" who would have the right to choose the president.

All the nation's slaves were disfranchised, and the problem of their representation—both in the House and in presidential elections—was a difficult one. Madison acknowledged that it was the severest obstacle in the way of adopting a direct vote of the people for president.[32] The convention finally compromised on counting three-fifths of the slave population in determining a state's congressional representation, and the final elector plan carried the same principle into presidential elections.

Thus the convention washed its hands of the problem of voting qualifications for white men, refused to offer any guarantee whatever of a popular role in presidential elections, and temporized on the question of representation that would account for the slave population. The political exigencies of the time apparently made this the only feasible course. As a result, a whole revolution in human and political rights was left for future generations to cope with.

THE PRESIDENTIAL ELECTION PLANS

Three major proposals for electing the president were debated during the convention: election by Congress (or the national legislature, as it was called through most of the debates), election by a direct vote of the people throughout the nation, and election by intermediate electors. In addition, numerous alternative plans were brought forward, ranging from proposals that the state governors choose the president to one that fifteen members of Congress be chosen by lot to elect the next chief executive. None of these alternatives aroused much interest, and all were shunted aside with little debate.[33]

Election by Congress

The idea of placing the choice in the hands of the national legislature appeared in the original Virginia and New Jersey plans, was specifically approved by votes of the convention on four occasions, and was incorporated in the important Committee of Detail draft in the latter stages of the proceedings. Basically, it was favored by the delegates who backed a strong legislature and weaker executive, while proponents of a strong executive opposed it. In the end, it foundered on the shoals of executive independence and was rejected.

Sherman stated well the definitive case for legislative election on June 1, the first day the convention debated the mode of choosing the executive. He said the executive "ought to be appointed by and accountable to the legislature

only, which was the depository of the supreme will of the society."[34] Looking
to the state governments of the time, the delegates could see that no fewer than
8 of the 13 states placed the choice of their executive directly in the hands of
the legislature. Moreover, the members of the national legislature—who themselves had been selected by the people and state legislatures—would certainly
be in the best position to judge the qualifications of the various candidates.
The chief advocates of legislative election, in addition to Sherman, were
Randolph and Mason of Virginia, Charles Pinckney and John Rutledge of South
Carolina, and William C. Houston of New Jersey.

The most vocal opponents included Gouverneur Morris and Gerry, joined
later by Madison. A chief executive chosen by the legislature, Morris warned,
would be "the mere creature" of that body. Should the legislature elect, "it will
be the work of intrigue, or cabal, and of faction: it will be like the election of a
pope by a conclave of cardinals; real merit will rarely be the title of the appointment." There was an "indispensable necessity," Morris said, of "making
the executive independent of the legislature." Gerry warned that election by
the legislature would not only lessen executive independence but "would give
birth to intrigue and corruption between the executive and legislature previous
to election and to partiality in the executive afterwards to the friends who pro-
moted him." Many delegates also feared the intervention of foreign powers if
the legislature were to choose the president. Madison went to the heart of the
opposition on July 17 when he said that "a dependence of the executive on the
legislature would render it the executor as well as the maker of the laws; and
then, according to the observation of Montesquieu, tyrannical laws may be
made that they may be executed in a tyrannical manner."[35]

The first vote on election by Congress came June 1, when legislative election of an executive with a seven-year term was approved by a vote of 8 states
to 2. The decision was confirmed July 17 by a unanimous vote. On July 19 the
convention shifted to an intermediate elector scheme, but it returned to election by the legislature on July 24 by a vote of 7 to 4. The motion for legislative
election of the president with a single seven-year term was formalized July 26
by a vote of 7 to 3, and this provision was written into the report of the
Committee of Detail, received by the convention on August 6. But a major
dispute erupted on the convention floor over the voting procedure in the
legislature—whether it should be by joint ballot (a proposal accepted by a 7 to
4 vote) or by a system under which each state would have an equal vote
(rejected by a 5 to 6 vote). The Committee of Eleven, appointed to break the deadlock, discarded the legislative election method in favor of intermediate electors. A motion by Rutledge to return to legislative election was rejected September 5 by a 2 to 8 vote, with one state divided, thus dooming the proposal.[36]
But the final draft of the Constitution did preserve some element of the plan by
providing that when the electoral college failed to produce a majority, the election would be thrown into the House of Representatives for decision.

Direct Vote of the People

Only a few delegates to the convention felt that American democracy had matured sufficiently for the choice of the president to be entrusted directly to the people. On the two occasions that the convention voted on direct vote, the proposal was resoundingly defeated. But the advocates of direct vote were among the convention's more illustrious members—James Wilson, Gouverneur Morris, and James Madison. In retrospect, the arguments they offered seemed better suited to future generations than their own.

Wilson was the first to take the floor for direct election, arguing that "experience, particularly in New York and Massachusetts [two of the states then electing their governors by direct vote], showed that an election of the first magistrate by the people was both a convenient and successful mode." Wilson said he wanted both houses of Congress and the president chosen by direct popular mandate, "to make them as independent as possible of each other, as well as of the states." Morris summed up the direct election argument by declaring that "the executive magistrate should be the guardian of the people, even of the lower classes, against legislative tyranny. . . . If he is to be the guardian of the people, let him be appointed by the people." Madison admitted that there were objections against virtually every possible mode of electing the president, but it was direct election, "with all its imperfections," that he "liked the best." After all, said Madison, "the President is to act for the *people*, not the states." He recognized the problem raised by disfranchised slaves in the South, which would reduce his native Virginia's relative vote under direct election. But "local considerations," he said, "must give way to the general interest." As a southerner, Madison said, he "was willing to make the sacrifice."[37]

Gerry, Sherman, Pinckney, and Mason led the opposition. "The people are uninformed and would be misled by a few designing men," Gerry warned. He found the proposal "radically vicious." Some cabal would control the presidency, such as the Order of the Cincinnati, a unified and influential group with connections throughout the country. "They will in fact elect the chief magistrate in every instance, if the election be referred to the people," said Gerry. Mason declared that "it would be as unnatural to refer the choice of a proper magistrate to the people, as it would, to refer a trial of colors to a blind man. The extent of the country renders it impossible that the people can have the requisite capacity to judge . . . the candidates." Sherman found the proposal impractical because the people would "generally vote for some man in their own state, and the largest state will have the best chance for appointment." Voicing an argument to be heard time and again through U.S. history, Pinckney said he feared that "the most populous states, by combining in favor of the same individual, will be able to carry their points."[38] Moreover, the opponents warned, dangerous commotions might well accompany direct election.

Wilson and Morris took up the debate in rebuttal, arguing that there were no grounds to anticipate disorder in a national election, since it would occur in polling places across a wide land. If the people failed to produce a majority for a single candidate in the first election, Wilson argued, the legislature could then be authorized to choose among the men nominated by the people. Replying to the assertion that the people of the populous states might combine and elect their own man, Morris said: "Just the reverse. The people of such states cannot combine. If there be any combination it must be among their representatives in the legislature. It is said the people will be led by a few designing men. This might happen in a small district. It can never happen throughout the continent. . . . It is said the multitude will be uninformed. . . . But they will not be uninformed of the great and illustrious characters which have merited their esteem and confidence."[39]

Twice the alternative of a direct vote was put to the convention, and each time the proposal was rejected—by a 1 to 9 vote on July 17 (only Pennsylvania in favor), and by a 2 to 9 vote on August 24 (only Pennsylvania and Delaware in favor).[40] But in the course of their arguments, the backers of popular election had destroyed the initial consensus for electing the president in Congress and laid the groundwork for a compromise proposal—the system of intermediate electors—that would eventually carry the nation most of the way down the road to a choice of the president by all the people.

The Intermediate Elector Plan

The proposal for choosing the president by intermediate electors possessed the virtue of being the second choice of many delegates, though it was the first choice of few, if any, when the convention began. The plan was first advanced on June 2 by Wilson when he decided that support was lacking for his proposal of a direct popular vote. Luther Martin of Maryland, a states'-rights man, next brought the idea forward on July 17. Gerry backed it as an alternative to direct election, suggesting that the state governors choose the electors. On July 25 Ellsworth endorsed an elector system that would go into operation only when a president was standing for reelection. Otherwise, he favored election by Congress. Morris of Pennsylvania, a strong direct-election advocate, recommended the elector plan as second best on August 24. Some historians believe that the genesis of the intermediate elector plan was the scheme that Maryland wrote into its constitution in 1777 for the election of its Senate.[41]

When the Committee of Eleven reported the intermediate elector plan to the convention on September 4, Morris, who served on the committee, cited six grounds. They were all essentially negative, centering around the dangers of legislative election. The only real advantage Morris could cite for intermediate electors was that "the great evil of cabal" could be avoided since the electors "would vote at the same time throughout the U.S. and at so great a distance from each other."[42]

The elector plan had actually come up for a convention vote on frequent occasions before the Committee of Eleven devised its final form. As proposed by
Wilson, with a provision for direct popular vote of the electors in districts, it
was rejected June 2 by a 2 to 8 vote. When Martin suggested on July 17 that the
president be chosen by electors designated by the state legislatures, the proposal was rejected by an identical 2 to 8 margin. But the mood of the convention had changed perceptibly two days later when a proposal by Ellsworth for
election of the President by electors was approved, 6 to 3 (with one state divided), and his motion that the state legislatures choose them passed, 8 to 2.
The convention then voted an apportionment scheme for electors, ranging between one and three a state, depending on population. On July 23, however,
the convention voted, 7 to 3, to reconsider its decision after William C.
Houston of New Jersey pointed out "the extreme inconveniency and the considerable expense of drawing together men from all the states for the single purpose of electing the chief magistrate."[43]

The Committee of Eleven, picked by ballot of the entire convention on August 31, included a remarkable aggregate of political talent—Rufus King of
Massachusetts, Gouverneur Morris of Pennsylvania, James Madison of Virginia, Daniel Carroll of Maryland, John Dickinson of Delaware, Abraham Baldwin of Georgia, Pierce Butler of South Carolina, Nicholas Gilman of New
Hampshire, David Brearley of New Jersey, Hugh Williamson of North
Carolina, and Roger Sherman of Connecticut. They set directly to work and
four days later were able to present their ingenious compromise plan to the
convention. Their skill as practical politicians, well aware of what could be
"sold" and what could not in their home states, was amply evidenced in the
scheme they produced. As John Roche has pointed out, "everybody got a piece
of the cake."[44] The big states got an element of population-based apportionment in choosing the electors; the small states got equal voting rights in the
contingent election plan when a majority of the electors failed to agree; the
feelings of states'-rights advocates were acknowledged by giving the state legislatures the right to decide how the electors should be chosen; and those who
wanted to entrust the choice of the president to the people could see at least the
potential for popular vote.

In a relatively brief debate ending September 7, the convention approved the
Committee of Eleven plan and incorporated it into the Constitution. A few
changes were made, the most significant in the method of contingent election.
The analysis below shows in italics the final wording, compares it to the original Committee of Eleven plan where different, and provides key votes.

*Article II, Section 1. . . . [The President] shall hold his office during the term of four
years, and, together with the Vice President, chosen for the same term, be appointed in
the following manner:*

The four-year term (with indefinite reeligibility) and the idea of having a vice
president were inventions of the Committee of Eleven. A motion to return to the

idea of a seven-year presidential term favored during most of the convention proceedings was offered by Williamson and Richard Spaight of North Carolina but rejected by a vote of 3 states to 8. The North Carolinians then moved for a six-year term but lost on a 2 to 8 vote. The four-year term was then formally approved with all states but North Carolina in favor.[45]

The convention spent little time debating the desirability of having a vice president. Williamson commented that "such an officer as the Vice President was not wanted. He was introduced only for the sake of a valuable mode of election which required two to be chosen at the same time."[46]

Each state shall appoint, in such manner as the legislature thereof may direct, a number of [Presidential] electors, equal to the whole number of Senators and Representatives to which the state may be entitled in Congress.

In opting for this intermediate elector scheme, the Committee of Eleven rejected the much-discussed legislative mode of election and returned to a proposal that had encountered stiff resistance earlier in the proceedings. Predictably, several delegates announced their opposition to the new scheme in its entirety. Rutledge of South Carolina moved on September 5 to return to the proposal for congressional election of a president limited to a single seven-year term. But the weary delegates were in no mood to return to that dead end. They rejected his motion by a vote of 2 states to 8. The only states supporting Rutledge were North Carolina and his own South Carolina, with New Hampshire divided.[47]

Interestingly, there was no debate in the convention on the elector apportionment formula recommended by the Committee of Eleven. Nor was there any debate on how the state legislatures should or would select electors— whether they would appoint the electors themselves, require that they be chosen by popular vote in districts, or provide for popular vote statewide. This knotty problem, which would cause endless debates and maneuvers in the state legislatures in the ensuing years, was completely ignored. The legislatures were simply granted complete discretion in the matter.

Nor was there any debate on the real role of electors. Should they be wise men endowed with a wide knowledge of the country and thus best entrusted with choosing a president? Or should they be simply representatives of the legislatures or the people who would designate them? The delegates may have debated the question after hours at the Indian Queen, the local tavern where many spirited discussion took place after the formal sessions. But they barely touched on the question on the convention floor, if Madison's meticulous notes are to be trusted. The nearest they came to the issue was when Pinckney of South Carolina charged that the electors would "be strangers to the several candidates" for president and thus "unable to decide on their comparative merits." Wilson replied that "continental characters will multiply as we more and more coalesce, so as to enable the electors in every part of the Union to know and judge of them."[48]

But no Senator or Representative, or person holding an office of trust or profit under the United States, shall be appointed an elector.

This wording was not included in the text of the Committee of Eleven but was proposed on the convention floor by King and Gerry of Massachusetts as a way to prevent congressmen or federal officials from having a hand in the election of the president, with the bribery and intrigue they feared might result. It was approved unanimously.[49]

The electors shall meet in their respective states, and vote by ballot for two persons, of whom at least one shall not be an inhabitant of the same state as themselves. And they shall make a list of all the persons voted for, and of the number of votes for each; which list they shall sign and certify, and transmit sealed to the seat of the Government of the United States, directed to the President of the Senate.

This wording, as recommended by the Committee of Eleven, was left almost untouched by the convention. The requirement that electors meet in their respective states resolved an objection to earlier forms of intermediate elector plans, which had aroused opposition because of the inconvenience of traveling to the national capital simply to cast ballots. Also, the framers had feared "cabal and corruption" if all the electors actually met at one place, a problem this new wording neatly solved—or so it seemed in the world of 1787, before the growth of national political parties.[50]

Electors were required to cast their ballots for two persons for president—the votes to be of equal weight—in the hope that at least one of them would be a man of "continental reputation" rather than a fellow citizen of the elector's home state. This requirement would raise enormous difficulties in the first elections, necessitating the 12th amendment in 1804 providing for separate voting for president and vice president.

The President of the Senate shall, in the presence of the Senate and House of Representatives, open all the certificates, and the votes shall then be counted. The person having the greatest number of votes shall be the President, if such number be a majority of the whole number of electors appointed;[51]

This section would cause prolonged disputes during the nineteenth century, because it did not say *who* should actually count the electoral votes—the president of the Senate or the members of the two houses of Congress—and did not stipulate who would have the authority to decide in the event that some electoral votes were challenged. It was little debated by the convention.

The majority requirement was expected to throw many elections into Congress for decision. A move by Mason of Virginia to strike out the requirement was rejected on September 5 by a vote of 2 states to 9, and the convention by the same margin turned down a motion by Madison and Williamson to substitute "one third" for a majority. Gerry argued that a one-third requirement would "put it in the power of three or four states to put in whom they pleased."[52]

If there be more than one [candidate for President] who have such a majority, and have an equal number of votes, then the House of Representatives shall immediately choose by ballot one of them for President; and if no person have a majority, then from the five highest on the list the said House shall in like manner choose the President. But in choosing the President, the votes shall be taken by states, the representation from each state having one vote. A quorum for this purpose shall consist of a member or members from two-thirds of the states, and a majority of the states shall be necessary to a choice.

The Committee of Eleven draft had differed in that it vested the contingent election authority in the Senate—a provision that aroused much opposition and the most debate on the committee's report. The provision was considered crucial, since many delegates apparently agreed with Mason "that 19 times in 20, the President would be chosen by the Senate."[53] Pinckney warned that with no limit on presidential terms, the president "will become fixed for life under the auspices of the Senate." Williamson feared that the foundation was being laid "for corruption and aristocracy." The Senate, after all, would itself be chosen by the state legislatures, not by the people directly. But when Wilson moved on September 5 to shift the contingent election to the House instead, he was defeated on a vote of 3 states to 7 (with one divided). The bulk of the opposition came from the smaller states.[54]

Undaunted, Wilson returned to the attack the next day, warning of the excessive power being placed in the hands of the Senate if control of the presidency were added to its powers over treaties, impeachments, and approval of appointments. Wilson saw a danger of blending the legislative, executive, and judicial functions into one branch of government. "According to the plan as it now stands, the President will not be the man of the people as he ought to be, but the minion of the Senate," Wilson warned. But again he was defeated, the convention voting 6 to 4 to retain the contingent election power in the Senate.[55]

The final compromise was then brought forward by Williamson and Sherman, who proposed that the contingent election be decided in the House but that each state have but a single vote. The convention quickly seized on this alternative by an affirmative vote of 10 states, with only Delaware opposed.[56]

The great debate on the election of the president was now over, but Madison the next day, September 7, warned of the problem of election in the House with each state enjoying a single vote. In some instances, he said, a single man might case his state's vote. This led to a "further weighty objection, that the representatives of a *minority* of the people might reverse the choice of a *majority* of the states and of the people." Gerry moved to require that a majority of the state delegations be obtained to elect a president in the House, thus meeting one part of Madison's objection, and the convention agreed.[57] But it would still be possible for a minority of the people to elect a president in this manner. Madison had detected the profoundly undemocratic potentialities of a contingent election in which each state would have a single vote—a problem the nation would still have to face nearly 200 years later.

Another problem was the provision that the contingent election should be from among the *five* candidates receiving the greatest number of electoral votes—a clear concession to the smaller states, since a restriction of the number of candidates to the two or three receiving the most electoral votes would more likely have confined the choice to candidates from the larger states. Mason and Gerry moved to reduce the number of candidates in the contingent election from five to three, but lost on a 2 to 8 vote. A small-state countermove to make the choice from thirteen candidates—apparently on the assumption that each state could then "nominate" a man—was rejected, with only the Carolinas in favor.[58]

Another floor amendment, that the contingent election take place "immediately" in instances where it was required, was approved without objection, probably in the belief that the outcome of the electoral vote would not be known until the count in Congress was announced and that a quick runoff would prevent corruption and cabal among the members of Congress called on to make the choice.[59]

In every case, after the choice of a President, the person having the greatest number of votes of the electors shall be the Vice President. But if there should remain two or more who have equal votes, the Senate shall choose from them by ballot the Vice President.

This proposal, from the Committee of Eleven, was not altered by the convention. It is interesting to note that a majority electoral vote for vice president was not required. A separate vote for vice president, together with a majority requirement, would be established by the 12th amendment.

The Congress may determine the time of choosing the electors, and the day on which they shall give their votes, which day shall be the same throughout the United States.

The last phrase, requiring that the electors meet on the same day, was inserted from the convention floor September 6 on an 8 to 3 vote.[60] It was apparently another device to prevent what the framers saw as "the great evil of cabal" between the electors.

No person except a natural born citizen, or a citizen of the United States at the time of the adoption of this Constitution, shall be eligible to the office of President; neither shall any person be eligible to that office who shall not have attained the age of thirty-five years, and been fourteen years a resident within the United States.

This language, from the Committee of Eleven, was accepted without debate.

In case of the removal of the President from office, or of his death, resignation or inability to discharge the powers and duties of the said office, the same shall devolve upon the Vice President, and the Congress may by law prescribe for the case of removal, death, resignation or inability, both of the President and Vice President, declaring what officer shall then act as President, and such officer shall act accordingly, until the disability be removed, or a President shall be elected.

This provision was suggested on the convention floor September 7 by Randolph of Virginia and approved by a vote of 6 states to 4, with one (New Hampshire) divided.[61] The questions of what constitutes presidential "inability," who shall decide when it has begun and ended, and whether a vice president succeeding to the office would enjoy its full powers were to provide major problems for presidential administrations and the Congress for the next 180 years. The Constitution would not be definitively clarified on this point until the ratification in 1967 of the 25th amendment, providing that the vice president "shall become President" on the death or resignation of the president, authorizing the president to nominate a new vice president (subject to approval of Congress) when the latter office becomes vacant, and spelling out the steps to be followed in the event of a temporary or permanent presidential inability.[62] The 25th amendment came into effect for the first time in 1973 following the resignation of Vice President Spiro T. Agnew and the appointment by President Richard M. Nixon of Gerald R. Ford to succeed him. The amendment was used a second time in 1974 following Nixon's resignation. Vice President Ford succeeded to the presidency and subsequently selected former New York governor Nelson A. Rockefeller to be his vice president.

THE RATIFICATION DEBATES

With the hindsight that history affords, it is remarkable to note how seldom the opponents of the new Constitution attacked the presidential election system in the sometimes tumultuous ratifying conventions that followed submission of the document to the states in September 1787.[63] In the Pennsylvania convention James Wilson went unchallenged when he declared that "the manner of appointing the President of the United States, I find, is not objected to."[64] In The Federalist paper no. 68, published the following March, Alexander Hamilton would confidently state: "The mode of appointment of the chief magistrate of the United States is almost the only part of the system, of any consequence, which has escaped without severe censure, or which has received the slightest mark of approbation from its opponents." The more reasonable opponents, Hamilton said, had even admitted "that the election of the President is pretty well guarded."[65]

The silence of the Constitution's enemies, who were utterly forthright in their critique of so many other portions of the document, is all the more remarkable in light of the inherent contradiction in the way that Madison, Hamilton, and the Constitution's other advocates explained the system. On the one hand, they suggested that the president would be the man of the people and spring almost directly from them. On the other hand, they either suggested that wise electors would make the choice or that the real power would lie in the hands of the state legislatures.

Madison was foremost in claiming the essentially democratic character of the election procedure. The president, he told the Virginia ratifying convention, "will be the choice of the people at large." It was only because of the difficulties of direct vote in as large a land as America, he indicated, that the indirect system was proposed, but the people would choose the electors.[66] In *The Federalist* paper no. 39, Madison announced: "The President is indirectly derived from the choice of the people."[67] Wilson told his fellow Pennsylvanians: "The choice of this officer is brought as nearly home to the people as practicable. With the approbation of the state legislatures, the people may elect with only one remove."[68] And Hamilton wrote in *The Federalist* no. 68: "It was desirable, that the sense of the people should operate" in choosing a president, and that the president should be dependent for his continuation in office on none "but the people themselves."[69]

Reading only these portions of the debate, one would assume that the people's voice was to be almost direct in choosing the chief executive. But the same proponents had another message to deliver. Wrote Madison in *The Federalist* paper no. 45: "Without the intervention of the state legislatures, the President of the United States cannot be elected at all. They must in all cases have a great share in his appointment, and will perhaps in most cases of themselves determine it." And Hamilton would depict the presidential electors as men of special "information and discernment" who would not be as corruptible as the people themselves might be and would be able to choose a chief executive "free from any sinister byass."[70]

Thus there was never a clear definition of how much electors should rely on their own inclinations rather than the popular will. Perhaps the issue lacked importance in the minds of many, since it was universal knowledge that George Washington would be picked as the first president with the virtually unanimous support of his countrymen.

Nor was there any substantial challenge to the double balloting system that would lead to the 12th amendment seventeen years later or to the Constitution's total silence on how state legislatures should arrange for selection of the presidential electors. In the Virginia convention Randolph did proclaim that "the electors must be elected by the people at large," but he could point to no provision of the Constitution to support his assertion. James Monroe, a future president, told the same Virginia convention: "I believe that he [the President] will owe his election, in fact, to the state governments, and not the people at large."[71]

The most frequent argument given in favor of the electoral system was that it would prevent what Hamilton called the "heats and ferments . . . tumult and disorder . . . cabal, intrigue and corruption" which might well accompany the election of a president. No corruption would be possible, he claimed, because of the "transient existence" and "detached situation" of the electors.[72]

Even though the country still lacked any semblance of an organized party system, it is hard to believe that hardheaded politicians like Alexander Hamilton could have believed that the election of a president would operate in a political vacuum. The historian Carl Becker has commented: "If the motives of the founding fathers in devising the electoral system were of the highest, it must be said that their grasp of political realities, ordinarily so sure, failed them in this instance. Of all the provisions of the federal Constitution, the electoral system was the most unrealistic—the one provision not based solidly on practical experience and precedent. It was in the nature of an academic invention which ignored the experience in the vain expectation that, in this one instance for this high purpose, politicians would cease to be politicians, would divest themselves of party prejudice and class and sectional bias, and be all for the time being noble Brutuses inspired solely by pure love of liberty and the public good."[73]

The most basic reason for the invention of the electoral college was that the convention was deadlocked on simpler schemes like direct election and choice by Congress. It devised a system that could be "sold" in the immediate context of 1787. The electoral college, John Roche has commented, "was merely a jerry-rigged improvisation which has subsequently been endowed with a high theoretical content. . . . The future was left to cope with the problem of what to do with this Rube Goldberg mechanism."[74]

James Madison, the "father of the Constitution," perhaps was as frank about the problem as any of the framers could ever be when he wrote some thirty-six years later: "The difficulty of finding an unexceptionable process for appointing the Executive Organ of a Government such as that of the U.S., was deeply felt by the Convention; and as the final arrangement took place in the latter stages of the session, it was not exempt from a degree of the hurrying influence produced by fatigue and impatience in all such bodies; tho' the degree was much less than usually prevails in them."[75]

3

The First Elections

The tender greens of a Virginian spring had begun to cover the land as General George Washington departed Mount Vernon on April 16, 1789, for his trip to New York to be sworn in as the first president of the United States. Normally, the stagecoach trip might have taken five days. But Washington would not reach Manhattan until the twenty-third of the month. Everywhere, the people turned out to welcome their new chief executive. Washington was feasted at Alexandria, warmly entertained at Georgetown, and when he arrived in Philadelphia was welcomed by the governor and his troops as the city's church bells rang and a *feu de joie* was ignited. At Trenton, the women of that city erected a triumphal arch at the Assumpink bridge over which Washington had led his little army twelve years earlier, on the night before the Battle of Princeton.

Local militia companies—veterans of the Revolutionary War and some of the French and Indian wars—escorted Washington through New Jersey: the Hunterdon Horse from Trenton to Rocky Hill, the Somerset Horse to Brunswick, the Middlesex Horse from Brunswick to Woodbridge, and finally the Essex Horse to Elizabethtown Pond. Thirteen pilots rowed the general's barge across the harbor to Murray's wharf, where Governor Clinton and the new United States senators and representatives were present to escort him through throngs of cheering New Yorkers to the house made ready for his use.

Seven days later, when the final touches had been completed on the refurnished Federal Hall that would house the first Congress, Washington appeared on the building's balcony to take the now-familiar oath of office, as prescribed in the Constitution: "I do solemnly swear that I will faithfully execute the office of President of the United States, and will to the best of my ability preserve, protect and defend the Constitution of the United States." Chancellor Robert Livingston of New York administered the oath, and when the ceremony was finished, turned to the multitude filling Broad and Wall streets and cried, "Long live George Washington, President of the United States!" As the crowd took up the cry and the cannon roared on the Battery, Washington withdrew to the Senate chamber to deliver his inaugural address. The presidency was born.[1]

It was nineteen months since the Constitutional Convention had completed its work. The framers stipulated that ratification by nine states would be required, and by the end of 1787, three states had done this—Delaware, Pennsylvania, and New Jersey. Often in heated debate, the other states followed suit until New Hampshire became the ninth on June 21, 1788. But without Virginia and New York, no viable union would have been possible. To the joy and relief of the Constitution's backers, these states followed suit on June 26 and July 26, 1788.[2] Now the initial steps could be taken to elect the first Congress and president of the United States.

The old Congress of Confederation bogged down in a dreary debate on where the new seat of government should be located but on September 18 finally decided on New York and passed a resolution proclaiming the new Constitution to be in effect. The first Wednesday of January 1789 was set as the date for the presidential electors to be appointed; they were directed to meet in their own states and ballot for president on the first Wednesday in February. The meeting day for the new Congress was set for March 4, 1789.

In reality it would be April 6 before both houses of the new Congress could muster a quorum and proceed to their first business: counting the electoral votes for president. In joint session the electoral returns from the states were opened, and the temporary president of the Senate, John Langdon of New Hampshire, announced that 69 votes—a unanimous tally—had been cast for George Washington. John Adams of Massachusetts received 34 electoral votes and was elected the nation's first vice president.

Thus, on its first try, the electoral college seemed to be a successful institution. But the appearance was deceptive. Two major sources of difficulty were already apparent.

The first lay in the method by which the presidential electors were chosen. The Constitution provided simply that each state would appoint electors "in such manner as the legislature thereof may direct." Did this mean that the legislatures should appoint the electors directly? Or would the people choose the electors? And if the people made the choice, would they choose by districts? Or would the election be on a statewide basis—a method that would come to be known as the general ticket system? In this first presidential election, five legislatures—those of Connecticut, New Jersey, Delaware, South Carolina, and Georgia—simply appointed the electors without reference to the people. The New York legislature undertook to do the same, but its two houses argued so long about the choice that the deadlock could not be broken before the day on which the electors were to vote. Thus New York lost its vote completely.

In Massachusetts the General Court (legislature) let the people choose electors in districts but appointed two at-large electors itself. Only four states decided to entrust the selection of the electors exclusively to the people— Maryland and Virginia on a district basis, and Pennsylvania and New Hampshire on the general ticket system. But under New Hampshire's complicated election requirements none of the candidates for elector received a popular vote majority and the legislature ended up appointing the electors itself.[3] Thus, while the president was to be the chief magistrate of all the people, there was no uniformity in the way the electors who chose him were elected. Acting under the specific mandate of the Constitution, the state legislatures had an open invitation to manipulate the electoral system in any way they thought might satisfy their immediate partisan purposes.

The second problem related to the system of "double balloting" prescribed by the Constitution. Each elector was required to cast two votes for president. He could not indicate he wanted one to be for president and the other for vice president. Yet the fact was that every elector from the first election on had a distinct preference for president and another distinct preference for vice president. In this year of 1789, there was no opposition to the selection of the revered George Washington as the first president, but there would have to be a vice president as well. A man from the North was sought to balance Washington's Virginia, and Adams of Massachusetts became the prevailing choice. Yet no one thought of Washington as a possible vice president, and no one at this point (except perhaps Adams himself) thought of Adams as a candidate for president.[4] The problem was that if all the electors had voted for *both* Washington and Adams, the two men would have been tied in the electoral vote and the choice would have been thrown into the House of Representatives. To avert such an outcome, Alexander Hamilton sent word to several states urging that a few of the electors withhold their votes from Adams. His counsel appears to have been followed by some Connecticut and New Jersey electors. In retrospect, Hamilton's action was probably not necessary, since Adams recieved no votes at all from Delaware, Maryland, South Carolina, and Georgia. Indeed, Adams was accorded less than half the electors' second votes. The tally was 34 for Adams, with most of the remaining 35 votes split among various states' favorite sons. (For voting in all presidential elections, see Appendix A.) But since the Constitution had no majority requirement for vice president, Adams was elected.

If all 13 states had voted, there would have been 91 votes—corresponding to the 65 representatives and 26 senators. But Rhode Island and North Carolina, with 3 and 7 votes respectively, had not yet ratified the Constitution. New York's delay in appointing electors cost that state its 8 votes, and two electors in both Maryland and Virginia failed to appear on the day of voting. Thus the total number of electoral votes was reduced to 69. According to one historian's account, the absenteeism in Maryland was explained by the ice on the rivers and the Chesapeake Bay, which prevented one elector from reaching Annapolis, while an attack of gout kept the other at home.[5] Had the election been close, such irrational factors could have swayed the future of the republic.

THE ELECTIONS OF 1792 AND 1796

Despite the vagueness of the Constitution on the electoral base of the president, the idea of the president as the one great national representative of the American people began to assert itself from the very year of the nation's birth. The welcome accorded George Washington wherever he went surely demonstrated the people's direct support for him—not simply as citizens of a particular state but as citizens of the United States. In the first Congress, Representative Thomas Hartley of Pennsylvania declared: "The President is the representative of the people in a near and equal manner; he is the guardian of his country. The Senate are the representatives of the state legislatures." Representative Thomas Scott of Pennsylvania found the president "justly and truly denominated the man of the people. Is there any other person who represents so many of them as the President? He is elected by the voice of the people of the whole Union. . . . No man in the United States has their concurrent voice but him."[6]

But though the concept of the people's president was gaining ground in many quarters, the state legislatures still had a different idea. In the election of 1792 the legislatures of 9 of the 15 states then in the Union took themselves the function of appointing the presidential electors directly (see chart, Appendix B). In New Hampshire and Massachusetts some of the electors were chosen by the people others by the legislatures. Only four states—Pennsylvania, Maryland, Virginia, and Kentucky—left the choice of electors entirely in the hands of the people. (Pennsylvania and Maryland used the general ticket system, Virginia and Kentucky the district system.)

By the time of this election the first party lines were becoming apparent. The ruling Federalist party was encountering more and more opposition from the group centered around Thomas Jefferson—the anti-Federalists, or, as they soon named themselves, the Republicans (and still later, the Democrats). This group did not criticize Washington directly or try to prevent his reelection. Instead, the chief criticism was aimed at Adams. The Republicans' 1792 candidate to oppose Adams for the vice presidency was George Clinton of New York. In most states, the choice of electors turned into a strict party contest. The Federalists had solid control of New England, while New York was moving toward the Republican column. The middle states were more Federalist, while North Carolina and Georgia supported Clinton. The final 1792 count showed that each of the 132 electors had cast a vote for Washington. Adams received 77 electoral votes, followed by Clinton with 50, Jefferson with 4, and Aaron Burr of New York with one.

Again in 1796 a majority of the state legislatures appointed the presidential electors directly. There were now sixteen states. Only six gave the people the exclusive right to pick electors—Pennsylvania and Georgia under the general ticket system, Maryland, Virginia, North Carolina, and Kentucky under the district method. A popular general ticket election was held in New Hampshire, but when no elector candidates amassed a majority, the legislature picked the electors. Massachusetts again had a mixed system of popular elections and electors chosen at large by the legislature.

Early in 1796 Washington told his intimates that he would not run for a third term—establishing a tradition that would remain unbroken until the election of Franklin D. Roosevelt for a third term 144 years later. Washington's decision did not become public until September, but the Federalist members of Congress had already caucused during the summer and decided to nominate Adams as their candidate for the presidency and Thomas Pinckney of South Carolina for vice president. A Republican congressional caucus selected the party's natural leader, Thomas Jefferson, for the presidency and decided to back Burr for vice president. These congressional caucuses were of special interest because they established the method of nominating candidates for the presidency that would survive until the overthrow of "King Caucus" in the 1820s. The rise of the caucus system destroyed forever any lingering pretense that the presidential electors, chosen later in the election year in each state, would be dispassionate searchers for the men of "continental character" who were fit to be chief magistrate of the republic. The founding fathers' conception of the disinterested elector vanished quietly into history, leaving its traces only in the constitution they created. Henceforth the electors would be little more than political puppets, mere tools of the political parties that had already decided on the nominees.

Now that there would be two bona fide candidates for president, the double-balloting system in the electoral college would cause even more difficulties. Not only was there the possibility—recognized since Washington's first election—that the man generally supported for vice president would get as many votes as the man intended for the presidency, thus throwing the election into the House, with unpredictable results. But now, with two clearly defined parties, each putting forward its candidates for president and vice president, the winning party might discover that if it instructed a number of electors to withhold their votes from the vice presidential choice to prevent an electoral college tie, the opposing party's presidential candidate might win the vice presidency instead. The result would be a president of one party and a vice president of the other.

In fact, this is just what happened in 1796. The dominant Federalists, anxious that their vice presidential choice, Pinckney, not receive as many votes as their presidential candidate, Adams, withheld 18 electoral votes from Pinckney in New England and 3 in Maryland. Pinckney received 8 votes with Jefferson in South Carolina and one more than Adams in Pennsylvania. The net result was that while Adams won 71 electoral votes, Pinckney lagged 12 votes behind with 59. But Jefferson's overall total was 68. Thus Jefferson, the Republican became vice president in the administration of Adams, the Federalist (Burr, the Republicans' vice presidential choice, received only 30 votes, and another 48 were scattered.) The election results also revealed a clear regional split. The Federalists carried all the states north of Pennsylvania, while the Republicans won all those from Virginia southward. The Federalists won 6 of the 10 Maryland districts, one of them by a margin of only 4 votes. A change of less than 100 popular votes in Pennsylvania, which unexpectedly elected 13 Republican electors out of 15, would have resulted in the election of Pinckney instead of Jefferson as vice president.[7]

The year 1796 also produced the first faithless elector. He was picked as one of the two Federalist electors in Pennsylvania, so that everyone expected he would vote for Adams, the Federalist candidate. Instead he decided to cast his vote for Jefferson. An exasperated Federalist complained in the *United States Gazette*: "What, do I chuse Samuel Miles to determine for me whether John Adams or Thomas Jefferson shall be President? No! I chuse him to *act*, not to *think*."[8]

The next winter, when Congress met in joint session for the official count of the electoral votes, Adams—the outgoing vice president and thus president of the Senate—presided and had the pleasure of declaring his own election as chief executive. Adams may have felt a few pangs of nervousness that day, however. An essential part of his majority was comprised of Vermont's four electoral votes, but there was an apparent deficiency in the Vermont electoral law. (The Vermont legislature had proceeded to appoint electors without first passing legislation specifying that designation would be by the legislature itself rather than by another method.) Happily for Adams, no objection was raised. If the Vermont votes had been invalid, Adams would have had only 67 votes. The total number of valid electoral votes would then have been reduced to 134, and Jefferson—with 68—would have had a bare majority and thus won the election.[9]

Commenting in February 1797 on the election results, the *New York Diary* wrote: "Mr. Adams' election is not owing to a fair, decided expression of the public voice, but to the different modes prescribed in the several states for the appointment of electors. A uniform rule on this subject is a desideratum of our Constitution. Accident alone gave Adams the Presidency."[10]

Thus the electoral college's propensity for razor-thin decisions and its susceptibility to political manipulation was abundantly clear as the nation headed for the climactic election of 1800.

THE ELECTION OF 1800

The four years of John Adams's administration had witnessed a rapid disintegration of the Federalist party. The disruption of relations with France, leading to talk of war in 1797–98, darkened the foreign scene, while at home the Federalists stirred up bitter opposition by enacting the repressive Alien and Sedition laws. The brilliant Alexander Hamilton sought to maintain his influence over the Adams administration of which he was not a member, a practice that led in 1800 to the dismissal of two of Adams's cabinet officers who followed Hamilton's lead on policy.[11] This was followed closely by a Republican victory in the New York elections in the spring of 1800 and the appearance of a letter by Hamilton attacking the president.

As the long-dominant party, however, the Federalists were not to be taken lightly, and the country girded itself for a heated contest. In 1799 some Federalist circles sought to induce General Washington to emerge from retirement and run again, but he refused. On December 14, 1799, Washington was dead. The Federalists really had no alternative to Adams, and a party caucus of the Federalists in Congress decided early in 1800 that their ticket would consist of Adams and General Charles Cotesworth Pinckney, a brother of Thomas Pinckney, the 1796 candidate. The selections were not authoritatively announced until June, however. Vice President Jefferson was the Republicans' obvious candidate, but a small congressional caucus was held to confirm his selection as the party's presidential candidate and to settle on Aaron Burr for vice president. Jefferson later wrote that Burr had been put on the ticket "out of respect for the favor he had obtained with the Republican party by his extraordinary successes in the New York election in [April] 1800."[12]

The closeness and bitterness of the impending campaign prompted the leading politicians of both parties to rig the methods of choosing electors in their respective states to maximize their own electoral vote and minimize the opposition's. Ironically, several members of the Constitutional Convention, men who had declared so confidently in 1787 that they had protected the election of the president against all intrigue and cabal, were at the forefront of the effort.

In Virginia, where the ruling Republicans had witnessed a number of Federalist inroads since 1796, James Madison introduced a bill in the House of Delegates to shift from the district system Virginia had employed in the first three elections to a general ticket system. The change was to be made "until some uniform mode of choosing a President and Vice President of the United States shall be prescribed by an amendment to the Constitution," and the preamble to the bill actually condemned the general ticket system. But as Madison told the House of Delegates, necessity had impelled the change. Jefferson summed up the reasons for the move in a letter to Monroe: "All agree that an election by districts would be best if it could be general, but while ten states choose either by their legislatures or by a general ticket, it is folly or worse for the other six not to follow."[13] The effect of the change in Virginia in 1800, of course, was to assure all the state's 21 electoral votes for Jefferson in that fall's election.

In New York state, where previously the legislature had chosen the presidential electors, the Federalists viewed with alarm the results of the April 1800 elections that had put Republicans in control. Alexander Hamilton wrote to Governor John Jay on May 7 urging that the lame-duck Federalist legislature be called quickly into session to adopt a popular vote district system that would prevent a solid New York electoral vote for Jefferson. Hamilton told Jay he was aware there were "weighty objections to the measure," but that "in times like these in which we live, it will not do to be overscrupulous." So long as nothing was proposed that integrity would forbid, he said, the scruples of propriety "ought not to hinder the taking of a legal and constitutional step to prevent an atheist in religion, and a fanatic in politics, from getting possession of the helm of state." Jefferson's party, Hamilton warned, was "a composition, indeed of very incongruous materials, but all tending to mischief—some of them to the *overthrow* of the government, by stripping it of its energies; others of them, to a *revolution* after the manner of Bonaparte." The text of Hamilton's letter found its way into print, occasioning strong criticism. The original letter was found years later among Jay's papers, on the back of which the governor had written: "Proposing a measure for party purposes, which I think would not become me to adopt."[14] In the fall the new Republican legislature would vote to cast all of New York's 12 electoral votes for Jefferson and Burr—a crucial factor in the Republican ticket's 8-vote lead in the electoral college.

In Pennsylvania, another key state, the old law providing for popular election of electors on a general ticket had expired and the Senate—under Federalist control by a 2-vote margin—refused to agree to renewal of the statute, fearing that the Republicans would capture the state's electoral votes. The Republicans already controlled the Assembly by a large margin and had won decisive control of both houses of the legislature and of the governorship in the 1800 elections. The refusal of the lame-duck Federalists in the Pennsylvania senate—a group of thirteen, known as the "Spartan band"—to agree on an election system prompted the Republican newspaper *Aurora* of Philadelphia to comment that because the Constitution lacked "explicitness on the momentous object of choosing electors of a chief magistrate, it is almost in the power of two or three abandoned individuals, by disenfranchising our state, perhaps, to impose a President on the Union contrary to the strongest wishes of the people."[15] Finally, a compromise was arranged that allowed the senate to choose seven electors and the Assembly to pick eight. Predictably, the senate picked Federalists, the Assembly, Republicans, so that the votes nearly canceled themselves out. "Thus," commented one observer of the past century, "was the vote of a state bargained away."[16]

In Massachusetts, to save the whole ticket for Adams and Pinckney, the General Court was summoned into special session and took up on itself the appointment of electors. New Hampshire also withdrew the privilege of voting for electors from the people and appointed six Federalist electors by action of the legislature.[17]

In the end, legislatures picked the presidential electors in ten of the sixteen states. The only states with popular election were Virginia and Rhode Island (employing the general ticket system) and Maryland, North Carolina, and Kentucky (under the district system).

The Federalists had remained confident that they could eke out another victory, and on December 13, 1800—after the electors had already met to cast their votes—the *Columbian Centinel* of Boston confidently asserted that "there cannot be a doubt" of the election of Adams and Pinckney. (This journalistic blunder would go unmatched until the night of November 2, 1948, when the banner headline of an early edition of the Chicago *Tribune* proclaimed: "Dewey Elected President.") One week later the *Centinel* was obliged to "concede" the "bad news" that Jefferson and Burr were chosen. The results were finally determined by the votes of South Carolina, which went for Jefferson and Burr despite the Federalists' expectations of victory.[18] The final electoral count would show 73 votes each for Jefferson and Burr. In amassing its victory, the Republican ticket had won New York, half of Pennsylvania, and every state from Maryland southward.[19] The Federalists were confined to their solid base of support in New England, plus scattered support in the middle states. Adams received 65 electoral votes, Pinckney 64, and John Jay one.

The Republicans, however, could not rejoice. They had failed to take the precaution of having just one of their electors withhold a vote from Burr with the result that Jefferson and Burr were in a dead tie, and there was no decision on a president in the electoral college. Ironically, the duty fell to Jefferson, as the vice president and president of the Senate, to preside over the joint session of Congress on February 11, 1801, where the electoral votes were opened and this unhappy result confirmed.

Now, for the first time in United States history, the House of Representatives was required to choose the president, acting under the contingent election procedure spelled out in the Constitution. Each state would have but a single vote, and if its representatives were equally divided, the state would lose its vote.

Since late December, when the outcome of the electoral vote had become common knowledge throughout the country, the Federalists had been laying plans to thwart Jefferson's election. The lame-duck Congress, with a strong Federalist majority, would still be in office, and the possibilities for intrigue were all too apparent. An initial Federalist plan was to block any candidate from receiving a majority of the states' votes in the House until March 4, when the offices of president and vice president would become vacant and a new election could be required under a 1792 law and under the original constitutional language regarding presidential elections, which was still in effect.[20] This course of action was soon abandoned, however, perhaps because such a naked power play would backfire and result in an easy election for Jefferson in any runoff.

The next plan developed was to throw the support of the Federalist House delegations to Burr, thus electing a cynical and pliant politician over a man the Federalists considered a "dangerous radical."[21] This became the general Federalist strategy, even though Alexander Hamilton remonstrated against it. "I trust the Federalists will not finally be so mad as to vote for Burr," Hamilton wrote to Gouverneur Morris. "I speak with intimate and accurate knowledge of his character. His elevation can only promote the purposes of the desperate and the profligate. If there be a man in the world I ought to hate, it is Jefferson. With Burr I have always been personally well. But the public good must be paramount to every private consideration." In a letter to Albert Gallatin, Hamilton said he "could scarcely name a discreet man of either party" who did not think "Mr. Burr the most unfit man in the United States for the office of President."[22]

When the House of Representatives retired to its own chamber to choose a president on February 11, it became apparent that Hamilton's powerful efforts to dissuade the Federalists from supporting Burr had been only partly successful. A majority of the Federalists insisted on backing Burr over Jefferson, the man they despised the most. Indeed, if Burr had given clear assurances that he would run the government as a Federalist, he might well have been elected. But Burr was unwilling to make those assurances; as one chronicler has put it, "no one knows whether it was honor or a wretched indecision which gagged Burr's lips."[23]

In all, there were 106 members of the House at this time, consisting of 58 Federalists and 48 Republicans. If the ballots had been cast per capita, Burr would have received 53 to Jefferson's 51. But the constitutional rule was for a single vote for each state, with a majority vote required to decide the election. On the first ballot, Jefferson received the votes of 8 states—one short of a majority of the 16 states then in the Union. Six states backed Burr, while Vermont and Maryland were evenly divided, so that their votes could not be counted. The rules of the House required that it remain in continuous session until a president was elected, but by midnight on the first day of balloting, nineteen ballots had been taken and the deadlock remained.[24] In all, thirty-six ballots would be required before the House came to a decision on February 17.

In the meantime, frantic efforts were under way to resolve the deadlock. Two men backing Burr held it in their power to switch their states to Jefferson—James A. Bayard of Delaware and Lewis R. Morris of Vermont. One more state for Jefferson would have given him nine and thus the election. On the other hand, Burr could have gained three states and thus been elected president if two Federalists from New York and one each from New Jersey and Maryland had decided to withdraw their support from Jefferson. Predictably, there were some who sought to exploit the situation for personal gain. Jefferson wrote to Monroe on February 15: "Many attempts have been made to obtain terms and promises from me. I have declared to them unequivocally that I would not receive the government on capitulation; that I would not go in with my hands tied."[25]

Hamilton directed his efforts of persuasion, which were considerable, to Bayard of Delaware, who initially voted for Burr in the hope Burr would govern as a Federalist. Bayard finally became convinced that Burr's Republicanism was unshakable, however, and announced to one of the Federalist caucuses that he intended to vote for Jefferson. "You cannot well imagine the clamor and vehement invective to which I was subjected for some days," Bayard wrote later.[26] Bayard was persuaded to hold off for a day, but on the thirty-sixth ballot on February 17 the impasse was broken. Morris of Vermont turned in a blank ballot, permitting his sole Vermont colleague, Matthew Lyon, to vote the state for Jefferson. The Burr backers in Maryland, sensing that the deadlock had been broken, also cast blank ballots, permitting the four Jefferson backers from that state to switch its support to Jefferson. Delaware and South Carolina likewise withdrew their support from Burr by casting blank ballots. Thus, at the completion of the thirty-sixth ballot, Jefferson had ten states and Burr four. Jefferson was elected the third president of the United States.[27]

But the nation had not survived its constitutional crisis without danger. The Republican governors of Pennsylvania and Virginia had reportedly been ready to call out their militia to block a Federalist usurpation of the presidency. Two years later Senator James Jackson of Georgia declared that if the scheme to elect Burr had "been pursued to consummation," Georgia "would have flown to arms, and South Carolina would have joined her to do justice in the interest of the nation."[28]

Once the presidency was decided in Jefferson's favor, Burr had the greatest number of electoral votes, and he became vice president. But Jefferson refused to consult Burr in patronage matters, and the Republicans dropped him from their ticket in 1804. Burr returned to New York, bargained for Federalist support in an unsuccessful race for governor of that state, and darkened his name forever by killing Hamilton in a duel on July 11, 1804.

As for the Federalist party, its day of power was finished. The Congress that was to take office on March 4, 1801, elected the previous autumn, would have strong Republican majorities in both houses. In the next presidential election only two states would cast their electoral votes for the Federalist candidate. The Federalists would never again elect a president.

THE 12TH AMENDMENT

The election of 1800 had demonstrated both the impracticality and the dangers in the Constitution's requirement that each presidential elector cast two equal, undifferentiated votes for president. The system had been designed in the hope that the vice president chosen would be a man of high character and ability who could easily assume the presidency if needed. But the early rise of the party system had altered the situation entirely. Each party decided on the person it wanted for president and selected another—often of inferior quality—for the vice presidency. The dangers in the system were threefold. First, there might be a tie vote, as occurred in 1800—bringing an inferior man like Burr perilously close to the presidency through the kind of intrigue and cabal the founding fathers had hoped most to prevent. Second, if some electoral votes were withheld from the person intended for vice president, there was a chance that the opposing party's candidate for president might win the vice presidency. This occurred with Jefferson's election as vice president in 1796 over Pinckney, the man the winning Federalists favored that year. And third, the minority party could, if it so chose, switch some of its votes to the vice presidential candidate of the opposing party and thus make him president. If Jefferson had received a few less votes than Pinckney in 1796, a solid bloc of southern Republicans might well have cast votes for Pinckney, making him president instead of Adams. This was seriously considered by many southern Anti-Federalists.[29] Thus an inherent weakness of the electoral system had been demonstrated after only three presidential elections. By a number of numerical vagaries, the will of the country could be frustrated in any relatively close election.

The first constitutional amendment proposing that electors vote separately for president and vice president was introduced in Congress in January 1797 by Representative William Smith of South Carolina. In 1798 John Marshall of Kentucky proposed a similar amendment in the Senate, and the following year Representative Abiel Foster of New Hampshire sought unsuccessfully to get the House to debate the proposition. The Vermont legislature in November 1799 and the Massachusetts General Court in early 1800 proposed similar amendments, but the Congress failed to take action on any of these proposals.[30]

After the 1800 election, pressure for an amendment to the Constitution to avoid the pitfalls of double-balloting was renewed. In 1801 and 1802 the New York legislature, partly on the urging of Alexander Hamilton, passed resolutions asking for a constitutional amendment obliging the electors to vote separately for president and vice president. (The New York proposals also urged that the system of choosing electors by popular vote in districts be made mandatory, but Congress failed to act affirmatively on this aspect of the recommendation.) An amendment incorporating the separate vote for president and vice president cleared the House on May 1, 1802, by a 47 to 14 vote, but in voting two days later the Senate failed to get the required two-thirds majority for approval.[31] The Senate vote would have been a bare two-thirds in favor if Gouverneur Morris of New York had not voted in opposition. Morris explained his vote in a letter to the president of the New York senate, referring to his role as a delegate to the Philadelphia convention: "The Convention not only foresaw that a scene might take place similar to that of the last Presidential election [1800], but even supposed it not impossible that at some time or other a person admirably fitted for the office of President might have an equal vote with one totally unqualified, and that, by the predominance of faction in the House of Representatives, the latter might be preferred," Morris said. "This, which is the greatest supposable evil of the present mode, was carefully examined, and it appeared that, however prejudicial it might be at the present moment, a useful lesson would result from it for the future, to teach contending parties the importance of giving both votes to men fit for the first office."[32] Morris's argument is an interesting one, but the records of the convention indicate that if any such discussion did take place, it was not on the convention floor. Hamilton easily demolished Morris's argument with the comment: "One such fact as the late election is worth a thousand theories." However, if Morris saw a danger in degrading the vice presidency, he was correct. Opposing the amendment in the House the same year, Roger Griswold of Connecticut warned prophetically: "What will be the effect of this principle? The office of Vice President will be carried to market to purchase the votes of particular states."[33]

The proposed amendment was brought up again and considered at length by the first session of the Eighth Congress, which met in October 1803. By this time, five legislatures were on record as favoring it—New York, Vermont, Massachusetts, North Carolina, and Ohio.[34] The opposition seemed to spring from two sources—the fear of some small states that their voice in the presidential election would be undercut, and the fear of some Federalists that they would have less chance of electing a vice president.

Senator William Plumer of New Hampshire, expressing the small-state fears, said that under the proposed amendment "the large states can with more ease elect their candidates." The reason was that there would be less chance of tie votes and thus less chance that the election might be thrown into the House, where the small states enjoyed equal voting power. Yet the Constitution, Plumer said, "is the great plan of compromise between the jarring and contending interests of the great and small states." Seeking to rebut the small-state attack, Senator Samuel Smith of Maryland said that no law could be found in the country's statute books that was produced by such a combination of large-against-small or small-against-large states. But Senator Jonathan Dayton replied angrily that under the proposed amendment, the smaller states would be "degraded to the dependent position of satellites." The people of his New Jersey, Dayton said, "will never willingly submit to such degradation."[35]

The Federalist opposition to a change was based on that party's hope that it could compel the Republicans to scatter enough of their second votes in the presidential election of 1804 so that the Federalist candidate for president could at least be elected vice president. Thus the Federalists hoped to exploit the anomalies of the electoral system to elect a vice president just as the Republicans had done in 1796. The Federalist John Quincy Adams said he considered the proposed amendment "as intending to prevent a federal Vice President being chosen." In the Senate, a dissident Republican, Pierce Butler of South Carolina, sought to pinpoint the motives for the Federalist opposition by saying: "If you do not alter the Constitution, the people called Federalists will send a Vice President into that chair; and this, in truth, is the pivot upon which the whole turns."[36]

The party lines were apparent when the Senate approved the 12th amendment by a 22 to 10 vote on December 2, 1803, with almost all the Republicans in favor and the Federalists almost solid in opposition. The House then approved it after considerable debate, by a vote of 84 to 42, with the Speaker (Nathaniel Macon of North Carolina) casting the deciding vote to achieve the required two-thirds. After some differences in wording were ironed out, the amendment was submitted to the states on December 8, 1803. The states ratified with unexpected rapidity, and the amendment was declared in effect September 25, 1804, in time for that year's election.[37]

The text of the 12th amendment—which, with slight changes, remains the law today—appears in Appendix G. It effected the following changes in the original Constitution:

1. The presidential electors must vote separately for president and vice president, instead of casting two undifferentiated votes.

2. If an election is thrown into the House of Representatives because no candidate has a majority, the House shall pick from the *three* top electoral vote recipients, rather than the five stipulated in the original Constitution.

3. If the House is called on to pick the president and does not make a selection by March 4 (this date was changed to January 20 by the 20th amendment, ratified in 1933), then the new vice president will become president. The original Constitution had no comparable provision.

4. A majority of electoral votes is also required for the election of the vice president. The original Constitution had simply provided that the person receiving the second highest number of electoral votes, regardless of whether they constituted a majority, would be elected vice president. The 12th amendment left the contingent election for vice president in the Senate. (The original Constitution had contemplated throwing the vice presidential choice into the Senate only if there was a tie for that office.)

5. The age, citizenship, and residence requirements for a vice president are to be the same as those for a president. The original Constitution was silent on this point.

CHOOSING ELECTORS: FROM VARIETY TO UNIFORMITY

The practice of shifting the method of choosing presidential electors from year to year for the benefit of ruling circles in each state, so apparent in the election of 1800, would continue for another quarter-century. The Constitution had given the state legislatures an absolute *carte blanche* in this regard, and they seemed to place partisan interests first whenever they had a choice. Massachusetts, for example, shifted its system of choosing electors no less than seven times during the first ten elections. In 1826 a Senate report authored by Thomas Hart Benton noted that the various states' methods of choosing electors "change with a suddenness which defies classification," a practice producing "pernicious effects."[38] The case was put even more strongly by Senator Mahlon Dickerson of New Jersey in 1818. "The discordant systems adopted by the different states," he said, "are the subject of constant fluctuation and change—of frequent, hasty and rash experiment—established, altered, abolished, re-established, according to the dictates of the interest, ambition, the whim or caprice, of party and faction."[39] (See chart showing the states' methods 1789–1836, Appendix B.)

Direct choice by the legislature was the most widely used method in the first four elections and was employed by a significant number of states until the 1820s. For the dominant political circles in a state, it was the simplest method, since it involved no reference to the people—that unpredictable and sometimes fickle electorate. In fact, when state legislatures saw a chance that the candidate of their party would be defeated in a popular choice of electors, they sometimes revoked previous laws permitting popular election and took the appointment of electors back into their own hands. This is exactly what the lame-duck Federalists in the Pennsylvania senate succeeded in doing in 1800, though they were unable to elect Federalists to more than half the elector slots because the Republicans controlled the other part of the legislature at the time (see page 38). The New Jersey legislature, under Federalist control, effected an even bolder coup in 1812, repealing the state law for popular choice of electors and designating the electors itself on the very eve of the statewide election. Dickerson of New Jersey related six years later in the Senate: "Expresses were sent into the different parts of the state, to give notice of this repeal, but not in time, for the citizens in many towns met and gave their votes for electors and Representatives without knowing of the repeal of the law. The Legislature appointed eight electors, not one of whom would have been appointed by the people under the late election law—and this the Legislature well knew; otherwise they would not have taken from the people the right of choosing the electors under the law."[40]

When the legislatures did appoint electors directly, there were many ways in which it was done. Sometimes the appointments were made by the joint vote of the two houses; sometimes the choice was by concurrent vote, requiring a majority of each house for each elector chosen. Under a New York law in effect from the first elections to 1825, each house nominated a slate of electors by majority vote. The two houses then met in joint convention to reconcile their differences, again by majority vote.[41] This procedure was spelled out in statute to prevent a recurrence of the circumstances in the first election, when neither house of the New York legislature would concur in the other's choice of electors, and the state lost its vote for president altogether.

The rise of democratic sentiment in the early nineteenth century was to doom the direct legislative choice of electors, however. In several instances, parties that used the legislative election to control a state's electoral votes subsequently found themselves thrown out of office by an enraged populace. Between 1812 and 1820, nine state legislatures still chose the electors for their states. In 1824, though, the figure dropped to six states, in 1828 to only two, and from 1832 to 1860, only one state—South Carolina—resisted the trend to popular selection of the electors. After the Civil War, finally, democracy came to that state as well.

Popular choice of electors by district was the system personally favored by many of the nation's most distinguished early statesmen, including Jefferson,

Hamilton, Madison, Andrew Jackson, John Quincy Adams, and Daniel Webster.[42] Madison wrote in 1823 that "the district system was mostly, if not exclusively, in view when the Constitution was framed and adopted."[43] Yet in practice the district system was never employed by a majority of the states in any election. Only two states adopted it in the first two elections, and reached its height in 1820 when six states utilized it. By 1836 it had disappeared completely from the scene until it was revived by Maine in 1969 in a form that would provide for the determination of two of its four votes on the basis of its two congressional districts. Under this arrangement the only possible divisions of electoral votes would be 4-0, or 3-1 (should one district be carried by the candidate losing the statewide vote as well as the other district). As of the end of the 1970s, the latter division had not occurred, and in effect Maine's electoral vote had been cast as if it still had a general ticket basis.

When the district system was employed, it appeared in many forms. Sometimes there was a district for each elector; sometimes a state had only two or four superdistricts, each electing several electors. Sometimes a majority of the district vote was required for election; sometimes a plurality was sufficient. Sometimes two electors were statewide, either by direct vote or by the legislature, while the remainder were chosen by popular vote in districts. Variations of this plan were tried several times in Massachusetts. Popular election was the basis of choosing electors in the great majority of district plans, but Tennessee offered a major exception in 1796 and 1800. So that the "electors may be elected with as little trouble to the citizens of the state as possible," the Tennessee legislature decreed that the state should be divided into three districts and that the appointment of the presidential elector from each district be given in turn to a group of "electors"—three citizens from each county who had been selected by the legislature itself.[44]

Popular vote under a general ticket system, the plan under which all presidential electors run for election on a statewide basis, was the simplest system used in the early years. It was employed by two to three states in the first four presidential elections and by five to seven states in the years between 1804 and 1816. Then it rapidly gained the center of the stage, as its usage rose from nine states in 1820 to eighteen states in 1828 and twenty-five states (all but South Carolina) in 1836.

Why did the general ticket win this wide acceptance? There appear to be two major reasons. First its provision for the popular choice of electors—whose party loyalties were generally well known—corresponded in substantial measure to the developing ideas of the people's president. By the 1820s, democratic ideals had advanced so far in the United States that the people of most states were simply unwilling to leave the crucial choice of presidential electors in the hands of state legislatures.

Secondly, the general ticket system suited the purposes of the ruling political faction in any state. No longer would it be necessary (as under the district system) to share the state's electoral votes with the opposing party. By the general ticket system, the ruling party could deliver an absolutely solid electoral vote bloc to its national candidates—and then be in a position to demand the dividends in patronage and power that the contribution warranted. Once the opposition party could be subdued within the individual state, it would have no voice at all in the presidential election. Thus the dominant politicians almost invariably lined up in favor of the general ticket system. The politicians out of power usually preferred the district system so that they could retain some voice. But, lacking power, they naturally had little to say about the system the state would adopt—and the general ticket system gradually prevailed.

The adoption of the general ticket in some states, moreover, virtually compelled the others to follow suit so that their strength in the electoral college would not be diluted. In the words of the Benton Committee in the Senate in 1826: "If uniformity by districts is not established by free consent of the states, uniformity by general ticket or legislative ballot must be imposed by necessity. For, when the large states consolidate their votes to overwhelm the small ones, those, in turn, must concentrate their own strength to resist them. A few states may persevere for some time, in which they believe to be the fairest system; but, when they see the unity of action which others derive from the general ticket and the legislative modes of election, they will not, they cannot, resist the temptation to follow the same plan."[45] (See Jefferson's comments along the same line, page 37.)

The first decades of the nineteenth century witnessed the first major effort to write into the Constitution some specific plan, such as the choice of electors by district, that would prevent the abuses so apparent in the early years of the republic. But the attempt would fail, because it was in the interest of the ruling political circles in some states to adopt the general ticket system, and once some states had taken the step, the others were eventually obliged to follow. The general ticket was not adopted out of high constitutional principle. Indeed, as Lucius Wilmerding points out in his study of the period, "the question of reform tended to be debated on grounds of state power rather than national principle."[46] Ironically, most Americans today—if they are aware of the electoral college at all—usually think that the general ticket system is part of the Constitution. The truth is that any state could follow the lead of Maine and abandon it in any election. But such state action is exceedingly unlikely. The arguments against change by any single state—arguments that spring from simple motives of political self-preservation—are the same today as they were a century and a half ago.

4

Years of Controversy

Any electoral system in a democratic country, where elections are marked by competing political parties and free expression of the popular will, is likely to produce close calls and cliff-hanger elections in which a slight shift in votes can alter the final result. Yet the American electoral system, with its two stages in choosing a president—first through the votes of the people and then by the votes of the presidential electors whom they have chosen—can magnify the uncertainties in any close election, and throughout our history it has fostered uncertainties and the kind of unsavory intrigue that can only weaken the presidency and the unity of the American people behind their chief executive.

We have already seen how, in 1796, the defeated Federalist candidate for vice president might have been propelled into the presidency by scheming electors of the other party if 100 votes had shifted in a single state, Pennsylvania (pages 35–36). The 1800 tie vote in the electoral college and the pressures for unprincipled agreements by the presidential contenders during the subsequent thirty-six ballots in the House have also been reviewed (pages 39–41). The 12th amendment was intended to correct the chief deficiencies, yet all it really did was to reduce sharply the possibilities of a tie in the electoral balloting.

Since the ratification of the 12th amendment, nine presidential elections have illustrated most clearly the anomalies, ambiguities, and undemocratic consequences of the system. The first three—those of 1824, 1876, and 1888—showed how the electoral college could elect the man the people had rejected. The 1824 election also showed the special danger of elections in the House, while the election of 1876 illustrated the ugly consequences of widespread disputed returns. Five later elections—1916, 1948, 1960, 1968, and 1976—demonstrated how close we have come to a miscarriage of the popular will in our own century and the dangers still inherent in vote frauds, splinter parties, and electors who may suddenly break the traces and exercise their own will against the people's will. The election of 1980, while decisive in its final result, raised speculation about the impact of a major nationwide independent candidacy. Each of these elections deserves closer scrutiny.

THE ELECTION OF 1824

Thomas Jefferson's election began a quarter-century of Virginian presidents, all members of his Republican party—or, as it was known by the 1820s, the Democratic party. James Madison won relatively easily in 1808 and 1812, and by the time James Monroe ran in 1816 and 1820, the once-powerful Federalist party was so weak that it could offer no organized opposition. The rise of new national issues—slavery in the new western states, tariffs, public works—brought an end to the "Era of Good Feeling" at the end of Monroe's second administration. But the Democratic party was the only recognizable national party, and thus the search for a new president was an entirely intraparty affair.

Though as many as seventeen men were prominently mentioned for the presidency, the field by the time of the election was narrowed down to four: John Quincy Adams of Massachusetts, the secretary of state and son of the former president; Henry Clay of Kentucky, who had won national prominence as Speaker of the House; William H. Crawford of Georgia, the secretary of the treasury; and Andrew Jackson of Tennessee, known as the hero of the Battle of New Orleans in 1815. Though each candidate sought a national following, their appeals were primarily sectional in character. Adams's major source of support lay with the eastern industrialists. Western businessmen tended to favor Clay, Crawford was the favorite of the southern planters, and Jackson had the western farmers on his side.

Through 1823 and into 1824 there was widespread controversy over the desirability of holding a congressional caucus to nominate candidates for president and vice president. Defenders of the caucus system, which had received increasing criticism over the years, argued that it was a tried method that offered the best expression of nationwide rather than strictly sectional interest in the presidential nomination. Opponents claimed that the caucus was simply a device to permit rule by powerful congressional cliques and that it would not represent the will of the people. In 1824, however, special opposition to the caucus developed because it was common knowledge that one of the candidates—Crawford—would probably receive its support. In a strategic blunder, Crawford's supporters did call a congressional caucus in February 1824. Supporters of the other contenders boycotted the caucus, making it a rump affair. Of the 216 party members in Congress, only 66 attended. Crawford was nominated with 64 votes. Not only the dispute over the caucus but Crawford's physical condition—he had suffered a paralyzing stroke in September 1823—would work to his disadvantage in the ensuing campaign.[1]

In the meantime, in November 1822, the Kentucky legislature had nominated Clay. Jackson was nominated by the lower house of the Tennessee legislature in 1822 and then by mass conventions of people in various parts of Tennessee and in other parts of the country. Adams's name was placed in nomination by most of the New England legislatures early in 1824. The names of two other men were also put forward: John C. Calhoun of South Carolina and De Witt Clinton of New York. But both withdrew before the election, Calhoun to run for (and win) the vice presidency.

In 18 of the 24 states, there was a popular vote for president. For the first time in U.S. history, something approximating a national popular vote could be compiled. The vote showed 152,933 for Jackson, 115,696 for Adams, 46,979 for Crawford, and 47,136 for Clay. The accuracy of this count as a valid reflection of the popular will is open to serious challenge, however, because the states still choosing their presidential electors by legislature included mighty New York. Even in Virginia, where there was a popular election, only 14,955 votes were cast from a white population of 625,000, and the vote was similarly low in many other states.[2] The popular vote count was important, however, for it would give Jackson's supporters an opportunity to claim that their man was the real choice of the people.

Results of the 1824 Election

	Popular Votes*	Electoral Votes
Andrew Jackson	152,933	99
John Quincy Adams	115,696	84
William H. Crawford	46,979	41
Henry Clay	47,136	37

* Returns from 18 of the 24 states then in the Union. In the other 6 states, the legislatures chose the presidential electors.

Since no candidate received an electoral vote majority, the election was thrown into the House, where Adams won on the first ballot. The count: 13 states for Adams, 7 for Jackson, 4 for Crawford.

The electoral count was widely split. Jackson won Pennsylvania, New Jersey, and a majority of the southern states; Adams took all of New England; Crawford drew his main support from Virginia and Georgia; Clay had little support outside of Kentucky and Ohio. On February 9, 1825, when the electoral votes were officially counted, it was apparent that no candidate had received a majority, and it fell to the House of Representatives—for the first time since 1801—to select the president. The House would have to choose from the three top candidates—Jackson, Adams, and Crawford. The real choice lay between Jackson and Adams, the top contenders, and the key man whose support had to be obtained was Henry Clay. From the start, Clay apparently intended to support Adams as the lesser of two evils; he is known to have regarded Jackson as a hotheaded military man with little qualification for the presidency.[3]

But before the House vote, a scandal erupted. The *Columbian Observer* of Philadelphia published an anonymous letter alleging that Clay had agreed to support Adams in return for being made secretary of state. The letter said that Clay would have been willing to make the same deal with Jackson. Clay immediately denied the charge and pronounced the writer of the letter to be "a base and infamous character, a dastard and a liar." Clay urged the anonymous letter writer to make himself known and challenged him to a duel. Representative George Kremer of Pennsylvania announced that he had written the letter but failed to take up the duel challenge. A slow-witted man, Kremer probably was a front for the Jackson faction. Jackson himself believed the charge, and his suspicions were clearly vindicated when Adams, after the election, actually did appoint Clay as secretary of state. "So you see the Judas of the West has closed the contract and will receive the thirty pieces of silver," Jackson wrote to a friend. "His end will be the same. Was there ever witnessed such a bare faced corruption in any country before?"[4] Representative John Randolph of Virginia termed the Adams-Clay alliance "the coalition of Blifil and Black George—the combination, unheard of till then, of the puritan with the black-leg." Clay challenged Randolph to a duel, which actually took place, though neither was hurt.[5]

As the day of decision in the House approached, Adams seemed assured of the six New England states and, in large part through Clay's backing, of Maryland, Ohio, Kentucky, Illinois, Missouri, and Lousiana. Thus he had 12 of the 24 states and needed only one more to win the election. The likeliest state to add to the Adams column appeared to be New York, since 17 members of its 34-man delegation were already reported ready to vote for him. Clay decided that the one uncommitted member of the delegation was Stephen Van Rensselaer, an elderly, deeply religious member of one of New York's aristocratic families. Van Rensselaer was invited into the Speaker's office the morning of the crucial vote and personally urged by Clay and Daniel Webster to vote for Adams. The entreaties from these two powerful men were reportedly unsuccessful, but the story is told that as Van Rensselaer sat at his desk in the House before the vote, he bowed his head in prayer to seek divine guidance. As he did this, his eyes fell on a slip of paper inadvertently left on the floor. The name "Adams" was written on the slip. Interpreting this as a sign from above, Van Rensselaer voted for Adams. Thus was New York's vote cast for the candidate. Added to the 12 states he already had, Adams thus enjoyed the support of 13 of the 24 states—and was elected president by the House on the first ballot.[6]

In his reply to the committee that notified him of his election, Adams alluded to the circumstances under which he had been chosen and expressed his wish to decline the office and submit the question once again to the people. But he noted that this avenue was not open, for "the Constitution has not disposed of the contingency which would arise in the event of my refusal."[7] Like his father, Adams would have but a single term in the presidency. The controversy and allegations that accompanied Adams's election would hang over him like a cloud for the next four years. This handicap, together with his natural limitations as a popular leader, made Adams's term a trying one.

Losing no time, the Tennessee legislature in 1825 nominated Jackson for the presidency in 1828. As the campaign approached, the Jacksonians harped increasingly on the basic issue given them by the 1824 election: that Jackson had won the most popular votes and had been the choice of the people, but the House of Representatives had frustrated their will. This simple, emotional appeal was more than Adams could withstand, and the 1828 election results showed an overwhelming triumph for Jackson, both in popular and electoral votes.

THE ELECTION OF 1876

The American nation was little more than a decade past the throes of its great civil war as it prepared to elect its nineteenth president in 1876, and the bitterness lingered on, in both North and South. While the states of the old Confederacy labored to cast off the last remnants of Reconstruction, Republican orators in the North waved the "bloody shirt" and warned of dire consequences if the Democratic party, the party of the former rebels, were to return to power. The country had come on hard times, and many had suffered in the financial panic of 1873. The midterm elections of 1874 had carried the Democrats into control of the House of Representatives, much to the dismay of Republican President Ulysses S. Grant and his administration, especially as committees of the House began to disclose corruption in high places. Against this background, the country entered the presidential campaign of 1876—a contest that would not be decided until two days before the inauguration in 1877, following a historic dispute over the counting of the popular and electoral ballots. Two decades later, Edward Stanwood, the distinguished historian of the presidency, would write: "It is to be hoped that the patriotism of the American people and their love of peace may never again be put to so severe a test as that to which they were subjected in 1876 and 1877."[8]

Meeting in Cincinnati the week of June 14, 1876, the Republican National Convention balloted seven times before it could agree on Ohio's governor, Rutherford B. Hayes, as its presidential nominee. A dark horse when the convention convened, Hayes received only 61 of the 754 votes on the first ballot but gradually drew ahead of James G. Blaine of Maine and other early favorites. Into the campaign Hayes would carry a reputation as an efficient three-term governor and Ohio's top vote-getter and a record free from any taint of scandal.

The Democrats met in St. Louis two weeks later and nominated Governor Samuel J. Tilden of New York on the second ballot. A corporate lawyer who had won a high reputation by his warfare against the "Tweed ring" in New York City, Tilden was known as a competent reform governor of his state. But he was an austere bachelor of sixty-two who lacked much of the fire and verve needed for an effective onslaught on the entrenched Republicans.

Following a relatively spiritless campaign, the people went to the polls on Tuesday, November 7. The real excitement began as the returns started to pour in. The Republicans' one-time strongholds in Connecticut, New York, New Jer-

Results of the 1876 Election

	Popular Votes		Electoral Votes, Count after Decisions of Electoral Commission
	Republican Count	Democratic Count	
Samuel J. Tilden (Dem.)	4,285,992	4,300,590	184
Rutherford B. Hayes (Rep.)	4,033,768	4,036,298	185
Minor Parties	94,935		

Tilden plurality: 252,224 (Republican count); 264,292 (Democratic count)

The above figures are based on contemporary accounts.[9] For slightly differing figures, based on modern-day analysis, see Appendix A.

sey, and Indiana went for Tilden, and with the expected outpouring of southern votes for the Democrats, Tilden looked like a winner on election night. Republican National Chairman Zachariah Chandler, discouraged with the reports, went to bed, and Hayes admitted his defeat in his diary.[10] The general expectation was that Tilden would have 203 electoral votes to Hayes's 166.

Early the next morning, however, Republican hopes began to revive. If South Carolina, Florida, and Louisiana could be held for Hayes, he would defeat Tilden by a single electoral vote—185 to 184. Chandler proclaimed Hayes's victory. Telegrams were rushed to Republican leaders in the doubtful states warning them not to accept the early returns, which were favorable to the Democrats, and Republican agents supplied with money were soon on their way south to help local Republican political leaders in the impending disputes over contested returns. In each of the disputed southern states, Reconstruction was still in force, and the Republicans controlled the state governments and election machinery. Republicans counted on masses of Negro votes to win, while the Democrats employed threats and intimidation and even violence on occasion to prevent the Negroes from casting ballots. The ensuing struggle would find agents of both parties using illegal and corrupt tactics to achieve their ends; there were even reports of a Democratic offer of a million dollars to a member of the Louisiana election board to achieve the certification of at least one Democratic elector from that state.[11] Both sides were keenly aware that the choice of a *single* Tilden elector in the disputed states would upset Hayes's alleged one-vote lead and result in a Democratic victory.

Eventually, double sets of elector returns were sent to Congress from four disputed states. In South Carolina, it was alleged that army detachments stationed near the polls had prevented a fair election. The official returns showed a slight lead for the Hayes elector slate, and the state board of canvassers so certified. But the state's Democratic elector candidates met the same day, voted for Tilden, and forwarded their ballots to Washington. In Florida, both sides charged fraud, and though the canvassing board and governor certified the election of Hayes electors, the Democrats won a court challenge and submitted electoral votes for Tilden. Anarchy reigned in Louisiana, where there were two governors, two canvassing boards, two sets of returns showing different results, and two electoral colleges. In Oregon, where the Republicans received a clear majority, Democratic Governor L. F. Glover discovered that one of the Republican electors chosen was a postmaster and thus ineligible under the U.S. Constitution. Glover thereupon certified the election of the top-polling Democratic elector candidate. But the Republican electors met, received the resignation of the ineligible Republican elector, and then elected the same man to the vacancy, since in the meantime he had resigned as postmaster. Two sets of returns were sent from the state to Washington.[12]

On two previous occasions, Congress had faced the problem of disputed electoral votes, but this was the first time in U.S. history that a decision would have to be made on competing sets of elector returns which would determine the actual outcome of the election. Nor would the conflict be easy to resolve, for although the House of Representatives was under Democratic control, Republicans still held a majority in the Senate. The fear of the time, expressed by Senator George F. Edmunds of Vermont in the *American Law Review* of October 1877, was that "the Senate would declare Hayes President, the House Tilden." In that case, he continued, "each of these gentlemen would have taken the oath of office, and attempted to exercise its duties; each would have called upon the Army and the people to sustain him against the usurpations of the other. . . . The solemn ceremonies and the grand pageant of inauguration would be only the first act in the awful tragedy and anarchy of civil war."[13] Indeed, there were threats that thousands would march on the Capitol to demand an honest count, and calls of "Tilden or Blood" came from some Democrats.

These dangers were keenly felt when Congress met in December 1876. The leaders of both parties quickly agreed that some compromise would have to be reached for the good of the whole country. No clear precedent existed for resolving electoral disputes. In fact, a rule that would have disqualified the returns of any state where one house of Congress objected had been allowed to lapse at the start of 1876. If the former rule had been in effect, the House could easily have objected to any of Hayes's disputed votes and thus brought about Tilden's election.

With a need for immediate action because of the impending electoral vote disputes, a joint committee was established to write a rule on resolving electoral disputes "by a tribunal whose authority none can question and whose decision all will accept as final." The Electoral Commission Law, to apply to the count of the 1876 electoral votes only, passed both houses late in January and was signed by President Grant on January 29—three days before the appointed day for opening and counting the electoral votes, February 1.[14]

Under the new law, both houses would have to agree upon rejecting the electoral votes from any state for those votes to be disqualified. A special blue-ribbon commission of fifteen members—five from the Senate, five from the

House, and five from the membership of the Supreme Court—was established to judge those cases in which more than one return from a state had been received. The decisions of this Electoral Commission would be final, unless overruled by both houses of Congress.

All commission members were required to take a solemn oath that they would unquestionably "dismiss every consideration that would cloud their intellects or warp their judgments." This heroic attempt to achieve nonpartisanship was underpinned, however, by a clear understanding of all parties concerned that the members appointed by the Senate would include three Republicans and two Democrats, while those from the House would include three Democrats and two Republicans. The names of four Supreme Court justices were designated in the bill—two Democrats and two Republicans. Thus it was known that the commission would have seven Republicans and seven Democrats. The crucial selection—on which the entire election was to turn—was the fifth justice. The bill specified that he would be selected by the four Supreme Court justices already designated, and it was generally understood that this final member would be Justice David Davis, a Lincoln appointee who was regarded as a political independent.[15]

If Davis actually had served, it is quite likely that he would have agreed with the Democrats in at least one of the disputed elector cases and thus brought about Tilden's election. But on January 26, the very day the commission bill passed Congress, startling news arrived from Springfield, Illinois. The afternoon before, the Illinois legislature had named Davis to a seat in the U.S. Senate. The historian Eugene Roseboom comments that "fortune seemed to reserve her smiles for the Republicans during these years, but in this case asinine blundering by the Illinois Democrats would seem to be a more logical explanation."[16] The four justices designated in the bill eventually chose another colleague, Justice Joseph P. Bradley, as the commission's fifteenth member. Democratic leaders approved of the choice, feeling Bradley was as independent as any of the remaining members of the Court. But the fact of the matter was that Bradley was a Republican, and on every disputed vote before the commission, he took the Republican side—giving the Republican cause an 8 to 7 edge and bringing about Hayes's election. Even though eight million people voted for president, as one newspaper charged, "the vote of one man—Justice Bradley—nullifies the voice of the majority and places the usurper in the chair."

As the electoral count began in Congress on February 1, each party was confident—the Democrats believing that at least *one* Hayes vote would be found invalid, the Republicans hopeful that the commission would confine itself to deciding which state elector certificates were official, without investigating the circumstances surrounding the actual balloting. As each disputed state was reached in the official count in the joint session of Congress, objections were raised to both the Hayes and Tilden certificates that had been submitted. The disputes were then automatically referred to the electoral commission, which met and made a decision on each of the disputes. In every instance, the commission split 8 to 7 in favor of accepting the Hayes votes and rejecting the Tilden votes. The decision was then referred back to each house of Congress, and in every instance the Democratic House voted against the electoral commission decision while the Republican Senate voted to uphold it. Under the new law, the result was that the commission's decision was sustained in every case.[17]

This long process of count and challenge stretched over a month and a day, and the final result was not announced until four o'clock in the morning on March 2. That same day, Hayes arrived in the capital, and he took the oath the next evening at the White House, because March 4 fell on a Sunday. A formal inauguration followed on Monday.[18]

As the disputed South Carolina votes were being counted, some Democrats in the House had suggested launching a filibuster that would block resumption of the joint sessions and the regular count beyond inauguration day—with unpredictable consequences. The crisis never developed that far, however, because negotiations had already been under way between associates of Hayes and a number of southern conservatives. Under the terms of the agreement, the Democrats would permit the electoral count to proceed without obstruction. In return, Hayes would agree to a number of concessions, the most important of which were the withdrawal of federal troops from the South and the end of Reconstruction. In return, the southerners pledged that Negro rights would be respected. Within a few months, Hayes had lived up to his part of the bargain by withdrawing the remaining federal troops in the Confederacy,[19] but the conservative southerners were unable to protect Negro rights. More violent forces in the South were soon to seize power and to deprive southern Negroes of their most basic right—the right to vote. It would be almost a century until the nation began to rectify the injustices to the southern Negro that stemmed from the price paid for peace in the land in 1877.

No public disturbances followed the announcement of Hayes's election. Even Tilden refused to offer public protest. "I can return to private life," he said, "with the consciousness that I shall receive from posterity the credit of having been elected to the highest position in the gift of the people, without any of the cares and responsibilities of the office."[20]

Democrats continued for years thereafter, however, to denounce the outcome as a fraud. A Democratic-controlled committee of the House reached this very conclusion in 1879. Many newspapers refused to speak of Hayes as the rightful president. That the public will had been frustrated there could be little doubt. For whether one accepted the Republican or Democratic version of the correct vote count, it was clear that Samuel Tilden had received some quarter-million more votes than Rutherford Hayes, the man whom the electoral college and political happenstance had made president.

Moreover, the 1876 election had demonstrated a grave defect in the Constitution: its failure to spell out exact responsibility for counting the electoral votes and resolving disputes, so that the resolution of the entire presidential election can swing on the intrigues and maneuvers in a partisanly motivated Congress, to the detriment of the people and the presidency alike. Today that basic constitutional defect remains uncorrected.

THE ELECTION OF 1888

From 1876 through 1900 the country experienced an unbroken line of exceptionally close presidential elections. In 1876 the shift of one state—indeed, the shift of one electoral vote—would have altered the outcome. Single-state outcomes also dictated the results in 1880, 1884, and 1888. Strategically placed shifts of less than 75,000 popular votes would also have altered the outcome in 1892, 1896, and 1900. But the election of 1888 has the distinction of being the last election, up to the present time, in which the electoral college clearly elected a man to the presidency over the candidate favored by most of the people.

In itself, the campaign of 1888 offered little excitement. Grover Cleveland was completing his first term in the White House, and the Democratic Convention in St. Louis nominated him by acclamation for a second term—the first time since Martin Van Buren's renomination in 1840 that a roll call had not been necessary. James G. Blaine could probably have had the Republican nomination for the asking; he had barely lost to Cleveland in 1884 and was still the party's most popular leader and powerful orator. But Blaine announced that he would not be a candidate, and when Republicans met in Chicago in June, eight ballots were required until General Benjamin Harrison of Indiana, a grandson of President William Henry Harrison, emerged as the nominee. The great issue of the campaign was the tariff, with the Democrats pressing for freer trade and the Republicans pledging that they would sweep away the entire internal revenue system before they would lower the protective duty on imports. With the end of Reconstruction the Democrats had seized complete control of the South and the question was whether the Republicans could prevent enough northern defections to overcome the solid South. The election turned on the doubtful states of Indiana and New York. Cleveland lost Indiana, and crucial New York also went to Harrison—by a margin of 13,373 votes out of the 1,321,897 cast in that state. Had Cleveland carried New York, he would have won the election.* Across the nation, Cleveland led Harrison by 95,096

---

* Four years before, in the election of 1884, the national result had also swung on the outcome in New York. Two trivial occurrences appear to have delivered the state to Cleveland over Blaine. The first occurred October 29, when Blaine, in an informal meeting with a group of ministers in New York City, failed to take exception to the allegation of one of the clerics that the Democrats were the party of "rum, Romanism and rebellion." Cleveland forces moved quickly to exploit Blaine's failure to object, and the incident may well have cost Blaine enough Irish votes to lose the state. Possibly even more important, election day brought a driving rain upstate and cut down the

popular votes. But the electoral college rendered a different decision: Harrison would be the next president, winning 233 electoral votes to Cleveland's 168.[21]

Results of the 1888 Election

	Popular Votes	Electoral Votes
Benjamin Harrison (Rep.)	5,445,269	233
Grover Cleveland (Dem.)	5,540,365	168
Minor Parties	404,205	—
Cleveland Plurality: 95,096		

THE ELECTION OF 1916

No American president of the twentieth century has been chosen by the electoral college after a definitive defeat in the popular vote. But on five occasions in this century, the nation has come perilously close to such an unjust outcome of the national election. The first occurred in 1916.

The election of 1912 had witnessed a historic schism in the Republican party between the Old Guard, under President William Howard Taft, and the Progressives, led by former president Theodore Roosevelt. The split opened the way for Woodrow Wilson to become the first Democratic president in two decades. As the 1916 contest approached, the Republicans sought a candidate who would be acceptable to both factions of the party. In Supreme Court Justice Charles Evans Hughes they felt they had the ideal candidate. Hughes had proven his administrative abilities as a reform governor of New York state, yet had been isolated from the internecine Republican warfare as a member of the bench since 1910. Against a split field, Hughes was nominated on the third ballot at the Republican National Convention in Chicago the second week of June. Roosevelt was nominated by the Progressives for a second time, but he declined the honor and campaigned for Hughes. No organized opposition materialized against Wilson in his own party, and he was renominated at the Democratic National Convention in St. Louis a week after Hughes.

Labor unrest and tariffs figured as campaign issues, but the overriding appeal on which the Democrats won, spelled out in their platform and repeated countless times up to election day, was that Wilson had "kept us out of war." Most Americans genuinely abhorred the idea of becoming involved in the great European war, even though the sinking of the *Lusitania* and other submarine horrors had aroused serious resentments against Germany. The Republicans found themselves occupying a middle ground between the country's pro- and anti-German factions, while the Democrats campaigned as the party that could

---

rural Republican vote. Cleveland's margin in the state was only 1,149 votes out of 1,167,169 cast. With New York, he won the nation and became the first Democratic president since the Civil War.[22]

preserve peace. The issue had great appeal, especially in the farm areas, known for their isolationism, and among women voters. Wilson carried nearly all the states in which the franchise had already been extended to women.

The best hope for Hughes was that the country's basic Republicanism, disrupted in 1912, could reassert itself in the presidential balloting. Roosevelt's decision to support Hughes increased his chances substantially. Indeed, as the first returns began to pour into New York on election night, a Hughes victory seemed imminent. The East, including New York with its 45 and Pennsylvania with its 38 electoral votes, went Republican, and when the Midwestern returns showed only Ohio in the Democratic column, President Wilson told his close associates that he was relieved to see the burdens of office lifted from him.[23]

Results of the 1916 Election

	Popular Votes	Electoral Votes
Woodrow Wilson (Dem.)	9,131,511	277
Charles Evans Hughes (Rep.)	8,548,935	254
Minor Parties	855,786	—
Wilson plurality: 582,576		

As more states reported, however, the race for electoral ballots grew closer and closer. The solid South held steadfastly Democratic, and Wilson won Kansas, most of the border states, and all of the mountain states. Finally, the outcome hinged on California and its 13 electoral votes. Excluding California, the electoral count stood at 264 for Wilson, 254 for Hughes. Whoever won California would be president. An agonizing delay in the vote count now occurred, and it was not until several days later that the California vote was finally tallied and Wilson found to be the victor. But Wilson had carried California by only 3,806 votes out of almost a million cast in the state. A shift of less than one-fifth of one percent of the California vote would have elected Hughes, despite Wilson's national popular vote plurality of well over half a million votes.

The nation was apparently spared this electoral travesty by a chance occurrence early in the campaign. Hughes, on a tour of California, had let the more reactionary Republican leaders plan his itinerary and failed to meet with Republican Governor Hiram Johnson, who had been the Progressive nominee for vice president in 1912 and was running for the Senate in 1916. Johnson gave at least nominal support to Hughes in the campaign that followed, but his more enthusiastic backing could well have delivered California to Hughes. Johnson won his own campaign for the Senate by almost 300,000 votes.

THE ELECTION OF 1948

Except for President Harry S Truman, virtually everyone in the country expected the Republicans to take over the White House in 1948, thus ending the period of Democratic dominance that had begun with Franklin D. Roosevelt's first election in 1932. Truman, a Missouri senator until Roosevelt chose him for the vice presidential nomination in 1944, had suddenly been catapulted into the presidency by Roosevelt's death in office in April 1945. But under Truman's leadership the Democrats were thrown for staggering losses in the 1946 mid-term elections, relinquishing control of Congress for the first time since the early 1930s.

Truman and the newly elected Republican eightieth Congress were able to work together fairly well on foreign problems and indeed launched such historic programs as the Marshall Plan to aid war-torn Europe. But bitter feuding erupted between president and Congress on domestic issues. In 1947, over the president's veto and the angry protests of organized labor, the eightieth Congress passed the landmark Taft-Hartley Labor-Management Relations Act. Congressional investigation of Communist infiltration of the government in the 1930s further exacerbated White House-Capitol Hill relations. In his 1948 State of the Union address, Truman shocked a budget-conscious Congress by simultaneously urging new social welfare legislation that would cost $10 billion and a $40 tax cut for every man, woman, and child in the country. Republicans promptly accused him of gross political opportunism, and that dispute had scarcely cooled before the president in February advocated a sweeping civil rights program that drew embittered protests from the southern Democrats. Truman had already won the enmity of the Democratic left wing by adopting a stiff policy against Soviet advances in Europe.

By the summer of 1948 the president's popularity had plummeted to such depths that many Democrats—conservatives and liberals alike—had cast around for another nominee to head the party's ticket. In the end, however, Truman was able to exert the massive political powers of an incumbent president and force his own renomination by the Democratic National Convention in Philadelphia on July 15. In his acceptance speech, Truman lashed out as the Republicans as "the party of special interests" that "favors the privileged few and not the common everyday man." Truman used the occasion to announce that he would call Congress back into special session on July 26 ("Turnip Day in Missouri") to enact an almost incredible array of welfare bills. "What that worst 80th Congress does in its special session will be the test," the president said. Naturally, the Republican Congress did little that Truman asked, and throughout the campaign Truman could concentrate his fire on the "do-nothing Republican Congress." The Republicans, Truman declared, were "predatory animals who don't care if you people are thrown into a depression." They had "murdered" housing legislation, he said, and the farmers should oppose the Republicans because "this Republican Congress has already stuck a pitchfork into the farmer's back." Truman made a special appeal to minority religious and racial groups, calling for strong civil rights legislation and condemning Republicans for passing the Displaced Persons Act, which he said discriminated against Catholics and Jews.[24]

One reason for the near-universal predictions of Truman's defeat was the split-off from the Democratic party of the southern segregationists on one side and the left-wingers on the other. The southern defection, brewing several months, came to a head at the Democratic National Convention when a tough civil-rights plank was adopted at the instigation of Minneapolis Mayor Hubert H. Humphrey and other party liberals. The Alabama and Mississippi delegations walked out on the spot, and rebellious southerners from thirteen states subsequently held a rump convention at Birmingham, Alabama, to nominate Governor Strom Thurmond of South Carolina as the States' Rights (Dixiecrat) party candidate. On the other extreme of the party, former vice president Henry A. Wallace organized a new Progressive party opposed to the United States' Cold War foreign policies. Though no one doubted Wallace's own loyalty, his new party was heavily influenced by Communists and others of the extreme left. Both the Dixiecrat and Progressive candidacies posed serious dangers for Truman. The former could deprive him of regular southern electoral votes counted on by Democratic presidential candidates ever since 1880, while the latter could cost him enough votes to lose a number of strategic urbanized states of the North.

Regardless of how they felt personally about Truman, most Americans had to admire his courage in launching an exhaustive, 31,000-mile barnstorming, whistle-stop train tour, crisscrossing the country in the face of almost unanimous predictions from pollsters, reporters, and sundry political "experts" that Thomas E. Dewey would win an overwhelming victory. A Republican of moderate persuasion in his second term as governor of New York, Dewey had emerged as his party's nominee on the third roll call at the Republican National Convention in Philadelphia on June 24. In New York, Dewey had first won fame as a tough and effective district attorney and was respected as an able state administrator. In 1944 he had run a creditable race against Roosevelt for the presidency. These factors helped him outrun Senator Robert A. Taft of Ohio, leader of the Republican conservative wing, and Harold E. Stassen, a

Results of the 1948 Election

	Popular Votes	Electoral Votes
Harry S Truman (Dem.)	24,179,345	303
Thomas E. Dewey (Rep.)	21,991,291	189
Strom Thurmond (States' Rights)	1,176,125	39
Henry A. Wallace (Prog.)	1,157,326	—
Minor Parties	289,739	—
Truman plurality: 2,188,054		

younger liberal leader, in the competition for the nomination. But in the fall campaign, Dewey made the fateful mistake of believing his election was already assured and thus refused to join Truman in a sharp partisan debate on substantive issues. Instead, Dewey concentrated on diffuse calls for "national unity," failed to excite the Republican partisans, and left most of the country indifferent to his fate.

As the first returns came in from the northeastern states the night of November 2, Truman seized the lead in the popular vote. As the night hours wore on, state after state that observers had marked as "safe Republican" moved into the Truman column. Massachusetts went Democratic, as did the border states. Truman lost only four southern states—Alabama, Louisiana, Mississippi, and South Carolina—to the Dixiecrat ticket. About half the farm belt was Truman's and he ran ahead in California despite the presence of that state's popular governor, Earl Warren, as the vice presidential nominee on the Republican ticket. Among the larger states, Dewey won only New York, Michigan, and Pennsylvania. When Ohio went conclusively for Truman at eleven o'clock on Wednesday morning, Dewey conceded.

The national popular vote total showed that Truman had won by more than two million popular votes and that he ran 114 votes ahead of Dewey in the electoral college. Truman's electoral vote margin was deceptive, however. A shift from Truman to Dewey of only 24,294 votes in three states (16,807 in Illinois, 8,933 in California, and 3,554 in Ohio) would have made Dewey president instead. The election would have gone into the House of Representatives for final resolution with a shift of only 12,487 votes in California and Ohio.

Even with the hindsight that history affords, it is impossible to determine just what might have happened if the House had been called upon to pick a president in the wake of the 1948 election. Control of twenty-five delegations (a majority) would have been required to elect. Loyalist Democrats would have controlled 21 delegations, Republicans 20, the Dixiecrats 4. Three delegations would have been divided equally between the major parties. In fact, an election by the House was precisely what Thurmond and his Dixiecrats had hoped for. They would undoubtedly have brought pressure on Truman to hold back on civil rights legislation or other steps designed to further racial integration, in return for which the Dixiecrat states would have thrown their support to Truman and made him president. Thus a splinter party that won only 2.4 percent of the national popular vote might have forced its terms on a president. The Dixiecrats probably would have been amenable to a similar deal with the Republicans, but even if their votes had been added to his, Dewey would have been one state short of a majority. These calculations assume, of course, that House members would invariably vote for their own party's presidential candidate or, in the case of the southerners from the four Dixiecrat states, would vote the way the people of their states had voted in the fall elections. There might have been "breaks" in this lineup or peculiar types of deals under the pressures of the moment.

One scarcely believable but distinct possibility, if the 1948 election had gone into the House, is that no decision at all would have been made there. Had the House deadlock held from the day of the electoral count, January 6, until inauguration day, January 20, the new vice president would have assumed the presidency under the terms of the 20th amendment. (That amendment, ratified in 1933, provided in part that "if the President elect shall have failed to qualify, then the Vice President elect shall act as President until a President shall have qualified.") But who would have been the new vice president? If Truman had failed to win an electoral majority, his vice presidential running mate, Senator Alben W. Barkley, would also have failed to win a majority. Under the Constitution the Senate would have had the task of electing the new vice president. The party lineup in the Senate was 54 Democrats, 42 Republicans. The senators would have had only two choices: Barkley or Warren. Barkley was a highly respected fellow-senator and member of its inner "club." Thus he could have expected solid backing from all the northern Democrats and probably from all but one or two of his colleagues and long-time associates from Dixiecrat states. The chances are very high that Barkley would have been chosen as vice president. And if the House had failed to break its deadlock by January 20, Barkley would have assumed the powers of the presidency—even though not a single American had voted to elect him to that position.[25] But Barkley would have been only acting president and would have been obliged to relinquish the office at any time in the following four years that the House resolved its deadlock and chose a new president.

The 1948 election did more than demonstrate anew the dangers of throwing an election into the House. It also provided a striking example of how the electoral college permits splinter parties, which receive only tiny percentages of the national popular vote, to play a decisive role in the ultimate allocation of large blocs of electoral votes. Truman apparently lost a massive bloc of 74 electoral votes—those of New York, Michigan, and Maryland—because Henry Wallace was on the ballot in those states. The Wallace vote, liberal and basically Democratic-inclined, accounted for more than the difference between Dewey and Truman in each of those states. Thus the electoral college permits splinter parties in big states to occupy the balance of power in the election of an American President.

THE ELECTION OF 1960

Republican President Dwight D. Eisenhower, the first of his party to win the presidency since the 1920s, was ineligible to seek a third term in 1960 because of the two-term limitation written into the Constitution through the 22nd amendment. The Democrats also felt obliged to come up with a new nominee because Adlai E. Stevenson, their standard-bearer in 1952 and 1956, had a record of two successive defeats behind him. For the Republicans, the choice of a presidential candidate was comparatively easy. Vice President Richard M. Nixon had been in the public eye for eight years, had been an exceptionally active vice president, and enjoyed strong support in the Republican organizations throughout the country. New York Governor Nelson A. Rockefeller, the only potential opponent to Nixon who might have amassed significant delegate strength, decided the odds against success were too high and declined to make the effort. Nixon was nominated by an almost-unanimous vote of the Republican National Convention on July 27 in Chicago.

Four formidable candidates entered the race for the Democratic nomination—Senator Hubert H. Humphrey of Minnesota, a leading spokesman for the party's liberal wing; Senator John F. Kennedy of Massachusetts, a liberal, a strong vote-getter and the first Roman Catholic to be seriously considered for the presidency since Alfred E. Smith in 1928; Senator Stuart Symington of Missouri, a former secretary of the air force; and Senate Majority Leader Lyndon B. Johnson of Texas, a skilled and powerful Democratic legislative leader since 1953. By winning the most important presidential primaries of the year and obtaining the support of the party's big-city leaders, Kennedy was able to win nomination on the first ballot at the Democratic National Convention in Los Angeles on July 13. In a surprise move, Kennedy picked Johnson as his vice presidential running mate. Many liberal leaders in the party expressed consternation at the selection of Johnson, but later it became evident that Johnson's presence on the ticket was probably an essential element in holding most of the South behind Kennedy and effecting Democratic victory in one of the closest elections of U.S. history.

Kennedy promised the voters a "New Frontier" to cope with "uncharted areas of space and science, unsolved problems of peace and war, unconquered pockets of ignorance and prejudice, unanswered questions of poverty and surplus." The central issue, he asserted repeatedly, was the need for strong presidential leadership to reverse the nation's declining prestige abroad and lagging economy at home. Nixon, on the other hand, pledged to "build on" the achievements of the Eisenhower administration and pictured himself as a man trained for the presidency and its trying problems, especially in the field of international diplomacy. He described Kennedy as "immature" and "impulsive" and said the Democratic platform pledges would add $18 billion to the government's annual budget. As the campaign entered its final weeks, Kennedy was thought to have gained significantly from an unprecedented series of four face-to-face encounters between the presidential candidates on national television.[26]

In some respects, the outcome was similar to that of 1948. The Democratic candidate won a substantial margin of electoral votes—303 compared to 219 for his Republican opponent. The substantial nature of Kennedy's electoral college victory belied the suspense of election night, November 8, as the nation watched the popular vote reports in what would prove to be one of the most closely contested presidential races of the century.

Early in the evening, as the polls began to close across the continent, it had looked like a national sweep for the Democrats. Led by bellwether Connecticut, the industrial states of the eastern seaboard had gone for Kennedy—Pennsylvania with its 32 electoral votes, New York with its gigantic 45-electoral-vote bloc, and Kennedy's native Massachusetts with 16 electoral votes, the last by a staggering half-million plurality in the popular vote.

But the East was not all of America, and the later the night grew, the less certain the result appeared. Kennedy may have been strong in his native East, but the Republican ticket of Nixon and Lodge showed remarkable strength as the other regions began to report. To the surprise of virtually every political analyst, Nixon won Ohio with its 25 electoral votes by a decisive margin and a quarter-million votes. The "new South" states of Virginia, Kentucky, Tennessee, and Florida were his. The midwestern Republican heartland delivered Indiana, Wisconsin, and Iowa into Nixon's hands, and as the night progressed it became apparent that virtually every prairie state, from North Dakota to Oklahoma, would be his and that he would capture every one of the western mountain states except Nevada. In addition, he defeated Kennedy in the Pacific states of Washington, Oregon, and Alaska. Several days later it would become official that Nixon also had won his native California, with its 32 electoral votes, by a fragile margin. In all, he would win 26 of the 50 states.

John Kennedy's eastern lead would never be overcome, however. To that solid base, Kennedy added industrial Michigan with its 20 electoral votes; he captured Illinois, too—by a much-disputed margin of 8,858 votes, which brought him 27 electoral votes. Border states like Maryland, West Virginia, and Missouri went for Kennedy, and his victory was clinched by his ability to seize 81 electoral votes from seven states of the old Confederacy—aided in no small part by his vice presidential running mate from Texas.

There was no left-wing splinter party of any consequence in the 1960 balloting, but the southern unpledged elector movement, a successor to the Dixiecrat movement of 1948, won 14 electoral votes in two southern states. The unpledged electors eventually cast their votes for Senator Harry Flood Byrd in the electoral college. In one major respect however, the results were markedly different from those of 1948. While Truman had amassed a popular vote plurality of over 2 million votes, Kennedy's popular vote margin was one of the smallest in the history of Presidential elections—apparently just over 100,000 out of a total of 68,738,000 ballots cast in the country.

In fact, it was impossible to determine exactly what Kennedy's popular vote plurality—if it existed at all—really was. With the exception of Alabama, where unprecedented difficulties arose in determining the popular vote, the national count was 33,902,681 for Kennedy and 33,870,176 for Nixon—a Kennedy lead of 32,505. In Alabama, the state law provided that the names of the individual candidates for presidential elector would appear separately on the ballot, with the voter allowed to vote for as many or as few members of any electoral slate as he liked. (For ballot diagram, see Appendix K.) Each elector slate consisted of eleven names—the number of electoral votes to which the state was entitled. All the Republican electors were pledged to vote for Nixon, and the highest Republican elector received 237,981 votes in the general election—establishing a clear Nixon popular vote total in the state.[27] There had been stiff competition in Alabama to determine who would be placed on the ballot as Democratic electors—those pledged to support the party's national nominee or unpledged electors opposed to the national policies of the party. A Democratic primary and runoff held in the spring had resulted in the selection of six unpledged and five loyalist elector candidates to compose the eleven-man Democratic elector slate in the general election. Thus the question arose: For whom should the votes cast for the Democratic elector slate be counted in the national popular-vote tally—for Kennedy or for the unpledged elector movement? On election day the highest unpledged elector on the Democratic slate received 324,050 votes while the highest loyalist or Kennedy elector received 318,303 votes. It appeared that, with few exceptions, the same people had voted for both the unpledged and the loyalist electors. The national wire services chose to credit Kennedy with the highest vote cast for any Democratic elector in the state—the 324,050 that one of the unpledged members of the Democratic slate received. The wire service accounts made it appear that no unpledged elector votes at all were cast in Alabama. The result, of course, was a gross misstatement of the actual vote in the state, an error that followed over into the wire associations' reports that Kennedy won the national popular vote by some 118,000 votes. The figure was open to criticism on two counts: first, because it included some 6,000 votes which were specifically cast *against* Kennedy by Alabama Democrats who would not support loyalist electors, and secondly because it totally disregarded the unpledged elector vote, even though it was higher than Kennedy's.

A preferable method of reporting the Alabama vote, adopted by coauthor Peirce of this book for the *Congressional Quarterly* and noted as "First Method" (see below), was to report the vote for the highest Kennedy elector (318,303) as part of his national count and the vote for the highest unpledged elector (324,050) as part of the national unpledged elector vote (eventually credited to Byrd). The result was a Kennedy plurality nationwide of 112,827 votes. In reporting this result, *Congressional Quarterly* took the care to note, however, that it was actually reporting the votes of the citizens who supported Democratic electors in Alabama twice—once for Kennedy, once for unpledged electors. The result involved a serious distortion, since it resulted in a double count of the votes of the Democratic voters in Alabama while the Republican

Results of the 1960 Election

	Popular Votes	Electoral Votes
First Method		
John F. Kennedy (Dem.)	34,220,984	303
Richard M. Nixon (Rep.)	34,108,157	219
Harry F. Byrd*	638,822	15
Minor Parties	188,559	—
Kennedy plurality: 112,827		
Second Method		
Kennedy	34,049,976	303
Nixon	34,108,157	219
Byrd*	491,527	15
Minor Parties	188,559	—
Nixon plurality: 58,181		

First Method involves counting split Alabama elector slate both for Kennedy and unpledged electors; *Second Method* involves dividing vote for Alabama Democratic elector slate proportionately according to its composition. See below.

* Byrd was accorded the votes of 14 unpledged electors from Alabama and Mississippi, plus one vote by a Republican elector in Okalahoma.

voters in the state—and the votes of citizens in every other state—were reported but once.

An alternative method, developed by the *Congressional Quarterly* and noted as "Second Method," (see table above), was to take the highest vote for any Democratic elector in Alabama—324,050—and divide it proportionately between Kennedy and unpledged electors. Since loyalists held five of the eleven spots on the slate, they were credited with five-elevenths of the party total—147,295 votes. The unpledged electors, holding six elector slots, were credited with six-elevenths of the Democratic vote—176,755. This procedure, while somewhat arbitrary, had the virtue of avoiding any double count of the Democratic votes in Alabama. The state totals would now read: Nixon 237,981; Kennedy 147,295; unpledged electors (Byrd) 176,755. But when these totals were added to the popular-vote results from the other forty-nine states, a significant change took place. Kennedy no longer led in the national popular vote at all. Instead, Nixon was the popular vote winner by a margin of 58,181 votes.[28]

Interestingly, Nixon never sought to use these figures to argue that he had been the people's choice for president in 1960. Since Kennedy was clearly the electoral college winner, Nixon may have felt that claiming a popular-vote victory would simply have made him out as a poor loser. Moreover, the complex issues raised by the Alabama count were not the kind that many people would fully understand. Thus, little public debate took place on the question of how Alabama's votes should be counted, and it seemed likely that the issue would not be raised again.

But in 1964 the problem of determining the 1960 Alabama vote did reappear. The Democratic National Committee, in allocating the number of delegate seats each state would have to the 1964 national convention, employed a formula that rested in part on the number of popular votes the party's nominee—Kennedy—had received in the last presidential election. The northern Democrats in control of the committee were anxious to minimize the weight of the southern states, especially those that had been disloyal to the national ticket in the 1960 election. So when it came to determining the number of Kennedy votes with which Alabama should be credited in determining the delegate apportionment, the national committee used exactly the same formula that the *Congressional Quarterly* had used following the 1960 election. It took the highest vote for a Democratic elector in Alabama, divided it in eleven parts, and credited five parts to Kennedy and six to the unpledged electors. As a result, the size of the Alabama delegation to the 1964 convention was reduced. But, by employing this stratagem, the committee was accepting the rationale of a counting system under which Nixon was the clear popular vote winner in 1960.

In the days and weeks following the 1960 election, however, the nation's attention was focused not on the Alabama vote count but rather on the question of fraud. Two days after the election, Republican National Chairman Thruston B. Morton sent telegrams to party leaders in eleven states asking them to look into allegations of voting irregularities. A Republican spokesman said many complaints alleging fraud, payment of money, and other irregularities had been received, most of them from Illinois, Texas, North and South Carolina, Michigan, and New Jersey. Republicans were especially bitter over the outcome in Illinois, where Kennedy had won by 8,858 votes out of 4,757,409 cast, and there were allegations of irregularities in the count in heavily Democratic Cook County (Chicago). The Cook County Republican chairman alleged that 100,000 fraudulent votes had swung Illinois to Kennedy through "systematic" looting of votes in twelve city wards and parts of two others.[29] Republicans laid stress on one precinct, virtually deserted because of highway demolitions, where the vote reported was 79 for Kennedy and 3 for Nixon though there were less than 50 registered voters on election day.[30] Widespread "tombstone" voting and tampering with voting machines were alleged. The Democrats replied angrily that the Republicans had no proof of substantial irregularities and that they were darkening the name of the city before the nation. The recounts in the city soon bogged down in legal maneuvering, and the Republicans were never able to produce hard evidence to show that fraud had been a big enough factor to give the state to Kennedy. (In 1962, however, three Democratic precinct workers in Chicago did plead guilty to "altering, changing, defacing, injuring or destroying ballots" in the 1960 election.[31]) Republicans were even less hopeful of a reversal in Texas, where the Kennedy-Johnson ticket led by 46,233 votes, though Republicans charged that the Democratic-controlled election boards had consistently invalidated Republican ballots with slight defects while counting Democratic ballots with identical deficiencies.

Despite the closeness of the election, the Republicans never publicly claimed that the alleged vote irregularities were sufficient to reverse the outcome. But for a while, between election day on November 8 and December 19 (when the electors met to vote), there was speculation that if Illinois' 27 electoral votes were lost to Kennedy through proof of vote fraud, thus reducing Kennedy's electoral votes to 273—only 4 more than the 269 needed for victory—southern electors might bolt and withhold votes from the Kennedy-Johnson ticket, thus throwing the election into the House of Representatives. This immediate fear was dispelled, however, when the Illinois electoral board, consisting of four Republicans and one Democrat, certified the election of the Kennedy electors from the state on December 14.

The close elections in the northern states had been watched with special interest by conservative southerners who hoped to thwart Kennedy's election. On December 10, Alabama's six unpledged electors met in Birmingham and announced their desire to cast their presidential vote "for an outstanding Southern Democrat who sympathizes with our peculiar problems in the South." They stated that "our position remains fluid so that we can cooperate with other unpledged electors for the preservation of racial and national integrity." The Alabamans specifically deplored the role of southerners who "ally themselves with a candidate [Kennedy] who avowedly would integrate our schools, do away with literacy tests for voting," and "otherwise undermine everything we hold dear in the South."[32]

Two days later, a joint meeting was held in Jackson, Mississippi, between the six unpledged electors from Alabama and the eight who had been chosen in Mississippi. The decision was made to throw the unpledged elector support to Senator Byrd of Virginia, and a joint statement was drafted calling on presidential electors from the other southern states to join the vote for Byrd in the hope that enough electoral votes might be withheld from Kennedy to throw the election into the House of Representatives. A defection of thirty-five additional southern electors from Kennedy would have been necessary to send the election to the House. Mississippi's Governor Ross Barnett, one of the South's strongest segregationists, sent letters to six other states asking for support in the move to block Kennedy. In Louisiana, leaders of the White Citizens Council were at the forefront of a move to have the state's Democratic electors withhold their support from Kennedy.[33] The stated hope of the unpledged electors was that if the election reached the House, all southerners would vote Byrd and that the Republicans, "being fundamentally opposed to the liberalism of Senator Kennedy," would follow suit.[34] The new party lineup in the House would consist of 23 states controlled by northern and border state Democrats, 6 controlled by Deep South Democrats, and 17 controlled by Republicans. Another four delegations were evenly split between the parties. Thus it is highly problematic what would have happened, even if the election had reached the House.

As it turned out, when the electors actually cast their votes on December 19, the only vote Byrd got outside of the anticipated ones from Alabama and Mississippi came not from another southern Democrat but from a Republican. He was Henry D. Irwin, who had been elected as a member of the winning Republican elector slate pledged to Nixon in Oklahoma. Irwin subsequently stated on a nationwide television program that he had performed "his constitutional duty" as a "free elector." The next July, subpoenaed to appear before a U.S. Senate judiciary subcommittee, Irwin said he had never planned to vote for Nixon, whom he "could not stomach." Irwin revealed that he had worked in concert with R. Lea Harris, a Montgomery, Alabama, attorney, in a national movement to get the members of the electoral college to desert Nixon and Kennedy in favor of a strongly conservative candidate. An alternative considered by Harris was to support a plan reportedly considered by some conservatives in the Louisiana legislature to call a meeting of conservative southern governors in Baton Rouge, to which Kennedy would have been invited and presented with the following conditions which he would have to meet to receive the southern electoral votes he needed for election: "(1) Eliminate the present sizable foreign aid we presently give to the Communist economy; (2) adhere to the spirit of the 10th Amendment [reserving powers not specified in the Constitution to the states], and (3) appoint one of these Southern Governors Attorney General."[35]

On November 20, Irwin had telegraphed all Republican electors in the country saying, "I am Oklahoma Republican elector. The Republican electors cannot deny the election to Kennedy. Sufficient conservative Democratic electors available to deny labor Socialist nominee. Would you consider Byrd President, [Barry] Goldwater Vice President, or wire any acceptable substitute. All replies strict confidence." Irwin received approximately forty replies, some of them favorable, but most of the electors indicated they had a moral obligation to vote for Nixon. Irwin subsequently asked the Republican national committeemen and state chairmen to free Republican electors from any obligation to vote for Nixon, but received only three sympathetic replies. Republican National Committeeman Albert K. Mitchell of New Mexico wired Irwin that he had taken up the idea "with some of the leaders of the Republican National Committee level and found that while everyone was in favor of the move, they felt that it should not be sponsored by the Republican organization." Mitchell encouraged Irwin, however, to take further steps to "eliminate Kennedy from the Presidency." Later, Republican National Chairman Morton said that if Irwin "had the support of the Republican National Committee, I knew nothing about it." Not a single additional Republican elector in the country followed Irwin's lead.[36]

Thus every move to upset the results of the 1960 election—from a Republican challenge of vote returns to the efforts of the southern unpledged electors and the machinations of Henry Irwin of Oklahoma—was to prove fruitless. But it was only by chance that the country was spared weeks or months of indecision following the 1960 contest. A shift of only 8,971 popular votes—4,480 in Illinois and 4,491 in Missouri—would have thrown the election into the House. If an additional 1,148 votes had shifted from Kennedy to Nixon in New Mexico, along with 58 in Hawaii and 1,247 in Nevada, Nixon would have become president. Whether that would have violated the popular will, one cannot say, because there is no obviously clear and fair way to count the popular vote for the 1960 election. Had it not been for the electoral college, each candidate might have conducted his campaign somewhat differently, and one candidate or the other might have won a clear-cut popular vote victory.*

In many ways, the 1960 election summed up the evils of the electoral college in our times. First it showed once again the irrational, chance factors that decide a close election, when the shift of a few votes can throw huge blocs of electoral votes in one direction or the other. Second, it underscored the danger of fraud deciding a presidential election, because Illinois, where the most ballot disputes arose, was the state that almost decided the entire election. Third, it showed the potentially decisive role that a narrowly based regional or splinter party can play in the choice of a president and how the system actually encourages independent elector blocs. Fourth, the election showed how a faithless elector, chosen to carry out a specific function, could suddenly break his trust and try to determine the choice of the chief executive for 180 million Americans. (What if Henry Irwin's vote had been the deciding vote in the electoral college in 1960?) And lastly, the election showed that as long as individual states have carte blanche in deciding how presidential electors will be chosen, it may be difficult and sometimes impossible to compile accurate national popular vote totals (as in Alabama in 1960) and to learn whom the majority of Americans really wanted to be their president.

---

* Kennedy's strategy was to carry the Midwest and the eastern industrial states, plus California, while counting on the normal Democratic vote from the majority of southern states. The Nixon strategy was to carry the normally Republican farm areas, run strongly in the Far West, and make sufficient inroads in the major industrial states and normally Democratic South to win a majority of the electoral votes. Perhaps one reason Kennedy won was that since 1956 he and his advisers had shown an extraordinarily keen perception of the workings of the electoral college and understood how an appeal centered on the major industrial states might win for a Democratic candidate. Nixon, on the other hand, pledged to visit every one of the fifty states in his campaign, a pledge that would bedevil him on the final weekend before the election as he spent valuable hours in a visit to Alaska (a state with 3 electoral votes) instead of concentrating on big doubtful states like Michigan and Illinois (with 20 and 27 electoral votes respectively). In retrospect, neither candidate could say his strategy had been completely effective. Kennedy, to be sure, did carry most of the big states. But he lost Ohio and California, and, by his failure to win the prairie or mountain states, came perilously close to defeat. Nixon did win a majority of the states, a fitting conclusion for his campaign. But Nixon had diffused his effort and fell short of victory. Without the electoral college, the campaigns might have been somewhat less oriented to specific states or blocs of states.

We have not so far, paid great attention to the *real* election—the moment when the electoral votes are counted before a joint session of Congress and the next president and vice president of the United States are officially proclaimed. The scene following the 1960 election was one such occasion of particular interest.

At 12:55 P.M. on the sixth of January, 1961, the doorkeeper of the House of Representatives announced the arrival in the House chamber of the vice president and the members of the Senate for the purpose of counting the electoral votes. Two handsome boxes of inlaid wood, holding the electoral votes submitted from all the states, had been brought by pages from the Senate chamber and were now taken down the center aisle of the House and placed on the desk of the Speaker's podium. For the Democrats it was a happy occasion, and their side of the chamber was almost filled, while only a few of the seats on the Republican side had been taken.

As the presiding officer of the Senate, Vice President Richard M. Nixon had the constitutional duty to preside at this joint session of Congress. It was the first time in a century that a vice president had been called upon to preside over an electoral vote tally that certified the election as president of the man he had run against. The last occasion had been on February 13, 1861, when Vice President John C. Breckinridge, who had run unsuccessfully for president the previous autumn, certified the election of Abraham Lincoln.

Before ordering that the ballot count begin, Nixon threw his arm around the shoulder of the Speaker of the House, Sam Rayburn of Texas, and, as applause mounted, offered the congratulations of the Senate to the venerable Speaker on his seventy-ninth birthday. Then the official business of the joint session got under way. Four tellers had been appointed—a Republican and a Democrat from both the Senate and the House. The senior man among them was Arizona's Senator Carl Hayden, whose congressional service had begun forty-eight years before, when his state entered the Union. Representing the Senate Republicans was Carl Curtis of Nebraska, while Representatives Edna F. Kelly of New York and Frances P. Bolton of Ohio had been designated from the Democratic and Republican sides of the House respectively.

The returns from Alabama, the first state by alphabetical order, were withdrawn from the boxes and handed to Nixon, who opened the certification and then handed it to the tellers, who announced the result. The count for Alabama showed 6 electoral votes for Senator Harry Flood Byrd of Virginia and 5 for Senator John F. Kennedy of Massachusetts. Nixon nodded to Senator Byrd and said it seemed that "the gentleman from Virginia is now in the lead." The count proceeded uninterrupted until Nixon announced that three certificates had been received from Hawaii—one certifying the election of Republican electors, one certifying the election of Democratic electors, and a third, from the governor of the state, certifying the proper election of the Democratic electors. The first official count in Hawaii had shown a Republican electoral victory by a margin of 141 votes, but on a recount the Democrats forged ahead by 115 votes. Nixon suggested that the governor's certification of the Democratic electors be accepted, and there being no objection, it was so ordered.

The count then proceeded through the last state on the list—Wyoming. Nixon had sought, more or less successfully, to maintain a cheerful demeanor through the long ballot tally, but now he fidgeted as the tellers assembled the documents that showed the final results. The count, reported to him by the tellers, showed:

For president, John F. Kennedy, 303 electoral votes; Richard M. Nixon, 219 electoral votes; Harry F. Byrd, 15 electoral votes.

For vice president: Lyndon B. Johnson, 303 electoral votes; Henry Cabot Lodge, 219 electoral votes; Strom Thurmond, 14 electoral votes, and Barry Goldwater, one electoral vote.[37]

THE ELECTION OF 1968[38]

The tumultuous events surrounding the presidential election of 1968 included massive riots and demonstrations—on college campuses because of the nation's involvement in the war in Vietnam, in the cities because of race tensions that culminated with the springtime assassination of civil rights leader Martin Luther King, Jr., in Memphis, Tennessee. President Lyndon B. Johnson, who had succeeded to the presidency on the death of John F. Kennedy in 1963 and won an overwhelming election victory in 1964, found himself under such heavy challenge for renomination that he withdrew shortly before the crucial Wisconsin primary. The majority Democratic party was wracked by dissension and disunity, culminating in a nightmarish convention in Chicago that ended with bloody street confrontations between antiwar protestors and Mayor Richard Daley's police. Robert F. Kennedy, former attorney general and brother of the late president, had entered the primaries, only to be cut down by an assassin's bullets in Los Angeles on the night the returns from the California primary were being counted.

The final nominees of the major parties were Vice President Hubert H. Humphrey for the Democrats and Richard M. Nixon—the vice president who had retired eight years before, now returned to political life—for the Republicans. But if there were an interesting figure in the 1968 elections, particularly for observing the workings of the electoral college, it was former governor George C. Wallace of Alabama, whose candidacy on the ticket of the party of his own creation—the American Independent party—presented America with the most formidable third-party candidacy of many decades.

In a sense, Wallace was simply a Dixiecrat—a direct descendant of the brand of anti-civil rights, southern politics that had propelled Strom Thurmond into the 1948 election and motivated the group of electors that eventually supported Harry F. Byrd in 1960. But Wallace had a much broader appeal. He had demonstrated that by strong runs in the 1964 Democratic presidential primaries and now proved it again by galvanizing supporters to place elector slates pledged to him on the ballots of all fifty states—an organizational miracle in modern-day politics. (Up to that time, it had been assumed it would be virtually impossible for an independent candidate to qualify so broadly; after Wallace, it would be clear that with sufficient planning and effort, candidates could indeed qualify without a major-party nomination.)

Nor was racism the only motivating factor of Wallace supporters. True, the Alabamian had declared in his 1963 inaugural address: "Segregation now—segregation tomorrow—segregation forever." Later he had "stood in the schoolhouse door" trying to prevent integration of the University of Alabama. But one needed to attend only one or two of his 1968 rallies to detect the broader attraction. They were half revival, half political meetings, with Wallace appealing to the plain folks present—those steelworkers and beauticians and cab drivers decked out in red, white, and blue—with his hot rhetoric about pseudo-intellectual government and long-haired students, bussin' and lenient judges, welfare loafers, and the fate that waited any anarchist "scum" "who lies down in front of our car when we get to be President." (The line that always brought down the house, reflecting the quintessential violence of the Wallace appeal: "It'll be the *last* car he'll ever lie down in front of.")

Wallace's southernism worked both for him and against him. He played strongly on the region's lingering sense of inferiority, telling southerners that they were tired of being looked down upon and repeating a sure-applause line: "Folks down here in Alabama are just as refined and cultured as folks anywhere!" But the provinciality doubtless hurt him in the North. When the election returns were in, Wallace had carried only five states, and all in the Deep South—Alabama itself, Mississippi, Louisiana, Georgia, and Arkansas. It was not much different from 1948, when Thurmond had won three of those states—Alabama, Mississippi, and Louisiana—and his own South Carolina. Ironically, South Carolina was denied Wallace in 1968 because Thurmond went all-out for Richard Nixon.

Opinions differ on whether Wallace ever believed he had a chance to win in 1968, but in addition to the build-up it gave him for future runs, he counted it a solid success. "I think my movement defeated Hubert Humphrey, which was something the majority of the people of my region wanted done," Wallace told coauthor Peirce.[39] "My running took away enough labor vote from Humphrey in California, in Ohio, in Illinois, in New Jersey and Missouri, so that those states went for Nixon." (Independent analysts think Wallace hurt Nixon much more than Humphrey, especially in the South, but the interesting point is his own analysis.) Wallace also thought he had changed the whole tone of the campaign, especially on issues like "law and order and tax exemptions for the multirich such as foundations and otherwise. Before it was over it sounded as if both national parties' speeches were written in Clayton, Alabama."

Wallace's 1968 campaign probably marked the high-water point of southern-based third-party politics in the twentieth century, and one of those tantalizing historical "ifs" is what would have happened if Nixon had received a few less electoral votes, so that he would have lacked a majority and George Wallace would have held the power to choose the next president through his forty-six electors.

When Peirce asked Wallace how he would have handled the situation, he first made it very clear that he would have instructed his electors how they should vote in the electoral college, which convenes in mid-December, and would never have permitted the choice of a president to remain unresolved there so that the House of Representatives would have chosen the following January. "Why," he said, "would I want to lose control of the matter by throwing the election into the House where we would have no control whatsoever? No, the matter would have been settled in the electoral college." And his own electors, Wallace said, "were pledged to go along with me in the matter, and they would have gone with me."

How would he have instructed his electors? "The chances are the votes probably would have gone to Mr. Nixon, because we were violently opposed to Mr. Humphrey's philosophy and ideology." Would he have demanded concessions, in advance, from Nixon? "We would probably have asked Mr. Nixon to reiterate some of his campaign statements he'd already made . . . just to restate what he had already said in substance: 'I want to work for world peace, I want tax reduction, tax reform. I want the neighborhood school concept protected. I'm in substance for freedom of choice in the public school system and against busing. . . .' " Wallace on other occasions talked of a "solemn covenant" to stop foreign aid to Communist nations and left-leaning neutrals, of a revamping of the U.S. Supreme Court, and a halt to federal civil rights enforcement. In other words, Wallace might well have forced on Nixon the same kind of a "hands-off" attitude toward the South that Rutherford B. Hayes had agreed to in 1877 in exchange for the electoral votes he needed to be elected. The South's price then had been termination of the first Reconstruction, a decision that would be followed by three-quarters of a century of impingement on black people's rights in the South. The net of Wallace's demands would have been to end the second Reconstruction—the civil rights advances of the 1960s.

It does seem unlikely that there could have been any secret deal between Wallace and one of the major-party contenders—some kind of selling off of the highest office to the highest bidder.[40] For the participants there would be the disastrous consequences of the almost inevitable disclosure—such a deal would involve too many people to be kept secret; and it is unlikely that Wallace would have wished to do so—a kingmaker enjoys real advantage from his actions only if he is recognized as being one. Given leaks about such arrangements, a major-party nominee would suffer the stigma of having bought the presidency by a deal, face possible threat of impeachment if the non-enforcement of existing laws were part of the understanding, and very likely find at least a few of his own electors in revolt and threatening to block the deal by abstaining on December 16.[41] This would be a very effective action on their part, since the needed majority of 270 electoral votes remains the same no matter how many electors might abstain.

The three-candidate nature of the 1968 election underscored other anomalies of the electoral college. It served as a reminder that under the unit rule a plurality of votes determines the entire electoral vote for a state, even if it is a distinct minority of the vote cast. The results of this feature can be clearly seen in the state-by-state returns. North Carolina, South Carolina, and Tennessee all exhibited similar patterns in which one candidate—Nixon—received 100 percent of the state's electoral votes by obtaining only 39.5 percent, 38.1 percent, and 37.8 percent, respectively, of the popular vote. Although Nixon did carry 17 of his 32 states with less than a majority of the votes cast, these three-way divisions did not always help him.[42] In Arkansas, for example, Nixon and Hubert Humphrey together split slightly over 61 percent of the popular vote, while Wallace, with 38 percent, received 100 percent of that state's electoral votes.

Of course, in most states outside the South, Wallace was not likely to receive a plurality—although to do so, he might need as little as 34 percent of the popular vote. His real impact came through his ability to draw off votes from the two major parties and possibly tilt a large state's bloc of 26 or 40 or 43 electoral votes one way or the other. In other words, it was the magnifying tendency of the unit rule, with its winner-take-all feature, that constituted Wallace's impact outside the South.

As election day approached, Wallace's popular vote strength and, more important, his electoral vote strength—at one point he had been expected to sweep the entire old Confederacy—had shrunk. Humphrey's popular and electoral vote strength, low during the early autumn, had rebounded—a not coincidental relationship. With Nixon and Humphrey running neck and neck, the potential of an electoral college deadlock seemed very real.

The results on election day, November 5, 1968, finally laid these fears to rest for the next four years. Wallace, with a national popular vote of 13.5 percent, received 45 electoral votes from his five Deep South states,[43] a low 8.4 percent of the total electoral vote. While Nixon, with a popular vote of 43.4 percent, led Humphrey by 0.7 percent nationally, the vicissitudes of the electoral

Results of the 1968 Election

	Popular Votes	Electoral Votes
Richard M. Nixon (Rep.)	31,785,480	301
Hubert H. Humphrey (Dem.)	31,275,165	191
George C. Wallace (A.I.P.)	9,906,473	46
Minor Parties	244,444	—
Nixon plurality: 510,315		

college resulted in Nixon receiving 302 electoral votes, or 56 percent of the total—a seeming comfortable 32 electoral votes over the 270 required.[44]

How close Wallace came to being the pivotal figure was illustrated by the fact that a shift of 53,024 votes from Nixon to Humphrey in New Jersey, Missouri, and New Hampshire[45] would have reduced the Nixon electoral vote to 269, one less than the needed majority, with Humphrey receiving 224 and Wallace 45. A shift of 111,674 votes in California alone—1.5 percent of the vote cast in that state—would have had the same result.

One factor could have affected the preceding analysis—a faithless elector who would cast his vote for president contrary to expectations. In fact, the 1968 election, like the 1960 election, did give rise to such an individual—the fifth in the history of the electoral college and the fourth in the postwar elections to vote clearly contrary to the expectations of those who had elected him. Not as colorful as Henry Irwin, the 1960 defecting elector, the 1968 individual was Dr. Lloyd W. Bailey of North Carolina, a Nixon elector. A member of the John Birch Society, Dr. Bailey finally decided that he could not vote for Nixon because of his concern over alleged leftist tendencies in the early Nixon appointments of presidential advisers and Nixon's decision to ask Chief Justice Earl Warren to continue on the Court for an additional six months. When the electoral college met on December 16, Dr. Bailey, therefore, gave his electoral vote to Wallace, thus increasing Wallace's final count to 46 electoral votes.[46]

The danger shown here is less in the action of one isolated individual—although voters of a state might wonder what their vote is really worth in such a situation—than in the possibility of electors deviating from their pledges on a multiple basis should an electoral vote majority rest on one or two votes—a very real possibility in both 1960 and 1968. One thing is certain: if Nixon had lost the three close states previously mentioned and thus had had only 269 electoral votes, one short of a majority, it would not have been Dr. Bailey who would have saved the day. He was a Nixon-pledged elector—and, in fact, if he had still switched, Nixon's revised total would then have been 268, 2 short of a majority.

In analyzing elections as close and precarious as that of 1968, it is important to remember that even if the general election did not produce a majority electoral vote winner, or even if it produced a winner who clearly lost in the popular vote, there might well be what has been termed "the legitimacy of the popular vote majority"[47]—the demand that the electoral college choose the winner in terms of the popular vote. These pressures would undoubtedly be exceptionally strong if the winner of the popular vote had fallen just a few votes shy of an electoral college majority. Along these lines, James Michener, the president of the 1968 Pennsylvania electoral college, tells how he had resolved that if this were the case, with Nixon leading, he would seek to swing enough electoral votes to Nixon so as to decide the election in the electoral college. He reports that he was both pleased and surprised to discover, on December 16, that

Thomas Minehart, the Pennsylvania Democratic state chairman, had had the same resolve.[48]

The candidates' knowledge of the prospective party lineup of the new House of Representatives, indicating their chances in a contingent election there, could also have played a heavy role.[49] Only nineteen House delegations were controlled by Republicans, so that Nixon, if he had trailed Humphrey in the popular vote and there was no electoral college majority, might well have seen that he had no hope of election and released some of his electors to Humphrey. Had the situation been reversed, with Nixon leading in popular votes but still short of an electoral majority, the "bargaining" with Wallace to obtain elector support, and prevent the contingent election procedure altogether, would have been quite strong.

But what if the election were not settled in the elector vote by explicit or implict deals, or through the switch of a few electors to prevent a deadlock? In this case, the electoral college meetings on December 16 would have resulted in a deadlock, with no candidate receiving 270 electoral votes, and the action would now shift to the newly elected House of Representatives, meeting at noon on January 6, 1969, only fourteen days before the constitutionally scheduled inauguration of the new president.[50]

The difficult and dangerous circumstances likely to attend any contingent election will be discussed in the following chapter (pp. 106–08). In 1968 it was widely assumed that the House, if it received the decision, would have elected Humphrey. Twenty-six state delegations were controlled by Democrats, nineteen by Republicans, and five were evenly divided and consequently would cast no vote.[51] However, this belief is based on one very questionable assumption: that each representative would have voted along party lines. A closer analysis shows that the complexity of the election in the House would have been much greater.[52]

The first complicating factor is that in many cases, House delegations that were split, and thus could cast no vote, or that had a narrow majority for one party or another, could be swung through the actions of a single House member seeking to express his independence or maverick tendencies, raise his price, or just seek mammoth publicity.

This problem, however, pales in comparison with another: How would the House delegations from the five Deep South states carried by Wallace, with percentages up to 66 percent, vote? While at least normally Democratic and thus counted in the twenty-six-state total, the representatives from these states would likely feel compelled to recognize and support Wallace in the House voting. On the other hand, if they broke party rank and failed to support the Democratic nominee at this critical moment, they would be subject to terrible retribution, including loss of patronage, party seniority, and committee chairmanships. The dilemma of these congressmen would be intense, and its resolution uncertain, although a likely pattern would be to support Wallace for a couple of ballots and then to switch to Humphrey. The problem here, then, would not be manipulation by Wallace, for his direct control over these unhappy congressmen would be comparatively weak, but whether sufficient Democratic leadership pressure would lead to an eventual Democratic House majority.[53]

One last factor in the actual 1968 election might have given rise to severe problems in reaching a twenty-six-state majority—and possibly have resulted in a House deadlock. This factor was the 1968 election-time pledges of a number of congressmen—mainly Southern Democrats in Wallace or Nixon-leaning districts—that if elected, and if the election came to the House, they would not automatically vote for Humphrey but would vote however their district had voted. In many states, this pledge would not have made a difference, but in several it would have.

Among at least thirty candidates for the House who had made such pledges prior to the election[54] were the six men who were elected to the House from South Carolina. All six were Democrats, but three of their districts went for Nixon, two for Wallace, and one for Humphrey.[55] If these candidates had honored their pledges, South Carolina's vote would have gone to Nixon, despite its solid Democratic representations.

The Virginia delegation would have been evenly divided between Republicans and Democrats. However, two Democratic representatives, David E. Satterfield III and John O. Marsh, Jr., had made the pledge; their districts were carried by Nixon. A third Virginia Democrat, W. C. Daniel, would have been pledged to Wallace. Thus Virginia's vote might have gone to Nixon.[56] Finally, Nevada's lone congressman, Walter S. Baring, a Democrat, would have been publicly pledged to cast his state's vote for Nixon.[57]

The results of these publicly recorded pledges, alone, would be—assuming complete party loyalty otherwise, and no Wallace defections—a House vote not of 26 to 19 and 5 states split but 24 to 22 and 4 states split. No majority of twenty-six states would have been immediately forthcoming, and political chaos could have resulted as the nation approached inauguration day.[58]

The 1968 election did not put the electoral college system to its greatest test; Richard Nixon did receive a majority of the electoral votes, and the nation was spared the opportunity of observing the dark nooks and crannies of the contingent election procedure in action. The 1968 election, however, did illustrate a broad range of electoral college perils: (1) the uncertainty of state winner-take-all results with a three-way split of popular votes; (2) the incentive given to regional third parties and the handicaps conferred upon nationally based third parties; (3) the likelihood of electoral college deadlock if a third-party movement coincides with an evenness of major party strength; (4) the possibilities that shifts of relatively few votes could deadlock an election; (5) the dangers of one of a few faithless electors affecting the electoral college results; (6) the opportunity for a third-party candidate to throw his electors one way or the other, with or without a deal; and (7) the likelihood of uncertainty, confusion, and even deadlock in the House contingent selection of the president.

THE ELECTION OF 1976[59]

Virtually every presidential election brings its share of surprises and "firsts," and the 1976 contest was clearly no exception. Out of a crowded Democratic field a man virtually unknown to most of the country when he started his campaign—Georgia's former governor Jimmy Carter—emerged victorious, winning enough primaries to arrive at the party's national convention in New York with sufficient votes to ensure his nomination on the first ballot. Carter, a moderate and an alien figure to the powerful national Democrat liberal establishment, made a bow to his adversaries by selecting as his running mate Senator Walter F. Mondale of Minnesota, a liberal and a close associate of Senator and former vice president Hubert H. Humphrey.

On the Republican side, Gerald R. Ford, Jr., had assumed the presidency following the August 1974 resignation, under threat of impeachment for his involvement with the Watergate affair, of Richard M. Nixon. A party moderate, Ford was actually the first appointed president of the United States. He had been selected for the vice presidency by President Nixon following the resignation of Vice President Spiro Agnew in 1973. (Agnew had been forced to resign and pleaded *nolo contendere* to income tax evasion following an investigation by the U.S. attorney in Baltimore who had proven a widespread pattern of Agnew acceptances of payments—some clearly kickbacks—from contractors and others doing business with the Maryland government during the time he was governor. Some of the payments had continued while he was vice president.) Under the 25th amendment regarding presidential succession, ratified in 1967, Nixon was empowered to appoint a successor to Agnew, subject to congressional approval.

Ford, who had spent most of a long political career as a Grand Rapids, Michigan, congressman, rising to the post of minority leader in 1965, had previously had no higher ambition than one day becoming Speaker of the House if the Republicans gained control. As president, he proved to be less than a dynamic leader. And he made what was to prove a fatal political error: he pardoned Richard Nixon, to the great resentment of millions of citizens, for any and all crimes he might have committed during his presidency. In the primaries, Ford was vigorously challenged by former California governor Ronald Reagan, a favorite of the party's right wing, and barely repulsed the Reagan onslaught. In the general election he consented to a series of nationally televised debates with Carter; though neither performed brilliantly, Carter probably emerged as the net winner.

But Carter, from a broad lead in the national polls at the time of his nomination, sank rapidly through the autumn months—partly because of a number of fumbled campaign issues. As election day approached, the outcome was very much in doubt. And as in all close elections, the functioning of the electoral college again became a crucial—and worrisome—factor in the selection of the next president.

The most obvious manifestation of the importance of the electoral college could be observed in the obsession of Carter and Ford strategists, in the closing weeks of the campaign, with the nine big electoral vote states, which together have 245 of the 270 electoral votes necessary to win an election. These campaign managers knew well what all campaign strategists realize—when a large electoral vote state is marginal, it is crucially important to commit an enormous amount of campaign resources to that state. A candidate's visit, additional advertising expenditures, more key campaign workers—any of these *might* be enough to win the few thousand popular votes sufficient to swing that state's *entire* bloc of 41 or 45 electoral votes—more than 15 percent total needed to win—to your side.

As a result, Ford and Carter campaign managers targeted these large states with an enormous commitment of resources in the closing weeks of the 1976 campaign.[60] In fact, this strategy proved to be wise: the contest in seven of these nine states turned out, in the final count, to be exceedingly close, with both candidates receiving at least 48 percent each state's vote.

Because of this obsession in the campaigns with large pivotal states, the electoral college does not treat voters alike—a thousand voters in Scranton, Pennsylvania, are far more strategically important than a similar number of voters in Wilmington, Delaware. This also places a premium on the support of key political leaders in large electoral vote states. This could be observed in Carter's desperate wooing of Mayors Frank Rizzo of Philadelphia and Richard Daley of Chicago because of the major roles these political leaders *might* have in determining the outcome in Pennsylvania and Illinois. The electoral college treats political leaders as well as voters unequally—those in large marginal states are vigorously courted.[61] (This point will be analyzed empirically, using computer-based data, in the next chapter.)

The electoral college also encourages fraud—or at least fear and rumor of fraud. New York, with more than enough electoral votes to elect Ford, would eventually go to Carter by 288,767 popular votes. Claims of voting irregularities and calls for a recount would be made on election night but later withdrawn because of Carter's clear national popular vote win. If there was fraud in New York, only 288,767 votes determined the election; under direct election, at least 1.7 million votes, Carter's national plurality, would have had to have been irregular to determine the outcome.

Another impact of the electoral college on the campaign arose from the independent candidacy of Eugene McCarthy, former Democratic senator from Minnesota. No one thought it at all likely that McCarthy would gather enough popular votes anywhere to win any electoral votes—or even that he would receive a significant total of votes nationally. Yet, there was considerable alarm over the impact of his candidacy. This was directly due to the fact that McCarthy had the possibility of drawing a few percent of usually Democratic votes in those very same large states that were judged to be pivotal between Carter and Ford. Concern was expressed that McCarthy had found another loophole avenue to electoral influence, complementing the Wallace electoral college stategy of 1968. While Wallace had sought power by winning enough electoral votes to deadlock the electoral college, McCarthy sought kingmaker influence by determining the election outcome. This potential power of McCarthy did not come because of his strong electoral appeal but solely because of where his limited electoral appeal was—in pivotal states where small numbers might determine a winner-take-all bloc of electoral votes. In other words, the electoral college was threatening to provide yet another minor-movement candidate with inordinate influence over who would be president.

In the final outcome, McCarthy received less than 1 percent of the national popular vote and in no state exceeded 4 percent (Oregon at 3.9 percent, and Arizona and Massachusetts both at 2.6 percent were his top states). Yet, in four states (Iowa, Maine, Oklahoma, and Oregon), totaling 26 electoral votes, McCarthy's vote exceeded the margin by which Ford defeated Carter. In those states, McCarthy's candidacy *may* have swung those states to Ford. Even more significantly, had McCarthy been on the New York ballot, it is likely his votes would have been sufficient to tip that state, with its micro-thin Democratic margin, from Carter to Ford. With that switch would have gone New York's entire bloc of 41 electoral votes, and with it also would have gone the presidential election—despite Carter's clear national vote margin of well over one and one-half million votes. Only by the dubious means of denying Eugene McCarthy a place on the New York ballot was McCarthy denied his goal—being the maker of the president in 1976.

Results of the 1976 Election

	Popular Votes	Electoral Votes
Jimmy Carter (Dem.)	40,829,046	297
Gerald R. Ford (Rep.)	39,146,006	240
Eugene J. McCarthy (Ind.)	756,631	—
Roger MacBride (Libert.)	173,019	—
Others	647,629	1
Carter plurality: 1,683,040		

The election results also show that in 1976 there was once again a faithless elector—and curiously enough once again, as in the previous three occurrences, a deviant *Republican* elector. Washington elector Mike Padden decided, six weeks after the November election, that Republican nominee Gerald Ford was insufficiently forthright in opposition to abortion and thereby unsuitable to be president. Mr. Padden instead cast his vote for Ronald Reagan. As we note elsewhere, similar defections from voter expectations had occurred in 1948, 1956, 1960, 1968, and 1972,[62] or in other words, in a total of six of the eight postwar elections. Even more important is that the likelihood of this occurring on a multiple basis would be greatly heightened in the case of an electoral vote majority resting on one or two votes—a very real possibility in 1976 as in other recent elections.

In fact, when one looks at the election returns for the 1976 election, one can observe that if about 5,560 votes had switched from Carter to Ford in Ohio, Carter would have lost that state and had only 272 electoral votes, two more than the absolute minimum needed of 270. In that case, two or three individual electors seeking personal recognition or attention to a pet cause could withhold their electoral votes and thus make the election outcome very uncertain.

A startling reminder of the possibilities inherent in such a close electoral vote election as 1976 has been provided by Republican vice presidential nominee Robert Dole. Testifying before the Senate Judiciary Committee on January 27, 1977, in favor of abolishing the electoral college, Senator Dole remarked that during the election count:

We were looking around on the theory that maybe Ohio might turn around because they had an automatic recount.
We were shopping—not shopping, excuse me. Looking around for electors. Some took a look at Missouri, some were looking at Louisiana, some in Mississippi, because their laws are a little bit different. And we might have picked up one or two in Louisiana. There were allegations of fraud maybe in Mississippi, and something else in Missouri.
We need to pick up three or four after Ohio. So that may happen in any event.
But it just seems to me that the temptation is there for that elector in a very tight race to really negotiate quite a bunch.[63]

In a less ominous vein, the 1976 election gave rise to another fascinating event. Following this election, a letter was sent to all members of the electoral college by Robert L. Brewster of Albuquerque, New Mexico, urging them to elect him as president in order to save the country from earthquakes and tidal waves. Nevertheless, Mr. Brewster received no electoral votes for president. There are no data available reporting unusual earthquakes and tidal waves.[64]

Besides the possibility of electors negotiating "quite a bunch" or being intimidated by imminent natural disaster, the electoral college in the 1976 election also held at least a possibility of electoral uncertainty. If slightly less than 11,950 popular votes in Delaware, and Ohio had shifted from Carter to Ford, Ford would have carried these two states. The result would then have been an exact tie in electoral votes—269–269! The presidency would have been decided not on election night, but through deals or switches at the electoral college meetings on December 13 or in the later uncertainties of the House of Representatives. What specifically might happen in the case of an apparent electoral college nonmajority deadlock? A first possibility, of course, is that a faithless elector or two, pledged to one candidate or another, might switch at the time of the actual meetings of the electoral college so as to create a majority for one of the candidates. This might resolve the crisis, although it is sad to think of the presidency as being mandated on such as thin reed of legitimacy.

If, however, no deals or actions at the time of the December 13 meetings of the electoral college were successful in forming a majority, then the action would have shifted to the House of Representatives for a contingent election—with all the possibility of political and social upheaval during the time before the November election and the January presidential vote in the House, as well as of the other dangers to the stability of the body politic we have previously reviewed in connection with the contingent election.

One final—and most definitely major—problem of the electoral college was demonstrated anew in the election of 1976. This is that under the present system there is no assurance that the winner of the popular vote will win the election. This problem is a fundamental one—can an American president operate effectively in our democracy if he has received fewer votes than the loser? An analysis of the election shows that if 9,246 votes had shifted to Ford in Ohio and Hawaii, Ford would have become president with 270 electoral votes, the absolute minimum, [65] despite Carter's 50 percent of the popular vote and margin of nearly 1.7 million votes.

One hesitates to contemplate the consequences of a nonelected president being inaugurated for four more years despite having been rejected by a majority of the voters in his only presidential election.

What, then, are the electoral college evils illustrated by the election of 1976? They are: (1) the distortions of campaign strategy resulting from candidates focusing on certain key, large, pivotal states, (2) the resulting inequities in candidate attention to voters and political leaders—some are viewed as vastly more important than others; (3) the fear of fraud or electoral accident tilting a large state's entire bloc of electoral votes and with it possibly the election; (4) the possiblities of a relatively insignificant minor-movement candidate being able to determine the election outcome if his limited support occurs in pivotal, large states; (5) the occurance of yet another faithless elector and the probable incentive for others should the electoral vote count be close; (6) the possibility of electoral college deadlock, even in an essentially two-candidate race, through an exact tie; and (7) the very real chance that the electoral college will elect the candidate who has run second in popular preference.

THE ELECTION OF 1980

The contest of 1980, in which Republican nominee Ronald Reagan swamped incumbent President Jimmy Carter with a 10 percentage-point lead in the popular vote and an overwhelming 91 percent of the electoral votes cast, scarcely ranks with the "years of controversy" in which the electoral college system was put to severe test.

There was, however, a wild card in the 1980 contest: the independent candidacy of John B. Anderson, a life-long Republican and veteran member of the U.S. House. Anderson initially sought the Republican nomination, only to find his brand of moderate Republicanism quite out of tune with the resurgent conservatism dominant in his party. In April 1980 he withdrew from the remaining Republican primary contests and announced his candidacy as an independent, calling on Americans of all political allegiances to join his "National Unity Campaign." Later he selected former Wisconsin Governor Patrick J. Lucey (Dem.) as his vice presidential running mate.

The Anderson campaign, though bedeviled by fund-raising problems, succeeded in qualifying for the ballot in all 50 states and the District of Columbia. Public opinion surveys showed voter discontent with both major party nominees. Carter had to battle Senator Edward M. Kennedy (Mass.) for his party's nomination and was gravely weakened by the nation's economic and foreign policy reversals of the preceding four years. Reagan appeared—especially at the campaign's outset—to represent a rigid conservatism outside the "winning" mainstream of American politics. At one point, in early summer, Anderson was the expressed preference of almost 25 percent in voter surveys.

But from that point, his support gradually evaporated. Reagan, in the general election campaign, was able to position himself as far more moderate than he had appeared in the early primary season. And Carter, although he would eventually lose by a large margin, drew many one-time Anderson supporters who feared the prospect of a Reagan presidency. By early September Anderson's poll readings had declined to the 15 percent range; by early October they were in single digit figures. Millions of Americans were clearly drifting back to the major party nominees. This illustrated first the continuing difficulty, despite the decline of party allegiance in the nation, of any independent candidate being considered a likely enough winner to maintain and build support during a general election campaign. The vast preponderance of Americans apparently still consider it a wasted vote to support a maverick candidacy. This is a phenomenon essentially unrelated to the electoral college. It is the reason that, with rare exceptions, third party or independent candidates are unable to win, or even score substantial support, in the direct vote that Americans cast for governors, U.S. senators, and other major officials. Even if the nation were to abolish the electoral college and substitute direct popular election, the "go with a winner" phenomenon would likely remain. Under the electoral college system it is probably exaggerated in states reported to be close, where people are particularly anxious to cast meaningful votes that might shift a bloc of electoral votes one way or another.

Had the 1980 election been close, however, the Anderson vote, even if small, could have thrown crucial states to one or the other of the major party contenders—and to a much greater extent than Eugene McCarthy, in fact, appeared to do in 1976. (See p. 82 above.) But in only 14 states with a total of

159 electoral votes did the Anderson vote exceed the margin of difference between the winning Reagan total and the trailing Carter count;[66] even in the unlikely event that Carter would have received all the Anderson votes if Anderson had not run, Reagan would still have won by a margin of 330 electoral votes to 208.

Results of the 1980 Election

	Popular Votes	Electoral Votes
Ronald Reagan (Rep.)	43,901,812	489
Jimmy Carter (Dem.)	35,483,820	49
John B. Anderson (NUC)	5,719,722	—
Ed Clark (Libert.)	921,188	—
Barry Commoner (Cit.)	234,279	—
Others	252,475	—
Reagan plurality: 8,417,992		

Had Anderson's support remained high enough to permit him to win some states in the three-way contest, he could have ended up—strategically though certainly not ideologically—in much the same swing position in electoral votes that George Wallace, running as a chiefly regional candidate, strove for in 1968. This eventuality evoked considerable media comment in the early stages of the campaign, as commentators speculated on what Anderson and his electors might do if they held the balance of power or what would result if there were no final electoral majority, throwing the election into the House of Representatives. (One fundamental difference between the Anderson and Wallace candidacies, of course, was the more national nature of Anderson's compared to Wallace's special regional appeal.)

A final feature of the 1980 election, similarly present in all contemporary presidential elections, was the potential for a faithless elector casting a vote contrary to expectations. Reagan was sufficiently concerned about this possibility to send a letter to each of his 538 elector candidates days before the election reminding them that he would expect them to fulfill their "obligation" to vote for him, even if President Carter should win the national popular vote.[67] In fact, no such faithless elector did appear when the electors convened in the various state capitals on December 15, 1980, making this presidential election the first since 1964 and only the third among the last nine in which no elector sought to act independently of the will of the American people in expressing his preference for president.

Reviewing the perils and close calls of all these elections, one recalls with amusement Hamilton's assertion in The Federalist concerning the method the Constitutional Convention chose for choosing the president: "I . . . hesitate not to affirm that if the manner of it be not perfect, it is at least excellent."[68] In the light of the history of these nine elections, the inevitable conclusion is that the electoral college system is far from perfect and hardly appears to be excellent.

Electing a President Today

The process by which the American people select their chief executive has two distinct aspects: the highly visible, popular campaign, which is seen, experienced, and participated in by millions of citizens, and, at the same time, the almost invisible workings of the constitutional mechanisms for elections, which go unnoticed by the vast majority of Americans. In most elections the electoral college manages to mirror the popular will, so that the two systems coincide in their results. But there are always the dangers that the electoral system may go awry and that the popular choice for president will be rejected by the electoral college. The interplay between these two systems—popular and constitutional—defines the subject of presidential election in America today. It is a necessary prelude to any discussion of the possibilities for reform and change.

THE POPULAR CAMPAIGN

Early in the year preceding a presidential election, the would-be candidates of each party begin their preliminary soundings across the nation, wooing influential party leaders and trying to establish a public image that will help them win the greatest prize the American electoral system has to offer. The first objective is to win the presidential nomination of one of the dominant national political parties, for under the country's prevailing two-party system no other road leads to the presidency.

The National Nominating Conventions

The historian Carl Becker has commented that "the national nominating convention is something unknown to the Constitution and undreamed of by the founding fathers. It is an American invention, as native to the U.S.A. as corn pone or apple pie. A Democratic or a Republican nominating convention, once it gets going, emits sounds and lights that never were on land or sea. Superficially observed, it has all the variety of a Slithy Tove. At different hours of the day or night, it has something of the painted and tinseled and tired gaiety of a four-ring circus, something of the juvenile inebriety and synthetic fraternal sentiment of a class reunion, something of the tub-thumping frenzy of a backwoods meeting." This is only the semblance, the picture to the outer world, however. "What goes on beneath the surface and behind locked doors," Becker adds, "is something both realistic and important. For it is here, un-exposed to the public eye, that deals and bargains, the necessary compromises are arranged—compromises designed to satisfy as well as possible all the diver-gent elements within the party. . . . What really goes on in a national nominating convention is the attempt, by the party leaders, to forecast the in-tangible and uncertain will of the people, as it will be registered in the state plu-ralities, and to shape the party policies in conformity with it."[1] Thus in many important respects the national conventions perform the task for the people that the Constitution's framers thought would be performed by the electors. But in-stead of settling on one candidate, the nominating conventions—and only those of the two dominant parties are usually of any lasting importance—propose the two presidential candidates from which the people and their agents, the electors, will choose the following autumn.

The Constitution's framers never contemplated national conventions for two reasons: because nationally organized political parties were unknown at the time, and because they dreaded the idea of partisan coalition and sought in the charter of government they wrote to isolate the presidential election from any pressures of faction or party.

By the early 1900s, however, national political parties were a fact of life in the United States. Institutions had to be developed by which each party could decide on its candidates for president and vice president rather than frag-menting its support in the election. The congressional caucus, operating from 1796 until 1824, was the first answer to this problem (see pages 35 and 49, above). In the era before the railroad, when travel from one part of the country to another was arduous and time-consuming, the congressional caucus pro-vided the only logical national forum for a political party. Ironically, the caucus placed the nomination of the president precisely where the Constitutional Con-vention had been determined not to place it: in Congress. Significantly, it was the supporters of frontier democracy and egalitarianism, grouped around Andrew Jackson, who effectively killed the caucus system in 1824. The caucus (or King Caucus, as its opponents derisively called it) could not survive an era of expanding democracy, because its power base was too narrow: congress-men were chosen by the people to make laws, not presidents.

In 1828, Jackson and Adams were nominated by a combination of state leg-islatures, public meetings, and irregular conventions scattered throughout the Union. The time was ripe for national nominating conventions to appear; the first was held by the Anti-Mason party in Baltimore in September 1831. The short-lived coalition called the National Republican party met in Baltimore in December 1831 to nominate Henry Clay for the presidency, and the Demo-crats held their first national convention in the same city in May 1832, nom-inating Andrew Jackson for a second term. The first Whig Convention was in

1839, the last in 1852. The first Republican National Convention was held in Philadelphia in 1856, nominating John C. Frémont for the presidency.

The delegates to each national convention come from every state and thus represent a broad geographic cross section of party and political activists. Some are governors, congressmen, and other prominent leaders from nonpolitical professions; some are simply party hacks who come to vote as party leaders tell them to; and many are individuals primarily loyal to their preferred candidate or to a particular cause or issue. Some are chosen by state party conventions, but the vast majority are elected in popular presidential primaries currently held in about thirty-five states. Collectively, the delegates to a national convention constitute the continuing entity of the national political party, a continental alliance that will continue to function and flourish only as long as it represents a significant cross section of the American people and reflects the major issues of the day.[2]

The rapid growth of presidential primaries in the 1960s and 1970s had the effect of transferring, more than ever, the decisive role in the selection of presidential nominees from the party powers of the day directly to the electorate. It became increasingly rare for a convention to be the arena of final decision; in most cases a clear decision had already emerged from the primaries. This tended to have a debilitating effect on the prestige and authority of the conventions—and thus of the established political parties.

The Presidential Campaign

In the early days of the Republic, the candidates for president remained quietly in their home cities and awaited the decision of the people. Today, through massive media coverage, every American is aware of the whirlwind of activity surrounding a presidential campaign. The candidates for president and vice president cover the face of the continent again and again, by air, rail, and motorcade, visiting every major population center at least once and even the smallest states of the Union. With the advent of radio, and especially of television in the years since World War II, the presidential campaign has been carried into the homes of all but a handful of the people. Whether the issues brought forth by the candidates be great or petty, the battle is distinctively national in character and is recognized by all as the decisive plebiscite on the course of the nation for four years to come.

Election Day

The grand climax of the race for the presidency comes as the people register their votes, starting with the stroke of midnight in a few early-voting hamlets in New England and ending some twenty-six hours later with the close of the last polling place in Alaska, four thousand miles to the west. In early American elections, it was days or weeks until the result was known; now, with quick reporting through the News Election Service, a cooperative ballot-counting operation of the three major television networks and the two major wire services, and rapid computer calculations by the national television networks, the result is generally known by mid-evening. A few hours later, except in the closest of contests, the losing candidate will concede, wishing his opponent all success in office and urging the nation to unify behind the winner. The drama seems to be closed for another four years.

THE CONSTITUTIONAL SYSTEM

As far as the Constitution is concerned, the popular election every fourth November is only the first step in a complex procedure that should culminate in the declaration of a winner a full two months later. In fact, under the Constitution, the November election is not for the presidential candidates themselves but for the electors who subsequently choose a president. And all the Constitution says of this stage of the election process is that "each state shall appoint, in such manner as the legislature thereof may direct, a number of electors, equal to the whole number of Senators and Representatives to which the state may be entitled in Congress." Thus the major controversies over the way the president is elected have centered on the presidential elector.

How Many Electors Are There?

Since each state's representation in the electoral college is equal to its representation in Congress, a state is guaranteed three electoral votes: two corresponding to the number of its United States Senators, and one corresponding to the minimum of one seat in the U.S. House that the Constitution assures each state. Additional House seats are apportioned on the basis of population following each decennial census. Congress has the power to decide the overall size of the House. The total number of representatives was set provisionally at 65 in the Constitution, rose to 106 after the 1790 census, and then increased gradually until the current level of 435 seats was established following the 1910 census. At this writing, with fifty states in the Union, the electoral college consists of 538 persons—435 corresponding to the number of representatives, 100 to the number of senators, and an additional 3 for the District of Columbia under the 23rd amendment to the Constitution.[3]

The relative power of various states in the electoral college has risen and fallen dramatically in the course of U.S. history (see Appendix C). Virginia, the early "mother of Presidents," swung the heaviest weight in the first years of the nation—21 out of a total of 138 electors in the last decade of the eighteenth-century. Today Virginia contributes only 12 electors in a vastly enlarged college. New York had 12 of the 138 electors in the 1791–1800 period but rose to a high for any state—47 electors—between 1931 and 1950. California, starting with only 4 electors when it entered the Union in 1850, had 45 electoral votes in the 1970s and was expected to control forty-seven of the 538 electoral positions in the 1980s.

A state's congressional apportionment—and thus its electoral vote—tends to lag behind actual population shifts. Since each census takes place in the first year of a decade (1790, 1960, etc.), the new apportionment cannot take effect until two years later. Thus the population figures from the 1790 census were not reflected in a new congressional apportionment until 1792, and the House elected under that apportionment did not take office until 1793. The same two-to-three-year gap has occurred after each subsequent census, except in the 1920s, when Congress failed to provide for any new apportionment whatever. If a presidential election falls in the same year as a census, it is still governed by the apportionment based on the census of a full decade before. The first presidential election under a new apportionment will take place either two years after the apportionment (as in 1952 and 1972) or a full four years later (as in 1964 and 1984) depending on the quadrennial cycle. For example, any state's increase or decrease in population since 1970 would not be reflected in that state's electoral vote apportionment until 1984.

Who Picks the Electors?

In practice, the people of the states have been given the power to choose the electors in statewide elections since the 1830s (see pages 44–47, above). The last instances in which a legislature chose the electors directly were in South Carolina through 1860, in the newly reconstructed state of Florida in 1868, and in the newly admitted state of Colorado in 1876. With these minor exceptions, the people have chosen the electors.

If any state legislature chose to, however, it would have the right under the Constitution to take the choice of the electors away from the people and do the job itself or deputize some other body to make the selection. In the words of a Senate committee in 1874, "The appointment of these electors is thus placed absolutely and wholly within the legislatures of the several states. They may be chosen by the legislature, or the legislature may provide that they shall be elected by the people of the state at large, or in district; . . . and it is, no doubt, competent for the legislature to authorize the Governor, or the supreme court of the state, or any other agent of its will, to appoint these electors." This language was quoted approvingly by the Supreme Court in a landmark 1892 case, McPherson v. Blacker, in which a group of Michigan citizens challenged the right of that state's legislature to shift to a district system for the 1892 elections.[4] The Court rejected the appeal, saying that the word "appoint" in the Constitution conveys the "broadest power of determination" to the legislatures. "There is no color for the contention," said the Court, that "every male inhabitant of a state being a citizen of the United States has from the time of his majority a right to vote for Presidential electors." The Court said the state legislatures have "plenary power" over appointing electors and could indeed refuse to provide for appointment of any electors at all if they so chose. During a debate in the House in 1826, Representative Henry R. Storrs of New York commented that nothing in the Constitution prevented a state legislature from vesting the power to choose presidential electors "in a board of bank directors—a turnpike commission—or a synagogue."[5]

Despite such sweeping language, there are some limitations on the discretion of state legislatures in setting the mechanism for presidential election in their respective states. Even *McPherson* v. *Blacker* recognized that *if* a state permits the people to choose the electors, then the 14th amendment protects citizens from having their vote denied or abridged. Congressional enactments designed to present fraud or regulate campaign expenditures in connection with presidential elections have been upheld by the Supreme Court.[6] The governor of a state, moreover, might well veto a legislative act abolishing popular election for presidential electors. In referendum states, a law abolishing popular election could be referred to the people, where it would almost certainly be defeated. Initiative measures could be used in a similar way.[7]

For the most part, however, it is not state or federal constitutional guarantee that assures the people the right to choose presidential electors. First of all, it would probably never occur to modern-day state legislatures to take the power of appointment of the electors directly unto themselves. And even if the temptation presented itself, fear of retribution at the polls would restrain them. After the 1960 election, segregationist forces in the Louisiana legislature suggested revoking the choice of the regular Democratic electors already elected by the people and substituting a new slate of electors that would oppose Kennedy's election. But despite the strong conservative sentiment in the legislature, the motion was withdrawn before it could come to a vote. Even if the motion had passed, it could probably have been subjected to successful challenge in the courts because it would have violated the congressional requirement that the electors be chosen on a uniform date—which had already passed. But a move by a legislature to take the appointment of the electors into its own hands before the nationally established date for choosing the electors would not be open to similar challenge.

Who Are the Electors?

The Constitution merely says that "no Senator or Representative, or person holding an office of trust or profit under the United States, shall be appointed an elector." The probable intent of the founding fathers was that the electors would be distinguished citizens, and such they were in some early elections. But in 1826 a Senate select committee said that electors were "usually selected for their devotion to party, their popular manners, and a supposed talent for electioneering."[8] As late as 1855, it was noted that the electors in Alabama and Mississippi were among the state's ablest men and went among the people to instruct, excite, and arouse them on the issues of the campaign.[9] Today, it is probable that not one voter in thousands knows who the electors are. Persons are usually nominated for elector on the basis of their service to their party. Since the only payment is normally a small per diem allowance on the day they cast their votes, some small measure of prestige is about all that electors can hope for from their selection. Democratic National Chairman John M. Bailey acknowledged in 1961 that the elector's role was "almost purely ceremonial" but said that the office should be continued because it "provides an honorary role for the people who devote themselves to making our political system work, and our society has too few such rewards."[10] Based on an entirely unscientific perusal of the pictures of electoral colleges convened in several states, it appears that such "rewards" are often reserved for women and party workers in the twilight of their lives. Many octogenarians are apparent. Thomas O'Connor was 93 years of age when he was elected president of the Massachusetts electoral college in 1960. Besides often being aged party workers, electors are frequently rewarded with the office because of their past financial generosity. As one well-known 1968 elector, author James Michener, honestly put it, "My finest credentials were that every year I contributed what money I could to the party."[11] The electoral college is far from being the assembly of wise and learned elders assumed by its creators; it is, rather, little more than a state-by-state collection of political hacks and fat cats.

A modern-day exception to the practice of having electors remain anonymous occurred in New York State in 1936, when the Democratic party put several trade-unionists, including Ladies' Garment Workers' chief David Dubinsky, on its electoral slate as a means of attracting the labor vote to Franklin D. Roosevelt. At the time, some fears were expressed that a "Tammany-izing" of electoral slates might occur, with the introduction of class, racial, and religious appeals through giving each of these groups some of the electoral nominations.[12] But the fears have not proved real; indeed, fewer and fewer states actually list the names of the electors on their ballots.

Nomination and Election of the Electors

Presidential electors for each party are today nominated by a variety of methods. The most widely used procedure—now in effect in thirty-four states—is for state conventions of the parties to nominate the electors. In ten states and the District of Columbia, nominations are made by the state political committees. One state, Arizona, authorizes nomination of the electors in primary elections. The remaining five states use a variety of combination methods. The most unusual nomination law is Pennsylvania's, which authorizes the presidential nominee of each political party to nominate electors on his behalf in the state (see Appendix J for state-by-state listing).

Before 1845, Congress refrained from setting any specific day for actual election of the electors. The Act of 1792, spelling out procedures for presidential election, stipulated only that the electors must be chosen within thirty-four days preceding the first Wednesday in December every fourth year.[13] A uniform national election date was established in 1845, however: the first Tuesday after the first Monday in November.[14] The date was especially appropriate for an agrarian society, for it fell after most of the autumn harvest had been gathered but before the rigors of winter set in. This date has been observed in every subsequent presidential election.

Since the advent of Jacksonian democracy, the states have almost exclusively used the general ticket for choosing electors. Under this system, electors are chosen "at large" (on a statewide basis) and the party with the most votes receives all the state's electoral votes.* Since 1832, only two states have reverted to the district system that several states used in the first years. The first instance occurred in 1892 in Michigan, where Democrats were temporarily in control of the legislature and hoped to divide the state's electoral votes so that they would not go en bloc to the Republicans, who normally had a majority in the state. Each of the state's twelve congressional districts became a separate elector district, and two "at large" districts, one eastern and one western, were established for the votes corresponding to Michigan's two senators. The plan was successful in dividing the Michigan electoral vote: nine electoral votes went for the Republican presidential ticket and five for the Democratic ticket in that year's election. But the national outcome was not close enough to be influenced by the Michigan returns. It was this Michigan plan that the Supreme Court refused to invalidate in *McPherson* v. *Blacker* (see page 91, above).

The other experiment with the district plan continues today. In 1969, Maine resurrected the district division of electoral votes by adopting a plan, which went into effect with the presidential election of 1972, that allowed for determination of two of its four votes on the basis of its two congressional districts. As of the 1980 election, however, an actual division of Maine's electoral votes 3 to 1 (the only division possible) had not yet occurred.

The virtual anonymity of the presidential elector has been reinforced in recent years by the marked trend, apparently spurred by the desire to simplify the vote count and the spread of voting machines, toward the use of the presidential "short ballot" in the November election. Instead of facing a ballot or voting machine with long lists of elector candidates, the voter sees the names of the parties' presidential candidates printed in large type, usually preceded (in small type) by the words "Presidential electors for . . ." Many states even omit the wording about presidential electors altogether, so that the voter, unless he is well versed politically, has no way of knowing that he is actually voting for electors rather than directly for president and vice president (see sample state ballots, Appendix K). The presidential short ballot was employed by fifteen states in 1940, by twenty-six in 1948, and was prescribed by the laws of thirty-

---

* A plurality is sufficient for election of electors in all states except Georgia, which requires an absolute majority. Georgia officials have ruled that if no elector slate won a majority, the two leading slates would participate in a runoff two weeks after the general election.

eight states by 1980. The names of both the presidential candidates and the electors appear on the ballots in eleven states. Most of these states require that the voter choose one slate or another as a unit, though three—Mississippi, Louisiana, and South Carolina—permit the voter to pick and choose among electors on various slates and permit write-ins. One unique state—Mississippi —prints the names of the electors but makes no mention of the presidential candidates they favor—unless the electors are pledged and wish to indicate their preference (for state-by-state listing, see Appendix J).

One beneficial result of the short ballot is to cut down the chances for voter confusion in marking ballots. History abounds with examples of spoiled ballots resulting from voter confusion over how to vote for electors. In the 1904 presidential election in Florida, the twenty candidates for elector, five from each of the four parties that qualified, were printed in a close column, one name below the other, with no line or space to separate the parties. Nor did the ballot carry any emblem or name to indicate which party each candidate for elector represented. The Democratic voter had to mark the first five electoral candidates, the Republican numbers six through ten, the Populist number eleven through fifteen, and so on. Naturally, a large number of voters were muddled, and 4,300 out of the 39,300 voters in the state failed to mark all the electors of their parties.[15] In Maryland in 1904 some 2,000 Republican voters marked only the square for the first Republican elector, thinking that that square represented a vote for all eight Republican elector nominees. The result was that the Republicans received only one instead of all eight Maryland electoral voters.[16] One of the most serious voter mix-ups of modern times occurred in Ohio in 1948. The state normally employs the short ballot, so that the names of the Republican and Democratic electors do not appear on the ballot. Henry Wallace's Progressive party was unable to qualify as a regular party for the general election ballot, however, so that the Wallace electors appeared on the ballot as individual names. Thousands of voters were confused by the double system and voted for some Wallace electors as well as marking ballots for Dewey or Truman. It has been estimated that more than 100,000 Ohio presidential ballots were invalidated for this reason. The confusion could well have determined the outcome in the state, which Truman won by a margin of only 7,107 votes.[17]

Under the general ticket ballot as employed by most states, the voter chooses one entire elector slate as a unit, and there is no chance for a split result—some electors elected from one slate and some from another. But where an elector can split his elector ticket, there is a chance for a divided result, as occurred in Maryland in 1904. It also occurred in California in 1912, when two Democratic electors and eleven Progressive electors were victorious because of slight differences in the vote cast for the various elector candidates on those two slates.[18] The spreading use of the short ballot has minimized the chances for such split results.

Electing a President Today

Electors: Bound or Not?

Since the first election, there has been controversy about the proper role of presidential electors. Are they to think and act independently or are they merely agents of the people who choose them? History records that in 1792 the electors chosen in North Carolina met and debated the respective merits of John Adams and George Clinton and finally decided to support Clinton.[19] Debates among the Virginia electors in the same year were reported to have shifted six votes from Adams to Clinton.[20] But even in the first elections, few electors really acted as independent agents. The newspaper *Aurora* said in 1796: "The President must not be merely the creature of a spirit of accommodation or intrigue among the electors. The electors should be faithful agents of the people in this very important business; act in their behalf as the people would act were the President and Vice President elected immediately by them. . . . Let the people then choose their electors with a view to the ultimate choice."[21]

With the passage of the 12th amendment in 1804, any semblance of the electors as independent agents faded. In his 1826 Senate committee report, Thomas Hart Benton of Missouri said that the founding fathers had intended electors to be men of "superior discernment, virtue and information," who would select the president "according to their own will" and without reference to the immediate wishes of the people. "That this invention has failed of its objective in every election," Benton said, "is a fact of such universal notoriety, that no one can dispute it. That it ought to have failed," he concluded, "is equally uncontestable; for such independence in the electors was wholly incompatible with the safety of the people. [It] was, in fact, a chimerical and impractical idea in any community."[22]

Thus by the early nineteenth-century, the function of the electors was little more than ministerial. Benton said the electors had "degenerated into mere agents"; and Justice Bradley, the famed "fifteenth man" on the Electoral Commission of 1877, characterized electors as mere instruments of party—"party puppets" who are to carry out a function which an automaton without volition or intelligence might as well perform.[23] Senator John J. Ingalls of Kansas commented in the same era that electors are like "the marionettes in a Punch and Judy show."[24] Reviewing the historical failure of the electors to be free agents as had been contemplated by the founding fathers, Supreme Court Justice Robert H. Jackson wrote in 1952: "Electors, although often personally eminent, independent and respectable, officially become voluntary party lackeys and intellectual nonentities to whose memory we might justly paraphrase a tuneful satire:

> "They always voted at their party's call
> And never thought of thinking for themselves at all."[25]

Jackson concluded that "as an institution, the electoral college suffered atrophy almost indistinguishable from *rigor mortis*."[26] Senator Henry Cabot Lodge of Massachusetts said in 1949 that electors "are mere rubber stamps—and inaccurate rubber stamps at that. The people know the candidates for President and Vice President; rarely do they know the identity of the electors for whom they actually vote. Such 'go-betweens' are like the appendix in the human body. While it does no good and ordinarily causes no trouble, it continually exposes the body to the danger of political peritonitis."[27]

Nevertheless, under the Constitution the elector remains a free agent and, if he chooses, can vote in any way he likes. At least as far as the law is concerned, Senator Benton warned, the elector "may give or sell his vote to the adverse candidate, in violation of all the pledges that have been taken of him. The crime is easily committed, for he votes by ballot; detection is difficult, because he does not sign it; prevention is impossible, for he cannot be coerced; the injury irreparable, for the vote cannot be vacated; legal punishment is unknown and would be inadequate. . . . That these mischiefs have not yet happened, is no answer to an objection that they may happen."[28] Since Benton's day, some efforts have been made to restrict the elector's independence, but his basic point still holds. In 1898 former president Benjamin Harrison suggested that "an elector who failed to vote for the nominee of his party would be the object of execration, and in times of high excitement might be the subject of a lynching."[29]

In fact, there have been a number of instances where presidential electors have broken their pledges. The first known case was recorded in Pennsylvania in 1796, when Samuel Miles, chosen as a Federalist, voted for Jefferson, prompting the much-quoted voter's remark that Miles had been chosen "to act, not to think" (see page 36, above). In 1820 former senator William Plumer of New Hampshire cast his electoral vote for John Quincy Adams rather than James Monroe, to whom he was pledged. Accounts vary about Plumer's motivation; he is reported to have said he felt only that George Washington "deserved a unanimous election"; but biographers also report that he wanted to draw attention to his friend Adams as a potential president and to "protest against the wasteful extravagance of the Monroe administration."[30] In 1824, North Carolina's 15 electors voted en bloc for Jackson, despite a reported agreement to divide their votes according to the result of a presidential preference vote, which the voters were allowed to make by writing on the ballot the name of the man they preferred. Adams's name was written in by about a third of the state's voters, so that he should have received about 5 electoral votes, according to the historian J. B. McMaster. Other authorities maintain, however, that it was understood that all of the state's votes would go to the more popular candidate.[31] In the same election the New York legislature picked a mixed slate of electors, including 7 electors expected to back Clay (from the state total of

36 in that election). One of the Clay electors was elected to Congress, however, and the man who replaced him voted for Adams. By the time the New York electors actually cast their ballots, they already knew that Clay would not even qualify for the runoff in the House. Two of the remaining 6 Clay electors from the state then deserted him—one to vote for Crawford, one to support Jackson.[32]

In recent times, six electors have broken their pledges. The first was Preston Parks, who was nominated on two elector slates in Tennessee in 1948—the regular Democratic (pledged to Truman) and the States' Rights (pledged to Thurmond). The regular Democratic slate, including Parks, was elected, but he voted for Thurmond anyway. In 1956, W. F. Turner of Alabama, a Democratic elector, voted for a local circuit judge, Walter E. Jones, for president, instead of supporting the regular Democratic nominee, Adlai E. Stevenson, to whom he was pledged. Turner subsequently commented: "I have fulfilled my obligations to the people of Alabama. I'm talking about the white people."[33] Henry D. Irwin, the renegade Republican elector in Oklahoma who voted for Harry Byrd in 1960 despite his pledge to vote for Nixon is another example (see pages 70–71, above). Irwin, who listed his occupation as "slave labor for the federal government," explained his action on a national television program: "I was prompted to act as I did for fear of the future of our republic form of government. I feared the immediate future of our government under the control of the socialist-labor leadership. . . . I executed my constitutional right . . . as a free elector." Irwin went on to say that the founding fathers were landowners and propertied people who never intended "that the indigent, the nonproperty owners should have a vote in such a momentous decision" as election of the president.[34]

In 1968 Dr. Lloyd W. Bailey, Republican of North Carolina, declined to abide by his pledge to support Nixon (see p. 77, above), and in 1972, Republican elector Roger MacBride of Virginia deserted his party's nominee, Richard Nixon (see chap. 4, n. 62). (The defection in 1972 made Nixon the only man in history to suffer elector defections on three different occasions.)

1976 saw yet another faithless Republican elector. (We are at a loss for any theory that could explain why every faithless elector for thirty years has been a Republican.) Mike Padden of Washington State cast his vote for Ronald Reagan instead of for Republican party candidate Gerald Ford (see pp. 82–83, above). This defection was the third occurrence of a faithless elector in successive presidential elections and the sixth such action in the eight elections since World War II. To the surprise of most observers, the presidential election of 1980 failed to produce a new faithless elector. When the electoral college met in the various state capitols on December 15, 1980, every one of the 489 Reagan and 49 Carter electors voted as anticipated. This was the first presidential election in sixteen years in which no individual elector had sought to replace state voters' preferences with his own.

Fortunately for the nation, Henry Irwin, Dr. Lloyd W. Bailey, Roger MacBride, Mike Padden, and the other self-willed men who broke electoral pledges before them were not able to change the outcome of the elections. Statistically, the chances are not very high that they could have. Between 1820 and 1980, 17,397 electoral votes have been cast for president. Only seven votes in all those years were indisputably cast "against instructions." If one also includes the disputed 1824 votes in New York and North Carolina, the total of bolting electors rises to fifteen. It should be noted, however, that the incentives for elector defections occurring on a multiple basis would be much greater in the case of a very close election. Should an electoral college majority rest on a margin of only one or two votes, then we might well witness faithless electors appearing in order to gain personal fame or draw attention to some favorite cause or issue. (For a discussion of some recent close elections, see chapter 4, especially the discussion of the elections of 1968 and 1976. Hairbreadth elections as a historical occurrence are analyzed in Appendix F.)

Most electors consider themselves irrevocably bound to support the presidential candidate on whose party ticket they were elected. In the disputed Hayes-Tilden election of 1876, James Russell Lowell, who had been chosen as a Republican elector in Massachusetts was urged to switch his vote from Hayes to Tilden—a move that would have given Tilden the election, since only one vote divided the candidates in the national count. Lowell refused to take the step, however. "In my own judgment I have no choice, and am bound in honor to vote for Hayes, as the people who chose me expected me to do," Lowell wrote to a friend. "They did not choose me because they have confidence in my judgment but because they thought they knew what the judgment would be. If I had told them that I should vote for Tilden, they would never have nominated me. It is a plain question of trust."[35] At the meeting of the California electoral college in Sacramento in 1960, former governor Goodwin Knight told his fellow Republican electors: "Before coming here today, many of us received messages by mail and wire urging that we cast our ballots for prominent Americans other than Richard Nixon and Henry Cabot Lodge. Among those mentioned were former Governor Allan Shivers of Texas, Senator Barry Goldwater of Arizona, and Senator Harry Byrd of Virginia. Conceding that these gentlemen have merit as statesmen," Knight said, "the fact remains it is our solemn duty, in my humble judgment, to vote for those men the people selected on November the eighth."[36]

In an effort to prevent the phenomenon of runaway electors, the party organizations in a few states require specific pledges by electors that they will support the national nominees of their party in electoral college balloting although these pledges are of dubious constitutionality (see below). Electors must now make such pledges in Alaska, Oregon, Oklahoma, and Florida—in the latter two by formal oath.[37] In a number of other southern states, the party committees are given sufficient discretion by state law to demand party loyalty pledges whenever they wish. Alabama has demanded such pledges in several elections, but not in those cases when the party machinery was generally supporting unpledged electors. In 1944 some Texas Democratic electors indicated that they might bolt the national ticket. A special party committee was convened. One of its members, Representative Wright Patman, later said the committee had "tried the proposed electors for disloyalty" and "put most of them off the ticket and put loyal ones on."[38] In 1972, in Minnesota, an already chosen Democratic-Farmer-Labor party elector indicated that he would be unlikely to vote for Democratic nominee George McGovern. That elector was promptly replaced by the state party.

In addition, a sharply increased number of states now have specific statutory provisions directing electors to vote for the candidates of the party that nominated them. Only five states had such laws in the 1940s, but today the list has expanded to fifteen, including the nation's two most populous states, California and New York. In the wake of the defection by Republican elector Irwin in 1960, the Oklahoma legislature added a new section to its election code stipulating that each elector candidate must take an oath to support his party's presidential and vice presidential candidates, and that if he votes for another person he will be guilty of a misdemeanor and fined up to $1,000.[39]

Serious constitutional questions are raised as soon as any effort is made to bind or control electors. Custom may have made electors into little more than instruments of party, but the Constitution provides that they shall vote by ballot, a procedure which would seem to imply that they are free agents. In 1952 the Supreme Court was called upon to judge the constitutionality of a requirement laid down by the Democratic Executive Committee of Alabama that candidates for elector pledge to support the presidential and vice presidential candidates of the party's national convention as a condition to being certified as a candidate in the Democratic primary. The Court, in a 5 to 2 opinion, held that the pledge requirement represented a legitimate exercise of the state's right to appoint electors under article II. The majority opinion noted the popular expectation that electors would vote for the party nominees and implied that the states' power to control electors was supported by the traditional practice of elector pledges. Even if a loyalty pledge were unenforceable, the Court said, it would not follow that a party pledge as a requisite for running in a primary was unconstitutional, since any person not wishing to take the oath could run independently of party.[40] But the Court did not rule on the constitutionality of state laws that require electors to vote for their party's candidates, or indicate whether elector pledges, even if given, could be enforced. The preponderance of legal opinion seems to be that statutes binding electors, or pledges that they may give, are unenforceable. "If an elector chooses to incur party and community wrath by violating his trust and voting for some one other than his party's candidate, it is doubtful if there is any practical remedy," in the view of James C. Kirby, Jr., an expert on electoral college law. Once the elector is appointed,

Kirby points out, "he is to vote. Legal proceedings which extended beyond the date when the electors must meet and vote would be of no avail. If mandamus were issued and he disobeyed the order, no one could change his vote or cast it differently. If he were enjoined from voting for anyone else, he could still abstain and deprive the candidate of his electoral vote."[41]

Conditionally Pledged or Unpledged Electors

Quite separate from the problem of elector fidelity is that of electors who either announce before the election that in certain circumstances they may support an alternative candidate or who simply refuse to be pledged in any way. An example of electors' announcing alternatives came in 1912, when South Dakota electors, nominally pledged to Theodore Roosevelt, let it be known before the election that if the returns from the rest of the country made it clear that Roosevelt could not be elected and the contest was between Woodrow Wilson and William Howard Taft, they would vote for Taft. The voters apparently found this assurance satisfactory, for the Roosevelt slate was victorious on election day in South Dakota. But Taft had run so far behind across the country that the state's electors stuck with Roosevelt anyway.

The concept of totally unpledged electors disappeared from the political scene around the time of the 12th amendment, only to reappear in the mid-twentieth-century as a device by conservative, segregationist-minded southerners to force the major parties to pay more heed to southern views. The genesis of the movement can be traced to the abortive States' Rights (Dixiecrat) third-party movement in the 1948 election (see pages 61 and 62, above). The Dixiecrat goal of 1948 was revived by the unpledged elector movement of 1960: to prevent either of the major party nominees from receiving a majority of the electoral votes. With the power to dictate the result of the election in their hands, the southerners then could extract pledges from one of the major party candidates with respect to southern positions on segregation and other issues, in return for the swing elector support from the South. If that strategy failed, the election would be thrown into the House of Representatives, where the southern states might also find themselves in a crucial bargaining position.

In 1948 the Dixiecrat nominees, Strom Thurmond (South Carolina) and Fielding Wright (Mississippi), won the elector votes of the four states where they actually appeared on the ballot as the Democratic nominees—Alabama, Louisiana, Mississippi, and South Carolina. Presumably, Thurmond and Wright would have released their electors to vote for one of the national party nominees if they had achieved enough votes to occupy a balance of power and could have struck a bargain with Truman or Dewey. Thus the Dixiecrat electors were technically pledged but would quickly have become unpledged if such an action had suited their purposes. A similar strategy was contemplated for the Wallace electors in 1968 in the event they held the balance of power between the major party candidates (see pp. 75–76, above).

In 1960 the unpledged electors chosen in Alabama and Mississippi decided to cast their votes for Harry Byrd when it appeared they were unable to achieve a balance-of-power position. Major preparations were made to launch another unpledged elector movement in 1964, but they were discarded when the Republicans nominated Barry Goldwater for president.[42] Goldwater's general conservatism and stand against civil-rights legislation satisfied most of the segregationist southerners, and of the six states he carried, four were the same ones that had gone Dixiecrat in 1948.

The Electors Cast Their Votes

The Constitution, in article II and the 12th amendment, provides that the electors shall meet in their respective states to vote by ballot for president and vice president. Congress is given the power to determine the day of voting, "which day shall be the same throughout the United States." This system of simultaneous elections in each state was adopted, according to one of the delegates to the Constitutional Convention, in the hope that "by apportioning limiting and confining the electors within their respective states, . . . that intrigue, combination and corruption would be effectively shut out, and a free and pure election of the President of the United States made perpetual.[43] The founding fathers had apparently hoped that the electors would be unaware of, and thus not influenced by, the action of their counterparts in all the other states.

Even in the first election, of course, the curiously naive hope for absolutely independent action by the electors in the various states was not fulfilled. But the form of election that the Constitution's framers prescribed has remained unchanged for almost two centuries, and on a specified day every fourth year a separate group, or "college," of electors meets in each state capital to vote for president. In 1792 Congress decreed that the day should be the first Wednesday in December. This provision remained in effect until 1877, when Congress shifted the date to the second Monday in January, reportedly to allow a state more time to settle any election disputes.[44] The final adjustment, to the first Monday after the second Wednesday in December—still the law today— was set by Congress in 1934 following ratification of the 20th amendment, which shifted inauguration day from March 4 to January 20.[45]

On the appointed day in December, the electors then convene, in most states at 12 noon. The meeting takes place in the state legislative chambers, the executive chambers, or the office of the secretary of state. Under federal law, the governor of the state must by this time have sent to the administrator of General Services in Washington a certificate showing the names of the electors appointed and the number of popular votes cast for them (for sample certification, see Appendix K). Copies of these certificates are presented to the electors when they convene, and the governor or secretary of state generally makes a short speech welcoming the electors to their august duty.[46]

Frequently, however, some of the electors fail to appear for their great day.

Congress, in a law first passed in 1845, has authorized the states to provide for filling of vacancies. In almost all the states today, the electors themselves are authorized to choose replacements. Sometimes the replacements are found by scouring the hallways of the state capitol for likely candidates. This process was followed by the Michigan electoral college in 1948, when only 13 of the 19 chosen electors—all pledged to Dewey and Warren—appeared. But one of the substitutes recruited on the spot, a Mr. J. J. Levy of Royal Oak, had to be restrained by his colleagues from voting for Truman and Barkley. "I thought we had to vote for the winning candidate," Levy was quoted as saying.[47] Substitute electors must frequently be designated because federal office holders have been chosen as electors, in violation of the Constitution.

While they have but one function—to vote for president—the electors in many states go through an elaborate procedure of prayers, election of temporary and permanent chairmen, speeches by state officials, appointment of committees and the like. Robert G. Dixon, in an interesting review of electoral college procedures, points out that the secretary of state is the "shepherd and guiding spirit of the electoral college in all states . . . the high priest who knows the ritual prescribed by laws and usages, federal and state, and under his prompting the electors go through their paces like obedient children."[48] In a speech accepting the chairmanship of the Ohio electoral college (for the fifth time) in 1948, Alfred M. Cohen said: "Our task is purely perfunctory if we are faithful to the trust confided in us." Cohen had apparently developed little love of the institution he headed, however, because he told his colleagues that he favored abolishing the system altogether in favor of direct popular voting for president.[49]

In 1976, while Wisconsin's electoral votes were being collected and tabulated, Wisconsin Governor and Electoral College Chairman Patrick Lucey invited a political scientist in the audience to speak to the electoral college. The resulting remarks were severely critical of the electoral college as an institution, describing it as "little more than a state by state collection of political hacks and fat cats."[50] The Wisconsin electors immediately proceeded to adopt a resolution calling for abolition of their office as well as of the entire electoral college system.

The Constitution provides specifically that the electors shall vote "by ballot" for president and vice president, which would seem to require a secret vote. In reality, the voting is not at all secret in many states. Dixon's survey showed that in 17 of the 40 states from which he received a response in 1949, the electors voted either by signed ballot, by oral announcement only (with no ballot whatever!), or by unsigned ballot accompanied by a public announcement of how each of them was voting. Fourteen states used paper ballots, 12 employed typewritten ballots, 8 printed ballots, 2 engraved ballots, and 5 the obviously unconstitutional practice of oral voting. Many of the printed ballots, in fact, actually list the names of the presidential and vice presidential candidates of the party that carried the state, thus destroying even the semblance of a free vote[51] (see sample electors' ballots, Appendix K). In 1800 one New York elector, Anthony Lispenard, insisted on his right to cast a secret ballot. It was reported, however, that Lispenard intended to forsake Jefferson and cast his double vote for Burr and someone else—a maneuver that would have given Burr the presidency. The prestigious De Witt Clinton was then brought into the meeting and his presence had such an impact that the participants showed each other their ballots before placing them in the ballot box. Lispenard hesitated but finally exhibited his ballot, marked properly for Jefferson and Burr.[52] Thus by common practice since the earliest days, the ballot is not secret and sometimes is not even a ballot at all. Actual use of the secret written ballot, as one observer has noted, "is an anti-democratic provision which may cause a blunder, and could be easily used to cover a crime. An agent of the people should never be permitted to act secretly in transacting their business, except in cases where the public safety may require."[53]

After balloting separately for president and vice president, as required by the Constitution, the electors are required to send lists of their votes by registered mail to the president of the Senate in Washington. This constitutional requirement has been amplified by statute to safeguard against loss of the first copy. Two copies are kept by the secretary of state of the state, two go to the General Services administrator and one to the judge of the local district court.[54]

The Count in Congress: Disputed Votes

Once the electors have balloted and the certificates of their votes have been forwarded to Washington, the scene shifts to Congress, where the votes are to be counted. The Constitution and 12th amendment provided simply that "The President of the Senate shall, in the presence of the Senate and House of Representatives, open all the certificates and the votes shall then be counted." In 1792, Congress provided that the joint session for counting the votes should take place on the second Wednesday in February; since passage of the 20th amendment, the date has been January 6. The count takes place in the hall of the House of Representatives, with the president of the Senate (who is the vice president of the United States) presiding.

Throughout the nineteenth-century the major controversy regarding the entire electoral college procedure centered on the technicalities of the vote count in Congress. By one theory, the president of the Senate had authority to count the votes; by another, the two houses present in joint session had the responsibility for counting; by still another theory, there was a *casus omissus* in the Constitution on who actually should do the counting.[55] The question was of great importance because of the number of disputed electoral votes. Obviously, the officer (or officers) responsible for the actual count enjoyed tremendous power, because, in effect, he was able to disqualify disputed electoral votes or to decide in the event of double returns from a state. During the first two decades of the nineteenth-century it was the unquestioned custom for the president of the Senate "to declare the votes." But from 1821 onward, his authority was undercut, and in the Reconstruction period, Congress itself exercised the power to judge disputed returns.

The major nineteenth-century ballot controversies centered on whether a state was fully admitted to the Union at the time its electoral ballots were cast (Indiana in 1817, Missouri in 1821, Michigan in 1837); whether certain southern states were properly readmitted to the Union when they sought to cast electoral votes immediately following the Civil War; and which ballots should be counted when two sets of returns were submitted by a state. Some of the objections raised during the century seem to have bordered on the trivial. In 1856, Wisconsin's electors met and voted one day later than the date set by Congress because of a blizzard that prevented their assembling on the proper date. The certificate of their vote was transmitted to the president of the Senate with an explanation of the circumstances that precluded their meeting on the appointed day. But though Wisconsin's vote would not have changed the national result, spirited argument began when the presiding officer in the joint session of Congress announced the count of the tellers "including the vote of Wisconsin." The arguments were ruled out of order, but the two houses withdrew to their own chambers for two days of bitter and inconclusive argument over whether the Constitution was inexorable in its requirement of the casting of the electoral vote on a single day. Among the more arbitrary actions of Congress was its vote in 1873 to exclude the electoral vote of Arkansas because the certificate of returns bore the seal of the secretary of state instead of the great seal—an article that the state did not possess at the time.[56]

In 1877, Congress finally enacted a law covering procedure in all disputed vote cases—a law still largely in force today. It seeks to shift the onus of decision in disputed vote cases back onto the states by providing that if a state has established a mechanism to resolve disputes, the decisions of the state officials will be binding on Congress. Congress may refuse to count votes from a state only if the two houses decide concurrently that the certification is invalid or that the electoral votes were not "regularly given" by the certified electors (for the text of existing statutes on the electoral count, see Appendix H).

Over the years the role of the president of the Senate has been reduced to little more than presiding at the joint session and breaking the seals on the ballots. The ballots are then given to tellers—two from each house—who actually announce each state's votes and make the national tally. The president of the Senate then has the honor of announcing the names of the new president and vice president of the United States—assuming that there has been a majority vote.

The counting and certification of electoral votes has become an entirely ceremonial act since the celebrated battle over the returns of the 1876 election—with the sole and important exception of the election of 1968. When the House and Senate met in joint session on January 6, 1969, to count the electoral votes, objection was made to the Wallace vote cast by Republican elector Dr. Lloyd W. Bailey. Those objecting included Senator Edmund Muskie (D., Maine)—the Democratic vice presidential nominee—and Representative James G. O'Hara (D., Mich.) along with six other senators and thirty-seven other representatives. Under the terms of an 1887 statute the two bodies then moved to separate deliberations on the disputed electoral vote, with a rejection of the vote by both House and Senate necessary to invalidate it.

The House debate was marked by the feeling of many members that elector Bailey had violated his trust, but Congress lacked any power to remedy the matter without a constitutional amendment. In contrast, the Senate debate explored some of the issue more fully. Senator Muskie, ironically fighting to preserve an electoral vote for the Nixon-Agnew ticket, argued that (1) electors, in effect, bind themselves when they agree to be part of a slate of electors in a state using the short ballot not listing individual electors; (2) the Supreme Court, in placing Wallace on the ballot in Ohio in 1968 had spoken of the need to ensure citizens an effective voice in the selection of the president—a concept violated by Bailey's action; and (3) to allow his act to stand unchallenged would be to establish a precedent encouraging future electors to unpredictable actions. To this, Senator Birch Bayh (D., Ind.) added the observation that he hoped this debate would "galvanize this Congress to find an equitable way of electing the President."

The dangers in congressional challenges to properly certified electoral votes, however, were stressed by Senator Howard H. Baker, Jr. (R., Tenn.), who also pointed out that this challenge, if successful, might "diminish pressures" for more basic electoral reform. Senator Sam J. Ervin, Jr. (D., N.C.) asserted that Congress has no control or review over electors. Senator Karl E. Mundt (R., S. Dak.), long a district plan supporter, observed that the congressional district in which Dr. Bailey lived had favored Wallace. Senator James B. Allen (D., Ala.) stressed the need for the "free elector system" and declared "the Senator from Maine would expect to make of the electors robots."

Throughout the debate in both houses, there was general dismay about the possibility of electors casting unexpected votes; however, there was also a feeling that after-the-fact congressional challenges were not the appropriate mechanism for eliminating this evil. The challenge to Dr. Bailey's vote was rejected by both the House (229 to 169) and the Senate (58 to 33). The result of the debates in both houses on January 6, was to give considerable new impetus in 1969 and 1970 to congressional attempts to abolish or modify the electoral college through the constitutional amendment process.[57] (See the discussion in chapter 7 of reform activities in 1969–70.)

Contingent Election

If no presidential candidate receives a majority of the electoral votes, the task of choosing a new chief executive is transferred to the House. This phenomenon has occurred twice in our history, following the elections of 1800 and 1824 (see pages 36–41 and 49–52, above). A minor shift of popular votes in the nation would have sent a number of other elections—including those of 1860, 1892, 1948, 1960, 1968, and 1976—into the House for decision. Under the 12th amendment, the House must choose among the three leading electoral vote recipients, rather than the top five originally stipulated in the Constitution. But the original system giving each state one vote in the House, regardless of size, remains in effect, and any state whose delegation is evenly divided loses its vote altogether (for rules of the House in a contingent election, see Appendix I).

Except for the founding fathers, few Americans have even found much commendable in the system of contingent election in the House. Thomas Jefferson wrote in 1823: "I have ever considered the constitutional mode of election ultimately by the legislature voting by states as the most dangerous blot on our Constitution, and one which some unlucky chance will some day hit."[58] Martin Van Buren in 1826 declared that "there is no point on which the people of the United States were more perfectly united than upon the propriety, not to say the absolute necessity, of taking the election away from the House of Representatives."[59] Senator Oliver P. Morton of Indiana said in an 1873 Senate speech: "The objections to this constitutional provision for the election of a President need only to be stated, not argued. First, its manifest injustice. In such an election each state is to have but one vote. Nevada, with its 42,000 population, has an equal vote with New York, having 104 times as great a population. It is a mockery to call such an election just, fair or republican." Morton showed that under the apportionment then in effect, 45 members of the House, drawn from 19 states, could control an election in a House then consisting of 292 members representing 37 states. The 19 states with an aggregate 1870 population of a fraction over 8 million people would be able to outvote 18 states with an aggregate population of 30 million. Morton declared that "the rotten-borough system was a mild and very small bagatelle" in comparison.[60] The comparable figures based on the 1960 census showed that 76 members of the House, drawn from 26 states, could elect a president in a House of 435 members representing 50 states. The 26 states with an aggregate population of 30.7 million people would be able to outvote 24 states with a total population of 148.6 million.

A number of other objections to election by the House are also apparent. First, representatives are elected not with an eye to their preference for president but for very different reasons. Many districts and states elect congressmen of one party and vote for the presidential candidate of another. Second, the choice of the president by Congress could place the chief executive under heavy obligations to the legislative branch. Third, the whole election could swing on one or two men from one or two key states, as it did in 1825. Fourth, the Constitution does not explain the procedure if a tie for third place occurs in the electoral balloting. Would the House consider just the top two, or in reality the top four candidates? After extensive research on these questions, one political scientist noted, somewhat wryly, "A certain amount of perseverance is needed in order to discover something good to say about the possibility of an election of the President in the House of Representatives."[61]

The rules of the House provide for continuous House balloting on president until a winner is declared. The balloting would start January 6, leaving fourteen days until the scheduled inauguration. In most cases, a speedy resolution could be hoped for. But a prolonged deadlock could occur, so that no president would be chosen by January 20. In that event the new vice president would become acting president under the specific mandate of the 20th amendment. If, as would be likely, there had also been no majority in the electoral college vote for vice president, he would have been chosen by the Senate. Since only the top *two* vice presidential elector candidates could be considered by the Senate, with each member having a single vote, a choice would almost certainly have occurred.

Only once in history has the Senate been called on to choose a vice president. In 1837, Van Buren won 170 of the 294 electoral votes in a split field. But his vice presidential running mate, Colonel Richard M. Johnson of Kentucky, had only 147 electoral votes—one less than a majority. Johnson, who had been hailed as the man who personally killed the Indian leader Tecumseh in the Battle of the Thames during the War of 1812, was boycotted by the Virginia electors, who voted for Van Buren for president but reportedly wanted to register disapproval of Johnson's social behavior.[62] The Senate proceeded to elect Johnson by a vote of 33 to 16 over Francis Granger of New York, the runner-up in the electoral vote for president.[63]

If a presidential election should ever be thrown into Congress again, at least the decision would not be made by lame-duck legislators as it was in 1801 and 1825. Under the 20th amendment, ratified in 1933, a new Congress—elected the same day as the presidential electors—takes office on January 3, three days before the official count of the electoral votes.

Death of a Presidential Candidate or President-Elect

Under the United States' multistage process of electing a president—stretching from the day that the national party conventions nominate candidates to the day in January that a new chief executive is inaugurated—a number of contingencies can arise through the death or withdrawal of a prospective president or vice president.

The first contingency may arise through the death of one of the nominees between the adjournment of the convention and the day in November when the electors are officially chosen. No law covers this contingency, though both the Democratic and Republican parties have adopted procedures to cover the eventuality. The rules of the Democratic party, approved by its national conventions, provide that the 108-member Democratic National Committee shall have the power to fill the vacancy, with each state or territory's delegates empowered to cast the same number of votes that the state or territory had at the original nominating convention. A resolution adopted by each Republican National Convention authorizes the Republican National Committee to fill any vacancy, with the same assignment of voting power to the committee members to correspond to voting strength at the convention. Alternatively, the Republican National Committee is authorized to call a new convention, a step it might well take if the election was not imminent.[64] Should they be called on to fill a vacancy caused by the death of a presidential candidate, the national committees might in most instances select the vice presidential nominee as the candidate for president and substitute a new candidate for vice president. If the death of a candidate took place just before election day—especially if he were one of the major presidential candidates—Congress might decide to postpone the day of the election, allowing the national party time to name a substitute and the new candidate at least a few days to carry his campaign to the people.

At no time in our history has a presidential candidate died before election day. In 1912, however, Vice President James S. Sherman, who had been nominated for reelection on the Republican ticket with President Taft, died on October 30. No replacement was made before election day, but thereafter the Republican National Committee met and instructed the Republican electors (only eight had been elected) to cast their vice presidential votes for Nicholas Murray Butler.[65] In 1860 the man nominated for vice president by the Democratic National Convention, Benjamin Fitzpatrick of Alabama, declined the nomination after the convention had adjourned. By a unanimous vote, the Democratic National Committee named Herschel V. Johnson of Georgia to fill the vacancy.[66] The Democratic vice presidential nominee in 1972, Senator Thomas F. Eagleton, resigned a few weeks after being nominated after it had been revealed that he had twice been hospitalized and had received electroshock therapy for depression. The Democratic National Committee hastily assembled and selected Sargent Shriver of Massachusetts as his replacement.

The second major contingency may arise if a presidential or vice presidential candidate dies between election day and the day that the electors actually meet—under current law, a period of approximately five weeks. Theoretically, the electors would be free to vote for anyone they pleased. But the national party rules for the filling of vacancies by the national committees would still be in effect, and the electors would probably respect the decision of their national committee on a new nominee. Again, the elevation of the vice presidential candidate to the presidential slot would be likely but not certain.

The only time that a candidate died in this period was in 1872, when the defeated Democratic presidential nominee, Horace Greeley, died on November 29—three weeks after the election and a week before the electors were to meet. Sixty-six electors pledged to Greeley had been elected, and they met to vote on the very day that Greeley was laid in his grave. Sixty-three of them scattered their votes among a variety of other eminent Democrats, but three Greeley electors in Georgia insisted on marking their ballots for him despite his demise. Congress refused to count the votes in the official national tally.[67]

The third contingency may occur through the death of a president- or vice president-elect between the day the electors vote in mid-December and January 6, the day that the votes are counted in Congress. There would likely be debate about whether the votes cast for a dead man could be counted, but most constitutional experts believe that the language of the 12th amendment gives Congress no choice but to count all the electoral votes cast, providing the "person" voted for was alive when the ballots were cast.[68] The U.S. House committee report endorsing the 20th amendment sustains this view. Congress, the report said, would have "no discretion" in the matter and "would declare that the deceased candidate had received a majority of the votes." The operative law would then be section 3 of the 20th amendment, which states: "If, at the time fixed for the beginning of the term of the President, the President-elect shall have died, the Vice President-elect shall become President."[69] And when the vice president-elect took office as president, he would be authorized under the 25th amendment to nominate a new vice president.

Similarly, if the vice president-elect should die before the count in Congress, he would still be declared the winner, and the new president would be able to nominate a replacement.

A fourth contingency may be caused by the death of either the president- or vice president-elect between the day the votes are counted in Congress and inauguration day. If the president-elect died, the foregoing provisions of the 20th amendment would elevate the vice president-elect to the presidency. In the event of the death of the vice president-elect, the 25th amendment would similarly authorize the new president to nominate a vice president, subject to the approval of Congress.

No president-elect has ever died in this period. But on February 15, 1933, a week after his election had been declared in joint session of Congress, and three weeks before his inauguration, president-elect Franklin D. Roosevelt barely escaped a would-be assassin's bullets in Miami, Florida.

In the event that neither a president nor a vice president qualified on inauguration day, January 20, then the Automatic Succession Act of 1947 would go into effect, placing the Speaker of the House, the president pro-tempore of the Senate, and then the various Cabinet officials in line for the presidency.

POPULAR VOTES VERSUS ELECTORAL VOTES

Though the term "popular vote" would seem to be simple and self-explanatory, its calculation can be quite complicated. As reported and generally understood in the United States, it is determined by taking the number of votes cast by the people on election day for each slate of electors in each state—Republican, Democratic or minor party—and then adding up the totals on a national basis. If a state requires that an elector slate be chosen as a unit, then the popular vote represents the number of ballots cast for that slate.[70] Thus in the 1964 election, 7,057,586 Californians voted for president. Of that total, 4,171,877 marked their ballots for the Democratic elector slate, and Lyndon Johnson was thus credited with that number of popular votes. The Republican slate pledged to Barry Goldwater received 2,879,108 votes, and he was credited with that total in the state. Minor party elector slates received 6,601 votes and were credited appropriately in the count. If a state permits its voters to ballot separately for presidential electors, then each elector is likely to have a slightly different total vote. In this case, the modern practice is to credit the presidential candidate with the number of votes received by the highest-polling elector pledged to him in the state.[71] The national popular vote total for any particular candidate consists of the aggregate of the votes cast for the electoral slates pledged to him in the various states.

With rare exceptions, this gives an accurate picture of the national will. There have been instances, however, in which a candidate's national vote was unnaturally reduced when state party rules or state laws prevented a slate of electors pledged to him from qualifying. In 1860 no electoral slate was pledged to Lincoln in 10 of the 33 states then in the Union. In 1912 the only way for California voters to cast ballots for President Taft was to write in the names of 13 elector candidates, since the Republican slot had been seized by Theodore Roosevelt's Progressives. In 1948 and again in 1964 the Dixiecrat and unpledged elector movements controlled the Alabama Democratic party machinery and appropriated the Democratic electoral slate for their own purposes. The Alabama voter had no way to register a vote for the national Democratic nominees in those years.

The percentage of electoral votes received by a candidate on a nationwide basis rarely coincides with his percentage of the popular vote for three reasons: (1) the general ticket (or unit vote) system, in which all the electoral votes of a state are credited to whichever elector slate receives a plurality of the state vote (minority votes in a state are washed out completely in the national electoral vote count); (2) the distortions caused by the existence of the two "senatorial" electoral votes in each state; (3) the fact that each state casts the number of electoral votes accorded it in the national apportionment, regardless of how few or how many citizens actually go to the polls.

Disparities from the General Ticket (Unit Vote) System

The operation of the general ticket system results in massive disfranchisement of minority voters. This effect of the winner-take-all procedure of the electoral college is perhaps unusually well expressed in Matthew 13:12: "For whosoever hath, to him shall be given, and he shall have more abundance; but whosoever hath not, from him shall be taken away even that he hath."

In 1960, 3,446,419, or 47.3 percent, of New York's voters cast their ballots for Nixon, but Kennedy's elector slate received a majority, and Nixon failed to receive a single one of the state's 45 electoral votes. In California, Kennedy won 3,224,099 votes, or 49.6 percent of the state total, but Nixon received all the state's 32 electoral votes. One calculation shows that in the 11 presidential elections from 1908 through 1948, a total of 372 million votes were cast for president, but 163 million (44 percent) of these votes were cast by minority voters in various states who failed to see a single electoral vote cast representing their votes:[72]

The electoral college can even under some circumstances disfranchise a majority of a state's voters. An example of this occurred in the election of 1968 in Arkansas. Major party nominees Hubert Humphrey and Richard Nixon together split slightly over 61 percent of the popular vote in that state; however George Wallace, with only 38 percent of the vote, received 100 percent of the state's electoral votes. The 61 percent of the voters of Arkansas who voted for Nixon and Humphrey received no electoral votes for their efforts.

A study of the impact of the general ticket system on a small number of states demonstrates its inherent inequality. For example, in the neighboring states of Illinois and Indiana in 1960, Nixon won a total of 3,554,108 votes to Kennedy's 3,330,204. But Kennedy had narrowly won Illinois, thus receiving its 27 electoral votes, while Nixon won a strong victory in Indiana, bringing him 13 electoral votes. Thus the two-state electoral vote was 27 for Kennedy, 13 for Nixon—or 67.5 percent for Kennedy, based on only 48.4 percent of the two-state popular vote total. In the adjoining states of Maryland and Virginia, the discrimination worked the other way. Kennedy won 50.9 percent of the two-state popular vote, but he received only 43 percent of the two states' electoral votes because he won by a large majority in Maryland (with 9 electoral votes) but lost by a smaller margin in Virginia (with 12 electoral votes).[73] Reviewing the operation of the general ticket system half a century ago, one observer said: "A plurality or majority in one section may, it is true, at times be counteracted by one in another section, and thus the net result be a rude approximation to fairness, taking the country as a whole; but this theory of averages may not work constantly, and the steady suppression of minority conviction in a state is an undisputed evil."[74]

Effect of Two Additional Electoral Votes
Corresponding to the Number of Senators

The weight of the population factor is further diminished in the electoral vote count by the two senatorial "counterpart" electoral votes that each state enjoys, no matter how few inhabitants it has. Based on the 1960 census, an electoral vote in Alaska corresponds to 75,389 persons, while one in California corresponds to 392,930 persons. On this basis, 35 states and the District of

Ratio of Electoral Votes to Population in Each State and the
District of Columbia for 1964 and 1968 Presidential Elections
(Based on 1960 Census)

Rank and State	Ratio	Rank and State	Ratio
1. Alaska	75,389	28. Kansas	311,230
2. Nevada	95,093	29. Connecticut	316,904
3. Wyoming	110,022	30. Washington	317,024
4. Vermont	129,960	31. Tennessee	324,281
5. Delaware	148,764	32. Louisiana	325,702
6. New Hampshire	151,730	33. Alabama	326,674
7. North Dakota	158,193	34. Georgia	328,593
8. Hawaii	158,193	35. Wisconsin	329,315
9. Idaho	166,798	36. Virginia	330,579
10. Montana	168,692		
11. South Dakota	170,129	National average	333,314
12. Rhode Island	214,872		
13. Utah	222,657	37. Kentucky	337,573
14. New Mexico	237,756	38. Minnesota	341,386
15. Maine	242,316	39. North Carolina	350,473
16. District of Columbia	254,652	40. Florida	353,682
17. Arizona	260,452	41. New Jersey	356,870
18. West Virginia	265,774	42. Indiana	358,654
19. Nebraska	282,266	43. Missouri	359,984
20. Oklahoma	291,036	44. Massachusetts	367,756
21. Colorado	292,325	45. Michigan	372,533
22. Oregon	294,781	46. Ohio	373,325
23. Arkansas	297,712	47. Texas	383,187
24. South Carolina	297,824	48. Illinois	387,736
25. Iowa	306,369	49. New York	390,286
26. Maryland	310,069	50. Pennsylvania	390,323
27. Mississippi	311,163	51. California	392,930

Columbia are technically "overrepresented" in the electoral college and 14 states are "underrepresented." The table above shows the disparities.[75]

Voter Turnout Disparities

Since each state has a set number of electoral votes, the actual vote total in a state has no relevance to its electoral votes. The electoral votes of a state will all be counted, whether one person or all the eligible persons go to the polls. In Mississippi, for example, only 25.5 percent of the adult citizens voted for president in 1960, so that 37,271 voters controlled one electoral vote. In Kansas, which had an identical number of electoral votes, 70.3 percent of the adult population voted, so that there was a ratio of 116,103 popular votes to every electoral vote.[76]

The net result of these distorting factors is that there is a gross disparity in most elections between the popular vote a candidate receives and his percentage of the electoral vote. The following tables illustrate five elections in which the disparities were most noteworthy.[77]

The Election of 1860

	Lincoln	Douglas	Breckinridge	Bell
Popular Vote	1,867,198	1,379,434	854,248	591,658
Electoral Vote	180	12	72	39
Percentage of Popular Vote	39.8	29.4	18.2	12.6
Percentage of Electoral Vote	59.1	3.9	24.0	13.0

Although Douglas was second in popular votes, he was last in the electoral college. And despite the fact that he won 74 percent as many popular votes as were cast for Lincoln, his electoral vote was only 6.7 percent of Lincoln's. Douglas' popular vote was 162 percent of Breckinridge's, but he received only 16.7 percent of the number of electoral votes for Breckinridge. Douglas's popular vote exceeded Bell's by more than twice, but Bell had three times as many votes in the electoral college.

The Election of 1912

	Wilson	Roosevelt	Taft	Debs (Socialist)
Popular Vote	6,301,254	4,127,788	3,485,831	901,255
Electoral Vote	435	88	8	0
Percentage of Popular Vote	41.9	27.4	23.2	6.0
Percentage of Electoral Vote	82.0	16.5	1.5	0

Taft had 85 percent as many popular votes as Roosevelt, but he carried only two small states, Vermont and Utah, with a total of eight electoral votes, or exactly one-eleventh of the Roosevelt electoral vote.

The Election of 1936

	Roosevelt	Landon	Others
Popular Vote	27,757,333	16,684,231	1,213,199
Electoral Vote	523	8	0
Percentage of Popular Vote	60.8	36.5	2.7
Percentage of Electoral Vote	98.5	1.5	0

In 1936 Landon received 36.5 percent of the total popular vote but only 1.5 percent of the electoral vote.

One of the greatest instances of a disparity between electoral votes and popular votes occurred in the 1970s. In the landslide presidential election of 1972, Nixon received over 60 percent of the popular vote but with that won over 96 percent of the electoral vote. McGovern saw his 37 percent of the popular vote transformed into a humiliating 3 percent of the electoral vote. The "multiplier effect" of the electoral vote percentage exceeding the popular vote percentage was a very high 36 percent—far above the twentieth-century average to date of 22 percent and less only than the elections of 1912, 1936, and 1980.

The Election of 1972

	Nixon	McGovern	Other
Popular Vote	47,170,179	29,171,791	1,385,620
Electoral Vote	520	17	1
Percentage of Popular Vote	60.7	37.5	1.8
Percentage of Electoral Vote	96.7	3.2	0.2

Finally, the first presidential election of the 1980s produced the greatest disparity between electoral votes and popular votes in the history of presidential elections. In a three-way division of popular votes somewhat parallel to 1912—the previous leader among elections—Reagan saw his winning popular vote margin of 50.7 percent swell into a landslide 90.9 percent of all electoral votes. The disparity between Reagan's popular vote and electoral vote percentages was 40.2—a new record for the forty elections for which popular vote totals are available.

The Election of 1980

	Reagan	Carter	Anderson	Others
Popular Vote	43,901,812	35,483,820	5,719,722	1,407,942
Electoral Vote	489	49	0	0
Percentage of Popular Vote	50.7	41.0	6.6	1.6
Percentage of Electoral Vote	90.9	9.1	0	0

Indeed, in few elections have the percentages of electoral votes received by candidates shown any reasonable semblance to the popular-vote breakdown. Since 1916 there has been only two elections—those of 1948 and 1976—in which the winning presidential candidate failed to run at least 10 percentage points better in the electoral college than he did in the popular vote (see chart, Appendix D).

CHANCES OF A MISFIRE

Despite the apparent tendency of the electoral count to inflate a winner's margin of victory, the fact is that in any close election, the disparity between popular and electoral votes can easily cause the man who lost the popular vote to win in the electoral college. In fact, in the nine presidential elections in which the leading candidate had a popular-vote lead of less than 3 percentage points over his closest competitor, the electoral college has elected the "wrong man"—the popular-vote loser—in three instances, or one-third of the time.*

Careful analysis shows that the danger of an electoral college misfire is not just historical but immediate in any close contest. In fact, only sheer luck has saved the nation from the choice of the popular-vote loser in the electoral college in several recent elections. These dangers lurking in the dual count system emerged clearly from a statistical analysis of presidential voting patterns commissioned for this book and prepared by Charles W. Bischoff of the Department of Economics, Massachusetts Institute of Technology. The experience of the past fifty years, Bischoff concluded, shows that in an election as close as that between Kennedy and Nixon in 1960, or between Carter and Ford in 1976, there is no better than a 50–50 chance that the electoral vote will agree with the popular vote as to the winner. When the leading candidate has a plurality of about 500,000 (or 0.57 percent, based on a 70-million-vote turnout), the verdict would still be reversed about one time in three. Even a plurality of 1 to 1½ million votes (a percentage point lead of 1.1 to 1.7) would provide not quite three chances out of four of winning the election, and a 2-million-vote plurality might not suffice one time out of eight. Projected 30 years hence (to the election of 2008), when the voter turnout will probably be at least 140 million, even a 1-million-vote plurality will fail to elect the popular vote winner in one election out of three. A plurality of 2 to 3 million votes will not quite provide three chances out of four of winning the election. A 4-million-vote plurality may still fail to elect the winner in one election out of eight.‡

* The elections included in this account are 1844, 1876, 1880, 1884, 1888, 1916, 1960, 1968, and 1976. The two that clearly misfired were those of 1876 and 1888, along with the less certain case of 1960. The count excludes the election of 1824, when Jackson ran 10.3 points ahead of Adams in the rather incomplete national popular-vote count yet lost in the electoral college.

‡ An alternative analysis of the misfire question by mathematician Samuel Merrill III utilizes an empirical model based on state-by-state presidential election results since 1900 as a means of

Bischoff counsels that it is not possible to make precise probability state-ments because the chance of a reversal depends in substantial measure on the particular candidate and the particular political climate in which an election takes place. For instance, when the South voted solidly Democratic, the Demo-cratic party almost invariably needed more than 50 percent of the national major-party popular vote to win an election—a result of large Democratic plu-ralities in southern voting, which in effect were wasted because they could not increase the region's electoral votes.

But Bischoff was able to arrive at some fascinating conclusions about the elections of recent decades by assuming various shifts in the popular votes be-tween the two leading candidates in each contest. These conclusions, in turn, cast light on the possible problems of the next decades, regardless of what the exact political conditions of the time may be.

Bischoff's method postulated a range of uniform shifts in the percentages of popular votes received by major party candidates in each election. The impact of these assumed shifts on the electoral vote results was then calculated for each election. In 1948, for example, Truman received 52.38 percent of the major-party vote. If his vote had been reduced by 1 percent, he would have re-ceived 51.86 percent of the major-party vote (52.38 percent less 1 percent of 52.38 percent, or .5238, = 51.86 percent). The method further assumes that the percentage reduction occurred uniformly in each state, with a correspond-ing increase in the popular vote for the opposing major-party candidate—in this example, Dewey—in each state.* Minor-party votes in each election were assumed to remain unchanged. In the 1948 example, the question may then be asked, would Truman still have won in the electoral college? The answer is no, for with a reduction of 1 percent of his vote total in all states, Truman would have lost Ohio, California and Illinois—three of the states he carried by the narrowest margins. This would have left him with only 225 electoral votes and would have given Dewey 267 electoral votes and the election. By repeating this experiment with different percentages, Bischoff discovered the minimum percentage of the major-party vote needed by each party to win an electoral college majority in the elections between 1920 and 1964:

---

estimating the likelihood of a divided verdict. Merrill's estimates are that in an election as close as 1960, there is a 0.23 probability of an electoral reversal by the electoral college; in the case of a vote as in 1976, there is a 0.5 probability of a misfire.

Merill's conclusions are a valuable extension and substantiation of the Bischoff analysis utilized here; both analyses are in substantive agreement. As Merrill concludes:

the likelihood of a divided verdict is significant when the winner's proportion of the major party popular vote does not exceed 52 or 53 percent and is most significant (rising to a probability of about .5) when that proportion falls below 51 percent. [p. 130]

Samuel Merrill III, "Empirical Estimates for the Likelihood of a Divided Verdict in a Presidential Election," *Public Choice*, 33 no. 2, 1978, pp. 127–33.

* Bischoff notes that some assumption about the distribution of the reduced vote is needed and that this symmetrical assumption seems to be the *most reasonable* one to make.

Minimum Percentage of Major-Party Popular Vote
Needed to Carry the Electoral College

Year	Needed by Democrats	Needed by Republicans
1920	51.34	48.66
1924	50.36	49.64
1928	48.75	51.25
1932	50.14	49.86
1936	52.25	47.75
1940	51.71	48.29
1944	51.36	48.64
1948	52.24	47.99
1952	50.32	49.68
1956	49.71	50.29
1960	49.82	50.31
1964	48.67	51.33

It is interesting to note that with growing two-party competition in the South, the Republicans have lost the comparative advantage they enjoyed up to the early 1950s. The year 1960 may be taken as a watershed when the parties seemed to be on a fairly even footing in terms of the percentage of the vote they need to win election.

But it would be incorrect to assume that the haphazardness of the system depends only on phenomena like solid-party voting in one region. Bischoff concludes that the more important, and perhaps more permanent, feature of the system depends on the existence of strong two-party systems in the large states like New York, California, and Illinois. As long as these states are likely to swing either way, thus throwing large blocs of electoral votes into one column or the other, the electoral college will often fail to reflect the popular vote in a close election. By rearranging and summarizing the data in the table above, Bischoff developed the following chart showing the number of electoral vote victories each party would have enjoyed at set percentages of the national vote in the twelve elections between 1920 and 1964:

The dangers of electoral defeat the Democrats faced in every close election, even when they won the most votes, are clear from the figures. But even with the advantage the Republicans generally enjoyed because of the Democrats' wasted popular votes in the one-party South, the Republicans would have lost from a third to a fifth of the elections in which they received from 50.2 to 51.0 percent of the total popular vote.[78]

The American public may have failed to notice the haphazard nature of the electoral college because of the runaway nature of many recent elections. But almost any halfway reasonable electoral system, Bischoff notes, can elect the right man in a landslide election. The times in which a good electoral system is needed are precisely those times in which it *does* make a difference—that is, in

Elections Won by Each Major Party, 1920–1964,
Assuming the Specified Division of Major-Party Popular Votes*

Division of Major-Party Vote	Democratic Victories	Republican Victories
Democratic 52.5% (5% point lead)	12	0
Democratic 52.0% (4% point lead)	10	2
Democratic 51.5% (3% point lead)	9	3
Democratic 51.0% (2% point lead)	7	5
Democratic 50.5% (1% point lead)	7	5
Democratic 50.4% (0.8% point lead)	7	5
Democratic 50.2% (0.4% point lead)	5	7
Tie Vote	4	8
Republican 50.2% (0.4% point lead)	3†	8†
Republican 50.4% (0.8% point lead)	2	10
Republican 50.5% (1% point lead)	2	10
Republican 51.0% (2% point lead)	2	10
Republican 51.5% (3% point lead) (or greater)	0	12

* The preceding chart, which was developed by applying uniform percentage shifts to the votes of each party, showed the percentage of the popular vote that would have given it a bare majority in the electoral college in each election. This chart simply adds up the number of elections either party would have won at any set percentage of the national popular vote. For instance, there were seven elections when the Democrats needed 51.0 percent *or less* of the popular vote to win the election—1924 (when they needed only 50.36 percent), 1928 (48.75 percent), 1932 (50.14 percent), 1952 (50.32 percent), 1956 (49.71 percent), 1960 (49.82 percent), and 1964 (48.67 percent). But in five other elections, the Democrats needed *more* than 51.0 percent of the popular vote to win, and thus would have lost, even if they had polled that much—1920 (when they needed 51.34 percent), 1936 (52.25 percent), 1940 (51.71 percent), 1944 (51.36 percent), and 1948 (52.24 percent). Therefore the fourth line on this chart, which assumes that the Democrats had received 51.0 percent in *all* elections between 1920 and 1964, shows that in that event the Democrats would have won seven elections and the Republicans five. The notation of a percentage-point lead on the chart is simply a translation of the absolute percentage-point figure. If a party has 51.0 percent of the major-party vote, the other party has 49.0 percent—2.0 points less.

† One election would have gone to the House of Representatives for decision.

close elections. With spirited two-party competition in every region of the country, there is every possibility that the nation may experience a string of close elections like those of the 1870s and 1880s. And if history and mathematics can be our guide, the country will run a high chance of electoral disaster in every such election.

THE BIASES OF THE ELECTORAL COLLEGE

Thus far, we have been stressing the disparities between popular votes and electoral votes in terms of overall electoral outcomes. The electoral college can reverse the lead of the popular vote winner and elect the popular vote loser as president (three times in our history), deadlock an election and force the utilization of House contingent procedures (twice—in the elections of 1800 and 1824), choose a president who did not receive a majority of the popular votes (15 elections—or 38 percent of the elections for which popular vote totals are available), and produce a hairbreadth election where relatively tiny popular vote shifts could have enormous consequences (22 elections—or 55 percent of the elections for which popular vote totals are available). (For tables summarizing all instances of these categories of electoral outcomes, see Appendixes E and F). Now we turn to a different aspect of the electoral college system—the way it makes some citizens' votes for president worth more than others. In short, we are interested in evaluating the biases of the electoral college in terms of individual voters.

Measuring State Biases of the Electoral College[79]

Major efforts have been made in recent years to measure the biases of the electoral college in terms of the ability of a voter to affect decisions through the process of voting. Methodologies based on the mathematical theory of games and utilizing computer simulations of thousands of elections have been developed to estimate the relative differences in voting power of citizen-voters in the different states. Additionally, some studies have sought to determine the voting power of various categories of voters, including residency, regional, ethnic, and occupational groups.[80]

The purpose of this research in every case is the same: to discover the advantage or disadvantage the electoral college gives to citizen-voters *solely according to where they chance to reside and vote*. Essentially, the "voting power" approach to the evaluation of the electoral college involves three distinct steps.

1. A determination is made of the chance that each state has in a "51-person" game (actually 50 states plus the District of Columbia) of casting a pivotal vote in the electoral college.

2. An evaluation is made of the proportion of voting combinations to the number of all possible voting combinations in which a given citizen-voter can, by changing his vote, alter the way in which his state's electoral votes will be cast.

3. The results of the first step are combined with the results of the second to determine the chance that any voter has of affecting the election of the president through the medium of his state's electoral votes.

These calculations are normalized with the power index of the state whose citizens have the least voting power set at one; all other states have voting powers greater than one; the result is an index of *relative voting power* of each citizen, vis-à-vis voters residing in other states.

Table 5.1 reports relative voting power figures under the electoral college for the electoral college apportionments of the 1960s for citizens of the 50 states and the District of Columbia. The voting power figures are normalized on the power index of the "state" with the least voting power (in this case, the District of Columbia). Citizens of the three most populous states have at least twice the relative voting power of the inhabitants of the least advantaged state—Pennsylvania with 2.011, California with 2.421, and New York with 2.478. Column 4 of this table reports the percentages by which the relative voting power (column 3) of citizens in each state deviates from the average (mean) relative voting power per citizen-voter. Thus 43 of the 51 states have *less* than the average relative voting power (in this case, 1.673); 8 (7 of which are the 7 most populous states) have *greater* than average relative voting power. The advantage that citizens in the most populous states enjoy *solely because of their place of residence* is a great as 48.1 percent.

Table 5.1. Voting Power under the Electoral College in the 1960s
Based on State Populations, Arranged by Size of State
(pivotal definition one)

State Name*	(1) Electoral Vote 1964, 1968	(2) Population 1960 Census	(3) Relative Voting Power†	(4) Percent Deviation from per Citizen-Voter Average Voting Power‡
Alaska	3	226,167	1.838	+9.9
Nevada	3	285,278	1.636	−2.2
Wyoming	3	330,066	1.521	−9.1
Vermont	3	389,881	1.400	−16.3
Delaware	3	446,292	1.308	−21.8
New Hampshire	4	606,921	1.384	−17.2
North Dakota	4	632,446	1.356	−18.9
Hawaii	4	632,772	1.356	−18.9
Idaho	4	667,191	1.320	−21.1
Montana	4	674,767	1.313	−21.5
South Dakota	4	680,514	1.307	−21.8
Dist. of Columbia	3	763,956	1.000	−40.2
Rhode Island	4	859,488	1.163	−30.5
Utah	4	890,627	1.143	−31.7
New Mexico	4	951,023	1.106	−33.9
Maine	4	969,265	1.096	−34.5

* Includes the District of Columbia.
† Ratio of voting power of citizens of state compared with voters of the most deprived state.
‡ Percent by which voting power deviated from the average per citizen-voter of the figures in column 3. Minus signs indicate less than average voting power. Average voting power per citizen-voter = 1.673.

Source: John H. Yunker and Lawrence D. Longley, *The Electoral College: Its Biases Newly Measured for the 1960s and 1970s,* Sage Professional Papers in American Politics. (Beverly Hills, Calif., 1976), pp. 10–11.

Table 5.1. Voting Power under the Electoral College in the 1960s
Based on State Populations, Arranged by Size of State
(pivotal definition one)—*continued*

	(1)	(2)	(3)	(4)
				Percent Deviation
	Electoral	Population	Relative	from per Citizen-
State	Vote	1960	Voting	Voter Average
Name*	1964, 1968	Census	Power†	Voting Power‡
Arizona	5	1,302,161	1.069	−36.1
Nebraska	5	1,411,330	1.026	−38.6
Colorado	6	1,753,947	1.120	−33.1
Oregon	6	1,768,687	1.115	−33.3
Arkansas	6	1,786,272	1.110	−33.7
West Virginia	7	1,860,421	1.224	−26.8
Mississippi	7	2,178,141	1.131	−32.4
Kansas	7	2,178,611	1.131	−32.4
Oklahoma	8	2,328,284	1.213	−27.5
South Carolina	8	2,382,594	1.199	−28.3
Connecticut	8	2,535,234	1.163	−30.5
Iowa	9	2,757,537	1.292	−22.8
Washington	9	2,853,214	1.270	−24.1
Kentucky	9	3,038,156	1.230	−26.5
Maryland	10	3,100,689	1.327	−20.7
Louisiana	10	3,257,022	1.295	−22.6
Alabama	10	3,266,740	1.293	−22.7
Minnesota	10	3,413,864	1.265	−24.4
Tennessee	11	3,567,089	1.382	−17.4
Georgia	12	3,943,116	1.352	−19.2
Wisconsin	12	3,951,777	1.351	−19.3
Virginia	12	3,966,949	1.348	−19.4
Missouri	12	4,319,813	1.292	−22.8
North Carolina	13	4,556,155	1.392	−16.8
Indiana	13	4,662,498	1.376	−17.7
Florida	14	4,951,560	1.506	−10.0
Massachusetts	14	5,148,578	1.476	−11.8
New Jersey	17	6,066,782	1.628	−2.7
Michigan	21	7,823,194	1.679	+0.4
Texas	25	9,579,677	1.844	+10.3
Ohio	26	9,706,397	1.916	+14.5
Illinois	26	10,081,158	1.880	+12.4
Pennsylvania	29	11,319,366	2.011	+20.2
California	40	15,717,204	2.421	+44.7
New York	43	16,782,304	2.478	+48.1

Table 5.2 presents similarly calculated state bias data for the electoral college apportionment for the 1970s. Although only 2 states have relative voting power ratios exceeding 2.0, the total range of inequities is greater than

Table 5.2. Voting Power under the Electoral College in the 1970s
Based on State Populations, Arranged by Size of State
(pivotal definition one)

State Name*	(1) Electoral Vote: 1972, 1976 1980	(2) Population: 1960 Census	(3) Relative Voting Power†	(4) Percent Deviation from per Citizen-Voter Average Voting Power‡
Alaska	3	300,382	1.587	−4.3
Wyoming	3	332,416	1.509	−9.0
Vermont	3	444,330	1.305	−21.3
Nevada	3	488,738	1.244	−25.0
Delaware	3	548,104	1.175	−29.1
North Dakota	3	617,761	1.107	−33.3
South Dakota	4	665,507	1.366	−17.6
Montana	4	694,409	1.337	−19.3
Idaho	4	712,567	1.320	−20.4
New Hampshire	4	737,681	1.297	−21.7
Dist. of Columbia	3	756,510	1.000	−39.7
Hawaii	4	768,561	1.271	−23.3
Rhode Island	4	946,725	1.145	−30.9
Maine	4	992,048	1.119	−32.5
New Mexico	4	1,016,000	1.106	−33.3
Utah	4	1,059,273	1.083	−34.7
Nebraska	5	1,483,493	1.035	−37.6
West Virginia	6	1,744,237	1.131	−31.8
Arizona	6	1,770,900	1.123	−32.3
Arkansas	6	1,923,295	1.077	−35.0
Oregon	6	2,091,385	1.033	−37.7
Colorado	7	2,207,259	1.137	−31.4
Mississippi	7	2,216,912	1.134	−31.6
Kansas	7	2,246,578	1.126	−32.0
Oklahoma	8	2,559,229	1.219	−26.5
South Carolina	8	2,590,516	1.212	−26.9
Iowa	8	2,824,376	1.160	−30.0
Connecticut	8	3,031,709	1.120	−32.4
Kentucky	9	3,218,706	1.244	−25.0
Washington	9	3,409,169	1.209	−27.1
Alabama	9	3,444,165	1.203	−27.5
Louisiana	10	3,641,306	1.281	−22.7

* Includes the District of Columbia.

† Ratio of voting power of citizens of state compared with voters of the most deprived state.

‡ Percent by which voting power deviated from the average per citizen-voter of the figures in column 3. Minus signs indicate less than average voting power. Average voting power per citizen-voter = 1.673.

Source: John H. Yunker and Lawrence D. Longley, The Electoral College: Its Biases Newly Measured for the 1960s and 1970s, Sage Professional Papers in American Politics. (Beverly Hills, Calif., 1976), p. 14.

Table 5.2. Voting Power under the Electoral College in the 1970s
Based on State Populations, Arranged by Size of State
(pivotal definition one)—*continued*

State Name*	(1) Electoral Vote: 1972, 1976 1980	(2) Population: 1960 Census	(3) Relative Voting Power†	(4) Percent Deviation from per Citizen-Voter Average Voting Power‡
Minnesota	10	3,804,971	1.253	−24.4
Maryland	10	3,922,399	1.234	−25.6
Tennessee	10	3,923,687	1.234	−25.6
Wisconsin	11	4,417,731	1.291	−22.2
Georgia	12	4,589,575	1.324	−20.1
Virginia	12	4,648,494	1.316	−20.6
Missouri	12	4,676,501	1.312	−20.8
North Carolina	13	5,082,059	1.462	−11.8
Indiana	13	5,193,669	1.446	−12.8
Massachusetts	14	5,689,170	1.459	−12.0
Florida	17	6,789,443	1.611	−2.8
New Jersey	17	7,168,164	1.568	−5.4
Michigan	21	8,875,083	1.648	−0.6
Ohio	25	10,652,017	1.815	+9.5
Illinois	26	11,113,976	1.888	+13.9
Texas	26	11,196,730	1.881	+13.5
Pennsylvania	27	11,793,909	1.913	+15.4
New York	41	18,236,967	2.360	+42.4
California	45	19,953,134	2.546	+53.6

for the 1960s, with one man's vote in California in the 1970s worth 2.546 times that in the District of Columbia. Percent deviations from average voting power also are somewhat greater in the 1970s than in the 1960s, now ranging from −39.7 percent (District of Columbia) to 53.6 percent (California).

The most disadvantaged citizens are those of the medium-to-small-sized states, with from 4 to 14 electoral votes. The citizens of Massachusetts, the nation's tenth most populous state, have a relative voting power approximately equal to that of the residents of Alaska, the least populous state. Therefore, the citizens of the 40 states with a population size between that of Alaska and Massachusetts are at a disadvantage in comparison with the citizens of these two states and the nine most populous states. The citizens of the nine most populous states have a disproportionately large relative voting power, which increases in a direct relationship with the population. In terms of the percent deviation data, it can be observed that 45 states have less than average voting power, and only 6 states have more—the 6 most populous!

In summary, the electoral college is formed to contain two major, partially countervailing biases, each favoring residents of quite different states. Voters in the very smallest states are found to have an advantage due to the constant two votes given every state regardless of population; voters in the larger states, however, have an even greater advantage due to the winner-take-all system. The *net* result, however, is an overall large-state advantage under the electoral college, with the most disadvantaged citizen-voters being residents in the medium-to-small states with from 4 to 14 electoral votes.[81] Specifically, a citizen voting in California in the electoral college, as apportioned for the elections of 1972, 1976, and 1980, is found to have 2.546 times the potential for determining the outcome of the presidential election of a citizen voting in the most disadvantaged area—the District of Columbia.[82]*

Measuring Regional and Group Biases of the Electoral College

The biases inherent in the present electoral college for inhabitants of different size *states* have thus far been shown. The data as presented up to now have not, however, dealt with the question whether various *groups* of voters may be similarly favored or disadvantaged because of their residency in various states. In order to examine this important question, the relative voting power data were used to determine the average voting power of various population categories under the electoral college as compared to the average voting power of the total population.

The groups chosen were placed in two categories: regional and population groups. Regions chosen were East, South, Midwest, Mountain, and Far West groupings of states. Population groups were blacks, and residents of urban areas, central cities, and rural areas (including rural nonfarm and rural farm areas).

The average voting power of urban residents for the present electoral college, for example, was calculated by multiplying each state's relative voting power index (Table 5.2, column 3) by its number of urban residents. The sum of these products divided by the total number of urban residents in the nation equals the average voting power per urban resident. Finally, the percent deviation of this average from the per citizen-voter average was obtained. This percent deviation gives an indication of how this particular group in the electorate fares in comparison with other groups, as well as with all of the electorate.

Table 5.3 presents regional and group biases for the electoral college in both the electoral college apportionments of the 1960s and 1970s. From this table, it

---

* Mathematician Samuel Merrill III recently has presented an alternative empirical model of voting power under the present electoral college based on state-by-state presidential election results since 1900. He concludes that the ratio of disparity ranges up to 10 to 1, somewhat higher than that suggested by our analysis. Merrill's model is based on a treatment of blocs of voters as individual voting units rather than as individual voters as we have done. In Merrill's analysis voting power tends to increase with the number of such blocs. (Samuel Merrill, personal letter to authors, June 21, 1979, and "Citizen Voting Power Under the Electoral College: A Stochastic Model Based on State Voting Patterns," *SIAM Journal on Applied Mathematics*, March 1978, pp. 376–90).

can be seen that the region most advantaged by the electoral college is the Far West, with its percent deviation from average increasing from 26.7 to 33.1 in the course of the decade. The East also has an advantage, but a decreasing one, from 13.8 to 8.9. The Midwest, South, and Mountain states are relatively less advantaged, with the Mountain states having a percent deviation disadvantage increasing insignificantly from −28.8 to −29.0 over the decade.

Estimates concerning various demographic groups under the electoral college are also reported in Table 5.3. Central-city and urban citizen-voters are the most advantaged (with the advantage slightly decreasing over the decade). Black citizen-voters are disadvantaged in both the 1960s and 1970s, yet their disadvantage is decreasing from −5.2 to −2.4. Rural voters maintain their position as the most disadvantaged demographic group, with their disadvantage slightly increasing over the decade, from −8.8 to −9.5.

Earlier it was found that the electoral college has countervailing biases, which result in a net large-state advantage and a disadvantage to states with from 4 to 14 electoral votes. To this, we can now add the additional information that the electoral college also advantages central-city and urban citizen-voters as well as inhabitants of the Far West and East. On the other hand, the

Table 5.3 Regional and Group Biases under the Electoral College
in the 1960s and 1970s

	(1) 1960s Percent Deviation from National Average Voting Power	(2) 1970s Percent Deviation from National Average Voting Power	(3) 1960s–1970s Net Change over Decade
Regions			
Eastern states	+13.8	+8.9	−4.9
Southern states	−15.0	−13.4	+1.6
Midwestern states	−5.6	−6.2	−0.6
Mountain states	−28.8	−29.0	−0.2
Far Western states	+26.7	+33.1	+6.4
Groups			
Rural citizen- voters	−8.8	−9.5	−0.7
Urban citizen- voters	+3.8	+3.4	−0.4
Central-city citizen-voters	+6.3	+5.7	−0.6
Black citizen- voters	−5.2	−2.4	+2.8

Source: John H. Yunker and Lawrence D. Longley, The Electoral College: Its Biases Newly Measured for the 1960s and 1970s, Sage Professional Papers in American Politics (Beverly Hills, Calif., 1976), p. 36.

present electoral arrangement discriminates against blacks and rural residents, as well as inhabitants of the Mountain, southern, and midwestern states.

As suggested by conventional wisdom, the South appears to be disadvantaged by the electoral college and would stand to gain from the direct vote proposal. However, it should be noted that this bias has nothing to do with the low turnout in southern states or with the supposed bloc voting of southerners for one party or another. It merely measures the disadvantage stemming from the effect of the unit rule and the constant two.

These data seem in most respects to confirm the often-stated hypothesis that the electoral college favors urban and ethnic interests. Urbanized areas and central cities are above the national average voting power for the electoral college. Rural voters, on the other hand, are found to be relatively disadvantaged by the present electoral college.

Further analysis finds one group that stands out as profoundly *advantaged* by the existing electoral college. This group is suburban residents.[83] For the electoral college in the 1970s, suburban residents are found to have an average voting power of 1.779 and a percent deviation from national average voting power of +7.3 percent, making this category of voters the most advantaged (nonregional) group studied.[84]

The Voting Power of Blacks in the Electoral College[85]

The findings for one group contradicts conventional wisdom concerning the biases of the electoral college. Table 5.3 reports that black citizen voters are *disadvantaged* by the electoral college, both in the 1960s and 1970s data sets. Other findings—that urban and central city voters are advantaged and rural voters are disadvantaged under the present system—seem to confirm widely held assumptions about the biases of the electoral college. However, the findings concerning black voters differ from those reached by many analysts.

Actually, one cannot say *all* blacks are advantaged or that *all* blacks are disadvantaged by the electoral college. A black voter in California has approximately two and one-half times the chance of affecting the election outcome that a black voter in the District of Columbia has (see Table 5.2 above). The differences in voting power arise because people live in different states, not because of differences in race.

The measurement of the bias affecting black voters as a group involves *averaging* the voting power of blacks in all 50 states and the District of Columbia. If blacks gain from the electoral college, that is, have above-average voting power, then they must be concentrated more heavily in the 6 most populous states than is the general population. However, that is indeed not the case. *Table 5.4* documents that blacks are less concentrated in these 6 states than the population as a whole.

This table lists the highest voting-power state, California, at the top of the list, with voting power decreasing as one goes down the list. The percent deviation from average voting power under the electoral college for each state is listed in column 1. Columns 2 and 3 display the percentage of the U.S. population and the percentage of the black population that lives in each state.

In which states is the black population significantly more concentrated than the general population? If we examine states in which the percentage of blacks is one percent or more above the percentage of the U.S. population located in that state, we find from Table 5.4 that generally these are southern states that are *disadvantaged* by the electoral college. Florida, North Carolina, Georgia, Virginia, Louisiana, Maryland, South Carolina, Alabama, Mississippi, and the District of Columbia are in this category, and all have below-average voting power. Floridians' voting power is 2.8 percent *below* average; North Carolina residents are 11.8 percent *below* average; and the rest have voting power ranging from 20.1 percent to 39.7 percent *below* average.

Likewise, we should examine those states in which blacks are significantly *less* concentrated than the general population. The states for which the percentage of the U.S. population is 1 percent or more above the percentage of blacks are California, Pennsylvania, Massachusetts, Indiana, Wisconsin, Minnesota, Washington, and Iowa. This group includes two of the largest states that benefit from the electoral college: California and Pennsylvania. In fact, California has 9.8 percent of the U.S. population but only 6.2 percent of the blacks in the United States. Furthermore, California is the most advantaged state, with voting power 53.6 percent *above* average! Thus, blacks are not any more heavily concentrated in the large states than is the general population.

Table 5.4 Voting Power under the Electoral College in the 1970s and Black Populations, Ranked by State Voting Power

State Name	(1) Percent Deviation from Average Voting Power	(2) Percentage of U.S. Population	(3) Percentage of U.S. Black Population
California	+53.6	9.8	6.2
New York	+42.4	9.0	9.6
Pennsylvania	+15.4	5.8	4.5
Illinois	+13.9	5.5	6.3
Texas	+13.5	5.5	6.2
Ohio	+9.5	5.2	4.3
Michigan	−0.6	4.4	4.4
Florida	−2.8	3.3	4.6
Alaska	−4.3	0.1	0.0

Source: Lawrence D. Longley, "Minorities and the 1980 Electoral College." Paper delivered at the Annual Meeting of the American Political Science Association, August 1980, Washington, D.C., p. 18.

State Name	(1) Percent Deviation from Average Voting Power	(2) Percentage of U.S. Population	(3) Percentage of U.S. Black Population
New Jersey	−5.4	3.5	3.4
Wyoming	−9.0	0.2	0.0
North Carolina	−11.8	2.5	5.0
Massachusetts	−12.0	2.8	0.8
Indiana	−12.8	2.6	1.6
South Dakota	−17.6	0.3	0.0
Montana	−19.3	0.3	0.0
Georgia	−20.1	2.3	5.3
Idaho	−20.4	0.4	0.0
Virginia	−20.6	2.3	3.8
Missouri	−20.8	2.3	2.1
Vermont	−21.3	0.2	0.0
New Hampshire	−21.7	0.4	0.0
Wisconsin	−22.2	2.2	0.6
Louisiana	−22.7	1.8	4.8
Hawaii	−23.3	0.4	0.0
Minnesota	−24.4	1.9	0.2
Nevada	−25.0	0.2	0.1
Kentucky	−25.0	1.6	1.0
Maryland	−25.6	1.9	3.1
Tennessee	−25.6	1.9	2.8
Oklahoma	−26.5	1.3	0.8
South Carolina	−26.9	1.3	3.5
Washington	−27.1	1.7	0.3
Alabama	−27.5	1.7	4.0
Delaware	−29.1	0.3	0.3
Iowa	−30.0	1.4	0.1
Rhode Island	−30.9	0.5	0.1
Colorado	−31.4	1.1	0.3
Mississippi	−31.6	1.1	3.6
West Virginia	−31.8	0.9	0.3
Kansas	−32.0	1.1	0.5
Arizona	−32.3	0.9	0.2
Connecticut	−32.4	1.5	0.8
Maine	−32.5	0.5	0.0
North Dakota	−33.3	0.3	0.0
New Mexico	−33.3	0.5	0.1
Utah	−34.7	0.5	0.0
Arkansas	−35.0	0.9	1.6
Nebraska	−37.6	0.7	0.2
Oregon	−37.7	1.0	0.1
District of Columbia	−39.7	0.4	2.4

And this unfavorable distribution of blacks among the various states accounts for the net voting disadvantage that blacks have, resulting from the electoral college.

Earlier we cited a number of ways by which the electoral college operates so as to distort popular votes when they are transformed into electoral votes. Among these are the constant two electoral votes given every state regardless of population, the unit rule by which all of a state's electoral votes are determined by a plurality of the state's voters, the constitutional basing of electoral votes on population figures independent from actual voter turnout, and the fact that these population figures are themselves based on census figures that freeze the electoral vote apportionments among the states for ten to fourteen years. The result of these various structural features of the electoral college is to ensure that the electoral college can never be a neutral counting device but inherently contains varieties of biases dependent solely upon the state in which a voter is casting his vote for president. The contemporary electoral college is not just an archaic mechanism for counting the votes; rather it is an institution that aggregates popular votes in an inherently imperfect manner.

6

Reform Efforts
of Two Centuries

In his remark about the road to electoral reform being "littered with the wrecks of previous attempts," the late Arthur Krock added: "Though the inequalities and other defects of the present system are generally conceded, it has been protected from change for more than 100 years by a mixture of natural American conservatism where the letter of the Constitution is concerned and a bipartisan political combination effected by what some major party politicians believe to be self-interest."[1] The actual count shows that in the first century of the Republic, 224 resolutions were introduced in Congress to amend the constitutional provisions for electing a president.[2] In the succeeding seventy-seven-year period, through 1966, another 289 amendments were offered, making a grand total of 513 to that point in American history.[3] Yet of all these proposals, only one has been successful—the 12th amendment, ratified in 1804, which was significant mainly in its requirement that presidential electors vote separately for president and vice president (see pp. 41–44, above).

In addition to the glaring objections to the existing system—the possibility of nonplurality presidents, the problem of faithless electors, the serious consequences of fraud in a state that might swing an entire election, and the undemocratic aspects of contingent elections in the House, with the invitation such elections offer for political manipulation and corruption—many of the reformers over the years have centered their fire on the general ticket or "winner-take-all" system of casting state electoral votes, with its resultant disfranchisement of the minority in each state in each election. This is particularly unfair, critics have said, in large states where some sections are urban and industrial, others rural and agricultural, some markedly Republican and some as heavily Democratic. In the words of Senator Thomas Hart Benton of Missouri in 1824, "To lose their votes is the fate of all minorities, and it is their duty to submit; but this is not a case of votes lost, but of votes taken away, added to those of the majority, and given to a person to whom the minority is opposed."[4]

In the twentieth century, many reformers have criticized the general ticket system for allegedly inflating the bargaining power of splinter parties and pressure groups, especially in large states fairly evenly divided between the parties.

This criticism has grown in significance with the urbanization of the country and the tension between various minority ethnic and economic groups, centered in the cities, and the remainder of the U.S. population. The current system, Senator Henry Cabot Lodge said in 1950, "not only permits but actually invites the domination of Presidential campaigns by small, organized, well-disciplined pressure groups within the large so-called pivotal states."[5]

Other criticisms of the existing general ticket system are that it effectively limits the choice of presidential candidates to men from the larger states and that it leaves no incentive for citizens to vote in states that are supposedly "safe" for one party or the other.

THE DISTRICT SYSTEM

The proposal to divide each state into separate districts for the casting of electoral votes was first made by Representative John Nicholas of Virginia on March 14, 1800, and was the subject of extensive debate in Congress and the state legislatures during the first decades of the nineteenth century. A significant minority (though never a majority) of the states employed the system during the first few elections (see page 45, above) and it was favored in some form by many leaders in the first half-century of the Republic. The major backing for the district system has always come from those who saw the general ticket or unit vote system of casting electoral votes as a chief evil of the American electoral system. Writing to George Hay in 1823, Madison said that "the district mode [of choosing electors] was mostly, if not exclusively, in view when the Constitution was framed and adopted; it was exchanged for the general ticket and the legislative election, as the only expedient for baffling the policy of the particular states which had set the example."[6]

The exact form of district system plans has varied widely over the years. The first proposal, which was the subject of some thirty resolutions in Congress between 1800 and 1826, would have created as many electoral districts in each state as the state had representatives and senators combined. Thus, even if a state had only three electoral votes altogether, corresponding to two senators and one representative, it would have been divided into three distinct districts for the choosing of electors. A second form, first advanced by Senator Mahlon Dickerson of New Jersey in 1817, called for the choice of one elector in each congressional district and the election of two or more, corresponding to the state's two senators, by some other method—usually statewide popular vote.[7] As a variant of both these plans, some proposed amendments retained the office of elector, while others abolished the office of elector, provided for direct vote of the people, but retained the basic form of the electoral system by providing that each candidate would be credited with as many electoral votes as the number of districts he carried. The first form, retaining the elector, was prevalent during the first decades of the nineteenth century, but the second, based on a direct vote by districts, gained popularity after Benton first introduced it in 1823.

The first district system plan, which contemplated retaining the electors and subdividing the states into the whole number of electors to which they were entitled, was proposed in resolutions by the legislatures of Vermont, New York, and North Carolina in 1802. But it was brushed aside in order to get a consensus for the 12th amendment, which provided simply for separate electoral votes for president and vice president. After the 1812 election, in which several state legislatures—notably those of Masschusetts, New Jersey, and North Carolina—arbitrarily shifted electoral systems for partisan advantage, another major effort was made to get this amendment through Congress. A newly elected legislature in North Carolina instructed Senator James Turner of that state to introduce the amendment in the Senate, where it passed by a 22 to 9 vote in 1813. But the House failed to take any action. The legislature of Massachusetts endorsed the district system in 1816, but despite the urgings of many senators and representatives, sponsors saw they could not achieve the required two-thirds vote. Commenting on the failure of Congress to act on these proposals to establish a uniform national elector system, the *Niles Register* noted in an editorial: "And we jog on in the old way, swindling and to swindle."[8]

The next major push for reform effort began in 1817 with Senator Dickerson's proposal—brought forward at the instruction of the New Jersey legislature—for a district system with two electors chosen at large. North Carolina instructed its senators to switch their support to the New Jersey Plan, and when it was brought to a vote in the Senate in March 1818, it achieved majority support but fell short of the required two-thirds. By the next session the legislatures of New York, New Hampshire, and Connecticut had added their weight to the movement. The Dickerson amendment finally passed the Senate in February 1819, on a 28 to 10 vote, but the House—as in 1813—again failed to act. Dickerson introduced his proposal again, however, and it passed the Senate early in 1820. The House refused to consider it at first but later in the year voted on a similar amendment by Representative James S. Smith of North Carolina. But the amendment fell just short of two-thirds—92 to 54—in House voting. If the House had approved the amendment, the Senate would surely have agreed to the House language and the amendment would have gone to the states for ratification. The district system would never again come so close to success.[9]

Dickerson continued to introduce his amendment through 1826, but Thomas Hart Benton had entered the Senate with the admission of Missouri to the Union in 1821 and became the great reform leader of the succeeding thirty years. Benton's first proposed Constitutional amendment on presidential election, introduced in 1823, broke fresh ground by proposing a district system based on a direct vote of the people rather than intermediate electors. A uniform election system throughout the United States, Benton told the Senate, would "give to each mass of persons entitled to one elector the power of giving an electoral vote to any candidate they preferred." Both the general ticket system and the choice of electors by state legislatures, he said, violated the rights of minorities, because "a majority of one in either case carries the whole state." But when a select committee of five senators reported Benton's amendment early in 1824, it was opposed by Martin Van Buren, then a senator from New York, who said that division into districts would tend "to reduce greatly the present weight of the large states in the general scale" by "preventing them from bringing their consolidated strength to bear upon the Presidential question."[10] This fear in the large states, that their comparative power in the electoral college might be reduced, helped to defeat the district plan whenever it was brought forward.

Benton not only failed to muster enough Senate support to risk bringing his amendment to a vote in 1824 but also failed to do so after an enlarged special committee he headed reported a widened plan for consideration in 1826, just a year after the Jackson-Adams election had been thrown into the House for decision. In an effort to replace the fallen caucus system with an election process that gave the people the right of nomination, as well as election, Benton's committee recommended not only a first election by direct vote of the people in districts but a runoff by the identical system if no candidate recieved a majority in the first contest. "No intervening bodies should stand between" the people and their president, Benton said in his report. "The President should be nothing but an emanation of their will." A uniform district system, Benton claimed, would "give to every state and to the several sections of the state, and, as far as possible, to every individual citizen of the whole Union, their legitimate share and due weight in the election of the chief officers of their country."[11] Similar arguments were raised by Representative George McDuffe of South Carolina in a six-week-long House debate during the 1826 session.

The entrenched forces that saw an advantage in the prevailing systems of choosing electors by general ticket or legislative action were too strong to be overcome, however. In 1826 the House rejected the district system proposal on a 90 to 102 roll call, and Benton withdrew his resolution when he saw that he could not muster the required two-thirds vote for Senate approval. But Benton refused to accept final defeat, saying he "would pledge himself to the Senate and to the American people to continue the subject with all the energy he was master of till he brought it to a conclusion."[12] Benton remained true to his word, presenting his district system amendment at different times until 1844. Among his allies over the years was President Jackson, a close friend and supporter. In his first annual message to Congress, Jackson urged that the people be allowed to vote directly for president, for, he said, "in proportion as agents to execute the will of the people are multiplied there is danger of their wishes being frustrated; some may be unfaithful, all liable to err."[13] Jackson repeated his plea in each of his succeeding messages to Congress. Special Senate committees again reported the Benton amendment in 1834 and 1836, but it was never brought to a vote.

Benton's plan for a direct vote of the people by districts was advanced again by Andrew Johnson, then a member of the House, in the early 1850s, and was debated extensively by the House in 1854—again without a conclusive vote. As president, Johnson urged a similar amendment in a special message to Congress in 1868 and repeated the recommendation in his annual message the following winter."[14]

The case for electoral reform was taken up and ably advanced during the 1870s by Senator Oliver P. Morton of Indiana. Like Benton, Morton was for abolishing the office of elector and letting the people vote directly for president by districts. But he modified the Benton formula by requiring that the statewide popular vote winner receive two electoral votes and that the number of districts correspond exactly to the number of representatives the state had in Congress. The provision for two statewide presidential votes corresponding to the number of senators was similar to Dickerson's plan earlier in the century, except that Dickerson had contemplated retaining the office of elector. In a major Senate floor debate on his amendment in 1875, Morton said that the theory of the electoral college had failed completely: "It has turned out in practice that the electors are pledged in advance to vote for a particular candidate. . . . The reasons for the electoral college have gone. Why not let the people vote themselves for the Presidential candidates, instead of voting for electors who are pledged to do the same thing?" He acknowledged that "by the election of districts you do not bring the vote absolutely home to the people, as you would by a vote as one community, but you come as near to it as possible." Morton explained that his amendment preserved two votes at large for each state so that "the autonomy and power of the small states" might be preserved. He sought to avoid the problem of contingent election altogether by eliminating the majority vote requirement, simply providing that the candidate with the most district and state votes would be elected.

Morton's amendment had reached the Senate floor in 1875 with the endorsement of the Senate Committee on Privileges and Elections, which he headed. A district system amendment similar to Morton's was also brought to the House floor for debate in the same Congress, and aroused considerable interest. But neither the Senate nor the House actually reached a vote on the merits of the proposals, for the general opinion was that the greatest immediate danger relating to the electoral college lay in the count of disputed electoral votes in Congress. In fact, Morton's opening remarks in the 1875 debate presaged the disputed election of 1876: "No more important question can be considered by the Senate at this session of Congress," said Morton, "for in my opinion, great dangers impend, owing to the imperfection of the present system of electing the President and Vice President. . . . Though the election may be distinguished by fraud, notorious fraud, by violence, by tumult, yet there is no method for contesting it."[15] Morton would see the problem at first hand as a member of the fifteen-man electoral commission established to decide the Hayes-Tilden election.

As soon as the disputed election of 1876 had been resolved, Morton renewed his campaign for electoral reform. In the *North American Review* of May 1877, he declared: "Experience, as well as reason, now suggests that the rubbish of the electoral college be brushed away entirely."[16] But eight months later, at fifty-four-years of age, Morton succumbed to a chronic disease. With his death, the cause of electoral reform lost its most eloquent spokesman of the latter nineteenth century. Indeed, it would be almost three-quarters of a century before an electoral reform leader of comparable stature emerged.

After Morton's death, the district system was incorporated from time to time in amendments proposed in Congress, but it aroused little interest. When it finally was revived in the era following World War II, the district system emerged in a form closer to that of the very early nineteenth century than the more democratic forms advocated by Benton and Morton. The first postwar sponsor was Representative Frederic R. Coudert, Jr., a conservative Republican representing Manhattan's "silk-stocking" East Side congressional district. Coudert submitted his amendment on several occasions, starting in 1949, and was joined in 1953 by an equally conservative Republican, South Dakota's Senator Karl E. Mundt. The Mundt-Coudert plan, as it came to be known, retained two features of the original Constitution that Benton and Morton had sought to abolish: the office of elector and contingent election in Congress. Mundt and Coudert did advocate, however, that the responsibility for a contingent election be expanded from the House to both the House and Senate, in joint session, with each member entitled to a single vote. Under their plan, each congressional district would choose one elector, and two electors would be chosen at large in each state, corresponding to its number of senators.[17] A majority of electoral votes would be necessary for election. (Table 6.1 summarizes the major provisions of the district plan along with those of three other major reform plans.)

The roster of supporters for the Mundt-Coudert plan was heavily weighted with conservative Republicans and former Dixiecrats. Senator Strom Thurmond of South Carolina, the 1948 Dixiecrat presidential candidate, became a sponsor, as did Senator Barry Goldwater of Arizona and a number of representatives from the Deep South states.[18] In 1956 the plan was reported to the Senate as part of a hybrid package giving each state a choice between a proportional

Table 6.1.   Major Provisions of Four Reform Plans

	District Plan	Proportional Plan	Automatic Plan	Direct Vote Plan
1. Individual electors retained?	Varies	No	No	No
2. Unit vote retained?	Partially	No	Yes	No
3. Constant two electoral votes per state retained?	Yes	Yes	Yes	No
4. Present House contingent procedure retained?	Usually Not	No	Usually not	No
5. Possibility that winner of popular vote might not win election retained?	Yes	Yes	Yes	Yes—with joint session contingent No—with runoff contingent

plan of dividing its electoral votes and the district system. (For details on the proportional plan, see p. 144, below.) Arguing for the compromise package on the Senate floor, Mundt said that it "would restore and preserve the balance of voting power between the rural and urban areas, between great states and small states, which was intended by our Constitutional forefathers."[19]

At the crux of Mundt's argument was the assertion that both the president and the Congress should have the same "constituency." The Congress, he said, was elected on an individual district system basis, while its counterparts in the electoral college were chosen in multi-member districts consisting of entire states. As a result, the political complexion of the electoral college, chosen at large in each state, could differ radically from the political complexion of the House of Representatives chosen in the same election. The district system, Mundt claimed, would end the political disparity between the "Presidential United States" and the "Congressional United States" and lead to more harmony in relation between the executive and legislative branches of government.

It was precisely this "counterpart" theory that Mundt's opponents, led by Democratic Senators Paul H. Douglas of Illinois and John F. Kennedy of Massachusetts, objected to. The nation's big cities and the many minority groups within them, Douglas and Kennedy argued, were seriously underrepresented in the state legislatures and in both houses of Congress. "In the 48 state legislatures," Kennedy said, "the urban areas representing about 60 percent of the nation's population are allotted 25 percent of the seats in the popularly contested houses." Douglas produced figures showing a ratio of 540 to one in population between the most heavily populated and the least heavily populated districts in Connecticut. The rations were 94 to one in Florida, 25 to one in Wisconsin, and 296 to one in California, he said. These rurally dominated state legislatures, it was alleged, in turn create congressional districts that are malapportioned and gerrymandered to favor rural areas and conservative interests. The populations of the congressional districts in Texas, for instance, varied in the 1950s from 226,739 to 806,701, while Georgia had a disparity of 246,227 to 618,431 between the smallest and largest districts. In addition, the constitutionally mandated requirement for two senators for each state, regardless of population, overbalanced that body to the small, predominantly rural states. The cities of the United States, Douglas said, simply "do not have their fair and just representation." The effect of the proposed amendment, he argued, would be "to deliver the cities bound hand and foot, into the power of the rural sections of the country" by removing the sole advantage of the urban areas in the existing electoral system—their power to swing the vote in the largest states and thus influence the presidential election in a significant way. Kennedy summarized the opposition argument in these much-quoted words: "It is not only the unit vote for the Presidency we are talking about, but a whole solar system of governmental power. If it is proposed to change the balance of power of one of the elements of the solar system, it is necessary to consider the others."[20]

Thus the 1956 debate resolved itself into a fundamental power struggle along liberal-conservative, urban-rural, and party lines. The district system's opponents were able to show that it would increase the power of the conservative elements in both the Democratic and Republican parties. Since the heavily populated, two-party states of the North would split their electoral votes fairly evenly, the balance of power in the Democratic party would shift to the conservative southern states that would still cast almost all their electoral votes for Democratic presidential candidates. And in the Republican party, conservative rural interests would increase their influence because of the decreased importance of the large states and large cities where liberal Republicanism had previously flourished. "If political realignment is the real purpose of electoral change," Douglas said, "let us debate the merits of a political realignment rather than sneak realignment under the cloak of 'electoral reform.' "[21]

As it had been reported from the Senate Judiciary Committee, the 1956 amendment incorporated the proportional plan only. Its sponsors had subsequently agreed to attach the district system as an alternative, and the debate was technically on the motion to substitute the hybrid proportional-district plan. On March 27 that motion passed by a 48 to 37 vote, enough to carry as a substitute but substantially short of the two-thirds vote that would be needed for final passage. Facing defeat, the sponsors then moved to recommit the whole package to the Judiciary Committee. No constitutional amendment for changing the electoral college system was to reach the floor of either house of Congress again until the events of 1969, as discussed in chapter 7.

Coudert dropped out of Congress at the end of 1958 but Mundt remained in the Senate and continued to introduce his district system amendment in every Congress. In 1961 it was considered with other proposed reforms in extensive hearings before the Constitutional Amendments Subcommittee of the Senate Judiciary Committee, chaired by Tennessee's Estes Kefauver. Appearing before the Kefauver subcommittee, Mundt said his resolution had been altered to meet previous criticism by inclusion of a provision requiring that presidential elector districts be composed of compact and contiguous territory, containing as nearly as practicable equal population. These districts, he said, might coincide with congressional districts, but then the congressional districts would naturally have to meet the same standards. Mundt contended that the antigerrymandering requirement in presidential elector districts could be enforced by a suit of a state's citizens in state courts, by a similar suit in federal courts because of the possible violation of a federal constitutional provision, and by the authority that Congress would have to reject any electoral votes improperly cast because of the failure to establish equally populated and compact districts. Kefauver replied, however, that "the same political pressures and opportunity for political advantage would operate on the legislatures in this Presidential electoral districting as now influence Congressional redistricting." Professor Robert G. Dixon, Jr., of the George Washington University Law School warned that there was "a strong line of federal precedent against judicial action in legislative or electoral district cases," and that if Congress tried to enforce standards, "interminable wrangles and interstate reprisals" would result, making the sanction "both inadvisable and politically unfeasible." Thus the districts might well lack real standards of population equality and compactness, Dixon warned, and "we shall have gerrymandered the Presidency."[22]

In a letter to the Kefauver subcommittee, former president Harry S Truman endorsed the district system. "The problem we face today is that of the emergence of the big cities into political overbalance, with the threat of imposing their choices on the rest of the country," Truman said. (Ironically, the big-city vote had been a key factor in his own victory in 1948). Other backers of the district system included the National Association of Manufacturers (NAM) and

William E. Miller, chairman of the Republican National Committee and the 1964 vice presidential candidate. The NAM contended that "the district system would make the President the man of all the people; would reduce the effect of accident and improper election practices; would reduce the exaggerated influence of groups and individuals in control of bloc votes; and eliminate the unfair system of having the votes of large minorities cast opposite to their wishes."[23]

In the wake of the Judiciary subcommittee's 1961 hearings, its chief counsel, James C. Kirby, Jr., prepared a detailed memorandum showing the impact that any of the propposed reforms might have on the operation of presidential elections.[24] Under the district system, he pointed out, the 5 states with one representative in the House (Alaska, Delaware, Nevada, Vermont, and Wyoming), plus the District of Columbia, would constitute elector districts in which the entire vote would go to the plurality winner. In the other 45 states, 90 electoral votes, corresponding to the two senators from each, would continue to be awarded to the statewide plurality winner in the same manner as the existing unit vote or general ticket practice. Each of the remaining 430 elector votes would go to the winners in individual districts of states. If party strengths were uniform throughout a state, all the votes would still go to the winner of the statewide plurality.

Historically, Kirby noted, the district system had had mixed results in breaking up state unit votes. Between 1789 and 1892 there were 52 instances in which states used some form of the district system. In 36 of these cases, all of the state's votes had been cast as a unit. In the 1960 election, if existing congressional districts had been employed as presidential elector districts, 21 states with a total of 119 electoral votes would still have cast their electoral votes as a bloc under the district system. In another 7 states, with a total of 51 electoral votes, only one vote would have gone contrary to the state unit. In 6 states, with a total of 75 electoral votes, the minority party would have captured less than 25 percent of the state electoral vote. But in many states, especially the most populous ones, the district system would have effectively split the state's votes. New York would have split, 25 to 20; California, 19 to 13; Illinois, 15 to 12; Pennsylvania, 17 to 15; and Michigan, 10 to 10. Kirby's analysis would seem to bear out the charge of critics that the district system would magnify the comparative strength of smaller one-party states and dilute that of large states that are balanced relatively evenly between the parties. For instance, New York's effective vote—the lead it gave one candidate over another— would have been 5 votes, Pennsylvania's 2, and Michigan's zero. But in states where one candidate won all the districts, a solid bloc of electoral votes would still have been cast. Massachusetts would have had a relative weight of 16 votes in the 1960 election, Georgia 12, North Dakota 4, Oregon 6, and Wyoming 3.

By the same token, the disfranchisement of minority voters within any state could still continue under the district system. In a state with just three electoral votes, minority voters would never have a chance to capture electoral votes for their presidential candidate. In large states that split their electoral votes, the minority in each district would be just as effectively disfranchised as minorities are on a statewide basis today. As Thomas Jefferson said in 1800 (basing his comment on the then-existing size of the Union and number of districts), "It is merely a question of whether we will divide the United States into 16 or 137 districts."[25]

Under other circumstances the vote of a *majority* of a state's voters could also be negated under the district system. This would occur if one presidential candidate won a minority of the districts by overwhelming margins while losing a majority of the districts by small margins. Though such a candidate might emerge with a substantial victory in the state's popular vote, the distribution of district strengths might be such as to give his opponent a majority of the state's electoral votes. (This feature of the district plan is further analyzed below, p. 142.)

The district system would also not prevent the election of a minority president. Two of the three distortions of the existing system—the wide disparity in the number of votes representing one elector between large and small states and the inequalities stemming from variations in the voter turnout—would continue in full force (see pages 111–13, above). The general ticket system, as noted, would in effect remain in operation in the substantial number of states that could be expected to cast all their district votes for one presidential candidate. This, in turn, could have a profound political impact. Most of the states that could be expected to continue casting their electoral votes en bloc would be the smaller states, which on the whole tend to contain larger metropolitan areas and be more liberal politically. Thus the district system would likely benefit small-state rural conservatism and harm big-state urban liberalism. It is hardly surprising to note that in 1960, while Kennedy won a substantial electoral majority under the existing system, Nixon would have been the clear winner under a district system—278 electoral votes to 245. Since Nixon won 26 states, including most of the more lightly populated ones, he would have had a solid small-state base (with its inflated electoral vote) to which he could add the substantial number of individual Republican-oriented districts in the large industrial states (New York, Illinois, Michigan, etc.) that Kennedy carried under the existing general ticket system.

The basic conservative bias of the district system could be expected to reassert itself in election after election because the balance of the existing general ticket system—the inflated electoral vote power of conservatives in small states versus the swing power of liberal groups in the large states—would be erased. Conservatives, moreover, would frequently win more of the districts in large states than their percentage of the statewide vote would justify, because

Table 6.2   Disparity Between District and Popular Vote, 1952–1976

Winning Candidate	Electoral Vote Under District System	Percentage of District System Vote	Percentage of Popular Vote	Disparity
1952 (Eisenhower)	375	70.6	55.1	15.5
1956 (Eisenhower)	411	77.4	57.4	20.0
1960 (Kennedy)	245	45.6	49.7	4.1
1964 (Johnson)	466	87.1	61.1	26.0
1968 (Nixon)	289	53.7	43.4	10.3
1972 (Nixon)	474	88.1	60.7	27.4
1976 (Carter)	269	50.0	50.1	0.1

the popular vote majorities in conservative suburban and rural districts generally tend to be less than the liberal majorities in center-city districts. These factors would continue to operate even with an end to the malapportionment of congressional districts on which opponents of the district system centered their arguments in earlier years. There would be a continuing danger of minority presidents in close presidential elections.

Statistics based on the past seven presidential elections show clearly that under a district system there would still be major disparities between a candidate's percentage of the national popular vote and his electoral vote. Reliable congressional district breakdowns for president are not available for the elections before 1952, but the figures since then show a wide disparity between the percentage of popular vote and vote under the district system.[26]

The pivotal state, Kirby noted in his survey, would be of less importance under the district system. In fact, states as units would cease to be the targets of special campaign efforts. The national campaigns would instead be concentrated on the seriously contested districts—depending on the political circumstances of any year, probably 100 to 200 of the 435 House districts. The votes of minority blocs in the large two-party states would be of substantially less importance, because they would lose any balance-of-power position they may enjoy under the existing system. The potentialities for fraud or accidents of weather to influence a large state's vote would likewise be minimized, with such factors confined to a more limited number of districts.

Mundt's district system amendment was reported to the full Senate Judiciary Committee by the Kefauver subcommittee on a 4 to 2 vote in 1962, but no further action was taken on it.

In 1966, Mundt appeared before the Constitutional Amendments subcommittee to press his amendment again, once more decrying the power of big-state minorities under the existing system. Mundt pointed out that the Supreme Court decisions of the early 1960s, requiring equally populated congressional districts, had removed any possibility of gerrymandering under a district system. "The judicial branch," Mundt said, "has very clearly and vigorously indicated they not only can but will enforce districting standards." Mundt said the district system should be approved because it was the only electoral reform proposal that would "bring about a needed reform without a basic change in our constitutional system."[27]

The district plan had its chief moment of glory in recent decades in the form of the Mundt-Coudert plan of the 1950s. Since then, it has been relatively less significant as a seriously proposed electoral college reform, although a few senators continued to advocate it into the 1970s. Nevertheless, it would be useful to assess this plan as a major reform alternative of the recent past—in terms of electoral results. Considerable caution must be exercised in interpreting the possible outcomes of alternative electoral count systems in past elections, since the campaign might well have been conducted in a different manner as the presidential candidates and their managers sought to exploit the differing types of electoral bases that would have been included. Keeping this important caveat in mind, we can analyze the eight presidential elections between 1948 and 1976. The comparative results of these eight elections under the present system as well as under three proposed alternatives are presented in Figure 6.1.

The analysis of possible results under the district plan is greatly complicated by the limitations of congressional district election data for many past presidential elections. However, an examination of the eight recent elections is illuminating. Except in 1948, in each election the second- and third-place candidate in electoral votes would have done better under the district plan than under the electoral college and would have done worse under either than under the proportional plan. In other words, the district plan represents state-by-state minority preferences better than the present system but less well than the proportional plan.

One additional assessment should be made of the district plan: How fair is it to the individual voter? Following the mode of analysis summarized in chapter 5 (pp. 119–30), we find that the district reform plan contains biases slightly greater than those of the unreformed institution—although quite different in terms of who is advantaged. While the electoral college was found to sharply advantage voters in the largest states, central city, urban, and especially suburban citizen-voters, and inhabitants of the Far West and East, the district plan favors voters in the very smallest states, rural areas, and the mountain and southern states. The electoral college was found to provide a voting advantage of 2.546 for a citizen in California; the district plan, on the other hand, would provide a resident of Alaska in the 1970s with 2.857 times the relative voting power of a citizen-voter in the most disadvantaged area—California! This assumes, of course, that the voting districts were equal in population and that no thought of political gerrymandering had occurred to the drafters. The district plan is a curious reform: it introduces a "reformed" electoral system at least as complicated as the present system, and one with somewhat greater—although fundamentally different—inequities.[28]

THE PROPORTIONAL PLAN

The proportional plan for choosing a president would retain the constitutionally mandated apportionment of electors to the states, based on their representation in Congress, but would divide each state's electoral vote to reflect the share of the popular vote for president cast by the voters of the state.[29] (See table 6.1, Major Provisions of Four Reform Plans, above.) The plan was first introduced in Congress by Representative William T. Lawrence of New York on December 11, 1848. Lawrence envisaged abolishing the office of elector and assigning each presidential candidate the proportion of each state's electoral votes that would reflect the popular vote. No action was taken on Lawrence's proposal, but twenty-one years later Representative James M. Ashley of Ohio suggested an almost identical plan, except that the office of elector would be retained and the state legislatures would be called on to appoint electors who would divide their votes proportionately to reflect the popular vote in each state.[30]

Between 1875 and 1889, twenty proportional system amendments were suggested in Congress. The first of them, by Representative H. Boardman Smith of New York, was designed as a substitute for the district system amendment reported by the House Committee on Elections in 1875. His amendment, Smith said, was framed "for the purpose of obviating the danger and difficulty of a large accumulation of contested election cases in the electoral districts proposed by the plan of the Committee on Elections, and to prevent the gerrymandering of states by partisan majorities in the construction of election districts, and to dispense with the cumbersome machinery of electoral districts, while preserving the autonomy of the states in the election of President and Vice President."[31]

Major interest in the porportional plan was aroused in the wake of the disputed election in 1876, as Congress sought a way to avoid the difficulties of disputed elector votes. Among the chief sponsors were Representatives Levi Maish of Pennsylvania, William Springer of Illinois, and Jordan E. Cravens of Arkansas. Most of the nineteenth-century proportional plans would have retained whole electoral votes, dividing each state in proportion to the largest fraction. Thus if a candidate received 54 percent of the popular vote in a state with 10 electoral votes, he would get 5 electoral votes; if he polled 56 percent, he would receive 6 electoral votes. The plan introduced by Cravens in 1877, however, contained the first formula for carrying the computation out to the nearest one-thousandth. This formula has been utilized in most proportional plans advanced since.[32]

Writing in the *North American Review* in 1877, Senator Charles R. Buckalew

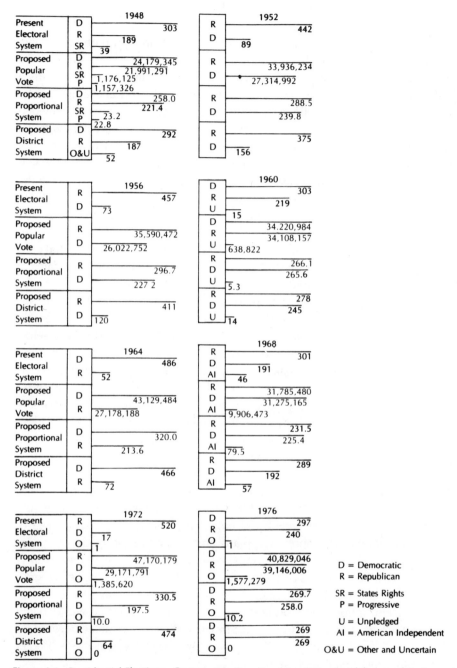

Figure 6.1 Presidential Elections: Comparative Results under Present and Proposed Systems

Sources: 1948–64: Legislative Reference Service, Library of Congress and Congressional Quarterly Service; 1968: Legislative Reference Service, Library of Congress, in U.S. Congress, House, House Judiciary Committee, *Hearings on Electoral College Reform,* 91st Cong. 1st sess., Feb. & Mar. 1969, p. 973; 1972: data supplied by the Library of Congress, Congressional Research Service, especially for this book; 1976: Government Division, The Library of Congress, and calculated from data in *Congressional Quarterly Weekly Report,* April 22, 1978, p. 971. The popular vote figures presented above, however, are drawn from the final official vote results contained in Appendix A and from the sources cited there.

of Pennsylvania claimed numerous beneficial results in a proportional system amendment: "It will greatly reduce, in fact, almost extinguish, the chance of a disputed election, by causing the electoral vote of the state to be very nearly a reflex of the popular vote, by confining the effect of fraud and other sinister influences within narrow limits, and by withdrawing the compact, undivided power of any one state from the contest. . . . Popular disfranchisement within a state will be swept away, while the supporters of no candidate will control more than their due share of electoral power." He said the amendment would "exclude the temptation to falsify or manipulate election returns, by which the whole vote of the state may be wielded in the interest of a party. Under it there would be no rival electoral colleges, or double returns of electoral votes, and pivotal states, inviting to profuse money expenditure, to fraud and to false returns, would no longer be known as a conspicuous feature of Presidential contests. It will render almost impossible the election of a minority candidate."[33]

In 1878 and again in 1880 a select committee of the House reported favorably on the proportional election plan. The 1878 report asserted that "it was not intended by the framers of the Constitution . . . that the state, as an entity, should cast the electoral vote *in solido* for a particular candidate." The select committee's minority, however, discerned a major threat to states' rights and declared that "the right to speak by a majority, when its fundamental laws permit, is a right inherent in every republic. This plan takes away from these republics, the states, this right *to speak by their majorities*, and confers upon the United States the right to say by a majority of the whole who shall be President and Vice President."[34] As reported to the House, the proportional plan required a simple plurality of electoral votes to win election. But it failed to come into a vote in the House in either year that it was reported.

It was almost fifty years before Congress again gave serious consideration to the proportional plan. In 1928, and in succeeding Congresses in a thirty-year congressional career that ended in 1948, Representative Clarence F. Lea of California introduced proportional plans and pushed for adoption of the reform. In 1933, at the end of the Seventy-second and again early in the Seventy-third Congress, committees of the House reported favorably on the Lea amendment, but it never came to a vote on the floor. Senator George W. Norris of Nebraska also introduced a proportional plan, and his proposal was debated fully by the Senate Judiciary Committee in 1934. But the committee decided instead to report out a resolution simply abolishing the office of elector while retaining the state unit vote system.[35]

Interest in electoral reform increased significantly following World War II, and the leadership for the proportional plan was undertaken by Senator Henry Cabot Lodge of Massachusetts and Representative Ed Gossett of Texas. The Lodge-Gossett plan, as it came to be known, was reported favorably by the Judiciary committees of both the Senate and House in 1948, but no further action was taken in that Congress. Lodge and Gossett renewed their efforts the following year, however, and the Judiciary committees of the two house reported favorably on the proposal in the summer of 1949.

On January 25, 1950, the plan was brought before the Senate, and Lodge delivered a major speech reviewing the deficiencies of the existing electoral college system and the benefits to be derived from a proportional plan. Under the proposed amendment, Lodge said, the anachronistic and potentially dangerous institution of the presidential elector would be abolished. The electoral vote per state, equal to its number of senators and representatives, would be retained, "but purely as an automatic counting device." The possibility than an election would be thrown into the House of Representatives would be eliminated, together with all "the turmoil, unrest, intrigue and possible frustration of the popular will by an election of the President in Congress."[36]

Because each state's electoral vote would be automatically divided to reflect the popular will, Lodge said, "all the evils inherent in the unit-rule method of counting electoral votes" would be eliminated. "No longer would millions of voters be disfranchised and their votes appropriated to the candidate against whom they voted. No votes would be lost. Every vote for President would count." The big pivotal states, Lodge said, would no longer receive a disporportionate share of presidential campaign efforts and spending. The proportional plan would "spread the campaign . . . into all the 48 states." As a result, it would "break up so-called solid or or one-party areas," since votes anywhere would have an impact on the national tally.

The major opposition raised against the Lodge-Gossett plan on the Senate floor came from Senators Homer Ferguson of Michigan and Robert A. Taft of Ohio. Ferguson charged that proportional voting would weaken federalism because the states, by being forced to break up their electoral vote to reflect popular sentiment, would be "required to surrender their sovereignty over the disposition of their own electoral votes." The idea of proportionalizing the vote of various states, Ferguson said, was "revolutionary" and should not be undertaken, because one could not foretell the political consequences.[37]

Taft said he would vote against the proportional plan "principally on the one ground, that it would give a tremendously disproportionate weight to one-party states." Taft was especially worried about the one-party Democratic South and the relative weight the southern states, voting overwhelmingly Democratic, would have compared to the northern states, where the vote is more evenly divided. Under the proporitonal system in 1900, Taft said, Mississippi would have had a relative weight of 7 electoral votes while Ohio, more closely divided, would have had a weight of only 1.6 electoral votes.[38]

Lodge dismissed the idea that the proportional plan might help one party over the other, pointing out that minority parties in one-party states would be encouraged if their votes counted nationally and that "the question of partisan advantage depends on the energy, imagination and ability of American party leadership. These are qualities which cannot be created by constitutional amendment." At any rate, Lodge contended, if one agreed that "the present system is wrong, dangerous and unfair, then it should be reformed regardless of party advantage."[39]

A major argument of the opponents was that the nation's two-party system would be endangered by proportional voting. Minority political groups, Ferguson charged, usually lacked enough power to carry states and thus win electoral votes under the existing system. But with proportional voting, he said, "their share of electoral votes in each state and accumulated total across the nation would provide a score card for their progress. The shining goal would be to divide and conquer the major parties by splintering."[40] Ferguson's argument paralleled, though it lacked a bit of the flamboyance evident in, a similar charge by Representative Wright Patman of Texas a year earlier that under the Lodge-Gossett plan there would be "the rise of many new parties—the Communist, the Dixiecrat, the Ku Klux Klan; parties representing the North, East and West; parties representing the farmers, the manufacturers, the laborers; parties representing racial and religious minorities,[41] all because they would now be able to obtain electoral votes. Replying to the splinter party argument, Lodge said the minor parties' hopes would actually be minimized, because they would no longer enjoy a balance-of-power position enabling them to throw large blocs of electoral votes one way or the other through their swing power in the big states—the practice that Henry Wallace's Progressives followed in 1948. On a related point, Lodge was obliged to deal with the argument that proportional voting for president might lead to a multiplicity of ideologically oriented splinter parties. Proportional voting for a single official, Lodge said, bears no resemblance to proportional representation in a legislative body. "Even the cleverest surgeon cannot divide one man up—proportionately or otherwise—and expect him to live," Lodge said.[42]

Lodge acknowledged that a candidate receiving a minority of the national popular vote could also be elected under a proportional system. That possibility, he said, could never be entirely eliminated without doing away with the two-electoral-vote bonus awarded each state regardless of population and resorting to direct popular election of the president. But Lodge said he thought the possibility would be much less likely under the proportional system.[43]

After rejecting alternative proposals for a direct vote or a general ticket system without electors, on February 1, 1950, the Senate approved the Lodge-Gossett amendment by a vote of 64 to 27, three votes over the required two-thirds majority. It was the first time in 130 years that the Senate had approved a constitutional amendment to alter the electoral college.[44] But, as time would show, it was the high-water mark for the proportional system.

In the 1950 Senate vote, the Lodge-Gossett plan had been supported almost solidly by Democratic senators and by moderate and liberal Republicans. The opposition came almost completely from conservative Republicans. But in the House, more Republicans moved to the opposition side, apparently sharing Taft's fear of increased electoral power in the Democratic South. And an even more significant block of opposition arose: from northern Democrats who likewise feared the political repercussions of the amendment. In the wake of the affirmative Senate vote, the Americans for Democratic Action in April 1950 went on record against the Lodge-Gossett plan unless it was modified to make a state's vote dependent on the actual voter turnout rather than population. In large part because of the growing northern Democratic opposition, the Lodge-Gossett plan became bottled up in the House Rules Committee, which exercised wide discretion in deciding which bills could be sent to the House floor for a vote. Of the 11 members of the Rules Committee, 7 opposed reporting out the amendment—4 northern Democrats and 3 northern Republicans. A minority of 4 favored reporting the bill for House debate—3 southern Democrats and one Republican, Representative Christian A. Herter of Massachusetts.

In a last-ditch effort to circumvent the Rules Committee, Gossett moved on July 17, 1950, to suspend the rules and bring the amendment to the floor. Motions to suspend the rules on controversial bills are rarely successful, and this was no exception. But Gossett in his introductory speech to the House adopted an additional strategy that only helped to solidify opposition: he actually named—"at the danger of stepping on some toes," as he put it—those minority groups in the large pivotal states who were said to have inordinate power under the existing unit vote system. "Is it fair, is it honest, is it democratic, is it to the best interest of anyone in fact," Gossett asked, "to place such a premium on a few thousand labor votes, or Italian votes, or Irish votes, or Negro votes, or Jewish votes, or Polish votes, or Communist votes, or big-city machine votes, simply because they happen to be located in two or three large, industrial pivotal states? Can anything but evil come from placing such temptation and such power in the hands of political parties and political bosses? . . . Both said groups and said politicians are corrupted and the nation suffers." The exaggerated electoral power of Negroes, Gossett said, had led to inclusion of fair employment practices platforms in the 1944 and 1948 national platforms. Likewise, "the radical wing of organized labor" in the Congress of Industrial Organizations had been appeased. And Jews had improperly influenced the parties by inclusion of planks backing the Zionist position on Palestine because "there are 2.5 million Jews in the city of New York alone."[45] Not surprisingly, only a handful of northern Democrats voted for Gossett's proposal.

The opposition to the Lodge-Gossett plan on the House floor was led by Representative Clifford P. Case of New Jersey, a liberal Republican. Case warned that the proposal would "reduce the Republican party to impotence" because it would need 52 to 54 percent of the popular vote to overcome the weight of southern electoral votes that would still be cast against its candidates. In the 1948 election, Case said, the electoral margin given by the state of Georgia alone would have been larger than the combined electoral margin given either party by the eleven most populous states of the country outside the solid South.[46] Republican Minority Leader Joseph W. Martin, Jr., of Massachusetts, who had been Speaker in the preceding Congress, warned that the amendment would "make it impossible for the election of a Republican President for a good many years." Martin said he held no "fetish and belief that the existing electoral college cannot be improved," but that a legitimate two-party system would first have to develop in the South.[47]

The final House vote, after the short forty minutes of debate permitted under the rules, was 134 in favor of the Lodge-Gossett plan, 210 opposed.[48]

In another round of hearings on electoral reform before the House Judiciary Committee in 1951, Gossett and Representative Lea (now retired but still active at the age of seventy-six) presented the familiar arguments for the proportional system. The hearings were more significant, however, for statements submitted by liberals explaining their opposition to the Lodge-Gossett plan. James Loeb, Jr., national executive secretary of the Americans for Democratic Action, charged that the Lodge-Gossett proposal would "make more secure the continued control of the government by the Democratic party, because of the disproportionate weight given the Southern states. But it would make even more certain the control of the Democratic party by the Southerns, including the Dixiecrats whose moribund movement would receive new life and influence. It would do all this without liberalizing the Republican party." Republicans, Loeb said, would be motivated to nominate more conservative men for the presidency to bid for their share of the southern vote—men like Robert Taft or John Bricker instead of Thomas Dewey or Wendell Willkie. Enacting a proportional plan would be unthinkable, Loeb said, as long as "the Fielding Wright machine in Mississippi and the Talmadge machine in Georgia remain free to maintain poll taxes, literacy tests, economic coercion or just plain terrorism in the electoral process." It would be like a united Germany with democratic elections in West Germany and one-party rule in East Germany, he contended.[49]

The National Association for the Advancement of Colored People, in a statement submitted by its Washington director, Clarence Mitchell, said the Lodge-Gossett amendment would "effectively draw the political eye teeth of all independent voters, including the Negro voter, as far as Presidential elections are concerned," since independent voters can swing doubtful states into one party column or the other. "Since 1909, in ever increasing numbers, the Negro has been migrating out of the South to the large industrial states of the North," most of which have large blocs of electoral votes and are doubtful politically, the NAACP noted. "If the Gossett proposal goes through, the Negro vote and the vote of other minority, national and religious groups will no longer be important in the great pivotal states of New York, New Jersey, Pennsylvania, Ohio, Indiana, Michigan, Illinois, California, West Virginia, Kentucky and Tennessee." But, said the NAACP, the South would continue to deliver a solid Democratic vote. "The only offset the Negro has to disfranchisement in the South . . . has been his political influence in the Northern pivotal states. The Gossett proposal would rob him of his influence without enfranchising him in the South." Thus, the NAACP concluded, "the Gossett proposal is antiurban, antinorthern and antiliberal."[50]

In 1951 the Lodge-Gossett plan was again endorsed by both the House and Senate Judiciary committees, but the proposal was not brought out for floor debate in either house. The Senate Judiciary committee held hearings again in 1953–54, but no further action was taken.

The next significant effort came in 1955, when the Senate Judiciary Committee, after a full round of hearings, reported out a Lodge-Gossett type of amendment. Lodge, however, had been defeated for reelection to the Senate in 1952 by John F. Kennedy, and the chief sponsorship of the proportional plan had been undertaken by Senators Estes Kefauver of Tennessee and Price Daniel of Texas. (Gossett had retired from Congress in 1950, but no prominent House advocate of the proportional plan arose to take his place.) A total of 30 senators sponsored the Kefauver and Daniel proportional amendments. By the time the measure was brought up for Senate floor action in March 1956, however, the supporters of the proportional and district methods had joined forces in an effort to gain enough votes for passage. The so-called "Daniel substitute," giving each state a choice between the proportional and district methods, had an astounding total of 54 Senate sponsors. Kefauver took the lead in floor debate, echoing many of the arguments for the proportional plan that Lodge had presented six years before.[51]

Senators Douglas and Kennedy, spearheading the opposition, employed basically the same arguments against the proportional plan aspect of the Daniel substitute that they employed against the district system alternative. Southern states could still be expected to cast the great bulk of their electoral votes for the Democratic candidates, while the closely divided northern states would split their votes more evenly. Thus a conservative bias would be introduced into presidential elections, compounding the alleged conservatism flowing from malapportionment of state legislatures and congressional districts. The proportional plan, Kennedy charged, "has been discredited in the past and . . . promises only doubt and danger for the future."

Seeking to demonstrate the danger of the proportional plan to the Republican party, Douglas produced statistics to show that in seventeen of the nineteen presidential elections between 1880 and 1952 the Democratic candidate would have received a larger electoral vote under the plan than he was entitled to by his percentage of the popular vote percentage in all 19 elections.[52] "The Lodge-Gossett formula would handicap the Republicans because the Democrats could secure large blocs of electoral votes in the South, where relatively few popular votes will capture an electoral vote," Douglas said. "In contrast, the Republicans would have to win the bulk of their electoral votes in the North, where more popular votes are required to gain an electoral vote."[53] Douglas also argued that many elections would have been thrown into the House under the proportional plan, because no party would have achieved 50 percent of the electoral vote in eight and possibly nine elections between 1880 and 1948. As reported to the Senate floor, the Daniel substitute required a majority of electoral votes for choosing a president, although other versions of the same plan in 1956 had alternatively set 40 and 45 percent of the electoral vote as the requirement for election.[54]

Kennedy and Douglas also took issue with the conservatives' allegation that minority voting blocs actually controlled elections under the existing electoral college system. "In politics," Kennedy said, "minority pressure groups almost always refer to those on the other side of an issue. Some of the proponents [of the proposed amendment] have been frank enough to admit they are talking about Negroes, Jews, Catholics and labor unions. . . . But to others, the term 'pressure groups' refers to farmers, doctors, veterans, the aged or someone else." Douglas quoted a 1948 editorial in the Vernon (Texas) Times to show the political motivation of some proportional system backers: "If the Republican party succeeds in having the Gossett-Lodge resolution adopted," the editorial said, "that will put an end to the bipartisan contest for Negro votes in pivotal states and eliminate the so-called civil rights issue from national politics." As for himself, Douglas had a quite different image of the minority groups in urban centers: "In our big cities, Americans of various races, religions and ethnic origins all live side by side as close neighbors," Douglas said. "The broadmindedness and tolerance which emanates from our cities is a leaven of our political parties. . . . Under the proposal before us, the major parties would give less attention to the legitimate interests of these minority groups; and this in turn would weaken our two-party system."[55] Ironically, the breakup of the minority vote alliance between Negroes and foreign ethnic groups like Poles, Italians, and Irish would contribute to Douglas' own defeat for reelection to the Senate ten years later in 1966.

Aside from their political attack on the proposed amendment, Kennedy and Douglas had two factors in their favor: the complex nature of the proposed compromise amendment, which Kennedy could label a "hybrid monstrosity," and natural disinclination to amend the Constitution without wide-ranging agreement on the change to be made and its necessity. Of the Daniel substitute, Kennedy said: "The two schemes joined together by this shotgun wedding . . . are wholly incompatible, the sponsors of each having thoroughly and accurately assailed the merits of the other over the years. The Mundt proposal multiplies the general ticket system; the Daniel proposal abolishes it. The Mundt proposal continues the importance of states as units for electoral purposes; the Daniel proposal reduces it. And yet it is now proposed that the Senate, being unable to give its approval to either system, should lump them together and give each state its choice. No surer method of introducing confusion and loss of public confidence in our electoral system could be devised."[56]

Douglas recognized evils in the electoral college system and personally favored a direct vote. But Kennedy saw no real need for reform at all. "No urgent necessity for immediate change has been proven," he said. "No minority Presidents have been elected in the 20th Century; no elections have been thrown into the House of Representatives; no breakdown in the electoral system, or even widespread lack of confidence in it, can be shown. . . . There is obviously little to gain—but much to lose—by tampering with the Constitution at this time." Kennedy then added: "It seems to me that Falkland's definition of conservatism is quite appropriate—'When it is not necessary to change, it is necessary not to change.' "[57]

On March 27, after a full week's debate, the Senate moved to final voting on the amendment. Proposed substitutes that would have instituted a direct vote were rejected, as was a proposal by Senator Clifford P. Case of New Jersey that the electoral vote of each state depend on the percentage of its eligible voters who actually vote. Case's amendment, which would have applied both to states using the proportional and to those opting for the district plan, was rejected by a 20 to 66 vote. The Senate then voted, 48 to 37, to accept the Daniel substitute, giving each state its choice of using the district or proportional plan. Significantly, 6 fewer senators voted for the Daniel substitute than the 54 who had placed their names on it as cosponsors before it came to the Senate floor. The margin of approval was substantially below the two-thirds needed for final passage, and the Senate by voice vote approved a motion by Daniel and Kennedy to recommit the amendment to the Judiciary Committee. In 1960, Kennedy would seek and win the presidency on a strategy geared to winning the large pivotal states of the North—a strategy that would have been denied him under either the proportional or district plans that he was instrumental in defeating in the 1956 debate.

Interest in electoral reform in Congress lagged seriously after the 1956 reverse and was not revived until the close 1960 election outcome raised questions about the safety of the existing system. In 1961 hearings before the Senate Judiciary Constitutional Amendments Subcommittee, Kefauver restated the classic arguments for the proportional system: It would, he said, "come nearer reflecting the popular will and would make each state just as important as any other. It would bring about a substantial two-party system in the United States. It would eliminate the evil that has grown up in the past of each party selecting the pivotal states and concentrating the election there."[58] Senator Thomas H. Kuchel of California supported the Kefauver position, saying that "a proportional system undeniably provides the best reflection of popular desire in the framework of a federal system that retains the states as voting units."[59]

The familiar argument about the threat to the two-party system in proportional voting was raised by Assistant Attorney General Nicholas deB. Katzenbach. "The chief and overriding objection against proportional division of electoral votes is that it would encourage the development of splinter parties," Katzenbach said. Senator Sam J. Ervin, Jr., of North Carolina took a different view, saying he saw no danger of splintering or other radical changes in the parties because, "after all, most Americans like to be on the winning side."[60] Kefauver later took the argument further, saying that the American voter, "whether his vote is counted out at the state or district level by a unit rule, or at the national level where it is insufficient by virtue of its total, . . . is not likely to waste his vote on a third party candidate who has no chance of winning."[61]

In a perceptive critique of the various proposals presented to the Kefauver subcommittee, Professor Paul J. Piccard of Florida State University said proportional voting would actually discourage splinter parties because they would lose their potential to "determine the outcome in a whole state and thereby control the balance of power in the entire nation," a practice Piccard said sometimes bordered on "political blackmail."[62] Nor did Piccard think that electoral vote counts reflecting minor party votes would encourage proportional representation. "As far as public opinion is concerned, all the candidates get credit under the present system anyway, for as soon as the election is over people discuss the size of the vote received by such gentlemen as Eugene V. Debs," said Piccard. (Debs was the Socialist candidate for president in five elections between 1900 and 1920 and actually polled 901,255 votes in 1912). Debs wanted to poll a million votes, Piccard said, "and he was not discouraged by the electoral college system which deprived him of official votes. Giving him a few electoral votes, calculated to three decimal places, would hardly have offered him new inducements." But Piccard did not endorse the proportional system. He suggested that fractionalized electoral votes would only create confusion and said he would "not like the job of explaining to the losers the significance of the third- or fourth-place decimal. . . . The question arises, is the labor of constitutional amendment justified for such an imperfect compromise?"[63]

The possibility that minority presidents might be elected under the proportional plan was also brought out in the 1961 hearings. In 1880, Winfield S. Hancock trailed James A. Garfield by more than 9,000 votes, but Hancock would have won by a margin of 6 to 8 electoral votes if the proportional system had been in effect. In 1896, William McKinley won nearly 51 percent of the popular vote to less than 47 percent for William Jennings Bryan. But proportionate voting would have elected Bryan by an electoral vote margin of 6. In 1900 the proportional division between Bryan and McKinley was so close—217.3 for McKinley, 217.2 for Bryan—that minuscule vote shifts could have determined the outcome, even though McKinley ran more than 6 percent points ahead of Bryan in the popular vote.

Figure 6.1 (p. 145) reported the election results of eight recent presidential elections under the proportional plan (as well as under three other electoral systems). Assuming that the proportional plan in effect required only 40 percent of the electoral vote for election, the only clear shift in outcome would have occurred in 1960. In that election the present electoral college elected Kennedy, the supposed popular vote leader. Under the proportional plan, however, Nixon might have been elected by 263.632 electoral votes to 262.671 for Kennedy; however, the result would actually depend upon the decision of votes actually cast for unpledged electors in Alabama and Mississippi.[64] If about half of these votes had gone to Nixon, he might have become president in 1960. (It should also be noted from the information in this figure that the same outcome would, without question, have resulted from the district plan: under it, Nixon would have had an undisputed 1960 victory, with 278 electoral votes to Kennedy's 245.)

Interestingly enough, the proportional plan also increases the uncertainty of electoral outcomes by removing the electoral college's multiplier effect, which usually—but not in 1976—transforms relatively thin popular vote margins (and sometimes nonmargins) into large electoral vote majorities. In each of the eight elections since 1945, the proportional plan would have produced an electoral vote lead substantially less than that resulting from the actual electoral college, and also in every case, less than that resulting from the district plan. As noted, in one case (1960), the popular vote lead would have been reversed by the proportional plan. In addition, in four cases (1948, 1960, 1968, and 1976), the proportional plan would have resulted in an electoral college deadlock—had there been a majority electoral vote requirement. This includes the election of 1976 that would have resulted in an electoral vote of Carter, 269.6645, Ford, 258.0255, and "other", 10.2371. A proportional plan with a majority electoral vote requirement (270 votes) would have given us a 1976 deadlock (by 0.3355 of an electoral vote); a 40 percent electoral vote requirement would have produced a Carter win—by 11 electoral votes rather than the actual margin of 57 votes.

The biases of the proportional plan should also be briefly mentioned. The major effect of the proportional plan lies in its division of the winner-take-all system. Each state's electoral vote—apportioned, however, as at present, with the small state advantage in the "constant two"—would be *divided*, in proportion to the popular vote. This would eliminate the inequities favoring the populous states arising from the unit vote, while retaining the inequities favoring the smallest states arising from the constant two. The result would be a *large systematic bias* favoring the *smallest* states—in fact, under this "reform" the relative voting power of a resident of Alaska in the 1970s would be 4.442 times that of a resident of New York. In effect, the proportional plan transforms the complex and partially opposing biases of the electoral college into a system containing substantially greater biases sharply favoring the smallest states. In terms of regional and group biases, it also greatly advantages inhabitants of the Mountain states and rural citizen-voters. Inhabitants of the South, Midwest, East, and Far West, as well as urban, black, and central city citizen-voters, are discriminated against by the proportional plan.[65]

Since the early 1960s the proportional system has made little headway in Congress and won few adherents. During a brief round of hearings before the Senate Judiciary Constitutional Amendments Subcommittee in 1966, Senator Spessard L. Holland of Florida did point to "new evidence and new developments" that he thought had removed some of the political objections to proportional voting for president—the decisions of the Supreme Court requiring equal apportionment on the basis of population at every governmental level and the eclipse of the one-party system in the southern states that culminated in Republican victories or near-wins in all the states of the old Confederacy in 1964. Holland predicted that the Republican party would "continue to grow and thrive in the South" and that in a few more elections there would be no substantial difference between the percentage of the total vote cast in the South and in the other states of the Union. The effort to overhaul the ancient electoral college machinery should be a bipartisan one, Holland suggested, adding: "No plan has yet been advanced, which preserves and safeguards our federal system, that better achieves the result of fair and democratic reform of the electoral system, than does the proportional plan."[66]

Opposition to the reform remained, however. Katzenbach, then the attorney general, opposed the proportional system because the existing balance—overrepresentation of the small states through the constitutional apportionment formula on the one hand and the unit rule advantage enjoyed by the large states on the other—would be destroyed. There would be a shift of power, Katzenbach charged, "to the rural states and perhaps those few states with historically a one-party political structure."[67]

Although the proportional plan surfaced at various points during electoral reform activities in the late 1960s and 1970s and was even the object of a half-hearted presidential endorsement in 1969 (see chapter 7, pp. 182–87), it had not proved to be a major reform alternative as electoral reform politics moved into the 1980s. Perhaps it is best described as an idea whose time came and went.

THE AUTOMATIC SYSTEM

In September 1801, just six months after he had taken office as president, Thomas Jefferson wrote of an "amendment which I know will be proposed, to wit, to have no electors, but let the people vote directly, and the ticket which has a plurality of the votes in any state to be considered as receiving the whole vote of the state."[68] It was a quarter of a century, however, until Representative Charles E. Haynes of Georgia in 1826 introduced this most modest of all electoral college reforms. Known by many names over the years, the proposal has best been described as "the automatic system," since it would simply write the general ticket or winner-take-all system of casting state electoral votes directly into the Constitution and abolish the actual office of elector.[69]

Haynes's proposal was a progressive one at the time it was offered, since it guaranteed to the people the right, by their vote, to decide for which presidential candidate the state's electoral votes should be cast. The state legislatures would have lost the right—which many of them still exercised—to appoint electors themselves, or to provide for district system elections as an alternative to the general ticket. Amendments similar to Haynes's were proposed eleven times over the next two decades, and three state legislatures—those of Georgia, Missouri, and Alabama—endorsed the idea. The Georgia General Assembly, however, took care to note that it favored a uniform method of electing the president and vice president through the suffrage of the people, "provided such alterations can be so made that the sovereignty of the states be not invaded and the weight of the states and the present basis of representation be retained according to the existing conditions of the Constitution." The Alabama and Missouri resolutions were similar in tone.[70]

An even more minimal proposal was put forth by Representative Thomas Whipple of New Hampshire in 1828. He suggested that the general ticket system be made mandatory for all states, but he would have retained the office of elector. Congress showed little interest in any of these proposals, however, and between 1844 and 1889 only two resolutions of a similar character were even proposed.[71]

When Michigan broke the national pattern of voting by general ticket by decreeing a district system for the 1892 election, there was concern that other states might follow suit. President Harrison, in his annual message to Congress on December 9, 1891, recommended that the permanency of the prevailing general ticket system should be secured by a constitutional amendment. If states went to the district system, Harrison warned, the evil influence of the gerrymander would be felt in presidential elections as well as those for Congress, and eventually the Supreme Court, indirectly through the power of appointment, would be infected as well. Again, Congress showed little interest in the proposal.[72]

Senator George W. Norris of Nebraska was a preeminent advocate of the automatic system during the 1920s and 1930s.[73] In 1922 he wrote a provision abolishing the office of elector and formalizing the general ticket system into a constitutional amendment that he was pushing to eliminate lame-duck sessions of Congress. But when opposition to the electoral college feature developed, Norris struck it from his amendment. After the 1932 election Norris advocated a proportional system, but the Senate Judiciary Committee modified it to an automatic system before reporting it for Senate consideration early in 1934, and Norris said he approved of the change (see p. 146, above). Even this minimal reform could not pass, however. The Senate vote on May 21, 1934, was 42 in favor, 24 opposed—7 votes short of the required two-thirds. Most of the opposition came from conservative senators who opposed any substantive change in the Constitution. Senator Arthur H. Vandenberg of Michigan charged that the automatic system would make it easier for independent candidates to get on the ballot, thus endangering the two-party system through a plethora of splinter parties, the "curse" and "plague" of European politics.[74]

During debate on the Lodge-Gossett plan in 1950, Senator Homer Ferguson of Michigan offered an automatic system as a substitute for the more comprehensive proportional plan then being debated by the Senate. The reformers, led by Lodge, rightly understood Ferguson's amendment as a move to block more thoroughgoing reform and combined to defeat it on a 20 to 71 roll-call vote.[75]

The possibility of an automatic system amendment was next raised seriously by Senator Kennedy during the 1956 Senate debate on electoral reform.[76] Kennedy said such an amendment would abolish the unnecessary office of elector and provide a more democratic manner of contingent election by having the entire Congress vote for the president if no candidate won a majority in the electoral college. But it would retain the state unit vote system, which Kennedy thought essential to the country's electoral balance. Kennedy did not bring this amendment to a vote during the 1956 debate, however, and did not actually introduce it in Congress until more than a year later.[77]

In the 1960 election the winner-take-all system of casting state electoral votes worked distinctly to Kennedy's advantage, and he showed little interest in the more comprehensive reform proposals urged in the wake of that year's elections. Assistant Attorney General Katzenbach supported Kennedy's earlier automatic system amendment in the Senate hearings of 1961. Senator Gale McGee of Wyoming, sponsor of a similar amendment, said the office of elector should be abolished because electors, "with sufficient collusion . . . could even overthrow the intent of the popular will on a nationwide scale." But the automatic system amendment, McGee said, "preserves that which has contributed so much to our political stability; namely, the great compromise among the diverse states and regions of the country." Little support was engendered for the Kennedy type of amendment, however. Professor Robert G. Dixon commented at the hearings that the breaking of pledges by electors "has been so infrequent and also so ineffective, that it may be questioned whether it warrants going through the whole process of constitutional amendment."[78]

The automatic system proposal was next revived by President Lyndon B. Johnson in a message to Congress on January 28, 1965. "Today there lurks in the electoral college system the ever-present possibility that electors may substitute their will for that of the people. I believe that possibility should be foreclosed," Johnson said. But he emphasized his support for the general ticket system: "Our present system of computing and awarding electoral votes by states is an essential counterpart of our federal system and the provisions of our Constitution which recognize and maintain our nation as a union of states." Johnson also maintained that the unit vote system supported the two-party system. The president's proposals were incorporated into resolutions by Senator Birch Bayh of Indiana, chairman of the Senate Judiciary Constitutional Amendments Subcommittee, and Representative Emanuel Celler of New York, chairman of the House of Judiciary Committee. The resolution provided that each state would have an electoral vote equal to its number of senators and representatives and that all of a state's electoral votes would go to the plurality winner in the state. Voters would cast their vote for president and vice president by one ballot. If no candidate won a majority of the national electoral vote, the choice would be made from among the top three electoral-vote winners by the Senate and House meeting jointly. The amendment also provided that if at the time of the congressional counting of electoral votes the winning presidential candidate had died, the vice presidential candidate who ran with him would become president. Congress was authorized to provide by law for the case of the death of both the president- and vice president-elect.[79]

Early in 1966, President Johnson reiterated his proposal in another special message to Congress, and it was considered in hearings before Bayh's subcommittee in the Senate. Opening the hearings, Bayh endorsed the automatic system and said that alternative proposals for reforming the electoral college "pose far greater dangers to the nation than the state-by-state, winner-take-all system." Katzenbach cautioned against discarding a tried and tested system of electing the president for proposals that would "change the basic system itself" with "grave risks" to the country's political structure. Senator Robert F. Kennedy of New York endorsed the administration's proposal, saying he believed "our electoral system on the whole has worked quite well." But Kennedy noted that a switch of a few thousand votes in key states in 1960, when his brother John F. Kennedy defeated Richard M. Nixon, "might have given a few electors the power to control the outcome. . . . It would be tragic for us as a nation if such a situation ever did come to pass."[80]

Even with full presidential backing, however, the automatic system gained little support. The advocates of virtually all the other proposed reforms opposed the automatic system because it would have given constitutional cognizance—for the first time in U.S. history—to the very winner-take-all system of casting state electoral votes that reformers have considered the chief evil of the existing system. The Chamber of Commerce of the United States, which had come out for comprehensive reform of the electoral college, said that the automatic system "would be worse than having no reform at all. Not only would it write into the Constitution the evils of the unit vote system, but its adoption would undoubtedly preclude meaningful reform indefinitely."[81] Opponents also said the automatic system incorporated such minor changes that it might never have a bearing on any election. "Indeed," said Senator Ervin on the Senate floor, "it is hardly worth cranking up the complex and protracted amendment process to accomplish so little—it would be almost like chasing a fly with an elephant gun."[82]

Senator Ervin's remark captured well the essence of the automatic plan—its overwhelming modesty. The primary defect of the electoral college the automatic plan would remedy is the possibility of a faithless elector. This problem the automatic plan would effectually deal with by abolishing the office of elector. Left untouched, however, would be other, even more serious problems of the electoral college: the distortions and inequities due both to the constant two electoral votes given to each state regardless of population and to the winner-take-all system, the possibilities of electoral college deadlock, and the potential for the election of a candidate who ran second in popular votes. The biases of the present electoral college (see pp. 119–30, above) would be retained in the "reformed" system; in fact, in the case of the unit rule, they would be written into the Constitution for the first time. Election outcomes under the automatic plan would also be identical to those that actually occurred under the present electoral college, less the incidence of faithless and unpledged electors.

The automatic plan is an unobjectionable yet extremely modest electoral college reform. It has proved to be the stepchild of electoral reform: a potential second choice of many but one enthusiastically loved by few.

The death knell for the automatic system was apparently sounded on May 18, 1966, when Senator Bayh, the Constitutional Amendments Subcommittee chairman and chief Senate sponsor of the Administration's plan, announced he was abandoning it in favor of direct popular vote of the people. "It may well be that mere procedural changes in the present system would be like shifting around the parts of a creaky and dangerous automobile engine, making it no less creaky and no less dangerous," Bayh said. "What we may need is a new engine, because we are in a new age."

DIRECT POPULAR VOTE

Of the more than five hundred constitutional amendments proposed in Congress during the course of U.S. history, well over one hundred have envisaged the simplest solution of all to the problem of electing the president: a direct vote of all the people, with no intermediate electors or electoral count standing between them and the choice of the chief executive. The arguments for and against this method have changed greatly in weight and significance over the years, but most of them were already clear on March 20, 1816, the day that direct national election was first proposed in Congress.

On that occasion, the Senate was debating the merits of a proposed district system amendment to the Constitution. Fittingly, it was Senator Abner Lacock of Pennsylvania, the state whose delegates had offered the strongest support for direct election in the Constitutional Convention, who offered the direct vote amendment.[83] Lacock said he could see no reason why agents such as the electors "should be employed between the people and their votes."

Supporting Lacock's position, Senator Rufus King of New York, who had been a delegate to the Constitutional Convention, said: "In time of difficulty and peril to the nation, when it is in utmost need of superior talent for its high stations, no tribunal is more competent to discern and select it than the people." In his judgment, King said, "the people are . . . the best keepers of their own rights; and any device to remove that power from them weakens the security of it."

Opposition was voiced immediately, however. Senator Jeremiah Mason of New Hampshire said the great disparities between voting qualifications in the various states would make direct election impracticable. Senator William W. Bibb of Georgia wanted to know what "would be the condition of the slaveholding states? They would lose the privilege the Constitution now allows them, of votes upon three-fifths of their population other than freemen. It would be deeply injurious to them." Senator James Barbour of Virginia warned of a "destruction of the balance of power in the Confederacy" because "it has pleased God to give the Southern country a population anomalous, having the double character of person and property; other states had none such."

Yet another objection was raised by Senator Eligius Fromentin of Louisiana. "Look at the vast expanse of our country, from Maine to Louisiana—no such election could here be made in case of emergency; before it could be consummated we should be devoured by the monster which threatened us."

It was left to Senator Robert G. Harper of Maryland to present the states'-rights argument, one that would return to plague direct election proposals for another century and a half. Election per capita, Harper charged, "threw out of view altogether the federal principle by which the states are represented, as well as the people, in the present mode of election. . . . It would destroy that influence of the smaller states in the Presidential election, which arises from their representation of the sovereign characters of the states—and thus destroy a very important principle of the Constitution."

Attempting to rebut the opposition arguments, Lacock admitted that there might be difficulties in instituting a direct national election, but asked: "What could make us so much one people, as to give to all the people this equal privilege? It will produce in the national habits, manners and love of country, more harmony than any other political measure which could be possibly adapted."

Whatever the merits of direct election might have been, the Republic was clearly not prepared for it. Lacock's motion went down to defeat, only 12 senators in favor to 21 in opposition.[84]

The election of 1824, which resulted in the election of Adams despite Jackson's lead in the recorded national popular vote, rekindled interest in a direct national election. On January 3, 1826, Representative William McManus of New York presented a direct vote resolution that declared: "Inasmuch as the people of the United States are subject to two distinct governments and their laws (the one state and the other national), and are citizens of, and owe allegiance to each government, they have the same equal and just right to elect, by their individual votes, the President and Vice President of the Union, that they have to elect the Governor and Lieutenant Governor of their respective states." McManus proposed that the plurality choice of the people of all the states be sufficient to elect the president and vice president.[85] Within the following four years the proposal was introduced eight more times in the House, twice on the instigation of individual state legislatures—those of Ohio and Missouri. Senator George M. Bibb of Kentucky made a similar proposal in 1833, but the committee to which it was referred recommended a district system instead.[86]

Though he was willing to let the states retain their weight in electoral voting, President Andrew Jackson can be counted as the spiritual godfather of the direct vote movement. "To the people belongs the right of electing their chief magistrate," Jackson said in his first annual message to Congress. "It was never designed that their choice should, in any case, be defeated either by the intervention of the electoral colleges, or by . . . the House of Representatives." Indeed, said Jackson, "the first principle of our system" is "that the majority is to govern. . . . It must be very certain that a President elected by a minority cannot enjoy the confidence necessary to the discharge of his duties."[87] Obviously, Jackson had the disputed election of 1824, and the election of Adams with fewer popular votes than he (Jackson) had received, in mind.

In the three decades from the mid-1830s to 1865, little interest in direct vote was apparent in Congress.[88] But in the period immediately following the Civil War it was frequently proposed. The chief exponents of the direct vote in this era were Senator Charles Sumner, Massachusetts' great reform leader and civil rights advocate, together with Representative James M. Ashley of Ohio and Senator Luke P. Poland of Vermont. Sumner advocated a direct vote because he found the existing system "artificial, cumbrous, radically defective and unrepublican." A direct election amendment, Sumner said, "would give every individual voter, wherever he might be, a positive weight in the election. It would give minorities in distant states an opportunity to be heard in determining who shall be chief magistrate."[89] Sumner's amendment, along the lines of Senator Benton's recommendations in earlier years, provided for a first election in the spring and then a national runoff in the autumn if no candidate won a majority on the first round. The intention—though it is questionable if it would have been realized—was to supersede the convention method of nominations.

Of the 25 direct vote resolutions in the immediate postwar era, 12 proposed a runoff popular election if no candidate received a majority in the first election, while 4 others provided for contingent election in Congress and several others required a mere plurality of the national vote for election. The greatest number of resolutions were proposed between 1872 and 1878, the majority of them by congressmen from the western states.

In the three-quarters of a century following the Reconstruction period, occasional proposals were advanced in Congress to abolish the electoral college and go to direct vote, but none of them made significant headway. A major reason seems to have been the almost universally held belief that a popular vote amendment would never be ratified by the required three-quarters of the states, because a majority of them would lose some percentage of their relative weight under the existing electoral college apportionment (see pages 112–13, above).

This gloomy belief failed to deter a number of prominent American statesmen from endorsing the idea of a direct vote. "I have favored the popular voting system for President and Vice President for 40 years," Senator (and former vice president) Alben W. Barkley said in the 1950s. "One of the first measures I introduced in Congress in 1913," he added, "was a resolution to adopt a constitutional amendment which would have allowed the people to vote directly for President and Vice President. . . . .It took a long time before the Constitution was amended to provide for the popular voting for United States Senators." Barkley said he realized the difficulties of achieving ratification, but "they do not dampen my belief or feeling that one of these days we shall have to give the American people the right to vote directly for President and Vice President."[90]

Indeed, by the 1950s Barkley was not alone among leading politicians who said they would accept popular vote for president. Senator Henry Cabot Lodge of Massachusetts introduced such an amendment in 1941 and in 1950 Senate debate (while pushing for the Lodge-Gossett proportional plan) said he had "never ceased to believe that this would be a desirable change." He had shifted to support of the proportion system, Lodge said, because he believed direct vote "utterly impossible of accomplishment, because it diminishes the relative importance of smaller states in a Presidential election. But I would not want it to appear that I oppose direct election." Lodge actually voted for direct vote amendments offered by other Senators to the Lodge-Gossett bill.[91] In the same 1950 debate, Senator Robert A. Taft of Ohio said: "Personally I will be willing under some circumstances to vote for a resolution based simply on the popular vote. Certainly it would be logical and reasonably defensible."[92] Senator (and later Vice President) Hubert H. Humphrey was one of the most prominent supporters of the direct national vote in the postwar era, offering an amendment to that effect during 1950 Senate debate on electoral reform. Under direct vote, Humphrey said, "every voter casts one vote, a whole vote, which is just as good and just as important as the vote cast by any other voter in the country. . . . This is the final step in the constitutional evolution which began with the Declaration that all men are created equal, and continued with the assertion that no man or woman may be denied the right to vote for arbitrary reasons. Now we must make the suffrage an equal suffrage, and repudiate arbitrary and discriminatory geographical bases for denying or reducing the importance of the votes of some of our citizens."[93] Senator Paul Douglas of Illinois, a leader in the 1956 Senate debate that ended in defeat of the Daniel proportional district system substitute, was a strong supporter of the direct vote alternative. And Senator Estes Kefauver of Tennessee, associated for years with the proportional system, said in 1950 Senate debate: "I, too, would be very happy if the President and Vice President could be elected by popular vote. . . . I would support . . . popular vote if it were possible to have the Constitution so amended."[94]

The prevailing mood of Congress in the postwar years was hostile to the direct vote alternative, however. In 1947 a combination direct vote—national nominating primary amendment was offered as a substitute for the proposal for a two-term limit on the president, then being debated in the Senate. It was rejected by a vote of 14 to 66.[95] In this instance, the vote for direct vote was doubtless reduced because it was not germane to the topic at hand and because it was sponsored by two political mavericks—Senators William Langer of North Dakota and Glen Taylor of Idaho (the latter subsequently ran for vice president on Henry Wallace's Progressive ticket in 1948).

During 1950 debate on the Lodge-Gossett proportional plan, two direct vote amendments were offered. The first, by Langer, would have substituted direct vote along with national nominating primaries. It was rejected by a vote of 31 to 60. The second, offered by Humphrey, provided only for election by direct national vote. It went down to defeat as well, by a vote of 28 to 63.[96]

Again in 1956, when the Senate was debating the Daniel substitute, amendments were offered to substitute a direct vote plan. On this occasion, they were defeated by even larger margins than in 1950. Langer's combined national primary—direct vote amendment was rejected by a margin of 13 to 69, and a simple direct vote amendment authored by Senator Herbert H. Lehman of New York lost by a vote of 17 to 66. John Kennedy was a leading opponent of direct vote in 1956. The Langer amendment, he said, "while purporting to be more democratic, would increase the power of and encourage splinter parties, and I believe it would break down the federal system under which most states entered the Union, which provides a system of checks and balances to insure that no area or group shall obtain too much power." Kennedy took a strong states'-rights view on the electoral college, saying, "I should hate to see the abolishment of state lines. . . . The Presidential election is determined on the basis of 48 separate units. I think the election should be decided in each one of them."[97]

One of the most fascinating parts of the 1956 debate, little noted at the time, was this colloquy between Kennedy and Senator John Pastore of Rhode Island, who favored direct vote:[98]

PASTORE: Why should one state be a pivotal state? Why should a group of states be pivotal states?

KENNEDY: Under the Senator's plan the pivotal states would be of infinitely more importance than they are today. Except in the Senate, Rhode Island would cease to be of any real importance. . . . Rhode Island is overrepresented in the electoral college today, based on its population.

PASTORE: I am not going into that question at all. I want to do away with the electoral college. I want to elect my President on election day. I say that when the people go to the polls the man who receives the greatest number of votes should be elected President of the people. He is the President of the people of the United States, and not the President of the states. It makes no difference to me how many electoral votes the people of Rhode Island have. What difference does it make? Why do we talk so much about the power of a state? . . .

KENNEDY: I must say that I disagree with the proposal of the Senator. In fact, it would not have a chance to get by. It would require a two-thirds vote, and the smaller states would not accept it.

PASTORE: I have never worried about what gets by and what does not get by. I am concerned with the principle involved. . . . Most of the people in my state, when they go to the polls on election day, think they are voting for President and Vice President. They do not vote for President if they must elect electors or delegates who meet later in the Governor's office and have a luncheon at 12 o'clock noon and then cast their ballot for President. . . .

KENNEDY: Would the Senator do away with the two electors which his state has by virtue of the fact that it has two Senators of the United States?

PASTORE: I would do away with the whole electoral college. I would do away with it completely. I would have the people elect the President of the United States on election day. I would not care where the candidates came from, whether they came from the North, the South, the West, or the East. They are all Americans. We are all one country. I say let us vote for the best man. Let the man who gets the most votes be

President. It is as simple as that. That is my idea of representative government. Everything else beyond that is a gimmick. . . .

The 1960 presidential election spurred renewed interest in the direct vote
alternative. Where only two direct vote amendments had been sponsored in
the preceding two sessions of Congress, a total of 12 were proposed in the
Eighty-seventh Congress, which convened in January 1961. The chief sponsors
included Senate Majority Leader Mike Mansfield of Montana, Senator
Margaret Chase Smith of Maine, and Senator Kenneth B. Keating of New York.
Their resolutions were debated extensively during the 1961 Senate Judiciary
hearings chaired by Kefauver.

"We must see to it," Keating said during the hearings, that "a majority of the
American people can and do determine who is to be our nation's Chief Executive. . . . I do not believe that any candidate would want to be elected to the
highest office of our land over an opponent who received a larger number of
votes." A large portion of the American electorate, the Kefauver subcommittee
was told, does not know of the existence of the electoral college, believing that
it actually votes directly for president. Professor Paul J. Piccard suggested that
the next time the popular vote winner loses in the electoral college, "even the
winning party is going to be sufficiently embarrassed to accept direct popular
election of the President. I think they will turn to that."[99]

Several witnesses expressed concern that direct national voting would
prompt the states to lower their voting qualifications, especially those of age,
to swell their vote total and their influence in the presidential balloting. Congress would have to be given power to fix uniform voting qualifications, Professor Robert G. Dixon argued, "in order to prevent one state or section of the
country from magnifying its voting age to ridiculous levels, or enfranchising
its cats and dogs." But other political scientists differed. Professor Kenneth
Kofmehl of Purdue University suggested that if the voting age, for example,
were reduced to 12, "these 12-year-olds will be picking their mayors, their
Governors, and their state legislatures also, and I don't think that the states are
going to commit political hara-kiri for some advantage in the Presidential election."[100] Most direct vote amendments have stipulated that the voting
qualifications for president would be the same as for the state legislature or
Congress, so that a state could not establish a special broadened voting base for
president alone. Even if permitted to do so, the states would probably not because of the obvious administrative difficulties in a dual-registration system.

The familiar states'-rights arguments were also raised again. "I think we are a
republic," said Senator Thurston B. Morton of Kentucky, "and as a republic, I
think the states, by virtue of being states, should have some additional weight
in the electoral college."[101] But Senator Mansfield argued that direct vote
would complement and strengthen the federal system rather than weakening it.
"The federal system," he said, "is not strengthened through an antiquated de-

vice which has not worked as it was intended to work when it was included in the Constitution and which, if anything, has become a divisive force in the federal system by pitting groups of states against groups of states. As I see the federal system in contemporary practice, the House of Representatives is the key to the protection of district interests *as* district interests, just as the Senate is the key to the protection of state interests *as* state interest. Those instrumentalities, and particularly the Senate, are the principal constitutional safeguards of the federal system, but the Presidency has evolved, out of necessity, into the principal political office . . . for safeguarding the interests of all the people in all the states."[102]

Even when they favored direct vote, many witnesses dismissed it as impossible of adoption because of small-state and particularly southern-state opposition. But a new counterargument was raised: that the power exercised by large states under the existing system had surely canceled out any advantage that the small states enjoy through their two extra electoral votes. "I do not think people in the small states are terribly anxious to preserve this alleged advantage if they could have a direct vote for President as the alternative," Professor Paul T. David of the University of Virginia said. Both he and Senator Mansfield suggested that a constitutional amendment instituting the direct vote could be put to special amending conventions chosen by the people of the states, rather than going through the usual state legislature role for ratification. The Constitution gives Congress an option in the matter, and Congress had actually provided for special state conventions to secure repeal of the 18th amendment in 1933, repealing prohibition. The experience of that year, David said, showed that delegates to the ratifying conventions were usually elected on a statewide basis permitting a clear yes-no vote on the proposed amendment.[103]

No significant move for the direct vote was made in or out of Congress in the wake of the 1961 hearings; indeed, actual sponsorships fell off to only four resolutions in 1963–64, and the reform looked quiescent if not dead. But in other fields there were major new developments that would have a profound bearing on the political complexion of the country. The Supreme Court reapportionment decisions of 1962 and 1964 pointed to a revolutionary new standard of political equality in state legislative and congressional districts. The 1964 presidential election broke down some of the last remnants of old one-party systems, in both the Democratic South and Republican states of the North. The Voting Rights Act of 1965 represented a national assurance that southern blacks, within but a few years, would enjoy full suffrage. Then, in 1966, came four highly significant developments for the direct vote cause.

The Chamber of Commerce of the United States announced on January 31, following a referendum of its member organizations, that it favored abolishing the existing system and shifting to either a nationwide popular vote or a district system. The final vote of the Chamber members in approving the new policy position was 3,877 in favor (91.5 percent) and 362 (8.5 percent) opposed.

A Gallup poll, released on May 18, showed that 63 percent of the people in a nationwide sampling favored amending the Constitution "to do away with the electoral college and base the election of a President on the total popular vote throughout the nation." The sampling showed 20 percent against the shift and 17 percent with no opinion. It was the first national poll on direct vote ever published.[104] The electoral college seems to be an institution in which familiarity breeds contempt. Breakdowns of Gallup surveys on the electoral college system show that the more educated a person is—and thus the more likely to be familiar with what the electoral college really is—the more likely he is to favor its abolition (see Appendix N).

Senator Birch Bayh of Indiana, who had taken over in 1963 as chairman of the Senate Judiciary Constitutional Amendments Subcommittee after Kefauver's death, announced on May 18 that he was abandoning his support of the automatic system amendment backed by the Johnson Administration and would henceforth work for the adoption of a direct popular vote.[105] This, too, was a first: the first time that the chairman of a major congressional committee or subcommittee charged with considering constitutional amendments had allied himself with the popular vote cause. Bayh had already won national prestige as chief congressional sponsor of the presidential inability amendment, approved by Congress in 1965. With the ratification of three-fourths of the states, it became the 25th amendment to the Constitution in 1967.

Senator Bayh's conversion to the direct vote cause was a major surprise, not only because he himself had been the chief sponsor of the Administration's automatic system amendment but because of his close association with Senators Edward M. and Robert F. Kennedy, both of whom still indicated reservations about a direct vote. Bayh acknowledged he had changed his position only "after a great deal of soul-searching," and that "the Justice Department is not at all happy with us." He had been asked by officials at Justice, Bayh said, why he was shifting to direct vote when it had been defeated so soundly in Senate votes during the 1950s. Bayh said his reply was that "a lot of history has been made since 1956, and a lot of freedoms given to our people since 1956." Specifically, he noted the 24th amendment abolishing the poll tax in federal elections, the Civil Rights acts of 1957, 1960, and 1964, and the Voting Rights Act of 1965. "Today, for the first time in our history, we have achieved the goal of universal suffrage regardless of race, religion or station of life," Bayh said.

In July, Delaware, subsequently joined by twelve other states, asked the U.S. Supreme Court to hear a suit challenging the constitutionality under the 14th amendment of the unit vote or winner-take-all method of casting state electoral votes. Delaware asked the Court to "open the door" to reform by granting interim relief that would require the states to divide their electoral votes in a way that would more accurately reflect popular sentiment. The suit acknowledged that a direct vote would be the only permanent remedy to the inequalities built into the electoral college system. On October 17 the Court refused to hear the case, giving no reasons for its action. Delaware's brief, however, served to compare the electoral college system with the "one man, one vote" standard being required by the courts in state legislatures and congressional districts.[106]

The American Bar Association in February 1966 established a blue-ribbon commission to study the problem of the electoral college and possible reform. Among the panel's members were several former ABA presidents; Paul Freund, constitutional law professor at Harvard Law School; C. Herman Pritchett, professor of political science at the University of Chicago and former president of the American Political Science Association; United Automobile Workers president Walter Reuther; Governors Otto Kerner, Democrat of Illinois, and Henry Bellmon, Republican of Oklahoma; and William T. Gossett, former general counsel to the Ford Motor Company. After a series of meetings the commission decided in the autumn that it would endorse the popular vote alternative. The commission's report, released officially on January 7, 1967, said that "the electoral college method of electing a President of the United States is archaic, undemocratic, complex, ambiguous, indirect and dangerous. . . . While there may be no perfect method of electing a President, we believe that direct, nationwide popular vote is the best of all possible methods."

The ABA recommendations, ratified by the association's House of Delegates in February 1967, were expected to carry special weight as ABA officials throughout the country brought pressure on members of Congress to consider the direct vote. It was a similar ABA commission, dealing with presidential inability problems, that had recommended the basic policies spelled out in the 25th amendment.

Both for Senator Bayh and for several members of the ABA commission, the fear of splinter parties appears to have been the major obstacle they had to overcome before accepting direct vote. Early in 1966, Bayh had actually announced his opposition to popular vote because "it would inevitably take this nation down the path of splinter parties that have plagued so many European nations for so many years." In May, Bayh said, "I hate to admit we were wrong, but I think we were." He said that under the constitutional amendment he was proposing, 40 percent of the popular vote, rather than a majority, would be sufficient for election. With that provision, he said, splinter parties would have little incentive to seek votes in the national election—perhaps less than under the existing system, since they would no longer have the hope of depriving both of the major parties of an electoral vote majority and thus putting themselves in a bargaining position. When the ABA commission announced its endorsement of the direct vote, Professor Freund said the fear of a proliferation of parties had been "the great stumbling block," but that "we were persuaded in the end that these fears were exaggerated." The ABA also recommended that 40 percent of the popular vote be required for election and went a step beyond Bayh's original direct vote proposal, which had provided for a contingent election in a joint session of Congress. The ABA recommended instead that a national popular vote runoff be held if no candidate won 40 percent in the first election. This provision, Freund said, would largely deter the splinter parties, because even if they prevented a decision in the first election, they would would have no opportunity to throw an election into Congress, with the deals and intrigues that might result. In January 1967, Bayh modified his direct vote amendment to provide for the national direct vote runoff recommended by the ABA.[107]

Professor Freund said the second difficulty the ABA commission had seen in direct vote was its possible impact on the federal system. But in voting for president and vice president, Freund noted, Americans vote as United States citizens, not as citizens of individual states. If one would preserve the federal system, he added, the presidential election was not the place to make one's stand. Direct vote, he added, might really strengthen the federal system, by making all votes equal and reducing the conflicts between large and small states.

Stressing the positive aspects of direct vote, the ABA commission said such a system "would do away with the ever-present possibility of a person being elected President with fewer popular votes than his major opponent. . . . It would abolish the office of Presidential elector, which is an anachronism and a threat to the smooth functioning of the elective process. It would minimize the effect of accident and fraud in controlling the outcome of an entire election. It would put a premium on voter turnout and encourage increased political activity throughout the country."

Finally, a poll of the members of the nation's fifty state legislatures, conducted by Senator Quentin N. Burdick of North Dakota, showed a strong majority for direct vote. During the summer of 1966, Burdick wrote to each of the state legislators asking if he or she thought the electoral college should be modified or abolished and, if so, what reform each legislator would favor. The results, based on replies from approximately 2,500 of the nation's 8,000 state legislators, showed a surprising 58.8 percent in favor of complete abolition of the electoral college and substitution of the direct vote. The proportional system was favored by 21.2 percent, the district system by 10.2 percent, and the existing system by only 9.7 percent. In all, 50 percent or more of the legislators replying from 44 of the 50 states supported direct election. And, contrary to the judgment of political observers since the early nineteenth century, the results showed the popular vote just as heavily favored in small states as in large states. Of the seven most heavily populated states, California legislators voted 73.5 percent for direct election, New York legislators 70.0 percent, Pennsylvania 55.8 percent, Michigan 52.4 percent, Ohio 57.1 percent, and Texas 52.3 percent. Illinois legislators registered only 37.0 percent for direct election, the lowest percentage among the "big seven." Among the smallest states—those with only three electoral votes—Alaska voted 50.0 percent for direct election, Delaware 53.8 percent, Nevada 62.5 percent, Vermont 68.9 percent, and Wyoming 55.5 percent.[108]

The momentum for the direct vote alternative carried into 1967, as the Bayh subcommittee in the Senate launched into a new set of hearings with testimony from ABA officials in favor of their commission's report. Senate Majority Leader Mike Mansfield reiterated his support for direct vote, and the cause won a major convert in the prestigious Senate Minority Leader, Everett Dirksen of Illinois. On the House side, Judiciary Committee Chairman Emanuel Celler of New York indicated his openness to the direct vote idea by introducing the same amendment drawn up for Dirksen by the ABA. Celler continued to introduced the Administration's automatic system bill as well, however.

The 1967 Senate hearings were noteworthy also for their academic testimony. Two political scientists who had previously backed other systems now announced they supported the direct vote—Lucius Wilmerding, Jr., hitherto a major spokesman for the district system, and Professor Joseph E. Kallenbach of the University of Michigan, a backer of the proportional plan in earlier years. What proved to be of even more importance, however, was the testimony on July 14, 1967, of a young New York lawyer, John F. Banzhaf III, who discussed his soon-to-be-published computer study of the electoral college and supplied the subcommittee with tables drawn from this study.[109]

Mr. Banzhaf's subsequent article, published early in 1968 in the *Villanova Law Review* under the intriguing title "One Man, 3.312 Votes: A Mathematical Analysis of the Electoral College," proved to have a major impact upon subsequent congressional and scholarly discussion about the biases of the electoral college.[110] Its first presentation in the 1967 hearings opened up an area of systematic analysis of the electoral college that had heretofore been marked by speculation and hunch.[111]

As such studies were released during the late 1960s and the 1970s, the obvious became accepted: in contrast to the inherent inequalities and distortions of any other method, the winner by direct vote, in terms of the number of votes received, would in fact *always* be the winner of the election. In terms of voting power, a vote cast anywhere would count equally in determining the presidency. If data on state or regional or group biases were presented, the percent deviations for any category from the citizen-voter average would be zero. In other words, under this reform plan, each citizen's voting power would be, by definition, equal. Among other things, the direct vote would also eliminate winner-take-all voting—except in the unavoidable final decision of who would be president, that office being indivisible under the Constitution.

The opposition in the 1967 Senate hearings tended to come from groups on the right, ranging from the American Good Government Society to the Liberty Lobby. The right-wing multimillionaire, Texas oilman H. L. Hunt, was one of the witnesses opposing a direct vote—because, as Hunt put it, "Dictators extend to their populace the privilege of going to the polls and casting a vote for their dictator and his stooges. They could laugh up their sleeves if they found the claimants of champions of freedom offering their populace a chance to case a direct vote." Opposition was also heard from some more moderate conservatives, including Nebraska's Republican Senator Roman L. Hruska and Florida's Democratic Senator Spessard L. Holland. Both professed to fear that a direct vote for president would somehow lead to demands that the states relinquish their equal voting rights in the U.S. Senate.*

Mid-1967 provides a convenient pausing point in our consideration of electoral reform politics, for by then the elements of the major reform battles of the late 1960s and the 1970s were all present: determined advocacy by congressional leaders such as Senator Birch Bayh; strong support for electoral reform from groups, including the American Bar Association and the Chamber of Commerce of the United States; supportive public opinion as measured in national polls; and new assessments concerning the electoral college by scholars and observers of the American political system. Together these ingredients would provide the basis for the push for electoral college reform by means of the direct vote plan, an effort that would peak in the late 1960s and continue to wax and wane throughout the 1970s and into the 1980s. The events concerning electoral reform politics over the decade from 1969 to 1979 are sufficiently dramatic and significant to require special examination and are the subject of the next chapter. Suffice it here to note that the dominant plan for electoral reform throughout this period was the direct vote plan, as finally modified by Senator Bayh in the late 1960s, to provide for a 40-percent requirement for election or national vote runoff between the two leading candidates. This contingency arrangement, urged upon Bayh by the ABA, would prove to be one of the most controversial aspects of the reform proposal yet would be retained as a central feature of the direct vote plan advocated throughout the 1970s. (For further discussion of contingent election variations, see pp. 177–79 below.)

HYBRIDS AND MISCELLANEOUS PLANS

The emergence, by 1967–68, of the direct vote plan as the preeminent reform plan does not mean that reformers since then—any more than in the

* The idea that the Senate could be "reapportioned" to conform to "one man, one vote" standards in other areas of government is obviously a red herring. Article V of the Constitution, which provides for amendments, stipulates specifically that "no state, without its consent, shall be deprived of its equal suffrage in the Senate." Yet as late in time as 1977, historian Arthur M. Schlesinger, Jr., would write an article for the Los Angeles Times suggesting that "should an abstract standard of equity require the abolition of large-state advantages in Presidential elections, then surely it requires the abolition of the small-state advantage in the Senate."[112]

past—have been willing to forego the opportunity to create sometimes astonishing varieties and permutations of electoral reforms. The electoral college
seems to be an institution that encourages political architects to try their hand
at devising change. In addition to the major electoral college reforms proposed
over the years, a number of alternative plans have been brought forward, some
of them serious attempts to effect a compromise based on the political conditions of the times, others so strange that they can only be described as grotesque
imitations of real reform.[113]

The first—and most delightfully outrageous plan—was suggested in 1808 by
Senator James Hillhouse, a Connecticut Federalist who said his intent was to
save the country from the evils of parties and party spirit. All United States senators would hold office for a three-year term, with a third of the senators
retiring annually. Each year the retiring senators would assemble and draw
balls from a box. One of the balls would be colored, and the man who drew it
would be president for a year. Old John Adams commented that the Hillhouse
plan "reduces the President's office to that of a mere Doge of Venice, a mere
head of wood, a mere tool of the aristocracy of the country."[114] His son, John
Quincy Adams, probably reflected prevailing opinion when he wrote in his diary that "a serious discussion of [Hilhouse's] amendments would be ridiculous."[115]

During the nineteenth century, a few proposals were made to elect the president by geographical sections. Representative Thomas Montgomery of
Kentucky introduced the first such resolution in 1822, providing that the country would be divided into four geographical sections, each of which would
elect a president in rotation. Montgomery felt impelled to tell his colleagues of
his plan: "However laughable it might appear to some gentlemen, [he] considered it a very serious matter." The reason for this proposal was doubtless the
jealousy felt in the Middle Atlantic states and New England, and still more in
the West, over the fact that all the presidents up to that time, except for John
Adams, had been from Virginia.[116]

Another sectional amendment, introduced by Representative Clement L.
Vallandigham of Ohio in 1861 on the eve of the Civil War, was apparently an
attempt to change the Constitution in a way that would persuade the South to
remain in the Union. Four geographical sections of the country would be established, and to be elected president a candidate would have to achieve a majority of the votes of the electors in each of the regions. A similar amendment, proposed by Andrew Johnson in 1860, would have had the president elected
alternately from the North and the South.[117]

One of the most byzantine plans of history was proposed by Senator Lazarus
W. Powell of Kentucky in 1864. The electors—from one to seven per state,
chosen by district—would all meet in Washington every fourth February and
form an electoral college with the Chief Justice presiding. By alphabetical order

of their names, the electors would be distributed into six groups, numbered from one to six. Each group would select one man from the next numbered group, and from the six persons so designated two would be selected by lot. The electoral college would then name one of these men as president, the other as vice president. If no one was elected in 24 hours, then the electoral college would be dissolved and a whole new election ordered. If no president were selected by June 1, then the Senate would choose a president—using the identical system. One of the provisions of Powell's amendment was that electors would declare that they had made no pledges to support any particular candidate or to aid any political party.[118]

In 1862 and on three subsequent occasions, Senator Jarrett Davis of Kentucky suggested that the states should nominate candidates for president in any way they desired and that Congress should then meet as a convention and choose one of the nominees as president. A unanimous vote for election was required. This was to be achieved by dropping candidates from the bottom of the list after a stated time had been reached in the balloting. If no choice were made, then the Supreme Court would pick the president.[119]

Trying to avoid all the problems of getting a specific new plan written into a constitutional amendment, Representative Charles R. Buckalew of Pennsylvania suggested in 1869 an amendment providing simply that "Congress shall have the power to prescribe the manner in which electors shall be chosen by the people." The intent was to assure a popular vote for presidential electors in each state and to permit Congress to adopt a district system or any other, depending on the times. During Senate discussion the same year on the 15th amendment (Negro suffrage), Senator Morton of Indiana brought up Buckalew's proposal as an amendment, and the Senate accepted the addition on a 37 to 19 vote. A two-thirds Senate vote (40 to 16) was then obtained for the combined Negro suffrage—Presidential election amendments. The House, however, took strong exception to the Buckalew amendment and refused on a 37 to 133 vote to accept the combined proposals. The 15th amendment was subsequently submitted to the states without any provision regarding presidential elections. Similar proposals to let Congress determine the system by which electoral votes are cast were proposed again in 1872 and 1888, but neither made any headway.[120]

An interesting hybrid proposal was brought forward by Senator Hubert H. Humphrey of Minnesota during the electoral reform debate in Congress in 1956. The Humphrey plan, based on a recommendation made to him by Professor Ralph M. Goldman of Michigan State University, retained the total electoral strength based on the number of senators and representatives combined, though there would no longer be actual electors. Each state would continue to cast two electoral votes (corresponding to its number of senators) for the plurality winner in the state. But the remaining electoral votes, corresponding to the number of representatives in Congress, would be divided on a national proportional basis reflecting the national popular vote for president. Thus the plan would have given predominant weight to the national popular vote but would have allowed some modification based on the traditional federal principle of guaranteeing a minimum of electoral votes to each state. The plan was rejected by voice vote of the Senate during the 1956 debate.[121] Had the Humphrey plan been applied to the 1960 election returns, Nixon would have been elected president, primarily because he carried 26 states to the 22 that went for Kennedy. The vote would have been Nixon, 268.562 electoral votes; Kennedy, 260.159; unpledged, 6.936; and minor parties, 1.377.[122]

Three specific plans that were advocated during the 1969 and 1970 debates over electoral college reform also deserve brief analysis here. The first of these, the Tydings-Griffin plan, became very important during 1970 Senate consideration of electoral reform. This plan would abolish the office of elector and provide that a candidate would be elected president if he received a plurality of popular votes of at least 40 percent *or* a plurality of popular votes less than 40 percent and a majority of electoral votes (apportioned and determined as at present). If neither of these possibilities occurred, the decision would go to a joint session of Congress for choice between the top two candidates. Because it was favored by a number of key senators who were seen as potentially crucial to the prospects of the basic direct vote plan, the Tydings-Griffin plan was finally reluctantly accepted by Senate direct vote advocates in the closing months of 1970 electoral reform activity as part of a last-ditch but unsuccessful effort to save the direct vote plan that year.

The second major plan of the late 1960s was truly a hybrid. With the impressive title of the Federal System Plan, this proposal, introduced in March 1970 by Senators Thomas F. Eagleton of Missouri and Robert Dole of Kansas, provided three distinctly different ways that the president could be elected. On election night a candidate would be elected president if he had received a national popular vote plurality and *either* pluralities in a majority of the states or pluralities in states containing a majority of the voters. If no candidate succeeded in meeting these requirements, the election would be determined by the present electoral college, modified by the automatic casting of electoral votes. If no candidate received a majority of these votes, then the electoral votes of any third-party candidates would be proportionally reallocated to the two front-runners in order to derive a majority electoral vote winner. This rather complex plan, explained at length by its sponsors, attracted little attention and support in the months following its introduction.

The last plan, the Spong plan, emerged out of the October-November 1970 deadlock over electoral college reform and was frankly designed to be a possible compromise plan or, failing that, to be a proposal around which support could muster in the new 1972 Congress. This plan, developed by Senator

William B. Spong, Jr., of Virginia, abolished the office of elector but provided that a candidate would have to receive both a majority of electoral votes (apportioned and determined as at present) and a plurality of popular votes to be elected. If this did not occur, the election would go to a joint session of Congress for the final decision. In essence, this plan would eliminate the faithless elector and would also make it impossible for the electoral college to elect a popular vote loser. The winner in popular votes could, of course, still lose in the joint session of Congress contingent procedure.

One final hybrid plan should be mentioned, a proposal more noteworthy for the stature of its advocates than for any immediate signs of widespread support. In early 1978, The Twentieth Century Fund, an independent research foundation that frequently undertakes policy studies of economic, political, and social institutions and issues, issued the final report of its Task Force on Reform of the Presidential Election Process. In its report, entitled *Winner Take All*, the task force pointed out that initially it had been deeply divided on the merits of the existing electoral college and the direct vote alternative but had finally reached agreement in supporting a new alternative electoral reform plan called "the national bonus plan." Such unanimity was especially noteworthy in light of the considerable breadth of perspective of the members of the task force. They included political scientists and historians Heinz Eulau, Jeane Kirkpatrick (who served as cochairman of the group), Thomas Cronin, Paul Puryear, and Arthur M. Schlesinger, Jr.; political journalists and writers Jules Witcover, Neal Peirce, and Stephen Hess (the other cochairman); and political strategists John Sears, Jill Ruckelshaus, and Patrick Caddell. This highly diverse group brought strong critics of the direct election plan such as Arthur M. Schlesinger together with committed supporters of direct election. Despite this variety of membership, the task force found itself in agreement on the national bonus plan as a desirable form of electoral college reform.

This plan would add to the existing 538 electoral votes 102 additional votes (two corresponding to each of the fifty states and the District of Columbia). These "bonus votes" would be awarded as a bloc to that candidate who received the most popular votes nationally. The bonus plan emerged during the last days of the task force's deliberations when Arthur M. Schlesinger suddenly suggested adding a 50-vote bonus for the popular vote winner. Peirce made a quick rejoinder—"How about 100?"—and Schlesinger agreed. For simplicity's sake, it was then decided to make the bonus twice the number of the 51 voting units. The attraction of the plan was that popular vote advocates could regard it as de facto implementation of what they had been seeking all along—assurance that the candidate receiving the most votes would become president*—while those fearing a weakening of geographic or federalist factors

---

* The claim that the national bonus plan effectively eliminates the possibility of a divided verdict has been challenged by mathematician Samuel Merrill III. Utilizing an empirical model based on

in the presidential selection process, or an undermining of the parties, could take comfort in the retention of the traditional state-by-state electoral vote count. (Analysis showed there had not been one election in U.S. history in which the national bonus plan, if in effect, would not have assured election of the popular vote winner.)[123]

The national bonus plan was introduced as a constitutional amendment by Senator Bayh (though he did not abandon his own stand for the direct vote) shortly after the report of the task force was made public. But no further legislative action occurred on it, or on the direct vote plan, during 1978 or 1979[+].

Time will determine whether the national bonus plan will turn out to be the ingenious breakthrough compromise its creators hoped it to be or just another of the variety of hybrids briefly considered and then discarded along the long road to reform of the system. At the least, however, 1978 had brought a fascinating *new* proposal for electoral college reform—one on which, initially, leading critics and supporters of the electoral college could agree.

CONTINGENT ELECTION

The Constitutional provision for a contingent election in the House of Representatives, which goes into effect if no candidate receives a majority of the electoral vote, has been almost universally condemned. The various reform proposals over the years have contained a myriad of alternatives ranging from participation of Congress in the election of the president to a runoff election under certain circumstances.

Many reform proposals have in recent years have retained the contingent

state-by-state presidential election results since 1900, he has estimated the likelihood of an electoral reversal in an election as close as that of 1960 as 0.11, and in an election such as in 1976 as 0.03. This is in contrast with his estimates of the probabilities of such a divided verdict under the existing electoral college as 0.5 (in 1960) and 0.23 (in 1976). He concludes: "Although the national bonus plan would, of course, reduce the likelihood of a divided verdict, it would by no means prevent it." Merrill further extends his analysis to find that "if a third party is able to obtain 100 Electoral votes in an election in which the two major parties receive approximately the same number of votes, then the probability under the national bonus plan that no candidate receive a majority of the Electoral votes is about 50% [.5]. Thus a deadlock would not be an 'extremely remote eventuality.' " (Samuel Merrill, personal letter to authors, May 26, 1979, and "Empirical Estimates for the Likelihood of a Divided Verdict in a Presidential Election," *Public Choice* 33, no. 2, 1978, pp. 127–33.)

[+] Samuel Merrill III has computed a "first approximation" of state voting power under the national bonus plan using 1970 population and electoral college vote apportionments. He estimates the ratio of voting power of a citizen-voter in California to one in the District of Columbia as being between 1.62 and 1.5. This contrasts with the comparable ratio of voting power under the existing electoral college, as discussed in chapter 5, pp. 120–25, of 2.5. Merrill concludes: "The disparity [of the existing electoral college] is reduced by the bonus plan, but certainly not to equality." (Samuel Merrill, personal letter to authors, June 21, 1979, and "Citizen Voting Power Under the Electoral College: A Stochastic Model Based on State Voting Pattersn," *SIAM Journal of Applied Mathematics*, March 1978, pp. 376–90.)

election in Congress but have provided that it will take place in a joint session of Congress with each senator and representative having a single vote. This procedure would at least eliminate the undemocratic procedure of each state in the House casting a single vote, as the Constitution currently requires. But it is still open to the objection that any president chosen in Congress might be required to make advance agreements that would limit his independence and power as the chief executive. In addition, senators and representatives would be forced, by this contingent arrangement, to decide whether to vote according to party or to allow their vote to be determined by which candidate had led in the national vote, or, alternatively, by which candidate had carried their state or congressional district. If congressmen voted according to party, as most members would likely feel compelled to do, then the joint session of Congress contingent procedure would elect the presidential candidate of the majority party in Congress—who might well be the candidate who had indisputably run second in popular vote.

Other contingent election procedures proposed over the years have included these alternatives as well: election by the House with each member casting a single vote; a runoff by popular vote but each state to have but one vote in the national tally; the state legislatures to choose; successive national elections until one candidate receives a majority; letting the House choose by any rules it may adopt; or, to prevent deadlock in the House, authorizing the House Speaker to choose a president by lot from the two top-runners after the second ballot.[124]

The simplest alternative, of course, is not to require an electoral majority at all, so that the possibility of a contingent election never arises. This was the course advocated by Senator Oliver Morton and a number of reform advocates of the nineteenth and twentieth centuries. The danger of a straight plurality election of the president is that under this system a candidate enjoying popular support of but 35 or 30 percent or even less could conceivably, in the case of a multiple candidate race, be elected president of all the people of the United States. The counterargument has been that such an outcome has always been, and remains, most unlikely and that the absence of any runoff or contingent plan would encourage voters to go for "a winner"—that is, a major-party candidate—in the election.

The most pervasive—and controversial—contingent election provision of the late 1960s and 1970s was the one adopted as part of the direct vote plan by Senate and House advocates in 1967. This arrangement provided that if no candidate should receive 40 percent of the national vote for president there would be a runoff election between the top two candidates.

The "40 percent or runoff" feature was introduced into the direct vote plan as part of a compromise between the goals of providing a sufficient presidential mandate and avoiding runoffs as much as possible. As Republican William

McCulloch of Ohio, the ranking minority member on the House Judiciary Committee, explained it in 1969:

The 40-per cent figure is obviously a compromise. A higher figure would encourage third parties and thus increase the possibility of a run-off which no one really deserves. A lower figure would provide a very small mandate for the man elected President. . . .[125]

This compromise is, like all compromises, somewhat contrived, yet it looks appealing in comparison with the massive problems that would arise under the present House contingent arrangement, the somewhat similar pitfalls of a joint session of Congress procedure, and the possible undermining of the mandate of the presidency that could result from a simple plurality election.

Opponents were able to argue, however, that the runoff possibility would motivate many splinter parties to enter the presidential election, hoping that their total vote would hold either major-party nominee under 40 percent and thus trigger the contingent election in which the splinter groups would be able to bargain with the serious candidates for concessions of one type or another. It was impossible to tell whether such a scenario would, in fact, evolve under the direct vote—40 percent requirement method of electing the president. Even if it did, it seemed probable that the minor and splinter groups, after an election or two in which the futility of their enterprise would likely be demonstrated, would forsake the strategy aimed at stalemate and special-interest bargaining and instead return to more traditional methods of seeking to influence the policy stands of the major parties and their candidates.

CONCLUSION

Constitutional Convention delegate James Wilson told the Pennsylvania ratifying convention late in 1787 that "the Convention [was] perplexed with no part of this plan as much as with the mode of choosing the President of the United States."[126] The founding fathers were well aware that they had failed to create a perfect vehicle for the choice of the chief executive, and during the entire course of American history few men have been willing to defend it. Yet despite lifetimes of exertion by the great reformers, no substantive changes have been made. Why?

First and foremost, the answer lies in the politics of each era. Amending the Constitution is an arduous process; to succeed, one must form and maintain a broad national consensus. Indeed, no constitutional amendment has much chance of ratification without the support or at least the acquiescence of all the major political forces in the country—the controlling groups in each major political party, the spokesmen for each section of the country, and state and national party leaders. The stakes in any presidential election are so high that no political group will consent to a change in the electoral system if it seriously fears that its power and influence will be undercut.

The first great proposed reform, the district system, appears to have lost out in the nineteenth century because it diluted the power of political leaders who thought they could deliver states for one candidate or the other. And by the time the district plan was revived in the twentieth century, it bore so many of the marks of a conservative-rural device to seize the presidency that it never had a serious chance of adoption. Nor are its chances likely to increase in future years, as the urbanization of America continues. By its very nature, the district system magnifies the power of small states and predominantly one-party areas. Large states and politically marginal areas of the country will never risk it, and they can easily block any proposed constitutional amendment.

For many of the same reasons, the proportional plan clearly seems to have run its course and has little chance of adoption in future years. While simpler in conception and operation than the district system, it can quite plausibly elect a minority president.

The automatic system is likewise destined for failure, because it enthrones the most repugnant features of the electoral college as it operates today—the winner-take-all system of casting state electoral votes, the constant two electoral votes given each state regardless of its population, uncertainties and inequities in contingent election procedures, and most of all, the very real possibility that the winner of the popular vote will be denied the presidency in favor of the candidate who had run second in popular preference.

What then of the direct popular vote? Is it also destined to failure because it would "gore the ox" of some major political group in America—the small states, or perhaps just the southern states, or the minorities in the big pivotal states? A few years ago, the answer would doubtless have been yes. But the past two decades have witnessed a revolution in the political life of this country—a revolution in party alignment, a revolution in voting rights, a revolution in concepts of voter equality. It is the fundamental alteration in the political landscape of the United States that has made the direct popular vote for president a viable alternative today and the central focus of electoral reform politics from the late 1960s into the 1980s.

A Decade of Electoral
Reform Politics: 1969–1979

By 1969 a powerful set of forces supportive of fundamental reform of the electoral college, and the direct vote in particular, had emerged. In the last chapter, we detailed the series of events building toward a critical mass of support for change. There was the 1966 endorsement of the direct vote by the Chamber of Commerce of the United States.[1] The 1967 American Bar Association vote endorsing the direct vote, following the recommendation of the ABA Commission on Electoral College Reform,[2] added the support of the official voice of the nation's legal community. President Lyndon Johnson in 1966 and 1967 sent Congress messages supporting electoral reform; although he would only go as far as the automatic plan, his messages served to focus attention on the electoral college. And one cannot underestimate the importance of Senator Birch Bayh's May 18, 1966, announcement that he now favored direct vote. The direct vote plan was thus provided with an undergirding it had never before enjoyed—the support of the chairman of one of the congressional committees concerned with constitutional amendments, who in addition would prove to be a skilled, persistent, and devoted advocate. (It is worth noting that when Bayh first endorsed direct election, it was with provision of contingent election by a joint session of Congress if no candidate received 40 percent or more of the popular vote. But soon after the ABA commission made public its amendment, providing for a popular vote runoff if 40 percent were not achieved, Bayh deferred to the ABA and modified his plan accordingly. Although this ensured that the popular vote choice would always become the president if the amendment were approved, it also opened the proposal to criticism and would play a role in its downfall in 1970.)*

By the last months of 1968, one factor overshadowed all others—the powerful and astonishing appeal of Governor Wallace of Alabama, who was playing

---

* This was not the first occasion on which Bayh and the ABA had worked in tandem. The Presidential Disability Amendment that Bayh, in an unusual accomplishment for a freshman senator, steered through Congress within two years of assuming his Judiciary Constitutional Amendments Subcommittee chairmanship in 1963, was also strongly supported by the ABA.

a scarcely disguised game pointed toward electoral college deadlock and bargaining with his electors to force concessions from one of the major party nominees. The 1968 election illustrated multiple deficiencies of the electoral college, ranging from the potential of Wallace-induced deadlock to the possibility that the popular vote winner might be denied the presidency (see pp. 73–80, above).

1969 AND HOUSE ACTION[3]

Alarmed by the close call of the 1968 election, and sensitized to faithless elector problems by the debate in both chambers over errant Nixon elector Lloyd W. Bailey, the members of the Ninety-first Congress were also exposed to a gushing outpouring of articles, essays, and pamphlets on the electoral college and its reforms.[4] Lengthy hearings began before the Senate Constitutional Amendments Subcommittee on January 23, 1969, and the full House Judiciary Committee on February 5.[5] At this point President Richard Nixon sent Congress a message asking that the office of elector be abolished (as in the automatic plan), that each state's electoral votes be divided in some manner (as in the district or proportional plans), and that a popular vote runoff (as in the direct vote plan) be held in case no candidate received 40 percent of the electoral votes.

The president's statement, which went on to suggest that Congress was not giving serious attention to electoral reform, was ill-received by congressmen deeply engaged in such efforts. In addition, his statement was subject to widespread criticism on the grounds that such a "conglomerate plan" made up of bits and pieces of various proposals confused and complicated reform activities.[6]

The major reform action now was to take place in the Judiciary committees. The 1969 House hearings, held over a period of five weeks, were unusual in that they involved the full committee rather than a subcommittee.[7] This proved to be of major importance. As testimony developed, and, as committee members would later say, often as a direct result of the testimony heard, the weight of opinion swung sharply to direct election and all Judiciary committee members, not just the leaders or a smaller subcommittee segment, were part of that shift in opinion. Initially, in fact, both Chairman Emanuel Celler (D., N.Y.) and ranking minority member William M. McCulloch (R., Ohio) were uncommitted and apparently undecided. The ambivalence of the committee's leadership created an atmosphere of open inquiry which permitted that somewhat rare event—actual education of committee members and leaders.

Over one hundred witnesses or statements came before the House Judiciary Committee in the course of the hearings, ranging from William T. Gossett, president of the ABA, to Chaim H. Zimbalist, a former member of the Missouri General Assembly. Of the major testimony, about seventeen people favored the direct vote plan, including William Gossett, Robert Storey, James C. Kirby, Jr., and John D. Feerick, all of the ABA's Commission on Electoral College Reform; John F. Banzhaf III, author of computer analyses of the electoral college; George Meany, the president of the AFL-CIO; and Clarence Mitchell, Jr., the director of the Washington Office of the NAACP. Testimony favoring retention of the present electoral college system in some form came from Alexander Bickel of Yale Law School and Harvie Williams, executive secretary of the American Good Government Society, Inc. The district plan was supported by Michael D. Jaffe, general counsel of the Liberty Lobby, John C. Lynn, legislature director of the American Farm Bureau Federation, and J. Banks Young, Washington representative of the National Cotton Council of America. Finally, the proportional plan was supported by Mr. Young (in addition to the district plan), I. Martin Wekselman of the American Jewish Council, Richard M. Scammon, director of the Elections Research Center (who, however, preferred the direct vote plan), and John N. Mitchell, attorney general of the United States.

The last testimony was to prove especially important, for the immovable insistence of the attorney general that direct vote lacked strong support in Congress[8] and in the states, while the proportional plan had much, considerably irritated Chairman Celler. He felt especially challenged by the Mitchell testimony about the lack of congressional interest in the direct vote plan, and, at least partially due to this, now took upon himself the task of selling the direct vote for president.[9]

Another individual's House testimony also proved to be of considerable although quite different importance. For the House committee this was a repeat performance of the 1967 Senate testimony of John F. Banzhaf III, now a George Washington Law School professor. His findings about the inequities of the present electoral college, as well as of the proportional and district plans, had enormous impact on the committee members, especially as it tended to "dispel [the] small state weighted power myth."[10]

One last feature of the committee hearing stage of the legislative process should be stressed. This was the strong, unified, and complementary activities of the several high-status associations now working for the direct vote plan. From the opening day of the hearings when Representative Celler noted that one of the measures under consideration "incorporates recommendations of the American Bar Association,"[11] to the final committee report three and a half months later when it was observed that "the Committee finds the statement of William T. Gossett, president of the American Bar Association, persuasive,"[12] the support of the ABA, United States Chamber of Commerce, and other groups for the direct vote plan was never far from the surface. These groups had considerable impact on the legislative process because of what political scientist

David Truman once identified as "the deference accorded a high-status group . . . [which] not only facilitates the acceptance of its propaganda but also eases its approach to the government."[13] In addition, these groups—especially the ABA—also have influence as providers of technical and expert knowledge that backstops allies and impresses the undecided. A final resource of the associations supporting direct vote lay in the very fact of their common cause. As Representative Celler later noted:

The hearings before the Judiciary Committee indicated that such diverse organizations as the AFL-CIO, the U.S. Chamber of Commerce and the American Bar Association have all united in support of the direct popular election method. I have been in Congress for a great many years. I know of no case or no bill where you had the unified support of such diverse groups as the American Bar Association, AFL-CIO, or the U.S. Chamber of Commerce representing business, large and small, and the labor organizations that I have mentioned. Yet they have all agreed not only to support this bill but to go out into the highways and byways after it is passed by the Congress and urge the voters in the various states to ratify this constitutional amendment.[14]

In April 1969 the House Judiciary Committee, having completed its extensive hearings, started to work in executive session on preparing its final bill. On April 17 the committee adopted a key section of the direct vote plan as a basic element of its "clean" bill. The next day, President Nixon spoke again on electoral reform, indicating his preference for a proportional plan, while also agreeing to work for a direct vote plan if one were to pass Congress. The impact on the committee members of the president's latest statement, however, seemed to be negligible.

In crucial committee votes on April 29 and 30, the committee first approved and then ordered reported a rewritten clean bill, House Joint Resolution 681, providing for a direct vote for president, essentially identical to that proposed by the ABA. The vote in each case was 28 or 29 for (one member was absent for the first vote) and 6 opposed.[15] This action was the first time since 1956 that any electoral reform amendment had been reported out of a congressional committee and the first time ever for a direct vote plan. On May 16 the committee issued its report on House Joint Resolution 681,[16] and the stage seemed set for floor action, after the House Rules Committee approved an appropriate rule.

After considerable delay, the House Rules Committee finally did, on July 24, issue a favorable rule, limiting debate to a total of six hours, three for each side, and allowing amendments. Why Representative Celler requested—as he in fact did—an "open" rule such as this is an interesting question. One line of speculation is that allowing amendments to be proposed and then voted down would be a convenient way of activating the strategy of turning proponents of other plans into "last chance for electoral reform" supporters of direct vote.

Meanwhile, in the Senate, things were not going at all well for direct vote advocates. The similarly exhaustive hearings by the Constitutional Amendments

Subcommittee of the Senate Judiciary Committee had not resulted in the near unanimity of opinion of the House Judiciary Committee. Rather, the Senate subcommittee proceeded to junk the direct vote bill of subcommittee chairman Birch Bayh, replacing it, by a 6-to-5 vote, with a district plan having few prospects. In effect, the result was greatly to increase the difficulties of direct vote supporters, since they would now have to convince the parent committee, chaired by direct vote opponent Senator James O. Eastland (D., Miss.) to override its "expert-matter" subcommittee and reinstate the direct vote plan. Senator Bayh expressed optimistic hope that his subcommittee could be so reversed; others, however, were far more pessimistic. The New York Times editorially expressed these doubts, declaring: "It is painfully apparent that the memory of what Senator Bayh called a 'brush with catastrophe' in last November's Presidential election has begun to recede; apathy is upon us."[17] At this point, it was becoming evident that favorable House action on electoral reform might be the desperately needed catalyst to get direct election moving again in the Senate.

On September 10, 1969, the House of Representatives commenced consideration of House Joint Resolution 681 in what was the first full-scale floor debate over electoral reform in the House since 1826. Representative Celler, as chairman of the House Judiciary Committee and author of the resolution, led off with a speech outlining five, by now familar, faults of the present electoral college system: the constant two allocation of electoral votes to the states, the winner-take-all procedure, the House contingent election of the president, the possibility of an election's winner losing the electoral college, and the occurrence of faithless electors.[18] The present electoral college system, Representative Celler concluded in his colorful manner, is "barbarous, unsporting, dangerous, and downright uncivilized."[19] Representative Celler would eventually top even this; in the closing minutes of House debate on September 18, prior to the final vote on direct vote, he would cry out:

I believe that if this joint resolution passes, it will be a crowning achievement in my own life. I am approaching my 82nd birthday. Fate has been kind to me in giving me many birthdays. The abyss awaits me. I have not too many years to live, and I am happy to know that the passage of this joint resolution, which I am hopeful will occur, is a real event in my life.[20]

Many amendments were offered on a variety of aspects of electoral reform, including one by Representative Joe D. Waggonner (D., La.) that would have raised the runoff percentage from 40 to 50 percent. This amendment was initially passed on a 43 to 33 standing vote but was then defeated on a subsequent 71 to 91 teller vote demanded by Representative Celler.

Another amendment was an innocuous proposal by Representative Richard H. Poff (R., Va.) to add the word "inability" to the conditions of death or withdrawal of presidential candidates, which proved to be the only amendment adopted. Sixteen other proposals, including automatic, proportional, and district plans were rejected by the House in a series of votes on September 17.

With most amendments out of the way, the House of Representatives prepared, on September 18, 1969, to move to a final vote. On the eve of the crucial final vote, Representative Celler and other direct vote supporters were reported to be concerned about their ability to muster the necessary two-thirds vote of the House. Defeating hostile amendments required only a majority, but final passage would necessitate a much more difficult two-thirds; and as many as 159 House members—well over one-third—had earlier expressed their preference for the district plan. The key to the two-thirds vote, then, would lie with the supporters of alternative plans that had been voted down. One such congressman was Representative Poff, who had joined with Representatives David and Dennis (R., Ind.) and John Dowdy (D., Tex.) to introduce a substitute district plan. On September 12 Poff stated that if his preferred electoral reform plan lost, he would support direct vote—a plan he had strongly opposed in the House Judiciary Committee—rather than have no reform. This action by a man who had been personally outspoken in opposition to the direct vote plan was thought by some observers to be important in "showing the way by which supporters of other plans could become supporters of direct vote."[21]

On September 18 one final attempt was made by direct vote opponents to block final action. Dennis, to the end a staunch opponent of direct vote, moved to recommit House Joint Resolution 681 to the House Judiciary Committee with instructions to substitute and report a district plan. This last-minute action was rejected by the members in a 162 to 246 roll call vote, and the House then proceeded to pass House Joint Resolution 681 by a resounding vote of 338 to 70, 66 more votes than needed—or, in other words, a margin of votes almost as large as the total opposition. Eighty-three percent of the House members voted for the direct vote plan—amazingly, the exact percentage of support that direct vote had received in the House Judiciary Committee five months earlier.[22]

The two House roll call votes of September 18 allow for some rather interesting analyses of patterns of support and opposition.[23] Research has found that neither size of state nor, to any great degree, region were important in the House votes; rather the recommittal vote was supported, and the final passage of direct vote opposed, by very conservative southern Democratic and Republican representatives. The direct vote amendment obtained its overwhelming final margin because of the last-minute shift of some southern Democratic and many Republican, less conservative, representatives to the direct vote plan.[24]

The approval, by the House of Representatives of the direct vote plan had considerable widespread impact. The New York Times, after reviewing some of the gloom surrounding Senate prospects for electoral reform, noted:

After Thursday's House vote, this pessimism lifted like a sunstruck marsh cloud. In the face of such a demonstration of popular support from wary and politically hard-nosed Congressmen, how could the Senate stand in the way? Or, at least, that was the warm flush of early reasoning.[25]

Anthony Lewis of the *New York Times* viewed the House action as demonstrating "a historical truth—that in choosing a President, at least, we are no longer a collection of states but a Nation."[26] Columnist Max Lerner, on the other hand, took the opportunity to decry the fact that now "each of us will become a statistical item in a single, vast national count."[27]

The assumption about the inevitability of final approval of the direct vote amendment was given additional support on September 24 with the timely release of the results of a Gallup poll on electoral reform taken in November 1968. At that time, the Gallup organization asked 1,530 respondents: "Would you approve or disapprove of an amendment to the Constitution which would do away with the Electoral College and base the election of a President on the total vote cast throughout the nation?" and found that 81 percent approved, 12 percent disapproved, and 7 percent had no opinion. With commentators making much of the similarity of this 81 percent popular support to the 83 percent approval the direct vote plan had received both in the House Judiciary Committee and in the full House, the direct vote plan seemed unstoppable.

Another event occurring in September ended an eventful month on a triumphant note for electoral reform advocates. President Nixon, who had been soundly criticized for his lack of leadership on electoral reform,[28] announced, on September 30, that he now supported the direct vote plan, and "unless the Senate follows the lead of the House, all opportunity for reform will be lost this year and possibly for years to come."[29] Representative Carl Albert (Okla.), Democratic floor leader in the House, acidly complimented the president for his belated support and added, "You can't criticize his flexibility."[30] As it turned out, however, the lack of timeliness of President Nixon's support for direct vote would be matched, in the Senate, by its lack of substance.

Another event of 1969 boosting the spirits of many electoral reform advocates was the publication by the *New York Times*, on October 7, of the results of a survey of state legislature leaders and governors concerning the prospects of state ratification of a direct vote constitutional amendment.[31] The *Times* found that, overall, 9 states could be said to strongly favor a direct vote amendment, 21 somewhat, 6 undecided, 6 somewhat opposed, and 8 strongly opposed. Most of the opposition was found to be in southern, midwestern, and Mountain states, yet even in those areas, nearly one-half of the states favored direct vote or were undecided.

One final item brought 1969 to a somewhat somber end. In spite of the House action of September and subsequent events, Senate Judiciary chairman Eastland announced on November 3 that full committee action on electoral reform—which direct vote supporters had been counting on to reinstate the direct vote plan in place of the subcommittee-approved district plan—was being "indefinitely" postponed, at least until after the committee had disposed of the disputed nomination of Clement Haynsworth to the United States Supreme Court. This delay in committee action, which was to stretch deep into 1970 as controversy developed first over Haynsworth and then over the succeeding G. Harrold Carswell nomination, caused electoral reform to lose the heady impetus developed from the events of September and October of 1969. By the time direct vote would be reported by the Senate Judiciary Committee late in April of 1970 and would come up for floor consideration in September 1970, the resounding House vote, the Gallup poll, President Nixon's support, and the *New York Times* survey of state legislatures would all seem distant and far removed. In 1969 direct vote for president achieved its peak of support; in the coming year, it would be subject to frustrating delay, massive debate, and—ultimately defeat.

1970 AND SENATE ACTION[32]

The immediate and urgent problem for Senate direct vote supporters in the early months of 1970 was to find some way to get the direct vote plan out of the Senate Judiciary Committee. Senate Joint Resolution 1 had been killed in the Subcommittee on Constitutional Amendments, and Eastland, the full committee chairman, seemed disinclined to allow his committee to resurrect it. Through the ample powers available to him as chairman, Senator Eastland might be able to delay committee action on electoral reform indefinitely—unless Bayh could outmaneuver him.

Much to the surprise of Senator Eastland (and perhaps also of Senator Bayh), such a successful outflanking did in fact occur on February 3. In an adroit parliamentary move, Bayh moved that the Judiciary committee vote on the pending nomination of Carswell to the Supreme Court on February 9 *and* vote on Senate Joint Resolution 1 and other electoral reform plans by April 24. By so linking the Carswell nomination, strongly supported by Eastland, to the direct vote plan, Bayh succeeded in making agreement on a voting date for electoral reform a condition for agreement on voting on the Carswell nomination. Senator Eastland, it was reported, noted the success of this maneuver "with some admiration."[33]

On April 13 Eastland announced a suitable surprise in return: supplemental hearings by the full Senate Judiciary Committee on electoral college reform, to be held starting in two days with himself presiding and featuring various witnesses hostile to the direct vote plan.[34] Bayh angrily responded to this insult to himself and his subcommittee's earlier hearings by terming Senator Eastland's move "the most blatant disregard for senatorial courtesy in my eight years in the Senate."[35] The only consolation offered him was the opportunity to add several witnesses favoring direct election on the last day, following testimony critical of the direct vote plan by initial witnesses such as Theodore H. White, Professor Alexander Bickel of Yale Law School, and Richard N. Goodwin, former assistant to Presidents Kennedy and Johnson.[36] In retrospect, it is unclear what real function these last-minute hearings served, except perhaps to provide a foretaste of the possibilities for obstruction by southern parliamentarians when aroused.

As the time for Judiciary committee voting on electoral reform drew near, it was reported that direct vote was having serious trouble in getting even the bare majority of 9 out of 17 committee votes.[37] On April 23 the decisive moment finally arrived as the Judiciary committee rejected an automatic plan by a vote of 7 to 9, a district plan by 6 to 10, and, in a crucial and close vote, a proportional plan by 8 to 9.[38] The committee then, by a vote of 11 to 6, ordered Senate Joint Resolution 1 reported. As Warren Weaver of the New York Times noted, the strategy of the direct vote supporters worked perfectly: they invited other reform plans to be brought out first and then voted down, leaving a simple choice—direct vote or nothing.[39] The result of the use of this strategy—which had earlier worked so well in the House—was again to give direct vote a strong mandate consisting of first-, second-, and even third-choice supporters. By the committee vote on April 23, the revived constitutional amendment emerged from the committee phase of the legislative process somewhat like the phoenix from the ashes—with renewed hope and expectations for final enactment.[40]

The electoral reform proposal was not, however, to move rapidly to the next stage of floor consideration buoyed by recent committee success. Rather, another long period of delay was to ensue before the final committee report was issued. The majority had agreed to write its majority report in a week; however, it found itself taking five weeks to do so. The minority of the committee had agreed to write its minority report in two weeks, but instead took eleven—starting after the majority completed its work.[41] Whether the Senate would have passed the direct vote plan if it had come to a floor vote soon after House approval will never be known; what is clear, however, is that, in the words of one legislative observer, "that year [between House and Senate action] really cooled things off."[42]

Finally, on August 14, 1970,[43] nearly four months after the favorable committee vote, the Judiciary committee formally reported Senate Joint Resolution 1 to the Senate floor.[44] In the committee report on the measure the majority argued, in a familiar manner, for direct election of the president with a runoff if no candidate received 40 percent of the popular vote. The committee minority, consisting of Senators Eastland, John L. McClellan (D., Ark.), Sam J. Ervin, Jr. (D., N.C.), Roman L. Hruska (R., Nebr.), Hiram Fong (R., Hawaii), and Strom

Thurmond (R., S.C.), was, however, not to remain silent in its views. In a dissent over twice as long as the majority statement, they outlined their convictions that the direct vote plan would destroy the two-party system, undermine federalism, damage the separation of powers, radicalize public opinion, encourage electoral fraud, and necessitate national control of the electoral process. They concluded their dissent with the ringing declaration:

It will not do to say that the electoral college is antiquated or outmoded; no more viable institution, nor a more salutary one, will be found today. Let us, if need be, repair it; but let us not abandon it for the sake of a mathematical abstraction, or because we are angry that the world is not perfect.[45]

By late August and early September, Washington activity on electoral reform had begun to pick up. By this time there had emerged an astonishing alliance among five major national interest groups in support of the direct vote plan: the League of Women Voters of the United States, the ABA, the UAW, the AFL-CIO, and the Chamber of Commerce of the United States.[46] This unity among groups more often found on opposing sides was unprecedented, especially the agreement between labor and the Chamber of Commerce. The series of group endorsements for direct vote stretching over the past four years had been an important factor in building and maintaining interest in electoral reform; now the very unity of their coordinated efforts would further enhance the attractiveness of the direct vote plan. As one involved lobbyist put it, "The effect is beyond the mathematics of 5 ones equal 5. There is a geometric effect far beyond that. . . . The march to Capitol Hill together is very significant. . . . The effect is magnified enormously."[47]

In addition to coordinated contacting of individual senators,[48] the five major groups also cooperated in a formal request for a meeting of President Nixon with their respective presidents. Three weeks went by without any answer, while the presidents of the different associations fretted about whether they should plan a Washington trip or not. Finally, on September 10, the day before the requested meeting date, a telegram was received from a rather low-level White House functionary stating that the president was unavailable for the hoped-for meeting with the organization presidents. No alternative time for such a meeting was mentioned, and it was indicated that the president's position on electoral reform was already quite clear.[49]

But was it? The most recent statement of the president on electoral reform had been nearly one year earlier, on September 30, 1969, when, in the flush of overwhelming House passage of House Joint Resolution 681, President Nixon had finally expressed support for the direct vote plan. As far as affirmative statements or actions on behalf of direct vote, however, there had been absolutely none.[50] On September 11, probably not by coincidence the day for which the association presidents had sought their meeting, President Nixon broke his silence by including electoral reform in a catch-all message to Congress on unfinished business. After restating his support for the House-passed plan, he chided the Senate, noting: "Unfortunately, the Senate has not completed action. Time is running out. But it is still possible to pass the measure and to amend the Constitution in time for the 1972 elections."[51]

This presidential expression of support for direct election was generally dismissed as weak, untimely, and as responding to events rather than showing leadership. One Senate aide characterized the president's position on electoral reform as one of "benign neglect"; another noted that Nixon was getting exactly what he wanted out of it: making liberals happy by being in favor of it, and yet not pushing hard enough to pass it.[52] That the president could exercise considerable leadership on the issue was evident: of the twelve or so undecided senators, eight were Republican and presumably subject to influence by administration pressure.[53] As one lobbyist put it, "if he issued strong marching orders, it could pass."[54] Yet, an aide to one of the key Republican opponents to direct vote acknowledged that there was no Nixon pressure on them as to their position nor had he seen any signs of administration pressure on Republican moderates.[55] Despite his offered support, President Nixon made little, if any, sincere effort to secure electoral reform in 1970.

Senate debate on Senate Joint Resolution 1 formally opened the day after Labor Day, September 8, 1970, ten days short of one year after House passage of the direct vote plan. Senator Bayh, as the floor manager of the bill, led off by calling direct vote "the only system that is truly democratic, truly equitable and truly responsive to the will of the people."[56] Major supportive efforts in the opening days were provided by Senators Howard H. Baker, Sr. (R., Tenn.) and Henry Bellmon (R., Okla.), both of whom stressed the small-state interest in the direct vote plan.[57]

Rhetorical counterattacks against the direct vote plan were launched and maintained by three leaders of the opposition—Senators Carl T. Curtis (R., Nebr.), Hruska (R., Nebr.), and Thurmond (R., S.C.). Curtis, for example, stressed the runoff provision as "the fatal defect" which could only cause "doubt and confusion." Senator Hruska expressed his opinion that direct election of the president was "the most mischievous and dangerous constitutional amendment that has ever received serious consideration by the Congress" and "to adopt it would be to set out on a vast uncharted sea, with no guarantee that the slightest political breeze might not capsize and destroy our ship of state."[58]

Most of the debate, however, was not up even to these rhetorical standards, but was, as one senator described it, "boilerplate"[59] designed to fill time and the *Congressional Record*. This was in spite of the fact that, starting on September 8, the Senate had been operating on an unusual double-shift schedule, debating electoral reform until 3 P.M., and then turning to other business late into the evening. This was necessary because of a push by the Senate leadership for adjournment by October 15, formalized in a bipartisan agreement of September 10,[60] which quickly broke down. The relation between the pressure of time and the desultory debate on Senate Joint Resolution 1 was simple: electoral reform was being killed by talk and inaction—in other words, by a filibuster. If direct vote opponents could delay long enough, the direct vote would likely be lost in the closing frenzy of the session without the possible awkwardness of an actual vote.

What made possible this type of cavalier treatment of a reform backed by 81 percent of the American people and voted for by 83 percent of the House was its peculiar character. Electoral reform is not a "gut issue" clearly determining gains and losses for affected interests. "For the lobbyists, this issue is not important to them. They will not hate you for how you vote."[61] Nor is the issue one on which there is clear constituency pressures generating clues or demands for action. Instead, it is one in which narrow advantage is neither clearly defined nor the deciding issue; one which calls for evaluations of a difficult type. For many senators, such an issue is somewhat a "pain in the neck" since they can in no way benefit or hurt themselves, yet a large amount of time is required in order to really understand it. The result of these aspects of the issue is a tendency to grasp at political symbols as a means of justifying political decisions and to build elaborate cases for dubious propositions. In short, electoral reform turned out to be an issue in which political rhetoric tended to create political realities.[62]

A political reality that Bayh and direct vote supporters found themselves facing in mid-September was a simple one—they did not have the votes. For over a year, the story had been the same: if direct vote could get to the Senate floor, it could count on 51, or 55, or 58 votes—always at least 7 to 10 short of the needed two-thirds vote of 66 or 67. After concluding yet another count, one senior Senate staff aide was reported, on September 10, to have flatly told a direct vote supporter, "You haven't got the votes now and you're not going to get them."[63] On September 14 the New York Times reported in one front-page article, "Electoral Reform Is in Deep Trouble," that Senator Bayh and allies were debating in an empty Senate chamber, there was no evidence of President Nixon pushing in any way for direct vote, five major interest group presidents had been unsuccessful in contacting or meeting with the president, Senate Joint Resolution 1 seemed stuck at the 58-vote level, and possibly the ghosts of Haynsworth and Carswell were indirectly killing electoral reform.[64]

The sources of the difficulties for the direct vote plan lay in several different directions. First, there was clear and outspoken opposition by southerners to the idea of abolishing the electoral college on the grounds that an important bulwark of states' rights would thus be breached. The president, they reasoned, is now elected by state voters; under a national popular election this "state element" of the presidency would be lost. In addition, concern was also expressed that abolishment of the electoral college's recognition of the role of individual states might lead to attacks on other institutions recognizing individual states—in particular, the United States Senate and its basis in equally weighted states. Other darker thoughts may have also occurred to southerners—that direct vote might increase voting turnout in their states, especially among the blacks, or that electoral reform was an attempt to block George Wallace and other traditional opportunities of the South in the electoral college system.

Opposition also came from nonsouthern sources: from staunch conservatives opposed to changing the Constitution, from some small-state senators convinced that direct vote would leave their states helpless in the hands of large populous states, and even from one liberal Democratic senator who found himself agreeing that direct vote might be "the most deeply radical amendment which has ever entered the Constitution of the United States."[65]

One issue, however, tended to cut across size, sectional, and ideological lines—a concern about the possible consequences of the runoff procedure incorporated in Senate Joint Resolution 1. As the legislative assistant to one direct vote supporter put it, "Everyone is much scared of the runoff feature."[66] Some compromise on this point seemed needed, but how would it be implemented, and along what lines?

As debate droned on into a second week, the fate of the direct vote plan became increasingly bound up in the pressure for adjournment. This took the form of lengthy negotiations between allies—partners, however, with different objectives. The goal of Senator Bayh, together with his chief aides Jason Berman and P. J. Mode,[67] was simple: to keep pressure up for Senate Joint Resolution 1 as long as necessary to bring it to a final vote. On the other hand, Senate Majority Leader Mike Mansfield, (D., Mont.), with his key aides Dan Leach and Charles Ferris, wished to see the Senate move as quickly as possible through its business on the way to the scheduled October 15 adjournment.[68]

On Monday, September 14, Senators Mansfield and Bayh and their aides spent more than six hours trying to work out, with direct vote opponents, a schedule for voting on electoral reform.[69] The alternative to some agreement with the opposition allowing for an eventual vote would be, all knew, a cloture motion.

Such a cloture petition was now prepared and ready for Mansfield to introduce. Bayh, however, tended to oppose its introduction—at least as long as any shred of hope remained that some compromise allowing for a vote would be worked out by other means. The reason for Bayh's opposition to use of a cloture petition at this time was a simple one: he did not have the votes to pass it. As he noted on September 14, two or three direct vote supporters would not vote for cloture of debate, thus making the necessary two-thirds vote almost impossible to obtain.[70] To Mansfield men, however, a cloture vote was really the last chance for getting a vote on electoral reform[71]—unless the opposition would agree to a voting timetable.

On Thursday, September 15, two important meetings of direct vote opponents were held: the southern Democrats in the morning, presided over by Senator Richard Russell (D., Ga.),[72] and the Republicans at midday. It was at the first caucus that the key decision dooming electoral reform was made: the southern Democrats would under no circumstances agree to any kind of vote on electoral reform. The decision to utilize (or, more exactly, to continue to utilize) a filibuster to defeat electoral reform was not necessarily a reflection of concern that they lacked votes to defeat the direct vote plan on an outright vote, but rather a coolly calculated strategy. The reliance upon extended debate was seen as the best tactic to be used to prevent any possiblity of Senate Joint Resolution 1 passing. As one key southern Senate aide put it, a filibuster was the safest way of assuring failure for electoral reform.[73]

In order for the southern filibuster to be effective, tacit acquiescence would be necessary from Republican opponents of Senate Joint Resolution 1. This, in fact, was obtained at midday on September 15, when the Republican opposition caucused. The decision was made not to go along with any voting agreement nor to try to force a vote on the southern Democrats through voting for cloture. As one key Republican aide explained it, there would be little advantage in treating an ally like that.[74]

Direct vote supporters had been aware of these crucial meetings occurring in the morning and midday of September 15[75] and were curious to find out what had been decided. Therefore, early in the afternoon of September 15, Senator Bayh rose on the floor of the Senate and announced that he was about to pose a series of unanimous consent requests pertaining to voting on electoral reform and wished senators to be notified and called to the floor. Senator Bayh then moved through a series of seven different unanimous consent requests on various pending electoral reform proposals. Senator Ervin objected to each, including one objection to voting on four of his own amendments. To this manifestation of the southern decision not to allow any vote on any electoral reform proposal, Senator Bayh responded with the biting observation: "I think it is unconscionable to suggest that the Senate does not have the courage to stand up and vote on the merits of an issue as vital as this."[76] Senator Bayh then yielded the floor to Senator Mansfield who, at 2:56 P.M., introduced the long-awaited cloture petition.[77] The Senate was now committed to a vote, but a vote on the very difficult matter of cloture of debate, to be held one hour after the 10 A.M. opening of the Senate session on Thursday, September 17.[78]

Supporters of direct vote at this time began to develop an important new issue in their favor—the propriety of unlimited debate or a filibuster being used against a constitutional amendment that would itself require a two-thirds vote of the Senate together with a subsequent three-fourths approval by the states in order to be enacted. As the *New York Times* editorially observed on September 18, "The excuse offered in defense of unlimited debate is that it can forestall precipitous action by a bare majority." Yet, direct vote could not be enacted by any such bare majority, but would rather require an "extraordinary majority" of two-thirds. As Senate Majority Leader Mansfield argued on September 18, the use of unlimited debate against such a measure "abuses the clear purpose and interests of the Senate rules." Similarly, Tom Wicker of the *New York Times* wrote on September 17, "There may be reason to vote against direct election of Presidents, but there is no reason for voting against consideration of the issue."[79]

It was the question whether the Senate would be allowed to vote on electoral reform that was before the Senate as it prepared to vote on cloture shortly after 11 A.M. on September 17. On a roll call vote of 54 to 36, the Senate then failed to invoke cloture on Senate Joint Resolution 1. With 90 senators present and voting, 60 were necessary for cloture to pass; consequently, the attempt fell 6 votes short. Even more disheartening was the realization that even if all 10 additional senators were present and voting unanimously for cloture, the vote still would be insufficient. The minority of 36 voting against cloture was, and would continue to be, sufficient to block voting on electoral reform until and unless significant defections occurred.

The reaction to the vote by direct vote supporters was guarded. Senator Mansfield observed that Senate Joint Resolution 1 was "still breathing," but he would have to examine the cloture vote closely to see where to go next. In words with an ominous ring, he added "I don't want to go through an exercise in futility."[80] Senator Bayh's aides, however, felt they had correctly predicted almost every vote, and with 97 instead of 90 senators present, cloture would have had 62 rather than 54 votes—still, however, 3 crucial votes short. In an interview only a few hours after the vote, the view was repeatedly stressed: Senator Mansfield could not deny them a second cloture vote when they were this close.[81]

Late in the following week, while consideration of Senate Joint Resolution 1 dragged on inconclusively, Senator Bayh moved to force Senator Mansfield's hand. Starting on Thursday, September 24, he began to object to all unanimous consent requests for the Senate to act on business other than the pending matter—electoral reform. In addition, he also objected to committees meeting while the Senate was in session, which was still for extraordinarily long hours. The Senate operates on the unanimous consent request;[82] with Senator Bayh making objection to any request other than an agreement for voting on Senate Joint Resolution 1, the Senate's business came to an effective halt. Senate Majority Leader Mansfield, by now despairing of any hope of an October 15 adjournment,[83] responded in the only possible way—he introduced a second cloture petition, to be voted on September 29.

The second vote was viewed by all as a crucial final vote. Senator Bayh termed it a test of the Senate's ability to function as a responsible instrument of government. The *New York Times* editorialized on the day of the vote: "A vote against cloture today is a vote against any reform of the Presidential electoral system within the foreseeable future." Senator Mansfield observed, not too subtly, "This is an extremely important vote. It could very well be the tell-tale vote."[84]

The second cloture vote was held shortly after 1 P.M. on Tuesday, September 29. In the closing minutes of debate on that day prior to the vote, direct vote opponent Senator Ervin urged the Senate not to invoke cloture, since there were many different ideas about the election of the president, and we "should not attempt to solve this problem in the last days of a harried and hurried session."[85] Following this summary of four years of congressional hearings and two years of congressional actions, the Senate proceeded to reject cloture on Senate Joint Resolution 1 a second time, by 53 to 34. With 87 senators present and voting, 58 votes were needed for cloture; consequently the second cloture attempt fell 5 votes short—an insignificant gain of one vote in return for ten days of effort. The minority of 34 was itself still sufficient to block cloture, even if all 13 missing senators supported cloture. Perhaps most discouraging was the absence of any signs of movement or change in voting patterns.

Following the vote, Senator Bayh ceased objecting to unanimous consent requests for the Senate to consider other business. Senator Ervin pledged a major effort in the next Congress for "genuine reform." The *New York Times* editorially concluded that "yesterday's vote in the Senate . . . all but dooms the nation to another round of electoral roulette in 1972."[86] One last act in the politics of electoral college reform, however, remained still to be played out—namely, a third cloture effort.

On October 2, perhaps out of despair of ever seeing the Senate resolve the issue, Senator Mansfield introduced a third cloture petition, to be voted on in the following week, on October 6. The purpose of this last gasp was somewhat unclear, unless it was to try one more time to persuade the reticent opponents of Senate Joint Resolution 1 to agree to a voting timetable that would give direct vote at least a decent burial. No matter what the motive for the cloture motion, the result was a meeting, on Monday afternoon, October 5, of the most unlikely people. Starting at about 3:30 in United States Capitol room number S220, the back portion of Senator Mansfield's Capitol office, the confrontation involved Senators Bayh, Baker, Griffin, Byrd, Spong, Dole, Ervin, and Hruska, as well as Bayh aides P. J. Mode and Jason Berman and Mansfield aide Charles Ferris. No one person presided; however, the purpose of the meeting was clear to all:

Could electoral reform—in any compromise form—be brought to a vote? After about one hour, the meeting in S220 adjourned and compromise efforts collapsed.[87]

With the failure of the October 5 meeting to lift the filibuster, electoral reform died in 1970. Within hours of the meeting, the third cloture petition was withdrawn and Senate Joint Resolution 1 was indefinitely postponed. The opposition to the direct vote plan was thus able to block in the Senate a plan that had exhibited so many signs of strength and support. Who were these successful opponents in the Senate?

A detailed analysis of the voting patterns on the two cloture votes of September 17 and September 29[88] has found that the supporters of cloture were a moderately liberal group of senators, while the opponents of cloture were somewhat more clearly conservative. More generally, size of state was not important in the Senate defeat of the direct vote plan; rather Senate Joint Resolution 1 was defeated by a filibuster strongly supported by southern senators and, to a lesser degree, by Mountain state senators together with allied support by Republicans. Together, these senators compromised a clear conservative opposition to electoral college reform.[89]

The result of these events was that electoral reform, which had started off the decade of the 1960s as an idea dismissed as without hope, ended in 1970 as a concept widely supported, but defeated. Support for reform of the electoral college, which had been building for five years, was ultimately stymied in the Senate. The electoral college would continue unreformed into the 1970s.

ELECTORAL REFORM IN THE 1970S

The defeat of Senate Joint Resolution 1 in October 1970 was a profoundly disheartening occurrence to electoral reform supporters. Not only was the momentum for the direct vote broken by the adjournment of the Ninety-first Congress but also any new electoral reform proposal would again have to follow the same tortuous Congressional route as before—of committee hearings, struggles for committee votes, floor consideration, and agonies in getting a final affirmative vote—and in both houses of Congress. Certainly discouragement over this prospect would have been sufficient to shake even the most committed direct vote advocate. Despite this, direct vote supporters, led by Birch Bayh in the Senate, continued to work to abolish the electoral college.

The landslide presidential election of 1972 seemingly did little to heighten any sense of urgency concerning reform of the electoral college. Although the direct election proposal was regularly introduced with each new Congress, it was gathering little new support. The only formal congressional actions during this period were the little-noticed 1973 hearings of the Senate Judiciary Subcommittee on Constitutional Amendments.[90] The printed record of the two days of hearings provided useful information on the status of electoral college reform as of 1973, but the hearings themselves were largely ignored by both press and public.

Indeed, prior to the 1976 election, much of the impetus for electoral reform appeared to have dissipated. But the potentially disastrous shortcomings of the electoral college system were dramatically revealed in the Carter-Ford contest (see pp. 80–84, above). This did serve to revive interest in electoral reform in the final three years of the 1970s.

THE POLITICS OF ELECTORAL COLLEGE REFORM: 1977–1979[91]

In January 1977, the Judiciary Committee[92] launched the most extensive Senate hearings on electoral reform since 1967–68.[93] In five days, thirty-eight witnesses testified, compiling a printed record (along with various exhibits and statements) totalling 600 pages. This activity itself generated additional press and editorial commentary concerning electoral reform.

The single most dramatic event of 1977 was the unexpected and strong endorsement of the direct vote plan by President Carter on March 22, despite widely reported assumptions that he would take a much weaker or limited reform position.[94] Thus, for the first time in the twentieth century, a president had personally committed himself to the abolition of the electoral college. It has been suggested by some that President Carter's conversion to direct election may have been due to the persuasive efforts of Vice President Mondale, long a supporter of direct election. It is also possible that missionary work by a coalition of interest-group leaders may have been significant. Certainly, Carter was not disposed to ignore a letter soliciting his support jointly signed by the presidents of the American Bar Association, the United Auto Workers, Common Cause, the AFL-CIO, the Chamber of Commerce of the United States, and the League of Women Voters.[95]

The significance of the Carter endorsement, however, would prove to be less than was initially thought. The direct vote plan was part of a package of presidential electoral reform proposals such as election-day voter registration and public financing of congressional elections. All the other proposals in the package proved to be politically weak, and all were dead within six months. Direct election suffered throughout 1977 from association with these political losers. In addition, the endorsement by the president also made abolition of the electoral college somewhat a partisan issue, putting Republican traditional electoral reform supporters such as Senators Baker, Bellman, and Dole somewhat on the spot. Finally, presidential support was not actively forthcoming, throughout 1977 and 1978, because of President Carter's deep and necessary preoccupation with crucial issues such as the Panama Canal treaty, energy legislation, and the Middle East.

After the Carter announcement, little immediate Senate activity was evident. Rather, what was underway was quiet vote-counting, both in the Senate committee, and on the floor. In mid-March, letters went out from Senator Birch Bayh (D., Ind.), leader of the direct vote advocates, to thirty-one uncommitted senators pointing out to them how recent studies by political scientists had shown that their states were disadvantaged by the electoral college.[96] Besides noting the disadvantages specifically suffered by the voters of their state, Senator Bayh went on to observe:

Contrary to the thinking that prevailed a few years ago, residents of small to medium sized states are the most disadvantaged group of voters under the electoral college system. I am sure you will share my concern over this latest evidence of the unfairness of the electoral college.

Despite this low-level activity, the direct vote constitutional amendment appeared by late spring to be losing momentum, and to be running into formidable committee difficulties and sticky floor scheduling problems should it even be able to get out of committee. Adding to the difficulties were the uncertainties as to the views of the Black Congressional Caucus and the outright opposition to electoral college abolition on the part of some black leaders such as Clarence Mitchell, revered (and retiring) head of the NAACP. Meanwhile, the floor calendar for Senate business in July and September-October was filling up, largely with energy legislation.[97]

On June 22, however, meaningful activity in the Senate Judiciary Committee finally took place. A test vote to refer the constitutional amendment back to subcommittee to kill it, was defeated by a 9-to-8 vote,[98] thus indicating the full committee votes were possibly there to pass the direct vote plan—if the committee would be allowed to come to a vote on passage.

This is not always easy, especially when a bill is strongly opposed by the committee chairman, as well as by both the ranking majority and minority members of the committee. Speculation grew that the bill floor manager, Senator Bayh, might be forced to try to bypass the committee totally by having the bill put directly on the Senate calendar.[99] This expedient, as difficult and even desperate as it might be, appeared to be possibly the only option left to electoral reform supporters in light of a committee filibuster that was begun and led by Senator William L. Scott (R., Va.), ranking minority member.

For five committee meetings following the June 22 test vote, Senator Scott held fast to his filibuster, preventing the committee from taking up the direct vote bill. Suddenly, on July 13, an agreement was struck allowing for a committee vote on passage of the direct vote plan "on or before September 16." In return, committee hearings on electoral college reform were reopened, with Scott selecting a number of the new witnesses.[100]

These renewed hearings were held on four days between July 20 and August

2, 1977, and included testimony supporting retention of the electoral college by political scientists Judith Best, Aaron Wildavsky, Herbert Storing, and Martin Diamond, who tragically died in the Committee room shortly after completing his testimony. Despite the compilation of an extensive additional hearing record during these reopened hearings totaling over 500 pages,[101] these July hearings seem not to have had any effect on either the perceptions or votes of the members of the Senate Judiciary Committee, as would be shown when the committee met to vote on September 15.

At this crucial committee meeting, three substitute amendments were first offered—to replace the direct election plan respectively with: the automatic plan (defeated 10 to 8), the proportional plan (defeated, but only just, by a 8-to-7 vote), and the district plan (defeated 8 to 6).[102] One more motion was finally made by the opponents: Senator Allen proposed that the runoff election be replaced by a joint session of Congress contingency arrangement. This also lost, but only by an 8 to 7 decision. Finally, Senate Joint Resolution 1 came to a final vote, and by the thinnest of margins—8 to 7—was approved by the Judiciary committee. The vote proved to be identical to that of the test vote nearly two months earlier, prior to the reopened hearings.[103]

As of September 1977, direct election had triumphed by emerging from committee. By being approved by the Judiciary committee, electoral reform appeared to some to be a proposal now ready to sweep through the Senate, subsequently to pass the House, and then to be ratified by the states. Once again, however, the Senate itself was to intervene, as in 1970, to stymie electoral college reform. What happened to electoral reform in the Senate in 1977 and 1978 can be summarized in two words: *agendas* and *procedures*.

Despite the favorable Judiciary committee vote in September, the business of the Senate, and especially the massive logjam resulting from the deadlocked energy conference committee, kept Senate Joint Resolution 1 from being scheduled for floor consideration during the remaining months of 1977. Further, Senate Majority Leader Robert C. Byrd (D., W. Va.) proved to be extremely reluctant to schedule the bill for any floor consideration throughout 1977 and 1978 until direct vote supporters could show him that they had 60 firm votes sufficient to impose cloture on the almost inevitable filibuster.

Throughout late 1977 and into 1978, the struggle for cloture commitments and floor time went on. By the summer of 1978, however, an additional problem was proving to be an overwhelming obstacle—the end-of-session crunch of legislative business. It should be noted that as the legislative calendar slips toward the end of any Congress, a controversial bill, such as the direct vote plan, becomes highly susceptible to filibuster and other delaying tactics, the fate of electoral college reform in 1970.

This also caused the demise of electoral reform efforts in 1978, as other legislation gained priority over direct election in the claim for precious floor time in the hectic final weeks. The result was that Senate Joint Resolution 1 died with the adjournment of Congress in October 1978, without even being taken up on the floor of the Senate. The most that direct vote supporters were able to salvage was a commitment on the part of the Senate leadership to bring electoral college reform to the floor early in the new Congress, in 1979. Once again, electoral reform, which had blossomed forth as a reform about to be accomplished, was put on the shelf to be considered at a later time.[104]

The direct vote plan did come before the Senate in the first half of 1979. One factor inhibiting reform efforts in 1979, however, was the realization that they would be irrelevant to the forthcoming presidential election of 1980. There was a feeling that it is better to wait and see what happens in the 1980 election—an attitude that so often has hindered electoral reform efforts in the last two years of a presidential term.

Enhancing electoral reform chances in 1979, however, were fundamental changes in the composition of the Senate Judiciary Committee. In January 1979, Senator Edward Kennedy (D., Mass.) assumed the chairmanship of that key committee from retiring Senator James Eastland (D., Miss.). With the retirement of reform opponents Eastland and William Scott (R., Va.) together with the deaths in 1978 of Senators John McClellan (D., Ark.) and James Allen (D., Ala.), the committee was a vastly more receptive forum for electoral reform efforts than it had been in the past.

On January 15, 1979, Senator Bayh introduced Senate Joint Resolution 28, incorporating the identical proposal for a constitutional amendment providing for the direct election of the president that had been debated for the preceding decade. This time the resolution was not referred to the Senate Judiciary Committee for possible hearings and delay as it had been in past years. In light of the sweeping changes in the leadership of that committee, there seemed little question the committee would favor direct election. Instead, the resolution was "held at the desk" for floor consideration early in the new Congress. Such early action would have the major advantage of minimizing the impact of a filibuster against reform. During this period both floor manager Bayh and Senate Majority Leader Robert Byrd were busily counting votes—both for passage (requiring two-thirds, or 67 votes if all senators were present) and for terminating debate (needing 60 votes).

Finally, on March 14, 1979, the direct vote plan was called up for Senate consideration—the first time any electoral reform plan had formally come before the entire Senate since the "Daniels substitute" involving the proportional and district vote plans twenty-three years earlier in March 1956 (see pp. 151–53 above). (Of course the Senate had debated electoral reform at length nine years earlier in 1970, but the question before it then was merely whether to "take up" the matter. The filibuster of that year precluded any formal consideration of direct election.)

The direct vote plan, however, did not stay on the floor very long. There was considerable criticism of the decision to bring the measure directly to the Senate without 1979 hearings on the part of the Judiciary committee. In a compromise move on March 15, Senator Bayh agreed to the referral of the resolution to the committee for such hearings. In return, however, he secured an agreement that the direct vote plan would be automatically reported back to the Senate for floor consideration by June 1 and that opponents would not filibuster a motion to bring it up on the floor. Thus, although some modest delay was the inevitable result, Bayh achieved the promise of floor action later in 1979 while avoiding the impression of trying to ram the measure through the Senate without following proper committee procedures.

The Judiciary Committee Subcommittee on the Constitution held four days of hearings in late March and April.[105] By the time the hearings were over, the committee had conducted a grand total of forty-seven days of hearings on the electoral college since 1966 and had produced seven volumes of testimony totaling 4,395 pages. Probably no issue of the 1960s and 1970s has been so overstudied and with less to show for it than electoral college reform.

Much of the testimony at the 1979 hearings was predictable and repetitive of earlier hearings. Law professor John D. Feerick, campaign consultant Doug Bailey, and author James A. Michener supported the abolition of the electoral college and the passage of the direct vote plan. Political scientists Harry Bailey, Walter Berns, Judith Best, and Jeane Kirkpatrick, along with columnist George Will and author Theodore White, urged its retention. Theodore White, for example, expressed grave concern over the possibility of fraud tainting a direct national vote for president. The present electoral college, he argued,

is like a vessel. We have a vessel now with 50 separate containers. They slosh around a bit, but they are contained. If you have this whole pack of 75 million votes cascading in all at once, the sloshing and the temptation to stall here or there will, I think, be enormous. This is such a gamble, Senator, that it appalls me to think of it.[106]

Two questions did arise that became central concerns later during floor debate: what states are advantaged or disadvantaged by the existing system, and what would be the consequences of its abolition for minority interests—and especially for black voting power? The question of state advantage was discussed in a pair of memoranda prepared by the Congressional Research Service and introduced into the record. The first analysis, prepared at the request of direct vote opponent Senator Strom Thurmond (R., S.C.) consisted of a table contrasting each state's percentage of the electoral college vote with its percentage of the 1976 presidential vote. The findings showed that 31 states (all small or medium-sized states) and the District of Columbia would lose influence by a change to direct election.[107] This analysis, of course, dealt only with state advantage arising from the constant two electoral votes allocated to each state independent of its population and failed to consider in any fashion state advantage or disadvantage resulting from the winner-take-all feature of the electoral college. (For a fuller discussion of the complex question of the biases of the electoral college, see chapter 5, pp. 119–30 and the sources cited there.)

The author of the Congressional Research Service study, Joseph B. Gorman, acknowledged the limitations of the analysis in a subsequent second, much more detailed evaluation that concluded:

There are two independent biases operating in the electoral college. One, which was illustrated by the March 5, 1979 computation . . . definitely favors the less populous states. A second, the general ticket, definitely favors the more populous states. It has thus far lain beyond the expertise of political scientists to prove quantitatively and conclusively which of these biases is more significant. The most persuasive evidence tends to support Yunker and Longley's conclusion that the present system gives a significant advantage to the most populous states, a smaller advantage to the less populous states, and disadvantages to the greatest extent the medium-sized states, having between 4 and 12 electoral votes, which are too large to benefit to any significant degree from the "constant two" but are too small to derive significant benefit from the general ticket system.[108]

The other issue underlined by the 1979 Senate hearings was that of minority interests. Two witnesses stated their strong opposition to the direct vote on the ground that it would diminish the political significance of their organization and the population it represented. Howard M. Squadron, president of the American Jewish Congress, testified on April 3 that "such innovations as a direct election would have unpredictable and possibly baneful results"[109] and agreed with the view that "the electoral college is a venerable institution that gives greater weight to Jews in the heavily populated states."[110]

On the same day, Vernon E. Jordan, president of the National Urban League, spoke, on behalf of a coalition of black organizations, of "what we believe would be the disastrous impact of direct elections on black people."[111] In colloquy with committee chairman Bayh, he emphasized: "As I said, Mr. Chairman, we like it [the electoral college]. We see our vested interest in it. We choose to retain it."[112]

The irony of these hearings was that they could not lead to any committee vote. By the motion adopted by the entire Senate on March 15, the committee was automatically discharged of the bill following the hearings, without a committee vote. A formal report, however, was necessary, and this was released in May.[113] The committee majority expressed its frustration with the entire issue:

The Committee has been impressed throughout the hearings on S. J. Res. 28 with the admissions of the Electoral College's most avid proponents that they themselves do not really know how it works. No better evidence of this imprecision exists than their willingness to defend the electoral college for reasons diametrically opposed to each other. Therefore, the Committee has heard that the present system favors large states and thereby urban interests; yet should be retained because it favors small states. That the unit rule serves to discourage third parties because they cannot pool votes across state lines; yet it benefits legitimate interest groups within states (although they too are prevented from pooling votes across state lines). That the electoral college pays special attention to the needs of minorities, yet it also magnifies the majority.[114]

Minority views were filed by three Republican senators, Orrin Hatch (R., Utah), Strom Thurmond (R., S.C.), and Alan Simpson (R., Wyo.), who stated their strong opposition to the direct vote plan and agreed that "if it passes, it will be the most deeply radical amendment which has ever entered the Constitution of the United States."[115]

Following these three months of hearings and the filing of majority and minority reports, the direct vote plan returned to the Senate floor. On June 21, Senate Joint Resolution 28 was called up for consideration, and debate continued on June 26 and 27. Following a week's recess for the Fourth of July, the Senate resumed its deliberations on Monday, July 9. After two weeks of off-and-on debate the New York Times reported, "Speakers frequently addressed an empty chamber, and leaders of both sides had difficulty findings enough participants to use up the allotted time."[116]

Behind the dreary debate, however, political strategies were being executed. Bayh had long worried about a filibuster sapping the momentum of electoral reform and had in fact filed a motion for cloture as early as June 27, the third day of debate. He argued that a cloture vote was necessary not only to assure that the Senate would finally have a chance to vote on electoral college reform but also to limit the "opponents' power to attach unrelated amendments to the measure."[117] As an example of such an amendment, Bayh cited the proposal by Senator Harry F. Byrd (Ind., Va.) requiring a balanced federal budget.[118]

There was, of course, a political motive for Senator Bayh's motion for a cloture vote. Such a motion required only 60 votes—less than the possible 67 necessary to pass a constitutional amendment. Cloture might provide an initial psychological victory, making that final 67-vote goal easier.

Late on July 9, direct vote opponents Hatch and Thurmond sprung a trap on Senator Bayh. Would Senator Bayh, they asked, be willing to let the resolution come up for a vote on the next day? After all, he had been insistent on a cloture vote allowing the Senate to vote. Let's now agree, they said, on such a vote being taken. Bayh was in an agonizing dilemma. For eleven years he had been fighting for a Senate vote on the direct vote plan. This vote had been prevented in 1970 by a filibuster on the motion to take up the topic. How could he resist this opportunity?

Direct vote supporters, however, were not ready for a final vote. For weeks they had been geared up for a numbing filibuster. It was unlikely that Bayh's forces could solidify 67 votes by the next day. Therefore, he suggested, perhaps some more time to evaluate the complex issues in the resolution would be helpful, especially in light of the unrelated pending amendments.

The direct vote opponents then closed the trap: if all amendments to the resolution were withdrawn,[119] would Senator Bayh agree to its being voted on the next day? Outflanked and outmaneuvered, Bayh had to agree. The Senate thereupon adopted a unanimous consent agreement providing that Senate Joint Resolution 28, the direct vote plan unencumbered by any side issues, would be voted on by the Senate at 5 P.M. on Tuesday, July 10.

The result was a debacle for electoral college reform. With 99 senators voting[120] and the resolution consequently requiring 66 votes for passage, it received 51 votes, 15 votes short. Forty-eight senators opposed it.[121] Electoral reform supporters, who for so many years had sought a Senate vote directly on the merits of the direct vote plan, had received a crushing setback. As the *Congressional Quarterly* concluded, "the conclusive margin of defeat July 10 may postpone for years any further effort to revamp the Presidential election system."[122]

What happened to account for this? Prior to the July 10 vote, growing weight had been given to the issue of minority interests. On July 4, the *New York Times* had reported: "In the foreground of the debate for the first time this year is an argument by minority groups that abolition of the electoral college would deprive them of political influence that is disproportionate to their numbers, of the asserted power to deliver large-state bonanzas through bloc voting."[123] This claim took several forms. Black leaders such as Vernon Jordan and Eddie Williams argued that a vote to abolish the electoral college was a vote to diminish black political power. Jewish spokesmen led by Howard M. Squadron of the American Jewish Congress[124] likewise lobbied strenuously against the resolution. The electoral college was portrayed as a bulwark of Jewish, black, and liberal interests. As Nathan Z. Deshowitz of the Ameircan Jewish Congress argued: "Most of the minorities and liberal influences are concentrated in urban areas, in the large electoral vote states. The present system favors liberal interests."[125] These pressures influenced "a group of liberal Senators of both parties who were apparently swayed by the arguments of black and Jewish groups that their members would lose political leverage that they enjoyed under the electoral college if that institution was abandoned."[126]

Key liberals who ended up voting *against* electoral reform were Senators Daniel Patrick Moynihan (D., N.Y.), Bill Bradley (D., N.J.), Paul S. Sarbanes (D., Md.), Charles H. Percy (R., Ill.), Lowell P. Weiker (R., Conn.), Edmund S. Muskie (D., Me.), and Wilbur S. Cohen (R., Me.). For opposite reasons, senators such as Moynihan, Bradley, and Percy from large states joined with senators such as Muskie and Cohen from small states in voting against the direct vote plan. An unusual voting configuration resulted, crossing party, ideological, and interest lines.[127]

The final vote of 51 for and 48 against was made up of 12 Republicans for, 28 against, and 39 Democrats for and 20 against. While most Democrats supported the direct vote plan and most Republicans opposed it, patterns were somewhat muddied by complex cross pressures. Eleven of the 18 southern Democrats opposed direct vote, but 7 supported it. This was an increase in support for electoral reform over 1970 when only 3 southern Democratic senators had voted for cloture on the direct vote plan. Republican support for the direct vote plan, however, fell in contrast with 1970: over two-thirds of the Republican senators opposed direct vote in 1979, whereas the party had been essentially split in 1970. Opposition to reform had also increased over the decade among northern Democrats: 9 of 41 voted against direct vote in 1979, while only 2 had voted against cloture in 1970. In short, the 1979 vote, in contrast to 1970, showed decreased Republican and northern Democratic support and somewhat increased southern Democratic support for direct vote.

In terms of regional patterns, direct vote enjoyed its greatest strength in the Midwest, where 16 of the 24 senators of both parties voted in favor. Electoral reform also did respectably in the South, receiving support from 10 of the 26 southern senators. Its weakest regions were the East and the West—areas containing both the very largest and the very smallest states. It is perhaps most revealing of the confusion of the July 10 vote that the 54 senators from the smaller states—with 8 electoral votes or less—split down the middle—26 for and 27 against.[128]

Regardless of the reason why each senator voted for or against the measure, the result was starkly clear. Electoral college reform, which had been seeking a clear Senate vote on its merits for a decade, had finally received that vote—and had conclusively lost. For the time being, until some electoral crisis should draw the attention of the American people and the Senate of the United States back to the necessity of electoral reform, the electoral college would continue into the 1980s with its quirks, peculiarities, and distortions unreformed.

Perhaps some future election will rekindle the fires. At that point, all that will be necessary to abolish the electoral college will be favorable committee action in the Senate, 60 votes in the full chamber for cloture of the likely filibuster, a final two-thirds vote in the Senate for passage, favorable committee action in the House, a two-thirds vote there for passage, and ratification by both houses of three-quarters of the state legislatures. The road to reform is rocky indeed and the prospects quite uncertain, yet it is to the credit of the direct vote supporters that they are willing to travel again and again down that difficult road.

8

Today's Alternative: Direct Vote or the Status Quo

The examination of electoral reform efforts over the years has shown how each halfway measure, from the district system of the nineteenth century to the proportional system advanced most prominently after World War II, has had its day and been found wanting. The alternatives have failed either because of inherent defects or because they would have wrought fundamental changes in the political power alignments of the nation. Thus the real choice today is between two alternatives. Either the country will continue with the existing electoral college system or it will shift to a direct popular vote.

The advantages of a direct vote are immediately apparent. There would no longer be the chance that the candidate who won the most popular votes could be deprived of the presidency through the mathematical vagaries of the electoral college. The massive disfranchisement of the minority voters in each state would be ended once and for all, with each person's vote registered directly and equally in the decisive national count. No one's vote would be totally eclipsed or magnified to many times its rightful weight because of the chance factor of state residence. Localized corruption in a single large state would be far less likely to determine the outcome of the national election. The office of elector would disappear, so that no "electoral Benedict Arnold" could take it in his own hands to sway the outcome of an election. Splinter parties would no longer have the ability to shift the outcome in pivotal states or to capitalize on their strength in a handful of states to throw an election into the House of Representatives for decision. If the direct vote system were properly devised, there would no longer be the possibility of a contingent election in Congress where a prospective chief executive could be subjected to unconscionable pressures to "sell out" on major issues as the price of his election.

BASIC ISSUES

Even if these apparent advantages are conceded, however, the opponents of direct vote can and do raise serious questions about its implementation: Are our politics advanced to a point where we are ready for a single national vote for president? Would it undermine American federalism and our two-party system? Would it have a disturbing impact on the political balance of the country, on our entire political stability? The late historian Clinton Rossiter, dubious about the advisability of change, warned that "we should hesitate a long time before replacing a humpty-dumpty system that works with a neat one that will blow up in our faces." Would-be reformers, he cautioned, "are digging into the foundations of the state—always a dangerous thing to do."[1]

The "Concurrent Majority" Arguments

Behind the arguments of many thoughtful opponents of the direct vote is a concern that we would be substituting a kind of naked, unrestrained majoritarianism for a system that obliges the national parties and presidential candidates to offer moderate programs acceptable to a wide range of economic, geographic, and political interests. The electoral college, Carl Becker argued, is a major factor in forcing both political parties to hew close to the middle of the road, in deterring them from the adoption of "pure" ideologies and taking an uncompromising stand in favor of any single economic or class group. "This system," he wrote, "makes it impossible for any political party to win a national election, even though it has a majority of the popular votes cast, unless the votes it polls are properly distributed throughout the country; and no party has much chance of getting such a distribution if it represents exclusively the interests of any section or class. It can get the necessary strategic distribution of the popular vote only if it is willing to appeal to the interests of many sections and to the interests of all classes—agriculture and industry, capital and labor, rich and poor, progressives and conservatives—in a sufficient number of states to win a majority of the electoral votes."[2]

The roots of Becker's argument may be found in John C. Calhoun's theory of the concurrent majority. "There are," Calhoun wrote, "two different modes in which the sense of the community may be taken; one, simply, by the right of suffrage, unaided; the other, by the right through a proper organism. Each collects the sense of the majority. But one regards numbers only and considers the whole community as a unit, having but one common interest throughout, and collects the sense of the greater number of the whole as that of the community. The other, on the contrary, regards interest as well as number—considering the community as made up of different and conflicting interests, as far as the action of the government is concerned—and takes the sense of each, through its majority or appropriate organ, and the united sense of all as the sense of the entire community. The former of these I shall call the numerical, or absolute majority; and the latter, the concurrent or constitutional majority."[3]

Calhoun, of course, developed his theory of the concurrent majority to justify the actions of states in nullifying the acts of the federal government. But the theory is still attractive and valid in many ways. Certainly the entire system of checks and balances, with its distribution of varying powers among federal, state, and local governments, is designed to prevent any temporary majority from assuming absolute power and negating the rights of minorities. It is one of the most vital—indeed indispensable—features of the American system of government.

But is the theory applicable to the election of a single individual—the president of the United States? Would the direct vote for president in any way negate or restrict the protections built into our constitutional system? The answer is clearly no. A president elected by direct vote would still have to win the approval of Congress for his major programs. Special district and state interests would still have a powerful voice through their regular representation in the U.S. Senate and House. The long chain of constitutional amendments designed to protect the rights of the people, starting with the Bill of Rights and extending into our own century, would remain in full force. The Judiciary would still function as an essential check on unbridled presidential power. The state and local governments would retain their special preserves of power and authority. One can recognize "concurrent majority" as a touchstone of the American system but still deny that it does or should have anything to do with the process by which the American people elect their chief executive.

What then of Carl Becker's argument? Would direct election of the president undermine the forces working for appeasement, for conciliation, and for compromise in the American political system? Would rigid ideologies and inflammatory class appeals become more dominant? Again, there is no palpable evidence to support the allegation. In fact, it must be acknowledged that the existing system does not invariably create perfect moderation and balance in our presidential campaigns. One may admire Harry Truman's political courage in 1948, but by any dispassionate analysis it must be conceded that his campaign was based on blatant class and ethnic appeals. For uncompromising ideology, no presidential candidates of modern times have outdone Barry Goldwater in the 1964 campaign and George McGovern in the 1972 contest. These campaigns may be more the exception than the rule, but they have happened, the electoral college notwithstanding.

Secondly, it may be asked if the actual operation of the electoral college has anything to do with the moderation of political life in the United States. If most Americans think they are voting for president directly anyway, it is hard to see how a constitutional legitimization of their direct participation would change their attitude or that of the political leaders. It is suggested that the electoral college makes presidential candidates and parties appeal to all sections and all classes. Senator Hugh Scott of Pennsylvania, chairman of the Republican National Committee in the 1948 campaign and a strategist in the Eisenhower and

Nixon races, suggested in an interview with one of this book's authors that the necessity of seeking state-by-state victories obliges a presidential candidate to recognize particular state and regional problems—irrigation and grazing problems in the West, the outmigration of industry in the East, TVA policies in the Tennessee Valley, or East-West trade in the Dakotas. Scott's argument— echoed by many opponents of the direct vote before and after him (we will spare the reader the dozens of possible citations)—is an interesting one; if valid it would be a compelling reason to resist the direct vote. But is it valid? Just because *states qua* states would not participate in the choice of a president, would a candidate be able to ignore vast classes or regions and have any prospect of winning? We think not. He would still have to fashion a national majority out of votes from hundreds of geographic areas, class and economic groups, and ideological camps. No single group could give him the election. In fact, the candidate might be more willing than now to consider special local problems, since every vote in every state would count—even if the opposing party was all but sure to carry that state.

In the final analysis, it must be recognized that the electoral college today—barring the catastrophe of rebel electors or an election thrown into the House—is nothing more than a counting device and a highly distorted one at that. Consciously or not, every candidate for president aims first at winning the support of a majority of the whole American people, because winning an electoral college majority without a popular vote majority is a risky undertaking. Before the 1964 election Barry Goldwater's strategists thought they might achieve an electoral college victory by combining the electoral votes of the South with those of the conservative western Mountain states and the farm-oriented Midwest. They consciously wrote off the popular-vote–heavy states like California, New York, Pennsylvania, and New Jersey, admitting, at least implicitly, a national popular vote defeat.[4] A similar hope for electoral college victory in the face of a popular vote loss was attributed to McGovern campaign strategists in 1972, though the seriousness with which the tactic was approached is not clear. Such strategies, bankrupt from the start, predictably end in overwhelming and deserved defeat. And if no serious presidential candidate will consciously design a strategy that admits popular vote defeat in the hope of electoral college victory, would it not be better to have a popular vote alone? Even if there were predictable regional patterns that permitted a candidate to localize his campaign to win in the electoral college while losing the popular vote, would we want to accept such a system? Should westerners or southerners or people from any region, by the way the electoral votes are distributed, be accorded some special privilege in electing the president that the rest of us are denied? Indeed, if the system *did* operate this way, there would be all the more reason to abolish it posthaste.

If a direct vote really did lead to increased class antagonisms, ideologically oriented campaigns, and a lack of political moderation, we should have seen these factors at work already in the states, where every governor is chosen today by direct vote of the people. The major states especially could be said to be microcosms of the entire nation. The 1960 census showed that New York and California both had four times as many inhabitants as the entire United States in the first census, that of 1790. Yet direct vote has not led to extremism in the states; indeed, the overwhelming majority of U.S. governors have tended to be practical problem-solvers rather than ideological zealots. Nor has the Senate become a stamping ground for extremists in the wake of the 17th amendment, which shifted the selection of senators from the state legislatures to direct vote of the people.

In fact, direct vote of the people is hardly a risky, untried governmental principle that could "blow up in our faces." It is the tried and true way of electing every nonappointive governmental official in the United States today, and for the most part it has been the common rule and practice since the birth of our nation. Norman Thomas stated the case with accuracy a few years ago when he commented that "no one in his right mind would suggest any way of electing the President of the United States, if you were starting *de nova*, other than by straight popular vote."[5]

The Two-Party System

One of the most frequent criticisms of the proposal for direct election of the president is that it would lead to a plethora of ideologically oriented splinter parties and thus undermine the prevailing two-party system and moderate political tone of the United States. Critics of direct vote have argued that splinter parties would be encouraged because they would see their votes, however small, reflected in the decisive national count, or because it might be easier for them to qualify for places on the ballot. The implication of the argument is that splinter parties are now discouraged because they rarely if ever can win a plurality of the popular votes in any state and thus capture electoral votes.

Replying to the party-splintering argument is complicated in present-day politics by the fact that the major parties appear anemic, if not splintered, even with the electoral college still in existence. In a minor way, one can be pleased that the direct vote was not instituted a decade or two ago, for now political scientists would be writing papers "proving" that the abolition of the electoral college was responsible for the parties' disintegration. The fact, of course, is that the parties are losing ground for a variety of reasons, ranging from mass communications and television commercials to the fact that all major institutions in American life, from business to unions to the press and universities, have dipped precipitously in public acceptance since the 1960s.

Whether the decline of the parties will continue and worsen is uncertain; what does seem clear is that the continued existence or demise of the electoral college will probably have little to do with the change, whichever way it goes. Earlier, when the two-party system seemed far more firmly entrenched than today, the most cogent reasons for its success never included the eighteenth-century presidential voting device of which, in any event, most Americans are ignorant. Rossiter, for instance, suggested that mere forms of government had little to do with two-partyism; rather: "The bounty of the American economy, the fluidity of American society, the remarkable unity of the America people, and, most important, the success of the American experiment have all mitigated against the emergence of large dissenting groups that would seek satisfaction of their special needs through the formation of political parties." Third-party politics is generally radical politics, Rossiter noted, and radical politics has not made much headway in the United States. "Socialism in particular (and in all its varieties) has sailed through rough seas in this country. It foundered long ago, as Werner Sombart remarked despairingly, 'on the shoals of roast beef and apple pie.' "[6]

Many institutional factors have also functioned to discourage third parties, including the basic American system of elections—electoral laws, campaign practices, social patterns, which make it extremely difficult for minor parties to attain even secondary nationwide influence. Contributing factors have been the high cost of political campaigning, the statutory obstacles to getting on the ballot in many states, and the legal status of the major parties as supervisors of elections in many areas.[7] V. O. Key, the noted political scientist, saw the very institution of the presidency as a major reason for the two-party system: "The Presidency, unlike a multiparty cabinet, cannot be parceled out among minuscule parties. The circumstances stimulate coalition within the electorate before the election rather than in parliament after the popular vote. Since no more than two parties can for long compete effectively for the Presidency, two contending groups tend to develop, each built on its constituent units in each of the 50 states."[8]

Many political scientists define the U.S. system of electing representatives in single-member districts, with the plurality deciding, as the basic support for the two-party system. The Frenchman Maurice Duverger and the American E.E. Schattschneider have been the most prominent advocates of this theory. As Schattschneider developed the case, the higher the percentage of the total vote that a party can win, "the more cheaply"—in terms of votes—can it win seats in Congress. Conversely, the smaller the party's percentage, the more "expensive" will be the seats it wins in terms of votes.[9] As an example, in 1964 congressional elections the Democratic party won 57.5 percent of the national vote for the U.S. House but 67.8 percent of the seats. The Republicans won 42.5 percent of the national House vote but only 32.2 percent of the seats. When the Republicans have controlled Congress, they have enjoyed the same inflation of their relative power. But while the system discriminates moderately against the runner-up party, the third, fourth, and fifth parties see their chances of winning actual seats reduced to the vanishing point. Though several hundred thousand votes are cast for minor parties in most congressional elections, minor parties have not held more than two of the 435 U.S. House seats at any time since 1944. The relatively rare occasions that a representative is elected without regular Democratic or Republican affiliation are usually due to intraparty feuds rather than being a mark of success of a minor party.

But why doesn't the single-member district system inflate the leading party's percentage so much that it crushes the second major party as well? The major reason, according to Scahttschneider, is that the defeated party is likely to have sufficient sectional strength to protect itself against annihilation even in a crushing defeat. In modern U.S. politics, it may hold certain center-city or rural districts, for instance, that are so impervious to national trends that they will indefinitely continue a party in power. A second reason is that the defeated party is able to retain a "monopoly of opposition" because it is the natural gathering point for critics of the party in power, and because it can claim that any votes cast for minor party candidates are wasted votes. In U.S. presidential politics, sectional third parties, even when they become strong, are unable to survive because they cannot make a serious bid for the great prize, the presidency.[10] They function only as spoilers as in the cases of George Wallace and Eugene McCarthy. Minor-party candidates could continue to attempt spoiler roles under direct election, but their strength would be only as great as the totality of votes they could muster nationwide. They would be deprived the current system's inducement for spoilers based only on the accident of regional strength (the Wallace model) or key-state support (the McCarthy model).

Another political scientist, Allan P. Sindler, said there is merit in the single-member district argument but that the system alone cannot guarantee the survival of major parties in all circumstances—witness the disintegration of the Federalists and Whigs in earlier years. Nor does the single-member district system, Sindler pointed out, prevent a one-party regional system such as the South has had until recently.[11] The broader reason for two-partyism, he suggested, is "the character of social conflict and consensus in the nation." There must be an acceptance of political disagreement to support a two-party system. Where conflicts are bitter and unreconcilable, Sindler said, "the raw materials for unstable multi-partyism are present," and under some circumstances—as in the U.S. in the 1860s—civil war may ensue. On the other end of the spectrum, there may be election areas so united in their political interests that they cannot generate enough conflict to support two parties. The South's involvement with the race problem is given as an example. "The continuance of stable and moderate two-party systems," Sindler concluded, depends "upon a happy balance struck between consensus and conflict." The United States has generally been able to keep the balance, helped in no small part by the federal structure that offers various levels for the release of political pressures that build up in the system.[12]

In short, the suggestion that the two-party system is primarily or even significantly sustained by the electoral college seems to be a classic case of putting the cart before the horse. And it totally ignores the obvious invitation to minor party manipulation that the electoral college, through its requirement of an absolute majority with contingent election in the House, has always afforded.

The Federal System

The direct election of the president, John F. Kennedy warned in 1956, "would break down the federal system under which most states entered the Union, which provides a system of checks and balances to insure that no area or group shall obtain too much power."[13] Kennedy was echoing the warning of critics, repeated thousands of times since the early nineteenth century, that a direct-vote amendment would be a betrayal of the Great Compromise between the large and small states that was reached at the Constitutional Convention. When the American Bar Association announced early in 1967 that it supported direct popular voting for the presidency, Senator Karl Mundt rose on the Senate floor to voice the argument once again, warning that the ABA's recommendations "would cut the heart out of our federal union of states" and substitute a "mathematical constituency" for the existing combination of geography and population in the electoral base of the Presidency.[14] In his testimony before Bayh's subcommittee just prior to his death in 1977, constitutional scholar Martin Diamond argued that the Constitutional Convention, after thorough-going dispute, had decided to include the states in the choice of the president and that the electoral college remains "a means of preserving Federal democracy, or a Federal element in the electoral process . . . . In my judgment, that has proven invaluable in this centralizing age. When all forces tend to homogenization and centralization, we have a saving remnant of decentralization in the Federal aspect of the election of the American President." To substitute the direct vote, Diamond warned, would be "a dangerous change and an unwarranted one."[15] Two years later, political scientist Aaron Wildavsky was in print with a warning of the dire effects of substituting for the electoral college "the plebiscitary Presidency."

The base of the federal system argument is that the allotment of two extra electoral votes given each state, to correspond with its number of senators, constitutes a central guarantee of the American system, stemming from the Constitutional Convention itself. Historically, however, the argument stands on shaky ground (see page 17, above). The Great Compromise was devised to settle the dispute over representation in Congress, *not* the electoral college. It was presented to the Convention on July 5, 1787, and constituted the agreement that made the federal Union possible. Today it represents a central pillar of the American federal system that few have seriously suggested disturbing. On the other hand, the terms of the Great Compromise, applied almost as an after-thought to electoral college apportionment, were not presented to the Consti-tutional Convention until September 4—a full two months after they had been considered in their essential form, relating to representation in Congress. At no point in the minutes of the Convention can one find any reference to the appli-cation of the Great Compromise to the electoral college's apportionment as im-portant to the federal system or to the overall structure of the Constitution that was adopted. Indeed, it was never mentioned directly at all. Only in *The Feder-alist Papers*, where James Madison argued at one point that the electoral base for the presidency would be a "compound" of national and state factors be-cause of the mixed apportionment base, does the argument appear.[16] But no more than indirect reference was made to the apportionment of the electoral college in the state ratifying conventions, or, in fact, by any of the nation's leaders, until some years after ratification of the Constitution. The argument that the founding fathers viewed the special federal nature of electoral college apportionment as central to the institution of the presidency, or to the entire Constitution, is simply false. The small states thought they would gain special advantage, but by another provision—their equal votes in the House in contin-gent elections.

In fact, the fear of small states that they might be "swallowed up" in a titanic struggle with the large ones has never come true in U.S. history. Experience has shown no clear set of interests held by small states as opposed to large ones. None of the great battles of American political history—in Congress or in presi-dential elections—has been fought on a basis of small versus large states. The arguments have been ideological, economic, and regional but never of the kind that neatly line up the small states on one side and the large ones on the other. The arguments over the years, starting at the Constitutional Convention itself, on the subject of big- versus small-state interests and advantages might well be termed the Great Irrelevancy.

Sometimes it is assumed that the Senate, because of the extra weight it gives to small states, should be a conservative body hostile to the needs of the large states with their large urban population centers. But in our political history, es-pecially in recent decades, this simply has not been the case. In fact, the Senate has generally been more liberal in its composition than the House of Repre-sentatives. The chief reason is probably that almost every senator, except a tiny handful from the most rurally populated states, has one metropolitan center or more within his state and must therefore be responsive to urban needs. On the other hand, there are many representatives from districts that have no metro-politan centers. These men have the freedom to be more conservative in their voting habits, and many of them are.

On paper, it may be shown that the people of thirty-five smaller states and the District of Columbia are "overrepresented" in the electoral college because under the existing apportionment fewer of their population correspond to a single electoral vote than the national average. In Alaska, for instance, the ratio for the 1960 electoral college apportionments and populations was one electoral vote for every 75,389 persons; in South Dakota, one electoral vote for every 170,129 persons (see chart, page 113). The thirty-nine smallest states (plus the District of Columbia), with only 43.2 percent of the national population, could theoretically have controlled an electoral college majority. The special small-state advantages have led observers to suggest that any direct vote amendment would be "butchered in the states." The "underrepresented" people are theoretically those in the fifteen larger states where the ratio shows more persons per electoral vote than the national average—from 337,573 per electoral vote in Kentucky in the 1960s to 392,930 per electoral vote in California.

Any advantage this disparity might be said to give to the people of the smaller states is largely illusory, however. The first reason is that the people of the fifteen states with the least favorable population-to-electoral-vote ratio still inhabit states with 312 electoral votes, easily a majority of the national total of 538. In any election the people of the larger states—if they chose to vote en bloc, which they rarely do—could outvote the people of the thirty-five smaller states and the District of Columbia. In fact, in the 1960s, the twelve largest states could have elected a president with the 281 electoral votes they controlled.* Politicians from the smaller states often complain that the electoral college, in actual practice, works against them, because by the very nature of the general ticket winner-take-all system, national candidates concentrate their efforts in the few biggest states where the shift of just a few hundred or thousand votes may change large blocs of electoral votes and determine the national outcome. Computer studies have in fact shown that the citizens of larger states have a greater chance to cast the decisive votes under the electoral college system than do citizens of smaller states, with the most disadvantaged states under the electoral college being the medium-to-small states with from 4 to 14 electoral votes (see "The Biases of the Electoral College," pp. 119–30, above).

A second reason that "overrepresentation" of a state is an illusory advantage is that the people of a state do not vote unanimously for one presidential candidate or another, although the unit vote system of casting electoral votes may make it look as if they had. But it is *people* who have preferences, not states. The right to cast one's vote for the presidential candidate one prefers—and to

* New York, California, Pennsylvania, Illinois, Ohio, Texas, Michigan, New Jersey, Florida, Massachusetts, Indiana, and North Carolina (1960s electoral vote apportionments. Those in the 1970s were not substantially different.).

see that vote added meaningfully to the votes of like-minded citizens throughout the United States and included in the national count—is the citizen's important right. If a voter finds he is in the minority in his state under the prevailing general ticket system, then he knows his vote will be completely negated in the national electoral vote count. His state may have enjoyed some theoretical right—and in fact cast an electoral vote several times over its actual right by population—but for the individual on the losing side, the alleged right is an empty one indeed.

To argue that these supposed mathematical advantages of small-state citizens under the federal system are important ones is to make a travesty of the entire federal system itself. For, in truth, there are rich benefits for the citizens of all the states stemming from federalism in America. But they stem from entirely different grounds: from the representation each district and state enjoys in Congress, from the right of each state to fashion governmental policies particularly suited to its own citizens, from the protections from overbearing federal power that stem from the special rights of the states under the Constitution. If one wants to preserve states' rights and the American federal system, there are many better ways to do so than by preserving the fictional advantages of the electoral college. Improving municipal government, strengthening state legislatures, getting the states to shoulder an increasing share of the complex problems of our modern-day industrialized society—these are the ways to make federalism a viable institution for the benefit of all.

Indeed, if the electoral college has had any real impact on American federalism, it may have been in a way that weakened the role of the small states rather than enlarging or guaranteeing it. For experience has shown that the natural emphasis on the electoral vote blocs of the biggest states under the existing system has eclipsed the presidential chances of many outstanding public servants who had the misfortune of coming from the smaller states. In a 1966 Supreme Court brief, the state of Delaware pointed out that 4 states—New York, Ohio, Massachusetts, and Virginia—had seen 21 of their citizens elected president for terms with a total of 111 years service. But Delaware pointed out that it was one of 36 states that had never witnessed the election of one of its citizens as president. Confining its analysis to the last century alone, Delaware showed that of the 100 major-party nominations for president and vice president from 1868 through 1964, citizens of New York were nominated in 24 instances and that citizens of 5 other large states—California, Illinois, Indiana, Massachusetts, and Ohio—had accounted for another 44 of the nominations. Twenty-six states, itself included, had been totally excluded from nominations. Of the 13 original states, the Delaware brief continued, 8 had never elected a president in the 45 elections since the founding of the country—Connecticut, Delaware, Georgia, Maryland, North Carolina, Rhode Island, South Carolina, and Vermont. In the 1960 census, these states had a combined population of

18,213,449—substantially more than the 16,782,304 population of New York, the modern-day "mother of presidents."

The natural rejoinder to Delaware's argument, of course, is that service in the state government of New York or another large state is more likely to train a man for rigors of the presidency and give him the national exposure he needs than is service in a small state. But even conceding that such factors may give large-state citizens a better break in many elections, the total from the presidency suggests real inequalities arising from the premium placed on big-state electoral vote blocs.*

Since the earliest days of the Republic, some American statesmen have recognized the dangers of placing states ahead of people in the election of the common national officer, the president. "The question of who shall be elected President is not a state, but a national question," Representative Jabez D. Hammond of New York declared on the House floor in 1816: "The President is an officer who exists for the benefit of the people of the United States, and not for any one state or states but by the people."[17] In 1848, President Polk declared: "If both houses represent the states and the people, so does the President. The President represents in the executive department the whole people of the United States, as each member of the legislative department represents portions of them."[18]

In 1956, Senator John Pastore of Rhode Island said that he had never heard—as a member of the Rhode Island legislature, as governor, or as senator from that small state—anyone in Rhode Island talk of the state's special power in presidential elections through its two extra electoral votes or "the power which would be abandoned if we went to popular elections." But Pastore said he had heard people say what "a shame" it was that the man who gets the most votes might lose the election.[19] At another point in the same year's debate, Pastore denied that his state of Rhode Island would be "making any sacrifice" if the electoral college were discarded for direct vote. "I believe that the power of a Rhode Islander lies in the fact that he has the right of franchise to vote for the President of the United States," Pastore said. "If more Rhode Islanders want a Republican to be President than a Democrat, and more people in the country agree with them than agree with other people who favor a different candidate, the more popular candidate should be elected President. . . . The man who has received the most votes is the man who ought to be President, whether he is from the South or the North or the East or the West. We are all Americans. We

* Major exceptions to party nominations of large-state candidates in recent times include the 1936 Republican selection of Alfred M. Landon of Kansas, the same party's 1964 nomination of Barry Goldwater of Arizona, and the 1972 Democratic nomination of George McGovern of South Dakota—ironically the three biggest losers of the last half-century. But the emphasis on candidates just because of their big-state ties, which Delaware complained of, may be dissipating in any event (see page 224, below).

are all one nation. . . . The President is the President of all the people, not the President of the states."[20]

The case for disentangling presidential elections from special state voting power was put another way, and with characteristic wisdom, by Norman Thomas. "Most of us people, when we are stirring up for political purposes, are not such terrific state patriots," Thomas said in 1949. "It seems to me, at least in the climate where I have spent most of my life, that the average American's great ambition is to get to Southern California or Florida or parts of Texas before he dies, perhaps to condition him for the hereafter in one way or another. Now, under those circumstances, I think it is rather ridiculous for us to claim such passion and fervor for 'Delaware über alles,' or something like that."[21]

Indeed, those who would preserve the existing electoral college because of its ties to the federal system ought to consider the effect on American federalism if the electoral college were again to elect a candidate who lost in the popular vote. How could this be explained to the people? That the voters of certain states—any way the mathematical vagaries of the electoral college might misfire—should have more weight in the election of the president than the voters of other states, which make up a majority of the country? That for some mysterious reason connected with the federal system, the votes of people from Wyoming and New Hampshire were to be given more weight than the votes of people from New York and California—or possibly the reverse? How would these inequalities be explained in the day of "one man, one vote"?

The question is by no means abstract. In 1976, for instance, our analysis has shown that the slightest variation in the electoral vote of some northern states would have elected Gerald Ford president despite Jimmy Carter's strong popular vote lead. The scenario of a potential Ford win in electoral votes while Carter won the popular vote was easy to foresee weeks before the election because of Carter's lopsided leads in many southern states that year. But consider what would have happened if Ford had actually won the electoral vote while Carter retained his popular vote lead. Would there be any rational way to explain to southerners that their votes—because they were geographically concentrated—were of less import and weight than votes cast elsewhere in America? That some hocus-pocus in an eighteenth-century vote-counting device was more important than the popular will? This is the one totally compelling, irrefutable argument that causes defenders of the existing system to founder time and again. There can be no rational explanation for retaining the arcane counting system when one projects it forward to the day that it actually causes the system to blow up in our faces again. To preserve such a system for abstract reasons incomprehensible to all but a tiny band of federalism savants would seem to be poor service to legitimate American federalism, a system and belief of immense inherent strength and importance.

Nor would the preservation of the electoral college seem to be an essential element in maintaining the "dual citizenship" of Americans—as citizens of the United States and of their particular states. Americans would still be citizens of their own states as they participated in state elections and took part in all the life of their states of residence. Abolishing the electoral college would simply create a direct relationship between the people and their president, who, after all, is a national, not a state, official. In the widest sense, direct voting would not be a contradiction of federalism but its natural culmination in a system of "one man, one vote" for every office, from city councilman to president of the United States, each in its proper sphere.

Pluralities, Majorities, and Runoffs

The system of plurality election, in which the man with the most votes is declared elected—regardless of his percentage—now applies almost uniformly in the U.S., with rare exceptions such as Georgia, which requires a majority vote for all state and federal offices, and Mississippi and Vermont, which require a majority vote for governor. In practice, the plurality system has worked well in the United States. In the great majority of elections, the winner receives a clear majority anyway. In a very close election one or more minor-party candidates on the ballot may pull him below 50 percent, but real three- or four-way splits are rare, and the plurality system has not encouraged minor parties in U.S. politics.

Nevertheless, there has been a feeling in the country that the president should be chosen by majority vote. Thus the Constitution requires a majority of the electoral college ballots to elect a president. In actual popular voting, there have been fifteen presidents who failed to achieve an absolute majority of popular votes—including Lincoln, Wilson, Kennedy, and Nixon in 1968 (see chart, Appendix E). But only in one election—1860—has one of the candidates failed to win at least 40 percent. Lincoln is credited with 39.8 percent but would certainly have received more than 40 percent if his name had not been kept off the ballot in ten states.

In company with many other constitutional amendments to reform the electoral college, direct vote proposals over the years traditionally maintained the majority requirement with a provision that Congress choose the president if no candidate were to achieve a majority, with each member accorded a single vote. Since the ABA's 1967 proposal of a popular vote runoff instead of a contingent election by Congress, that has become the dominant reform proposal. The reasons for it are obvious. As Wicker of the *New York Times* summed up the case: "Congress would not necessarily be controlled by the party of the leading Presidential vote-getter; its members might choose the second man, just as Georgia's Legislature did [January 10, 1967] in choosing Lester G. Maddox for Governor. In a closely divided Congress there might be excessive log-rolling, arm-twisting, promise-making, wheeling and dealing and even fraud to win the necessary votes. And particularly after such an episode, Congress might then be able to exert an undue influence over a President it had directly and specifically chosen, thus breaching the doctrine of separation of powers."[22]

The ABA suggested that the 40 percent figure, combined with a national runoff, would assure a reasonable mandate for any elected president and function to discourage splinter parties from trying to infuence the outcome of the election. The 40 percent figure, the ABA said, "would render extremely remote the possibility of having to resort to the contingent election procedure." Based on past experience, there would probably be no more than one election in a century when a runoff was actually required under the ABA system.

Nevertheless, the runoff does pose some problems. At the end of an already lengthy campaign, it would place added burdens on the presidential candidates and especially on their already depleted campaign treasuries. This disadvantage could, of course, be alleviated in part by a generous allowance of free national television time before the runoff. There would be no equal time requirements after all the minor-party candidates had been eliminated in the first election.

Second, a runoff would require an even more rapid count and certification of ballots, including the resolution of all disputes, than would otherwise be necessary. This would probably not be an insurmountable obstacle, however. The states that now provide for runoff elections in their primaries currently allow between two and five weeks after the first primary.[23]

The states might also be reluctant to undergo the major expense involved in a special runoff. This objection, though, could be met by a special congressional appropriation to cover costs at a reasonable figure per vote cast.

There is also the problem of whether the leading candidates might be tempted to make unconscionable concessions to the runners-up in a runoff. Experience shows this has often occured in southerns primary runoffs, but it may be argued that if a candidate cannot garner 40 percent of the vote in the first presidential election, his appeal is too narrow and he should be obliged to accommodate the minority candidates and the feelings of their followers before submitting hinself to the people again in the runoff.

Runoff elections often tend to be a contest in which the voters whose candidates were eliminated on the first round simply vote against the man they like the least. But if there is to be a contigent election at all, it is unquestionably preferable to let the people make that judgment rather than Congress.

Finally, there is the problem of whether there would be a significant drop-off of votes in the runoff. On the average, the vote is somewhat lighter in runoffs. An examination of a set of gubernatorial runoffs in ten southern states in the mid-1960s revealed that the total vote was less than that of the first primary in five instances and greater in five instances. Overall, however, the runoff vote was off only 2.38 percent from the first primary in these states. In a presidential election, with all the interest it arouses, the problem might not be too great.[24]

On balance, a runoff election provision is probably not necessary. An analysis of 170 gubernatorial elections, occurring in the 30 most competitive states between 1952 and 1964, showed that the winning candidate polled less than 45 percent of the total vote in only two cases and less than 40 percent in no case at all.[25]

Doing away with the contingent-election requirement altogether would be in the tradition of the great nineteenth-century electoral college reform effort in the United States. "Dispense with the requirement of a majority and adopt the plurality system, and avoid an election by the House altogether," Senator Oliver P. Morton of Indiana proposed in 1875. "The plurality rule is adopted by all the states except three in the election of state officers," Morton noted, "and by all in regard to election of Members of Congress. . . . It has worked well in the states and no state now proposes to go back from the plurality to the majority system."[26]

Even if the runoff provision is not particularly necessary, however, the ABA and other modern reformers may have been wise to adopt it as a counterploy to anticipated charges that they are undermining the two-party system. Minor parties would have to obtain at least 20 percent of the vote, and probably more in most years, to prevent one of the major candidates from winning election. Their incentives for making an effort at the presidential level would be reduced drastically from what they are today. The very fact that the Constitution provided for a runoff might mean that the country would never have to go through one.*

THE DIRECT VOTE AND NATIONAL POLITICS

Precisely because the popular vote corresponds so closely to the way the American people already think about their president and appears to coincide so well with the existing political institutions of the United States, its institution would not be likely to cause any major change in the political alignments of the country or in the way that presidential campaigns are conducted. In this respect the direct vote parts company with the district and proportional systems pro-

---

* In a 1967 statement endorsing the ABA direct vote recommendations, the New York City Bar Association commented that a runoff system could conceivably encourage third parties to enter candidates in the hopes of forcing a runoff and then wringing concessions from front-runners in return for their support. "On balance, however, we believe that the 40-percent runoff provision is necessary to avoid the possibility of a relatively small minority electing a President," the association said. Not only would runoffs be extremely unlikely, but "so uncertain a prospect of 'leverage in the sky' would be unlikely to induce a proliferation of political parties, particularly in view of the manifold difficulties, monetary and otherwise, in the way of mounting a serious Presidential campaign."

posed in earlier years, which opponents could claim—with substantial evidence—would do much to alter the political balance of the nation.

In a series of interviews with national party professionals, men who had managed or advised in presidential campaigns of the last decades, the authors asked for their analysis of the impact that a direct vote might have. Almost without exception, they replied that they saw few if any substantive changes that might result in presidential campaigns, and none felt that a direct vote would pose any special threat or give any special advantage to his party.

There was some thought that television and radio would take on more importance in campaigns, though most managers acknowledge it would be difficult to increase the existing usage of those media. Candidates would still feel obliged to make speeches to veterans and to labor and business conventions and to show particular concern for certain specialized geographic interests. Some minor "prop stops" might be cut from schedules, it was felt, but candidates would still have to "show the flag" to some degree, even in relatively sparsely populated regions of the nation.

One of the most delicate balances in U.S. politics is that between the national party structures and the state political organizations beneath them. Most of the men interviewed envisioned little change in the existing balance—presuming that the national convention method of nominating presidential candidates, with the special power and influence it gives to state party organizations, was retained. Some of the political managers interviewed believed the presidential candidate might be more distant from state leaders, since he would be a national candidate instead of a contender for any state's specific electoral votes. But the preponderant opinion was that the role of the state organizations might become more important because of the vital function they would play in maximizing voter registration and election day turnout under a direct vote system. Substantial additional funds might flow from national headquarters in Washington to the state organizations to help them in this function. Increased emphasis on voter registration and turnout efforts emerged as the most important effect the party professionals expected to see stem from institution of a direct vote.

Both political managers and political scientists analyzing the potential impact of a direct vote agree that it would serve to foster two-party competition in all the states of the Union. The basic goal of any presidential campaign in future years would be to get every possible vote in every state, since each vote would count. Simply carrying a state would no longer be of such paramount importance. Instead, the basic question would be a candidate's margin of victory—the net "plus" any state's votes would give him in the national tally. And even if a candidate had little hope of winning a plurality in a given state, he would be vitally concerned with the size of the vote cast for him in the state, bending every effort to minimize any margin against him.

The growing nationalization of U.S. politics in recent decades has already served to minimize the traditional emphasis on a potential candidate's home state and the bloc of electoral votes it can swing in the fall election. The presidential election of 1948 may well have been the last one in which the home state of one of the candidates—in that case, Thomas E. Dewey of New York—played an appreciable role in winning a major party nomination. Dwight D. Eisenhower, Adlai E. Stevenson, John F. Kennedy, Richard M. Nixon, Lyndon B. Johnson, Barry Goldwater, Hubert Humphrey, George McGovern, Gerald Ford, Jimmy Carter, Ronald Reagan—all were chosen because of their national stature or regional strength, not because they represented a certain state with a mighty bloc of electoral votes. This trend could be expected to continue under a direct vote system. The talents and leadership qualities of candidates would count much more than their state of origin. It would still be easier, of course, for a governor of New York or California to win a presidential nomination than for the chief executive of Vermont or Wyoming. But citizens of the latter states —especially if they distinguish themselves in Congress or in other national service—would no longer be almost automatically excluded as was once the case in U.S. politics.

A final concern with the institution of direct voting for president is whether it would work substantially to the detriment of one political party or one political bloc—conservatives or liberals, civil rights advocates or white supremacists. Ideally, this should not be a paramount concern, for the important question in establishing a presidential election system is more properly which system corresponds best to the standards of political democracy held by most Americans, and which system best guarantees that the popular will is reflected in the final outcome. But if it *could* be shown that one political group would lose out seriously through institution of the direct vote, then the proposal might be doomed from the start.

The fact is that no such case has been made, although some persons have attempted it. The groups backing the direct vote, from organized labor to conservative business groups, cover a wide spectrum, as have the congressional sponsors. Among informed political leaders, there seems to be a consensus that there is no longer a "solar system" of balanced injustices in U.S. politics, requiring preservation of the electoral college for the kinds of reasons John Kennedy advanced in the 1950s (see page 138, above). "One man, one vote" decrees have destroyed any special conservative advantages in legislatures and congressional districts, and the broadening of national suffrage has created a base for national presidential voting in which all groups, liberal and conservative alike, can have a fair voice.   ·

In recent years the most prominent opposition has been from the conservative/small-state camp. (It formed, for instance, the core of the opposition that prevented the direct vote amendment from clearing the Senate in

1970). Yet this opposition may stem more from the leaders than from the public. Most opinion samplings, even in small states, have suggested broad public support for the direct vote. And there are many small-state leaders who discern that their states' electoral college power is already severely eclipsed by the swing power of large states.

That raises, of course, an interesting question: should the big states fear a dimunition of their power under direct voting? Under direct vote, the election of the president would be far less likely to swing, as it may under the electoral college, on the turn of a few thousand votes in California, Illinois, or New York. But this is not to say that the *people* of the big states would have anything to lose. Indeed, individual citizens of the large states would know that their votes would be counted meaningfully, even if they found themselves in a minority in their own state.

Moreover, it seems certain that no presidential candidate, almost regardless of the election system in effect, will ever risk ignoring the vital interests of citizens in the large metropolitan areas of the country, which form the bulk of the big-state populations. An exclusive appeal to rural or small-town voters would have little viability in a country where the vast (and increasing) preponderance of the population lives in the cities and their immediate suburbs.

But what then of the minority groups—Catholics, unionists, blacks, Jews, assorted ethnic blocs—who are said to have a special swing power in modern presidential elections because of their alleged ability to shift a few thousand votes one way or the other and thus determine the outcome in pivotal states? Would these groups lose a special privilege they enjoy today? The answer is clearly no, for three specific reasons.

First, while it is true that a handful of votes can swing pivotal states in some (but certainly not all) elections, there are clearly limits to the ability of leaders of special ethnic, religious, or economic groups, in the heat of an election campaign, to persuade their followers to break radically from their traditional political loyalties and vote in any other way than they were planning to in the first place. Actually, studies on the voting behavior of such groups over several elections indicate a remarkable stability in their political preferences, even if their overwhelmingly Democratic preference in presidential contests has unquestionably weakened since the early 1960s. Over decades, these groups may make basic shifts in political allegiance, and their support for any party will naturally fluctuate slightly from election to election. But to suggest that they can shift more rapidly than other groups in the population for immediate political bargaining purposes in the midst of a campaign is to disregard the conclusions of most political science analyses.[27] On an emotional issue such as Israel, Jews might be able to switch rapidly in a campaign, though even this instance the unity of the move would be questionable. (The Jewish vote has in fact split sharply in some recent campaigns.) The existence of some magical swing group may also be highly illusory. One could argue just as logically that suburbanites or American Legionnaires or Rotarians or Episcopalians—or any group imaginable—constitute the swing vote in the pivotal states and thus control the presidential elections.

Second, even if one were to concede that certain groups in big states could mobilize to shift their votes back and forth for purposes of controlling large blocs of electoral votes, it is not clear that it would always be liberals who enjoy that special advantage. In fact, the white backlash vote among some groups could presumably be mobilized to defeat a presidential candidate who took a strong civil rights stand. Or some militant right-wing group might suddenly seize the swing position in the pivotal states that blacks, Jews, and a whole multitude of ethnic Americans have been said to occupy in the past. To say that the electoral college should be retained to defend liberalism or big cities leads down two odious roads: first, a political opportunism in which one would rather have a minority president he agrees with than a popularly chosen one he disagrees with; and secondly, a possibly fatal misreading of the political tea leaves, in which one assumes that the political balances and realities of the past decades will hold true for the 1980s and for time to come.

A third reason that the nation's minority groups would not be losing any special advantage in direct voting is that they would be able to transfer their voting strength to the national stage instead and be just as effective there. Scattered labor union members in the South would suddenly find themselves able to unite their votes with those of unionists from the industrialized states of the North. The newly enfranchised blacks from southern states like Mississippi and Alabama would be able to combine their votes with blacks from New York, Illinois, and Michigan and thus constitute a formidable national voting bloc that the parties would ignore at their peril. Of course, owners of expensive homes would also be able to unite their voting strength across state lines if they wanted to, and so would migrant workers (if they could manage to establish residence long enough to vote) or schoolteachers or retirees or segregationists. But there is nothing inherently evil about this process, for politics in the long run must be, and is, the process by which the competing demands and needs of a pluralistic society are met. The direct vote for president simply means that everyone would approach the game on equal terms.[28]

As late as the latter part of the 1970s, however, there were still black leaders who proposed retaining the electoral college because of its alleged special benefit for black persons. National Urban League Executive Director Vernon Jordan, Jr., was one of these; another was Eddie N. Williams of the Joint Center for Political Studies. In 1977 testimony before the Senate Judiciary Subcommittee, Williams said: "Blacks are 10 percent of the national electorate; they are strategically concentrated in the metropolitan areas of key states with large numbers of electoral votes. Historically, they have tended to vote as a block, and they are widely regarded as being able to wield a balance of power in close elections in key states."[29] This conclusion was apparently bolstered by the Joint Center's calculations that black voters were directly responsible for Jimmy Carter carrying a number of states in the 1976 election—among them Ohio, Pennsylvania, Missouri, Texas, Louisiana, Mississippi, and Maryland—clearly enough to swing the presidential contest to the Democrats.

But as Tom Wicker subsequently noted in the *New York Times*: "That leaves out of account the fact that Mr. Carter *lost* Illinois, in which he had heavy black support, as well as Michigan, Indiana and Virginia, in each of which more than 90 percent of black voters supported Mr. Carter. The winner-take-all effect of the electoral college nullified every one of those black votes; and it greatly diminished the electoral significance of hundreds of thousands more in states Mr. Carter won by wide margins."[30]

The irony, in our view, is (1) that black leaders have not made a convincing argument that the existing system aids blacks, and (2) that the research we cited earlier (see pp. 127–30) shows that black voters are in fact *dis*advantaged by the electoral college because of their distribution among the states. This suggests that under direct vote black influence on the election would, if anything, increase slightly.

IMPLEMENTING THE DIRECT VOTE

Because of its very simplicity, the direct vote for president would pose few difficulties in administration. But there are several problem areas that must be dealt with, both by Congress as it seeks to frame a direct vote amendment to the Constitution and later in terms of actual operation. Among the thorniest of these are the counting of the votes and the qualifications of voters.

Obtaining an Accurate National Vote Count

Each state today has a well-established, reliable method of counting the votes for local and state officials and certifying the winners. The popular vote for president would simply constitute the addition of the popular votes cast in each state and the District of Columbia to obtain a national total.

The only problem that could arise under this system would have to do with certifying the winner in an exceptionally close election. "The possibility of close elections," Senator Kefauver commented a few years ago, "will always be with us, and in a federation of 185 million people from Maine to Hawaii, uncertainty and suspense will attend the final determination under any system."[31] Some observers have suggested that the problem of local fraud would be magnified under the direct vote system, since any irregularity in the voting in any state could influence—and if great enough, actually determine—the outcome of the national election. Some have contended that actual federal administration of elections would be necessary.

On balance, such fears are probably exaggerated. The argument could as easily be made that federal administration of election laws is already necessary, since fraud in a closely contested state with a large bloc of electoral votes may already be enough to swing the entire national election. Some Republicans, indeed, suggested that an honest count in Illinois, Texas, and other states would have shifted the outcome of the 1960 contest. Regardless of the system of election employed, there has always been and will always be a possibility that irregularities could influence the outcome. Mathematically, there is probably no greater, and possibly much less, chance that there can be enough irregularities to cloud the outcome under the direct vote system than there is today, when the shift of a few hundred or thousand votes in crucial states can determine who will be the next president. The fact is that fraud, while it frequently appears in the United States, is almost always found in local elections—for sheriff or some other office extremely important to the persons committing the fraud. The motivation to engage in vote fraud, with its high legal penalties, is far less in the case of the rather abstract office of president of the United States.

A legitimate question may be raised, however, with regard to the winner in an exceedingly close election. Recalling the suspense of election night in 1960 and the hairbreadth popular vote margin that separated Nixon and Kennedy, some have suggested that the process of recounting, challenging, and litigation might have gone on well beyond inauguration day in January.

As an objection to popular voting, the problem of determining the winner falls on two points. First, as previously noted, the uncertainty of the outcome in one or just a handful of pivotal electoral vote states could easily create the same conditions of uncertainty about the winner under the electoral college system. Indeed, it was many weeks after the 1960 election before it was known who had carried Hawaii, and several days after the election before the California outcome was clear. The 1976 election produced a long period of indecision regarding the outcome in Ohio. Secondly, the chances that the two major candidates would come within a few hundred or thousand votes of each other are minuscule when 70 million or more persons are participating in the election. Tom Wicker of the *New York Times* points out that there was only one other presidential election—the Garfield-Hancock contest of 1880—when the popular vote was "so close that counting a winning total would have been difficult, or that any but the most massive and wholesale fraud could have changed the outcome."[32] Garfield's actual plurality was 9,457 out of 9.2 million votes cast. Proportionately, that would have been 69,036-vote plurality out of the total of 70.6 million votes cast in a national election such as in 1964. Admittedly this is a narrow margin on a national basis. But it would still be a clear and unambiguous national plurality, barring allegations of voting irregularity on a scale that the country has in fact not experienced in modern times. More than 1,000 votes would have to be stolen or lost in every state to change the outcome. Long-term projections of the growth of the total U.S. population, and of the size of the electorate, suggest increasingly less likelihood that only a few thousand votes might separate candidates in a presidential election.[33] Indeed, assuming a 55-percent voter turnout in presidential elections, by 1990 the difference between candidates of a narrow half of one percent would be a substantial 465,460 votes, and by 2010, 679,833 votes. A difference of a tiny one-tenth of a percentage point would be 93,092 votes in 1990 and 123,606 in 2010.

Statistically, it is doubtful whether there would be more than one election in a century, and probably not more than one every three or four centuries, in which the popular vote would be so close that there could be real dispute about the outcome. And the fact of the matter is that the American people are accustomed to witnessing razor-thin vote margins in individual state races: note the 91-vote margin by which Karl Rolvaag won the Minnesota governorship in 1962 and the 84-vote margin by which Senator Howard W. Cannon won reelection to the Senate from Nevada in 1964. Recounts are invariably ordered in all such close races, but it is rare indeed that the results of the first canvass, no matter how narrow, are upset. An exception was the 1960 presidential race in Hawaii, where the Republican electors led by 141 votes on the first official count but trailed by 115 after a recount.*

The most publicized close election of recent years was the 1974 New Hampshire Senate race between Democrat John Durkin and Republican Louis Wyman. When the initial vote tally was completed, Wyman was shown to be the winner by a margin of 542 votes. Durkin demanded a recount and emerged with an incredibly slim lead of 10 votes—out of 221,838 cast. The matter was eventually submitted to the U.S. Senate, where a committee spent months laboriously reviewing thousands of disputed paper ballots and eventually gave up, so that the new election (easily won by Durkin) had to be called.

The Durkin-Wyman race is cited by some as an example of the confusion that should never be allowed to surround a presidential election and thus as a rationale for opposing the direct vote for president. But is should be noted that it was paper ballots, now used in a small and declining portion of the nation's voting precincts, that caused the real difficulty in the New Hampshire contest.

---

* One of the more unusual arguments advanced against a direct vote system has been that it could result in a shifting of the political center of gravity of the country if accidental factors such as a severe storm in the northwestern states materially reduced the vote from one region.[34] Presumably, storms could influence the outcome only if the national vote balance was exceedingly close. Under the existing system, bad weather was reported to have reduced the upstate Republican vote in New York in 1884, helping the Democrats carry the state and, because of it, the entire nation. In the days of the automobile and mass transit, Americans are less likely to be deterred from voting by bad weather. But if weather really were the stumbling block in the way of adopting a national direct vote, alternative solutions like an extended 24-hour voting period in a storm-hit area could be instituted.

Elmer W. Lower, when president of ABC News, rightly noted that paper ballots are "a relic of the nineteenth century, inefficient and inaccurate." When recounts are required, incredible potential for ambiguity in how a voter really intended to mark the ballot emerges. The simplest solution to this problem would seem to be for the federal government to insist that automatic vote registering and counting procedures (by voting machine, punch card, etc.) be required in all precincts in federal elections. That precise recommendation was made in 1978 by the Twentieth Century Fund's Task Force on Reform of the Presidential Election Process.[35] The elimination of paper ballots would be the single most important step possible in assuring honest and undisputed elections.

But all the potential election irregularities fade in importance when it is recalled that under the existing electoral college system, the greatest fraud of all can be perpetrated, legally—the elevation to the presidency of a person who was specifically rejected by the people, even by a margin that could go as high as *several million* votes. A proportionate extension of the 1876 and 1888 vote counts to 1964 turnout levels indicates that Tilden would have won in 1876 by 2.1 million votes and Cleveland by 590,000 votes in 1888, despite the fact that the electoral college elected their opponents.

Short shrift may also be given to the argument that the existing electoral college should be retained because in a close and bitterly contested election its normally inflated majorities give the impression that the country stands overwhelmingly behind the winner, thus promoting national unity. Senator Margaret Chase Smith of Maine suggested that of all the arguments for the existing system, this is "the most fatuous and guilty of sheer sophistry."[36] The argument takes no account of the possibility that the candidate whose electoral victory looks so substantial may actually have lost in the popular vote, or of the possibility that the electoral vote (as in 1876) may also be sufficiently close to throw the country into turmoil. Nor can it be seriously suggested that very many of the people are fooled by an inflated electoral college majority when they know the popular vote margin was narrow. Former president Truman, himself a defender of the electoral college, suggested that "there is something to be said for the narrow margin of victory in a Presidential election. It makes the new President realize in a very dramatic and material way that there is more than one side to a question. And where there are two strong, major parties, there are bound to be reasonable differences of opinion on many issues and conflicts of interest." In the eyes of the president-elect, Truman said, the "voices and ideas" of the millions who voted for the losing candidate should be "just as important as those of the victorious millions."[37]

In addition to dramatically reducing the opportunities for fraud, modern, automated voting equipment should also help to solve another problem in American elections—the slowness of the count, recount and challenge procedure, which can sometimes delay certification of the winner in an election for weeks or, in the most extreme cases, for months after an election. In contrast to Great Britain, where a change of government takes place within hours of the popular mandate, the pace of the official ballot count in the United States (as opposed to the unofficial counts reported by networks and new services) is torturously slow. Many states are unable to report an official vote count until several weeks after election day, as local boards of elections languidly carry out their duties. If recounts are necessary or challenges reach the courts, the process of establishing an offical final count can drag on well into the term of the official who has been elected. It is in this area of the speed in the count and challenge procedure, rather than in obtaining, finally, a conclusive national count, that the direct vote for president raises the most serious problems. The presidential election takes place early in November, but the welfare of the country cannot permit slow vote count and challenge procedures that would prevent official certification of the new president until the eve of inauguration day, the next January 20, or beyond. A new president needs to know if he is elected almost immediately after election day, so that he can begin the delicate and difficult business of choosing a cabinet and other top aides, formulating a program for Congress, and letting foreign powers know what they may expect in the future international policy of the United States. No competent observer would doubt that prolonged uncertainty about the outcome of a presidential election could be injurious to the welfare of the entire nation.

Some rather ingenious proposals to get around this difficulty have been presented. The 1978 Twentieth Century Fund Task Force, for instance, recommended that within a very few days of the election, federal law require an *automatic, mandatory* retally of all votes cast, to assure that the official vote totals are accurate. As a special safeguard against abuse, it was also proposed that a second, independent authority or agency be the body instructed to undertake this retally. The second total would be considered the final, official one, even if the election were neither close nor disputed. The task force said its proposals were "specifically designed to lessen the possibility of errors, whether human or mechanical."[38]

The logical question arises, of course: If this type of automatic retally by an independent authority, obviating the necessity for recounts or delays in almost all cases, is so desirable, why not implement it whether the electoral college is abolished or not? The Twentieth Century Fund panel recognized that question by saying that its recommendations for enhancing the integrity of the voting process should be implemented regardless of the formal presidential election system used. But then it added that "an accurate national count, however, would be absolutely essential if direct election were adopted."[39] To that, we take exception. Why should an accurate count be more important under direct election than any other system? It may be that irregularities can now be isolated within states, but that makes them no less serious if the choice of the next president is affected. Since in every close election there are a number of close states, a national system of counting and preventing fraud that is as foolproof as possible is a reform that should long since have been adopted. Moreover, the very reforms the Twentieth Century Fund panel recommended to prevent irregularities and assure a rapid, twice-checked count should effectively allay fears of having to recount votes in every precinct in a close election. In effect, that recount would happen automatically.

Another interesting proposal to assure a rapid, reliable national count was put forth some years ago by L. Kinvin Wroth in the *Dickinson Law Review*.[40] Wroth's proposal was advanced for use under the existing electoral college system and might be largely obviated by a reform of the type suggested by the Twentieth Century Fund panel. But it is still worth consideration, whether or not the direct vote is implemented. Wroth's suggestion was that while the states continue to conduct elections, the federal courts be given exclusive jurisdiction in the event of contested presidential vote returns. The federal courts would be more appropriate than state courts in this regard, Wroth said, because they enjoy immunity from political pressures, stemming from the life tenure of federal judges, which state courts—where the judges are often subject to periodic reelection—do not enjoy. Congress, he said, could provide a schedule for the filing, hearing, and decision of all contests, including the selection of federal judges on an impartial basis determined in advance, perhaps by requiring each circuit to establish an election contest calendar prior to the election. The importance of the matter, Wroth said, might well justify special three-judge federal courts. They would have "jurisdiction of all questions arising out of the popular election which affect the validity of votes and the accuracy and fairness of the count and canvass." But the federal courts, he suggested, would be instructed to apply *state* election law in these matters. They would have express power to order the preservation of the ballots for a recount under the direction of a court-appointed master, Wroth proposed. Provision could be made for direct appeal to the Supreme Court—but all within a specified time limit that would result in a final determination of all contests before an appointed date.

"The President of the United States will increasingly require strength based on national and international respect if he is to guide the nation through times of mounting crisis," Wroth said. "This respect will not come to one who is elected under the slightest suspicion of error or fraud. To insure that no electoral contest will mar or disrupt the orderly succession of the Presidency in the difficult future, Congress must give to the federal courts the power to reach a timely, final and binding decision of all controversies."[41]

With reforms of the types suggested by the Twentieth Century Fund Task Force and Wroth, it is hard to imagine anyone or any group considering it really worthwhile to attempt fraud, delays in counting votes, or other irregularities in presidential elections.

Qualifications for Voters

A major danger to any direct vote amendment, as it is considered by Congress and later by the states, would be to infringe too far on the states' traditional right to set voting qualifications. The ABA and other chief congressional backers of the direct vote thus recommend a relatively simple formula: To vote for president, a person must have met his state's requirements to vote for members of Congress. Thus the voter for president would be subjected to the traditional state residence and age limitations, which are approaching universal adult suffrage today. Any state could specifically provide less stringent residence requirements for presidential elections alone, however. This would preserve the state laws already passed that set much shorter residence requirements for presidential balloting. Congress would be given a reserve power to set uniform residence and age requirements. "It is probable that, as with other reserve powers, Congress might not have to exercise this power, particularly in view of the increasing tendency on the part of the states to make uniform their qualifications for voting in elections," the ABA report noted. Senator Bayh stated the case in less formal language: "If we see some mad scramble by the states to lower voter qualifications willy-nilly, then Congress can step in and establish uniform standards."

A familiar argument of opponents of the direct vote is that the states would embark on a race to debase their voting qualifications. But since the qualifications for voting for U.S. congressmen are almost invariably the same as those for state legislators, it is doubtful that this would really happen. Local politicians who lowered the voting age just to increase a state's influence in presidential voting "would be cutting off their noses to spite their faces," Senator Pastore remarked a few years ago. "Does any Senator mean to tell me that he is going to say, 'Let us do this, because we in Rhode Island will control the election of the President of the United States'? The minute he gets himself into setting up such reckless and callous qualifications, he destroys the efficacy and the effectiveness and the dignity of his own local government."[42]

Opponents of the direct vote may well argue that even if Congress fails to exercise its reserve power there will be subtle influences on the states to conform to uniform age and residence requirements—thus reducing, to some extent, the states' traditional discretion in this field and the full extent of state sovereignty. The argument may be a fair one; indeed, Professor Paul Freund of the ABA commission acknowledged in 1967 Senate hearings that the logic of direct popular vote would draw in its train the concept of uniform voting qualifications prescribed by Congress, although he thought that step would be unnecessary if the states maintained relatively uniform requirements. Another direct-vote proponent, Professor Robert G. Dixon, Jr., said a direct vote amendment ought to include "standards and national police power regarding uniform voting qualifications and open, honest, unintimidated balloting," or that Congress should at least be required to enact legislation prescribing such standards. We believe there would be little immediate likelihood of Congress taking the steps Dixon recommended. Others differ, however. Elections expert Richard G. Smolka of American University has suggested that Congress, under a direct vote system, would feel itself obliged to deal with a whole host of election law details now left to the states. His list of areas in which he thought Congress would be compelled to act include: (1) uniform qualifications for voting; (2) how political parties and candidates obtain a ballot position; (3) the type of uniform ballot arrangement to be prescribed—office block, party column, straight ticket option, party position on the ballot, etc.; (4) rules governing voting—hours, places, method of voting: and (5) the standards and procedures for vote tallying and recounts.[43] If Smolka is correct, Congress would face a formidable set of problems and find itself interfering in broad areas now covered entirely by state laws.

We recognize that the problems in conducting elections enumerated by Smolka are quite real. Indeed, it can easily be argued that differences in state laws presently can so heavily influence the conduct of presidential elections that they might be determinative in a close election. But is it simply because of the mechanism of the electoral college and state-by-state counts that Congress now declines to interfere in these areas more deeply? The commonsense position is that under direct election, on some issues of compelling *national* interest—the use of automatic voting machines to prevent fraud, automatic retallies by independent authorities, and deadlines for submitting certified state totals—Congress could and perhaps would set down broad guidelines and requirements. On other, less vital issues (ballot position and arrangement, for instance) Congress could remain silent unless abuses appeared, at which point Congress could always step in if it were deemed necessary.

One may note parenthetically that the proposal for abolishing the electoral college perennially encounters the type of analysis of political scientists and politicians that alleges that "If *A* (abolishing the electoral college) happens, then *B* must follow." But *why* should *B* follow? Can a likely chain of cause and effect be established? We find that rarely takes place: the observer has a hunch about what might happen and then procedes to establish a case as if the consequence he foresees would be virtually inevitable. Prime examples are the suggestions that Congress would instantly rewrite all state election laws or that the nation would by necessity abolish nominating conventions and embrace a single national primary election for presidential candidates, just because such a primary would seem more logically consistent with the unmediated form of choice represented by the direct vote in the final election. We fail to see why the country would necessarily have to be bound by such sequiturs. Political debate would continue. It would remain obvious that dictation by Congress of minute details of state election laws would immerse the federal government in an unnecessary morass. And the political figures—probably a solid majority in Congress and the state legislatures—who today feel a national primary would be a grave error would not be forced to change their minds.

Direct election, of course, would produce some changes in American politics. History shows us that every electoral reform has brought changes—and often ones quite unforeseen. But because direct election conforms so closely to the way most people believe the president is elected, the strong likelihood is that such changes would prove something less than revolutionary.

Qualifying for the Ballot

The people of all the states should certainly have the right to vote for any major-party candidate, and the ABA suggested that Congress be given the power to deal with cases where a state seeks to exclude the presidential candidate for one of the major parties from the ballot, as Alabama did in 1948 and 1964. With Congress given this reserve right, it is likely that the states themselves would see to it that major-party candidates were given places on their general election ballots—if for no other reason, to avoid congressional intervention. There might, of course, be considerable debate in Congress about which parties are "major" enough to be entitled to inclusion on all states' ballots. Should modern replicas of the 1948 Dixiecrat and Progressive parties, for instance, be guaranteed ballot positions by Congress? In all likelihood, Congress—itself dominated by the two major parties—would leave this problem where it is now, in the hands of the states, where election laws generally make it fairly difficult for new parties to qualify.

Running as a Team

Most modern proposals for direct vote amendments require that the candidates for president and vice president run as a team. The advantages of this are obvious. It would prevent the distractions of separate appeals by presidential and vice presidential candidates in the general election, prevent any chance that these two officials might be from opposing parties, and assure reasonable harmony between the president and his vice president in the new administration.

"A MORE PERFECT UNION"

In one respect, the proposal for abolishing the rickety old electoral college and substituting a direct vote of the people seems to be little more than a housekeeping item on the agenda of pressing national and international problems that face the American people as they enter the closing decades of the twentieth century. Yet the importance of the presidency in American life can scarcely be underestimated, and thus the way that office is filled must be a matter of major national concern. As Estes Kefauver commented in 1961, "Every four years the electoral college is a loaded pistol aimed at our system of government. Its continued existence is a game of Russian roulette. Once its antiquated procedures trigger a loaded cylinder, it may be too late for the needed corrections."[44]

Of course, it is possible that even if the electoral college sent the popular-vote loser to the White House, the people would find a way to live with the situation—even though the authority of the presidency and the quality of American democracy would certainly be undermined. But even if one assumes that the country *could* somehow exist with a president the people had rejected, the question still remains: What good reason is there to continue such an irrational voting system in an advanced democratic nation, where the ideal of popular choice is the most deeply ingrained of governmental principles?

Democratic elections do not always guarantee that the best man will win. Even when we have scraped the barnacles of the electoral college from the ship of state, there is no guarantee that we or our descendants may not one day elect a charlatan or an ideologue to the presidency. For all our talk of great American presidents, we have elected some pretty grim mediocrities to that office, and we could again—although we would like to believe that the modern levels of education and political sophistication in the United States today make it far less likely. But even when one admits that the vox populi may err, the fact remains that through our entire national experience we have learned that there is no safer, no better way to elect our public officials than by the choice of the people, with the man who wins the most votes being awarded the office. This is the essence of "the consent of the governed." And no matter how wisely or foolishly the American people choose their president, he *is* their president. No one has been able to show how the preservation of a quaint eighteenth-century voting device, the electoral college, with all its anomalies and potential wild cards, can serve to protect the Republic. The choice of the chief executive must be the people's, and it should rest with none other than them.

The framers of the Constitution sought to embody the essence of American nationality in the opening words of the Preamble: "We the People of the United States, in order to form a more perfect Union . . ." Yet the perfection of the Union has more than once been marred by the workings of the electoral college, and every four years the nation runs the risk that a malfunction of the presidential voting system could disrupt "the domestic tranquility" and threaten "the general welfare" of which the preamble also spoke. By amending the Constitution to provide a direct vote of all the people for their president, the nation would strike a serious defect from its charter of government and lay a sound foundation for a fuller realization of that "more perfect Union" in the times to come.

Appendixes

Appendix A • The National Vote for President, 1789–1980

The United States has entrusted no single national agency with the official tabulation of the popular votes cast for presidential electors, although the electoral vote itself is certified every four years before a joint session of Congress. The chart below records the official electoral vote and indicates the best available tallies of the national popular vote, based on the method of translating votes for electors into a popular count described in chapter 5 (pp. 110–11). Sources* for the popular vote: for the elections of 1824 (the year for which the first national count could be compiled) through 1916, Svend Petersen, *A Statistical History of American Presidential Elections* (New York, 1963); for the elections of 1920 through 1964, Richard M. Scammon, *America at the Polls* (Pittsburgh, 1965); for the refinements of the 1960 vote, where a split Democratic elector slate in Alabama raised difficult problems in evaluation, Congressional Quarterly Service; for the elections of 1968 and 1972, Congressional Quarterly, *Guide to U.S. Elections* (Washington, D.C., 1975); for the election of 1976, Congressional Quarterly, *Guide to 1976 Elections* (Washington, D.C., 1977); and for the election of 1980, *Congressional Quarterly Weekly Report*, January 17, 1981, p. 138.

In the elections of 1789 through 1800, each presidential elector cast two equal votes, without distinguishing the person he favored for president from his choice for vice president. The candidate with the most electoral votes was elected president if his total constituted a majority of the number of electors. The runner-up, without a majority requirement, was elected vice president. The 12th amendment, adopted in 1804 and applicable to the election of that year and all subsequent elections, required the electors to cast separate votes for president and vice president.

The elections of 1800 and 1824 were decided by the House of Representatives because no candidate for president received a majority of electoral votes.

The name of the winning candidate is given first for each election year.

* Material reprinted with permission of the indicated authors or publishers.

Key to party designations:

F Federalist	P Prohibition
D Democratic	PO Populist
NR National Republican	S Socialist
AM Anti-Masonic	PR Progressive
W Whig	U Union
L Liberty	SR States' Rights
FS Free Soil	AIP American Independent Party
R Republican	Amer. American Party
LR Land Reform	Peop. People's Party
CU Constitutional Union	NUC National Unity Campaign
G Greenback	Libert. Libertarian
	Cit. Citizens Party

Party designations pose special problems in the early years, when national political parties in the sense understood in modern times were still emerging. The designation (D) for Democrat is used in this chart for the factions called Anti-Federalist, later Republican, and eventually known as Democratic by the 1820s.

Year	Candidates	Popular Vote Total Percentage		Electoral Votes Received
*1789	George Washington (F)	Not Available		69
	John Adams (F)	"	"	34
	John Jay (F)	"	"	9
	Others	"	"	26
*1792	George Washington (F)	"	"	132
	John Adams (F)	"	"	77
	George Clinton (D)	"	"	50
	Others	"	"	5
*1796	John Adams (F)	"	"	71
	Thomas Jefferson (D)	"	"	68
	Thomas Pinckney (F)	"	"	59
	Aaron Burr (D)	"	"	30
	Samuel Adams (F)	"	"	15
	Oliver Ellsworth (F)	"	"	11
	Others	"	"	22
*1800	Thomas Jefferson (D)	"	"	73
	Aaron Burr (D)	"	"	73

* See p. 245 for explanation of symbols * and †.

Year	Candidates	Popular Vote Total	Percentage	Electoral Votes Received
	John Adams (F)	"	"	65
	Charles C. Pinckney (F)	"	"	64
	John Jay	"	"	1
1804	Thomas Jefferson (D)	"	"	162
	Charles C. Pinckney (F)	"	"	14
1808	James Madison (D)	"	"	122
	Charles C. Pinckney (F)	"	"	47
	George Clinton (F)	"	"	6
1812	James Madison (D)	"	"	128
	DeWitt Clinton (F)	"	"	89
1816	James Monroe (D)	"	"	183
	Rufus King (F)	"	"	34
1820	James Monroe (D)	"	"	231
	John Quincy Adams (D)	"	"	1
*1824	John Quincy Adams (D)	115,696	31.9	84
	Andrew Jackson (D)	152,933	42.2	99
	William H. Crawford (D)	46,979	13.0	41
	Henry Clay (D)	47,136	13.0	37
1828	Andrew Jackson (D)	647,292	56.0	178
	John Quincy Adams (NR)	507,730	44.0	83
1832	Andrew Jackson (D)	688,242	54.5	219
	Henry Clay (NR)	473,462	37.5	49
	William Wirt (AM)	101,051	8.0	7
	John Floyd (D)	—	—	11
1836	Martin Van Buren (D)	764,198	50.9	170
	William H. Harrison (W)	549,508	36.6	73
	Hugh L. White (W)	145,352	9.7	26
	Daniel Webster (W)	41,287	2.8	14
	Willie P. Mangum (D)	—	—	11
1840	†William H. Harrison (W)	1,275,612	52.9	234
	Martin Van Buren (D)	1,130,033	46.8	60
	James G. Birney (L)	7,053	0.3	—
1844	James K. Polk (D)	1,339,368	49.6	170
	Henry Clay (W)	1,300,687	48.1	105
	James G. Birney (L)	62,197	2.3	—
1848	†Zachary Taylor (W)	1,362,101	47.3	163
	Lewis Cass (D)	1,222,674	42.5	127
	Martin Van Buren (FS)	291,616	10.1	—
	Gerrit Smith (L)	2,733	0.1	—

Year	Candidates	Popular Vote Total	Percentage	Electoral Votes Received
1852	Franklin Pierce (D)	1,609,038	50.9	254
	Winfield Scott (W)	1,386,629	43.8	42
	John P. Hale (FS)	156,297	4.9	—
	Others	12,445	0.4	—
1856	James Buchanan (D)	1,839,237	45.6	174
	John C. Frémont (R)	1,341,028	33.3	114
	Millard Fillmore (W)	849,872	21.1	8
	Gerrit Smith (LR)	484	—	—
1860	Abraham Lincoln (R)	1,867,198	39.8	180
	Steven A. Douglas (D)	1,379,434	29.4	12
	John C. Breckinridge (D)	854,248	18.2	72
	John Bell (CU)	591,658	12.6	39
	Gerrit Smith	172	—	—
1864	†Abraham Lincoln (R)	2,219,362	55.2	212
	George B. McClellan (D)	1,805,063	44.9	21
1868	Ulysses S. Grant (R)	3,013,313	52.7	214
	Horatio Seymour (D)	2,703,933	47.3	80
1872	Ulysses S. Grant (R)	3,597,375	55.6	286
	†Horace Greeley (D)	2,833,711	43.8	—
	Others	35,052	0.6	63
*1876	Rutherford B. Hayes (R)	4,035,924	47.9	185
	Samuel J. Tilden (D)	4,287,670	50.9	184
	Others	94,935	1.1	—
1880	†James A. Garfield (R)	4,454,433	48.3	214
	Winfield S. Hancock (D)	4,444,976	48.2	155
	James B. Weaver (G)	308,649	3.4	—
	Others	11,409	0.1	—
1884	Grover Cleveland (D)	4,875,971	48.5	219
	James G. Blaine (R)	4,852,234	48.3	182
	Benjamin F. Butler (G)	175,066	1.7	—
	John P. St. John (P)	150,957	1.5	—
*1888	Benjamin Harrison (R)	5,445,269	47.8	233
	Grover Cleveland (D)	5,540,365	48.6	168
	Clinton B. Fisk (P)	250,122	2.2	—
	Others	154,083	1.4	—
1892	Grover Cleveland (D)	5,556,982	46.0	277
	Benjamin Harrison (R)	5,191,466	43.0	145
	James B. Weaver (PO)	1,029,960	8.5	22
	Others	292,672	2.4	—

Year	Candidates	Popular Vote Total	Percentage	Electoral Votes Received
1896	William McKinley (R)	7,113,734	51.0	271
	William J. Bryan (D)	6,516,722	46.7	176
	Others	317,219	2.3	—
1900	†William McKinley (R)	7,219,828	51.7	292
	William J. Bryan (D)	6,358,160	45.5	155
	Others	396,200	2.8	—
1904	Theodore Roosevelt (R)	7,628,831	56.4	336
	Alton B. Parker (D)	5,084,533	37.6	140
	Eugene V. Debs (S)	402,714	3.0	—
	Silas C. Swallow (P)	259,163	1.9	—
	Others	149,357	1.1	—
1908	William H. Taft (R)	7,679,114	51.6	321
	William J. Bryan (D)	6,410,665	43.1	162
	Eugene V. Debs (S)	420,858	2.8	—
	Eugene W. Chafin (P)	252,704	1.7	—
	Others	127,379	0.9	—
1912	Woodrow Wilson (D)	6,301,254	41.9	435
	Theodore Roosevelt (PR)	4,127,788	27.4	88
	William H. Taft (R)	3,485,831	23.2	8
	Eugene V. Debs (S)	901,255	6.0	—
	Others	238,934	1.6	—
*1916	Woodrow Wilson (D)	9,131,511	49.3	277
	Charles E. Hughes (R)	8,548,935	46.1	254
	Allan L. Benson (S)	585,974	3.2	—
	Others	269,812	1.5	—
1920	†Warren G. Harding (R)	16,153,115	60.3	404
	James M. Cox (D)	9,133,092	34.1	127
	Eugene V. Debs (S)	915,490	3.4	—
	Others	566,916	2.1	—
1924	Calvin Coolidge (R)	15,719,921	54.0	382
	John W. Davis (D)	8,386,704	28.8	136
	Robert M. LaFollette (PR)	4,832,532	16.6	13
	Others	155,866	0.5	—
1928	Herbert C. Hoover (R)	21,437,277	58.2	444
	Alfred E. Smith (D)	15,007,698	40.8	87
	Others	360,976	1.0	—
1932	Franklin D. Roosevelt (D)	22,829,501	57.4	472
	Herbert C. Hoover (R)	15,760,684	39.6	59
	Norman M. Thomas (S)	884,649	2.2	—
	Others	283,925	0.8	—

Year	Candidates	Popular Vote Total	Percentage	Electoral Votes Received
1936	Franklin D. Roosevelt (D)	27,757,333	60.8	523
	Alfred M. Landon (R)	16,684,231	36.5	8
	William Lemke (U)	892,267	2.0	—
	Others	320,932	0.7	—
1940	Franklin D. Roosevelt (D)	27,313,041	54.7	449
	Wendell Willkie (R)	22,348,480	44.8	82
	Others	238,897	0.5	—
1944	†Franklin D. Roosevelt (D)	25,612,610	53.4	432
	Thomas E. Dewey (R)	22,017,617	45.9	99
	Others	346,443	0.7	—
*1948	Harry S Truman (D)	24,179,345	49.6	303
	Thomas E. Dewey (R)	21,991,291	45.1	189
	J. Strom Thurmond (SR)	1,176,125	2.4	39
	Henry A. Wallace (PR)	1,157,326	2.4	—
	Others	289,739	0.6	—
1952	Dwight D. Eisenhower (R)	33,936,234	55.1	442
	Adlai E. Stevenson (D)	27,314,992	44.4	89
	Others	299,692	0.5	—
1956	Dwight D. Eisenhower (R)	35,590,472	57.4	457
	Adlai E. Stevenson (D)	26,022,752	42.0	73
	Unpledged Elector Slates	196,318	0.3	—
	Others	217,366	0.3	1
*1960	†John F. Kennedy (D)	34,220,984	49.5	303
	Richard M. Nixon (R)	34,108,157	49.3	219
	Unpledged Elector Slates	638,822	0.9	15
	Others	188,559	0.3	—

Alternate Computation: This method avoids a major defect of the method used above, which counted Alabama Democratic votes twice, once for Kennedy and once for unpledged slates. The alternate computation credits five-elevenths of Alabama's Democratic votes to Kennedy and six-elevenths to the unpledged electoral slate totals. (See pages 66–68.)

	John F. Kennedy (D)	34,049,976	49.2	303
	Richard M. Nixon (R)	34,108,157	49.3	219
	Unpledged Elector Slates	491,527	0.7	15
	Others	188,559	0.3	—
1964	Lyndon B. Johnson (D)	43,129,484	61.1	486
	Barry M. Goldwater (R)	27,178,188	38.5	52
	Others	336,838	0.4	—

Year	Candidates	Popular Vote Total	Percentage	Electoral Votes Received
*1968	Richard M. Nixon (R)	31,785,480	43.4	301
	Hubert H. Humphrey (D)	31,275,165	42.7	191
	George C. Wallace (AIP)	9,906,473	13.5	46
	Others	244,444	0.3	—
1972	†Richard M. Nixon (R)	47,170,179	60.7	520
	George S. McGovern (D)	29,171,791	37.5	17
	John G. Schmitz (Amer.)	1,090,673	1.4	—
	Benjamim Spock (Peop.)	78,751	0.1	—
	Others	216,196	0.3	1
*1976	Jimmy Carter (D)	40,829,046	50.1	297
	Gerald R. Ford (R)	39,146,006	48.0	240
	Eugene J. McCarthy (Ind.)	756,631	0.9	—
	Roger MacBride (Libert.)	173,019	0.2	—
	Others	647,629	0.8	1
*1980	Ronald Reagan (R)	43,901,812	50.7	489
	Jimmy Carter (D)	35,483,820	41.0	49
	John B. Anderson (NUC)	5,719,722	6.6	—
	Ed Clark (Libert.)	921,188	1.1	—
	Barry Commoner (Cit.)	234,279	0.3	—
	Others	252,475	0.3	—

* Election Year Notes:

1789–for further background, see pp. 31–33.
1792–see pp. 33–34.
1796–see pp. 34–36.
1800–see pp. 36–41.
1824–see pp. 49–52.
1876–see pp. 52–57.

1888–see pp. 57–58.
1916–see pp. 58–59.
1948–see pp. 59–63.
1960–see pp. 63–73.
1968–see pp. 73–80.
1976–see pp. 80–84.
1980–see pp. 84–86.

† Notes on Candidates:

William Henry Harrison died in office April 4, 1841, and was succeeded by Vice President John Tyler.

Zachary Taylor died in office July 9, 1850, and was succeeded by Vice President Millard Fillmore.

Abraham Lincoln was shot April 14, 1865, and died the following day. He was succeeded by Vice President Andrew Johnson.

Horace Greeley died Nov. 29, 1872, before the counting of the electoral votes, which the Democratic electors divided among a scattering of candidates.

James A. Garfield was shot July 2, 1881, and died Sept 19, 1881. He was succeeded by Vice President Chester A. Arthur.

William McKinley was shot Sept 6, 1901, and died Sept. 14, 1901. He was succeeded by Vice President Theodore Roosevelt.

Warren G. Harding died in office Aug. 2, 1923, and was succeeded by Vice President Calvin Coolidge.

Franklin D. Roosevelt died in office April 12, 1945, and was succeeded by Vice President Harry S Truman.

John F. Kennedy was assassinated Nov. 22, 1963, and was succeeded by Vice President Lyndon B. Johnson.

Richard M. Nixon resigned Aug. 9, 1974, and was succeeded by Vice President Gerald R. Ford who had become vice president following the resignation, on Oct. 10, 1973, of Vice President Spiro T. Agnew.

Appendix B • The Choice of Presidential Electors, 1788–1836

The Number of States Using Each Method of Elector Selection

| Election Year | Legislature Selected | Popular Election | | | Mixed Systems |
		By General Ticket	By Districts	Total	
1788–89	4	2	2	4	2
1792	9	3	2	5	1
1796	7	2	4	6	3
1800	10	2	3	5	1
1804	6	6	5	11	—
1808	7	6	4	10	—
1812	9	5	4	9	—
1816	9	7	3	10	—
1820	9	9	6	15	—
1824	6	12	5	17	1
1828	2	18	3	21	1
1832	1	22	1	23	—
1836	1	25	—	25	—

State-by-State Breakdown on Methods of Choosing Electors, 1789–1836

Key	L chosen by legislature				G general ticket (at-large)		
	P chosen by popular vote				D district system		
	C combination of methods						

				Election Year			
State	1789	1792	1796	1800	1804	1808	1812
Connecticut	L	L	L	L	L	L	L
Delaware	P/D	L	L	L	L	L	L
Georgia	L	L	P/G	L	L	L	L
Maryland	P/G	P/G	P/D	P/D	P/D	P/D	P/D
Massachusetts	C	C	C	L	P/D & G	L	P/D
New Hampshire	C	P/G	C	L	P/G	P/G	P/G
New Jersey	L	L	L	L	P/G	P/G	L
Pennsylvania	P/G	P/G	P/G	L	P/G	P/G	P/G
South Carolina	L	L	L	L	L	L	L
Virginia	P/D	P/D	P/D	P/G	P/G	P/G	P/G
Kentucky	—	P/D	P/D	P/D	P/D	P/D	P/D
New York	—	L	L	L	L	L	L
North Carolina	—	L	P/D	P/D	P/D	P/D	L
Rhode Island	—	L	L	P/G	P/G	P/G	P/G
Vermont	—	L	L	L	L	L	L
Tennessee	—	—	C	C	P/D	P/D	P/D
Ohio	—	—	—	—	P/G	P/G	P/G
Louisiana	—	—	—	—	—	—	L

State	1816	1820	1824	1828	1832	1836
Connecticut	L	P/G	P/G	P/G	P/G	P/G
Delaware	L	L	L	L	P/G	P/G
Georgia	L	L	L	P/G	P/G	P/G
Maryland	P/D	P/D	P/D	P/D	P/D	P/D
Massachusetts	L	P/D & G	P/G	P/G	P/G	P/G
New Hampshire	P/G	P/G	P/G	P/G	P/G	P/G
New Jersey	P/G	P/G	P/G	P/G	P/G	P/G
Pennsylvania	P/G	P/G	P/G	P/G	P/G	P/G
South Carolina	L	L	L	L	L	L*
Virginia	P/G	P/G	P/G	P/G	P/G	P/G
Kentucky	P/D	P/D	P/D	P/G	P/G	P/G
New York	L	L	L	C	P/G	P/G
North Carolina	P/G	P/G	P/G	P/G	P/G	P/G
Rhode Island	P/G	P/G	P/G	P/G	P/G	P/G
Vermont	L	L	L	P/G	P/G	P/G
Tennessee	P/D	P/D	P/D	P/D	P/G	P/G
Ohio	P/G	P/G	P/G	P/G	P/G	P/G

	Election Year					
State	1816	1820	1824	1828	1832	1836
Louisiana	L	L	L	P/G	P/G	P/G
Indiana	L	L	P/G	P/G	P/G	P/G
Alabama	—	L	P/G	P/G	P/G	P/G
Illinois	—	P/D	P/D	P/G	P/G	P/G
Maine	—	P/D	P/D	P/D	P/G	P/G
	—	& G	& G	& G		
Missouri	—	L	C	P/G	P/G	P/G
Mississippi	—	P/G	P/G	P/G	P/G	P/G
Arkansas	—	—	—	—	—	P/G
Michigan	—	—	—	—	—	P/G

* South Carolina chose electors by the legislature until 1860.

Source: Adapted from data in Charles A. Paullin, "Political Parties and Opinions, 1788–1930," Atlas of the Historical Geography of the United States (Washington, D.C., 1932).

Appendix C • Electoral
College Membership

Total Membership of the Electoral College Since 1789
(together with totals for selected states)

Election Years*	Number of States†	Total Electoral Vote†	Calif.	Ill.	N.Y.	Va.
1789	13	91	—	—	8	12
1792–1800	16	138	—	—	12	21
1804–1808	17	176	—	—	19	24
1812–1820	23	232	—	3	29	25
1824–1828	24	261	—	3	36	24
1832–1840	26	294	—	5	42	23
1844–1848	31	294	—	9	36	17
1852–1860	33	303	4	11	35	15
1864–1868	36	315	5	16	33	13
1872–1880	38	369	6	21	35	11
1884–1888	44	420	8	22	36	12
1892–1900	45	447	9	24	36	12
1904–1908	46	483	10	27	39	12
1912–1928‡	48	531	13	29	45	12
1932–1940	48	531	22	29	47	11
1944–1948	48	531	25	28	47	11
1952–1960	50	537§	32	27	45	12
1964–1968	50	538‖	40	26	43	12
1972–1980	50	538‖	45	26	41	12
1984–1988	50	538**	47	24	36	12

* See p. 252 for explanation of symbols.

Sources: Biographical Directory of the American Congress (Washington, D.C., 1961), p. 45; *Representation and Apportionment* (Washington, D.C., 1966), pp. 53, 61; *Congressional Quarterly Weekly Report*, January 10, 1981, p. 71.

Electoral College Membership, State by State, 1904–1988*

State	1904–1908	1912–1928‡	1932–1940	1944–1948	1952–1960	1964–1968	1972–1980	1984–1988
Alabama	11	12	11	11	11	10	9	9
Alaska	—	—	—	—	3	3	3	3
Arizona	—	3	3	4	4	5	6	7
Arkansas	9	9	9	9	8	6	6	6
California	10	13	22	25	32	40	45	47
Colorado	5	6	6	6	6	6	7	8
Connecticut	7	7	8	8	8	8	8	8
Delaware	3	3	3	3	3	3	3	3
District of Columbia	—	—	—	—	—	3	3	3
Florida	5	6	7	8	10	14	17	21
Georgia	13	14	12	12	12	12	12	12
Hawaii	—	—	—	—	3	4	4	4
Idaho	3	4	4	4	4	4	4	4
Illinois	27	29	29	28	27	26	26	24
Indiana	15	15	14	13	13	13	13	12
Iowa	13	13	11	10	10	9	8	8
Kansas	10	10	9	8	8	7	7	7
Kentucky	13	13	11	11	10	9	9	9
Louisiana	9	10	10	10	10	10	10	10
Maine	6	6	5	5	5	4	4	4
Maryland	8	8	8	8	9	10	10	10
Massachusetts	16	18	17	16	16	14	14	13
Michigan	14	15	19	19	20	21	21	20
Minnesota	11	12	11	11	11	10	10	10
Mississippi	10	10	9	9	8	7	7	7
Missouri	18	18	15	15	13	12	12	11
Montana	3	4	4	4	4	4	4	4
Nebraska	8	8	7	6	6	5	5	5
Nevada	3	3	3	3	3	3	3	4
New Hampshire	4	4	4	4	4	4	4	4
New Jersey	12	14	16	16	16	17	17	16
New Mexico	—	3	3	4	4	4	4	5
New York	39	45	47	47	45	43	41	36
North Carolina	12	12	13	14	14	13	13	13
North Dakota	4	5	4	4	4	4	3	3
Ohio	23	24	26	25	25	26	25	23
Oklahoma	7	10	11	10	8	8	8	8
Oregon	4	5	5	6	6	6	6	7
Pennsylvania	34	38‡	36	35	32	29	27	25
Rhode Island	4	5	4	4	4	4	4	4
South Carolina	9	9	8	8	8	8	8	8
South Dakota	4	5	4	4	4	4	4	3
Tennessee	12	12	11	12	11	11	10	11
Texas	18	20	23	23	24	25	26	29

State	1904–1908	1912–1928‡	1932–1940	1944–1948	1952–1960	1964–1968	1972–1980	1984–1988
Utah	3	4	4	4	4	4	4	5
Vermont	4	4	3	3	3	3	3	3
Virginia	12	12	11	11	12	12	12	12
Washington	5	7	8	8	9	9	9	10
West Virginia	7	8	8	8	8	7	6	6
Wisconsin	13	13	12	12	12	12	11	11
Wyoming	3	3	3	3	3	3	3	3
Total†	483	531	531	531	537§	538‖	538‖	538‖**

* Apportionments are based on the last decennial census preceding the actual year of the election. Thus the electoral college membership for the presidential elections of 1792 through 1800 was based on the 1790 census, that of 1804 and 1808 on the 1800 census, etc. The electoral college membership for the first presidential election, in 1789, was based on the temporary apportionment specified in the Constitution.

† Figures given are those at the end of the decade, including temporary apportionment for states that may have joined the Union since the preceding census.

‡ Congress made no reapportionment following the 1920 census.

§ Total rose temporarily to 537 for the 1960 election to allow the newly admitted states of Alaska and Hawaii to cast electoral votes.

‖ Increase to 538 from 535, which would be the 50-state base, accounted for by the 23rd amendment, giving the District of Columbia a minimum of 3 electoral votes.

** In late 1978, Congress proposed a constitutional amendment to the states providing for congressional and electoral college representation for the District of Columbia "as if it was a state." This amendment, if ratified, would have the effect of increasing temporarily the size of the electoral college from 538 to 539 members because of the likely fourth electoral vote for the District of Columbia. This temporary increase would exist only until the next congressional reapportionment of seats among the states (1991), which would return the size of the House from 437 to its usual 435 members and the electoral college from a temporary 539 to a permanent 537 members—corresponding to 435 House members and 102 senators.

Appendix D • Comparison of Popular and Electoral Vote Percentages, 1824 – 1980

Year	Winning Candidate	Percent of Popular Vote	Percent of Electoral Vote	Disparity (in percentage points)
1824	John Quincy Adams (D)	32	32	0
1828	Andrew Jackson (D)	56	68	12
1832	Andrew Jackson (D)	55	77	22
1836	Martin Van Buren (D)	51	58	7
1840	William H. Harrison (W)	53	80	27
1844	James K. Polk (D)	50	62	12
1848	Zachary Taylor (W)	47	56	9
1852	Franklin Pierce (D)	51	86	35
1856	James Buchanan (D)	46	59	13
1860	Abraham Lincoln (R)	40	59	19
1864	Abraham Lincoln (R)	55	91	36
1868	Ulysses S. Grant (R)	53	73	20
1872	Ulysses S. Grant (R)	56	82	26
1876	Rutherford B. Hayes (R)	48	50	2
1880	James A. Garfield (R)	48	58	10
1884	Grover Cleveland (D)	49	55	6
1888	Benjamin Harrison (R)	48	58	10
1892	Grover Cleveland (D)	46	62	16
1896	William McKinley (R)	51	61	10
1900	William McKinley (R)	52	65	13
1904	Theodore Roosevelt (R)	56	71	15
1908	William H. Taft (R)	52	66	14
1912	Woodrow Wilson (D)	42	82	40
1916	Woodrow Wilson (D)	49	52	3
1920	Warren G. Harding (R)	60	76	16
1924	Calvin Coolidge (R)	54	71	17
1928	Herbert C. Hoover (R)	58	84	26

Year	Winning Candidate	Percent of Popular Vote	Percent of Electoral Vote	Disparity (in percentage points)
1932	Franklin D. Roosevelt (D)	57	89	32
1936	Franklin D. Roosevelt (D)	61	98	37
1940	Franklin D. Roosevelt (D)	55	85	30
1944	Franklin D. Roosevelt (D)	53	81	28
1948	Harry S Truman (D)	50	57	7
1952	Dwight D. Eisenhower (R)	55	83	28
1956	Dwight D. Eisenhower (R)	57	86	29
1960	John F. Kennedy (D)	50	62	12
1964	Lyndon B. Johnson (D)	61	90	29
1968	Richard M. Nixon (R)	43	56	13
1972	Richard M. Nixon (R)	61	97	36
1976	Jimmy Carter (D)	50	55	5
1980	Ronald Reagan (R)	51	91	40

Appendix E • Problem Elections

There are four major types of problem elections with regard to the electoral college's determination of the presidency. These are: (1) elections in which there was an electoral college reversal of the popular vote winner; (2) elections in which there was an electoral college deadlock and use of the House contingent procedure; (3) elections in which the president-elect did not have a majority of popular votes; and (4) elections in which minor vote shifts could have changed the outcome.*

Electoral College Reversal of Popular Vote Winners†

Year	Candidates and Popular Vote Results			Electoral College Results		
1876‡	Tilden (D)	4,287,670	50.9%	Tilden (D)	184	50%
	Hayes (R)	4,035,924	47.9%	Hayes (R)	185	50%
	Tilden popular vote margin of 251,746			Hayes winner with electoral vote margin of 1		
1888	Cleveland (D)	5,540,365	48.6%	Cleveland (D)	168	42%
	Harrison (R)	5,445,269	47.8%	Harrison (R)	233	58%
	Cleveland popular vote margin of 95,096			Harrison winner with electoral vote margin of 65		
1960	Nixon (R)	34,108,157	49.3%	Nixon (R)	219	41%
	Kennedy (D)	34,049,976	49.2%	Kennedy (D)	303	59%
	Nixon popular vote margin of 58,181			Kennedy winner with electoral vote margin of 84		

Note: The popular vote totals for 1960 used here are computed by the second method discussed in chapter 4, which consists of crediting Kennedy with five-elevenths of Alabama's Democratic votes and the unpledged elector slate with six-elevenths. See pp. 66–67.

† The election of 1824 also resulted in a reversal of the popular vote winner, but through use of the House contingent procedure. See pp. 49–52.

‡ The electoral vote results in 1876 were arrived at by a bipartisan election commission, voting along party lines, which awarded 20 disputed electoral votes to Hayes. See pp. 52–57.

* Adapted from Lawrence D. Longley and Alan G. Braun, *The Politics of Electoral College Reform*, 2nd ed. (New Haven, 1975), pp. 33, 36, and 38–40.

Appendix E contains summary information concerning the first three categories of problem elections. Information on the fourth category of problem elections appears in Appendix F.

Electoral College Deadlock and Use of House Contingent Procedure*

Year	Candidates and Popular Vote Results			Electoral College Results	House Result
1800	Jefferson (D)	not available		73	*Jefferson* winner with
	Burr (D)	"		73	10 states to 4 for Burr
	Adams (Fed.)	"		65	after 36 ballots
	Pickney (Fed.)	"		64	
	Jay (D)	"		1	
1824	Adams (D)	115,696	31.9%	84	*Adams* winner with 13
	Jackson (D)	152,933	42.2%	99	states to 7 for Jackson
	Crawford (D)	46,979	13.0%	41	and 4 for Crawford on
	Clay (D)	47,136	13.0%	37	the first ballot
	Jackson popular vote margin of 37,237				

* The Senate contingent procedure for selection of the vice president in case of no electoral college majority has been used only once, in 1837, after Democratic electors from Virginia refused to vote for the Democratic vice presidential nominee, Richard M. Johnson. He was subsequently elected by the Senate by a vote of 33 to 16.

Presidents Elected without a Majority of Popular Votes
(for full returns, see Appendix A)

Year	Winning Candidate in Electoral College	Percent of Popular Vote
1824*†	Adams (D)	31.9
1844	Polk (D)	49.6
1848	Taylor (Whig)	47.3
1856	Buchanan (D)	45.6
1860	Lincoln (R)	39.8
1876*	Hayes (R)	47.9
1880	Garfield (R)	48.3
1884	Cleveland (D)	48.5
1888*	Harrison (R)	47.8
1892	Cleveland (D)	46.0
1912	Wilson (D)	41.9
1916	Wilson (D)	49.3
1948	Truman (D)	49.6
1960‡	Kennedy (D)	49.5
1968	Nixon (R)	43.4

Note: Number of times a president was elected whout a majority of popular votes is 15, or 38 percent of the elections for which popular vote totals are available.

* Election where the winner did not have the most number of popular votes as well as lacked a majority of popular votes.

† Adams was elected president in 1825 through use of the House contingent procedure, although he lacked both a popular vote majority and a plurality. See pp. 50–52.

‡ Depending on the calculation of returns from Alabama, this election may be one where the winner did not have the most number of popular votes as well as lacked a majority of electoral votes. The popular vote totals used here are computed by the first method discussed in chapter 4, which consists of crediting Kennedy with all of the popular votes received by the most popular of his pledged Alabama electors. See pp. 66–68.

Appendix F • Elections in Which Minor Vote Shifts Could Have Changed the Outcome

Listed below are a number of elections in U.S. history in which a strategically placed, relatively small shift in the popular vote could have resulted in either the election of the other candidate or in electoral college deadlock.

Hairbreadth Elections

Year	Shift Needed	In What States	Outcome
1828	11,517	Ohio, Ky., N.Y., La., Ind.	Other candidate elected
1836	14,061	N.Y.	Electoral college deadlock
1840	8,386	N.Y., Pa., Maine, N.J.	Other candidate elected
1844	2,555	N.Y.	Other candidate elected
1848	3,227	Ga., Md., Del.	Other candidate elected
1856	17,427	Ind., Ill., Del.	Electoral college deadlock
1860	18,050	Calif., Oreg., Ill., Ind.	Electoral college deadlock
	25,069	N.Y.	Electoral college deadlock
1864	38,111	N.Y., Pa., Ind., Wis., Md., Conn., Oreg.	Other candidate elected
1868	29,862	Pa., Ind., N.C., Ala., Conn., Calif., Nev.	Other candidate elected
1876	116	S.C.	Other candidate elected
1880	10,517	N.Y.	Other candidate elected
1884	575	N.Y.	Other candidate elected
1888	7,189	N.Y.	Other candidate elected
1892	37,364	N.Y., Ind., Wis., N.J., Calif.	Other candidate elected
1896	20,296	Ind., Ky., Calif., W.Va., Oreg., Del.	Other candidate elected
1900	74,755	Ohio, Ind., Kans., Nebr., Md., Utah, Wyo.	Other candidate elected
1908	75,041	Ohio, Mo., Ind., Kans., W.Va., Del., Mont., Md.	Other candidate elected
1916	1,983	Calif.	Other candidate elected
1948	12,487	Calif., Ohio	Electoral college deadlock
	29,294	Calif., Ohio, Ill.	Other candidate elected

Year	Shift Needed	In What States	Outcome
1960	8,971	Ill., Mo.	Electoral college deadlock
	11,424	Ill., Mo., N.Mex., Hawaii, Nev.	Other candidate elected
1968	53,034	N.J., Mo., N.H.	Electoral college deadlock
1976	11,950	Del., Ohio	Electoral college deadlock
	9,246	Hawaii, Ohio	Other candidate elected

Note: Number of hairbreadth elections is 22, or 55% of the elections for which popular vote totals are available. An important qualification to keep in mind concerning this table is that shifts in voting patterns are seldom isolated in individual states but are usually part of regional or national trends. The changes that would have accomplished the electoral results outlined here would have most likely been part of national or regional shifts not limited to just a few states. Or, expressed differently, to win these key states, there would likely have to be vote switching of considerably greater magnitude than the minimum show here. This table does serve, however, as a demonstration of the relative closeness of many elections, as an illustration of how mighty results can come from relatively small voting shifts, and as evidence of the real potential for electoral college crisis in many of our past elections.

Hairbreadth elections are defined as elections in which a strategically placed shift in the popular vote amounting to less than one percent of the national vote cast, could have changed the outcome of the contest for presidency.

As we note above, however, a vote shift larger overall than the mathematical minimum first indicated would undoubtedly have been necessary, since any significant change in voting patterns would have been general, not selective in a few crucial states. To give some idea of the magnitude of the national vote shifts that would have changed election results, an additional percentage is noted: the percentage of switched votes required in the key states. In most elections a similar shift of the overall natural popular vote would have been required actually to change the outcome of the election. In 1892, for instance, a shift of 37,364 votes in five states would have elected Harrison instead of Cleveland. Those 37,364 votes constituted 0.317 percent of the national popular vote. But the shift in the five key states alone would have been 1.349 percent. Thus it is likely that a general national shift of between 1.0 and 1.5 percent of the popular vote would actually have had to take place for the five closest states to change, giving Harrison the election.

Pioneer research in the field of hairbreadth elections appears in Svend Petersen, *A Statistical History of American Presidential Elections* (New York, 1963). The list below however, contains a number of computations not made by Petersen and rests on data other than his for presidential elections since 1920.

1828. Andrew Jackson received 647,292 popular and 178 electoral votes, while John Quincy Adams received 507,730 popular and 83 electoral votes. A shift from Jackson to Adams of 11,517 votes in five states (Ohio, Kentucky, New York, Louisiana, and Indiana) would have elected Adams. The required shift was 0.997 percent of the national vote cast. But a shift of 2.189 percent in the five crucial states would have been needed to change the indicated number of electoral votes.

1836. Martin Van Buren received 764,198 popular and 170 electoral votes, while

William Henry Harrison received 549,508 popular and 73 electoral votes. A shift from Van Buren to Harrison of 14,061 votes in one state—New York—would have deprived Van Buren of an electoral college majority and probably would have encouraged the Whigs to unify their electoral votes behind Harrison and thus make him president. As it was, two other Whig candidates received a total of 40 electoral votes. The required shift was 0.937 percent of the national vote cast. But a shift of 4,600 percent in New York would have been needed to change the indicated number of electoral votes.

1840. Harrison received 1,275,612 popular and 234 electoral votes and Van Buren 1,130,033 popular and 60 electoral votes. A shift from Harrison to Van Buren of 8,386 votes in four states (New York, Pennsylvania, Maine, and New Jersey) would have elected Van Buren. The required shift was 0.349 percent of the national vote cast; a shift of 0.949 percent in the four crucial states would have been needed to change the indicated number of electoral votes.

1844. James K. Polk received 1,339,368 popular and 170 electoral votes, while Henry Clay received 1,300,687 popular and 105 electoral votes. A shift of 2,555 votes from Polk to Clay in one state—New York—would have made Clay president. The required shift was 0.097 percent of the national vote cast; a shift of 0.544 percent in New York would have been needed to change the indicated number of electoral votes.

1848. Zachary Taylor received 1,362,101 popular and 163 electoral votes, while Lewis Cass received 1,222,674 popular and 127 electoral votes. A shift from Taylor to Cass of 3,227 votes in three states (Georgia, Maryland, and Delaware) would have given Cass the presidency. The required shift was 0.125 percent of the national vote cast; a shift of 1.824 percent in the three crucial states would have been needed to change the indicated number of electoral votes.

1856. James Buchanan received 1,839,237 popular and 174 electoral votes, while John C. Frémont received 1,341,028 popular and 114 electoral votes; Millard Fillmore received 849,872 popular and 8 electoral votes. A shift of 17,427 votes from Buchanan to Frémont in two states (Indiana and Illinois) and from Fillmore to Frémont in one state (Delaware) would have deprived Buchanan of an electoral majority and thrown the election into the House of Representatives for decision. The required shift was 0.432 percent of the national vote cast; a shift of 3.554 percent in the three crucial states alone would have been needed to change the indicated number of electoral votes.

1860. Abraham Lincoln received 1,867,198 popular and 180 electoral votes, while Stephen A. Douglas received 1,379,434 popular and 12 electoral votes; John C. Breckinridge received 854,248 popular and 72 electoral votes, and John Bell received 591,658 popular and 39 electoral votes. A shift of 18,050 votes from Lincoln to Douglas in four states (California, Oregon, Illinois, and Indiana), or of 25,069 votes from Lincoln to Douglas in New York, would have deprived Lincoln of an electoral college majority and thrown the election into the House, where Lincoln's Republicans controlled only 15 of the 34 state delegations. The required shift of 18,050 votes was 0.772 percent of the national vote cast; a shift of 2,677 percent in the four crucial states alone—or a shift of 3.713 percent in New York—would have been needed to change the indicated number of electoral votes.

1864. Lincoln received 2,219,362 popular and 212 electoral votes, while George B. McClellan received 1,805,063 popular and 21 electoral votes. A shift of 38,111 votes in seven states (New York, Pennsylvania, Indiana, Wisconsin, Maryland, Connecticut, and

Oregon) would have elected McClellan. The required shift was 0.947 percent of the national vote cast; a shift of 1,994 percent in the seven crucial states would have been needed to change the indicated number of electoral votes.

1868. Ulysses S. Grant received 3,013,313 popular and 214 electoral votes, while Horatio Seymour received 2,703,933 popular and 80 electoral votes. A shift of 29,862 votes in seven states (Pennsylvania, Indiana, North Carolina, Alabama, Connecticut, California, and Nevada) would have elected Seymour. The required shift was 0.522 percent of the national vote cast; a shift of 1.923 percent in the seven crucial states would have been needed to change the indicated number of electoral votes.

1876. After the disputed ballot count in several states was settled, Rutherford B. Hayes received 4,035,924 popular and 185 electoral votes, while Samuel J. Tilden received 4,287,670 popular and 184 electoral votes. A shift of 116 votes in South Carolina would have transferred one electoral vote from Hayes to Tilden and made Tilden president. The required shift was 0.0056 percent of the national vote cast; a shift of 0.0635 percent in the South Carolina balloting would have been needed to change the electoral vote.

1880. James A. Garfield received 4,454,433 popular and 214 electoral votes, while Winfield S. Hancock received 4,444,976 popular and 155 electoral votes. A shift of 10,517 votes in New York would have elected Hancock. The required shift was 0.118 percent of the national total; a shift of 0.965 percent in New York would have been needed to change the indicated number of electoral votes.

1884. Grover Cleveland received 4,875,971 popular and 219 electoral votes, while James G. Blaine received 4,852,234 popular and 182 electoral votes. A shift of 575 votes in one state—again New York—would have made Blaine president. The required shift was 0.006 percent of the national vote; a shift of 0.051 percent in New York would have been needed to change the indicated number of electoral votes.

1888. Benjamin Harrison received 5,445,269 popular and 233 electoral votes, while Grover Cleveland received 5,540,365 popular and 168 electoral votes. A switch of New York's electoral votes, in this instance through a shift of 7,189 votes from Harrison to Cleveland, would have elected Cleveland. The required shift was 0.065 percent of the national vote; a shift of 0.589 percent in New York would have been needed to change the indicated number of electoral votes.

1892. Cleveland received 5,556,982 popular and 277 electoral votes, while Harrison received 5,191,466 popular and 145 electoral votes. A shift of 37,364 votes from Cleveland to Harrison in five states (New York, Indiana, Wisconsin, New Jersey, and California) would have reelected Harrison. The required shift was 0.317 percent of the national vote; a shift of 1.349 percent in the five states would have been needed to change the indicated number of electoral votes.

1896. William McKinley received 7,113,734 popular and 271 electoral votes, while William Jennings Bryan received 6,516,722 popular and 176 electoral votes. A shift of 20,296 votes in six states (Indiana, Kentucky, California, West Virginia, Oregon, and Delaware) would have given the election to Bryan. The required shift was 0.150 percent of the national vote; a shift of 1.207 percent in the six states would have been needed to change the indicated number of electoral votes.

1900. McKinley received 7,219,828 popular and 292 electoral votes, while Bryan received 6,358,160 popular and 155 electoral votes. A shift of 74,755 votes in seven states (Ohio, Indiana, Kansas, Nebraska, Maryland, Utah, and Wyoming) would have elected Bryan. The required shift was 0.551 percent of the national vote cast; a shift of 2.848 percent in the seven crucial states would have been needed to change the indicated number of electoral votes.

1908. William Howard Taft received 7,679,114 popular and 321 electoral votes, while Bryan received 6,410,665 popular and 162 electoral votes. A shift of 75,041 in eight states (Ohio, Missouri, Indiana, Kansas, West Virginia, Delaware, Montana, and Maryland) would have given Bryan a majority in the electoral college. The required shift was 0.533 percent of the national vote; a shift of 2.204 percent in the eight states would have been needed to change the indicated number of electoral votes.

1916. Woodrow Wilson received 9,131,511 popular and 277 electoral votes, while Charles Evans Hughes received 8,548,935 popular and 254 electoral votes. A shift of 1,983 votes from Wilson to Hughes in California would have cost Wilson the election. The required shift was 0.0112 percent of the national vote cast; a shift of 0.0214 percent in California would have been needed to change the indicated number of electoral votes.

1948. Harry S Truman received 24,179,345 popular and 303 electoral votes, while Thomas E. Dewey received 21,991,291 popular and 189 electoral votes. A shift of 29,294 votes in three states (Illinois, California, and Ohio) would have made Dewey president. A switch of 12,487 votes in California and Ohio would have denied both candidates an electoral college majority and would have thrown the election into the House, where neither candidate was favored by a clear majority of states. The shift required to elect Dewey was 0.063 percent of the national vote cast; a shift of 0.275 percent in the three states would have elected Dewey, and an 0.186 percent shift in the two states would have sent the election to the House for decision.

1960. John F. Kennedy received 34,220,984 popular and 303 electoral votes, while Richard M. Nixon received 34,108,157 popular and 219 electoral votes. A shift of 11,424 votes in five states (Illinois, Missouri, New Mexico, Hawaii, and Nevada) would have elected Nixon. A shift of only 8,971 popular votes from Kennedy to Nixon in Illinois and Missouri would have prevented either candidate from receiving an electoral college majority and given the balance of power to the unpledged electors who eventually voted for Harry F. Byrd of Virginia. If the election had gone to the House for decision, neither Kennedy nor Nixon would have been assured of a clear majority of the states. The shift required to elect Nixon was 0.0167 percent of the national vote cast; a shift of 0.157 percent in the five crucial states would have been needed to change the indicated number of votes, and a shift of 0.134 percent in the two states would have been enough to prevent either candidate from gaining an electoral college majority.

1968. Richard Nixon received 31,785,480 popular and 301 electoral votes, while Hubert H. Humphrey received 31,275,165 popular and 191 electoral votes and George C. Wallace received 9,906,473 popular and 46 electoral votes. A shift of 53,034 votes in three states (New Jersey, Missouri, and New Hampshire) would have resulted in an electoral college deadlock. If the election had not been decided at the time of the meetings of the electoral college, it would have gone to the House for final decision, where the outcome would have been very uncertain (see the discussion chapter 4, pp. 78–79). The shift necessary to deadlock the national election was 0.0724 percent of the national vote total and 1.07 percent of the vote in the three states.

1976. Jimmy Carter received 40,829,046 popular and 297 electoral votes, while Gerald R. Ford received 39,146,006 popular votes and 240 electoral votes. A shift of 11,950 votes in two states (Delaware and Ohio) would have resulted in an exact electoral vote tie, with each candidate having 269 votes. If the election had not been decided by a defecting elector at the time of the meetings of the electoral college, it would have gone to the House for final decision. This vote shift would be 0.0147 percent of the national vote total and 2.75 percent of the vote in the two states. If 9,246 votes had shifted in two other states (Hawaii and Ohio) Ford would have been elected (despite Carter's national vote margin of nearly 1.7 million votes). This vote shift is 0.0113 percent of the national vote total and 0.21 percent of the vote in the two states. If Republican elector Mike Padden (see p. 82) had withheld his electoral vote from Ford, the result of the 9,246 vote shift would have been not the election of the other candidate but rather an electoral college deadlock.

Appendix G • Constitutional Provisions Relating to Presidential Election and Succession and the Elective Franchise

Section 1.   The executive Power shall be vested in a President of the United States of America. He shall hold his Office during the Term of four Years, and, together with the Vice President, chosen for the same Term, be elected, as follows.

Each State shall appoint, in such Manner as the Legislature thereof may direct, a Number of Electors, equal to the whole Number of Senators and Representatives to which the State may be entitled in the Congress; but no Senator or Representative, or Person holding an Office of Trust or Profit under the United States, shall be appointed an Elector.

* [The Electors shall meet in their respective States, and vote by Ballot for two Persons, of whom one at least shall not be an Inhabitant of the same State with themselves. And they shall make a List of all the Persons voted for, and of the Number of Votes for each; which List they shall sign and certify, and transmit sealed to the Seat of the Government of the United States, directed to the President of the Senate. The President of the Senate shall, in the Presence of the Senate and House of Representatives, open all the Certificates, and the Votes shall then be counted. The Person having the greatest Number of Votes shall be the President, if such Number be a Majority of the whole Number of Electors appointed; and if there be more than one who have such Majority, and have an equal Number of Votes, then the House of Representatives shall immediately chuse by Ballot one of them for President; and if no Person have a majority, then from the five highest on the List the said House shall in like Manner chuse the President. But in chusing the President, the Votes shall be taken by States, the Representation from each State having one Vote; a quorum for this Purpose shall consist of a Member or Members from two thirds of the States, and a Majority of all the States shall be necessary to a Choice. In every Case, after the Choice of the President, the Person having the greatest Number of Votes of the Electors shall be the Vice President. But if there should remain two or more who have equal Votes, the Senate shall chuse from them by Ballot the Vice President.]

The Congress may determine the Time of chusing the Electors, and the Day on which they shall give their Votes; which Day shall be the same throughout the United States.

No Person except a natural born Citizen, or a Citizen of the United States, at the time of the Adoption of this Constitution, shall be eligible to the Office of President; neither

* Paragraph in brackets superseded by the 12th amendment (see below, p. 265).

shall any person be eligible to that Office who shall not have attained to the Age of thirty five Years, and been fourteen Years a Resident within the United States.

In Case of the Removal of the President from Office, or of his Death, Resignation, or Inability to discharge the Powers and Duties of the said Office, the Same shall devolve on the Vice President, and the Congress may by Law provide for the Case of Removal, Death, Resignation or Inability, both of the President and Vice President, declaring what Officer shall then act as President, and such Officer shall act accordingly, until the Disability be removed, or a President shall be elected.

The President shall, at stated Times, receive for his Services, a Compensation, which shall neither be encreased nor diminished during the Period for which he shall have been elected, and he shall not receive within that Period any other Emolument from the United States, or any of them.

Before he enter on the Execution of his Office, he shall take the following Oath or Affirmation—"I do solemnly swear (or affirm) that I will faithfully execute the Office of President of the United States, and will to the best of my Ability, preserve, protect and defend the Constitution of the United States."

Section 2. The President shall be Commander in Chief of the Army and Navy of the United States, and of the Militia of the several States, when called into the actual Service of the United States; he may require the Opinion, in writing, of the principal Officer in each of the executive Departments, upon any Subject relating to the Duties of their respective Offices, and he shall have Power to grant Reprieves and Pardons for Offenses against the United States, except in Cases of Impeachment.

He shall have Power, by and with the Advice and Consent of the Senate, to make Treaties, provided two thirds of the Senators present concur; and he shall nominate, and by and with the Advice and Consent of the Senate, shall appoint Ambassadors, other public Ministers and Consuls, Judges of the supreme Court, and all other Officers of the United States, whose Appointments are not herein otherwise provided for, and which shall be established by Law: but the Congress may by Law vest the Appointment of such inferior Officers, as they think proper, in the President alone, in the Courts of Law, or in the Heads of Departments.

The President shall have Power to fill up all Vacancies that may happen during the Recess of the Senate, by granting Commissions which shall expire at the End of their next Session.

Section 3. He shall from time to time give to the Congress Information of the State of the Union, and recommend to their Consideration such Measures as he shall judge necessary and expedient; he may, on extraordinary Occasions, convene both Houses, or either of them, and in Case of Disagreement between them, with Respect to the Time of Adjournment, he may adjourn them to such Time as he shall think proper; he shall receive Ambassadors and other public Ministers; he shall take Care that the Laws be faithfully executed, and shall Commission all the Officers of the United States.

Section 4. The President, Vice President and all Civil Officers of the United States, shall be removed from Office on Impeachment for, and Conviction of, Treason, Bribery, or other high Crimes and Misdemeanors.

AMENDMENT XII
(Declared ratified Sept. 25, 1804)

The Electors shall meet in their respective states and vote by ballot for President and Vice-President, one of whom, at least, shall not be an inhabitant of the same state with themselves; they shall name in their ballots the person voted for as President, and in distinct ballots the person voted for as Vice-President, and they shall make distinct lists of all persons voted for as President, and of all persons voted for as Vice-President, and of the number of votes for each, which lists they shall sign and certify, and transmit sealed to the seat of the government of the United States, directed to the President of the Senate;—The President of the Senate shall, in the presence of the Senate and House of Representatives, open all the certificates and the votes shall then be counted;—The person having the greatest number of votes for President, shall be the President, if such number be a majority of the whole number of Electors appointed; and if no person have such majority, then from the persons having the highest numbers not exceeding three on the list of those voted for as President, the House of Representatives shall choose immediately, by ballot, the President. But in choosing the President, the votes shall be taken by states, the representation from each state having one vote; a quorum for this purpose shall consist of a member or members from two-thirds of the states, and a majority of all the states shall be necessary to a choice. And if the House of Representatives shall not choose a President whenever the right of choice shall devolve upon them, before the fourth day of March next following, then the Vice-President shall act as President, as in the case of the death or other constitutional disability of the President—The person having the greatest number of votes as Vice-President, shall be the Vice President, if such number be a majority of the whole number of Electors appointed, and if no person have a majority, then from the two highest numbers on the list, the Senate shall choose the Vice-President; a quorum for the purpose shall be necessary to a choice. But no person constitutionally ineligible to the office of President shall be eligible to that of Vice-President of the United States.

AMENDMENT XIV
(Declared ratified July 28, 1868)

Section 1.   All persons born or naturalized in the United States and subject to the jurisdiction thereof, are citizens of the United States and of the State wherein they reside. No State shall make or enforce any law which shall abridge the privileges or immunities of citizens of the United States; or shall any State deprive any person of life, liberty, or property, without due process of law; nor deny to any person within its jurisdiction the equal protection of the laws.

Section 2.   Representatives shall be apportioned among the several States according to their respective numbers, counting the whole number of persons in each State, excluding Indians not taxed. But when the right to vote at any election for the choice of electors for President and Vice President of the United States, Representatives in Congress, the Executive and Judicial officers of a State, or the members of the Legislature thereof, is denied to any of the male inhabitants of such State, being twenty-one years of age, and citizens of the United States, or in any way abridged, except for participation in rebellion, or other crime, the basis of representation therein shall be reduced in the proportion which the number of such male citizens shall bear to the whole number of male citizens twenty-one years of age in such State.*

Section 3.   No person shall be a Senator or Representative in Congress, or elector of President and Vice President, or hold any office, civil or military, under the United

---

* The sections of this amendment which would reduce a state's congressional representation (and thus its votes in the electoral college) have never been enforced.

States, or under any State, who, having previously taken an oath, as a member of Congress, or as an officer of the United States, or as a member of any State legislature, or as an executive or judicial officer of any State, to support the Constitution of the United States, shall have engaged in insurrection or rebellion against the same, or given aid or comfort to the enemies thereof. But Congress may by a vote of two-thirds of each House, remove such disability. . . .

Section 5. The Congress shall have power to enforce, by appropriate legislation, the provisions of this article.

AMENDMENT XV
(Declared ratified March 30, 1870)

Section 1. The right of citizens of the United States to vote shall not be denied or abridged by the United States or by any State on account of race, color, or previous condition of servitude.

Section 2. The Congress shall have power to enforce this article by appropriate legislation.

AMENDMENT XVII
(Declared ratified May 31, 1913)

The Senate of the United States shall be composed of two Senators from each State, elected by the people thereof, for six years, and each Senator shall have one vote. The electors in each State shall have the qualifications requisite for electors of the most numerous branch of the State legislatures. . . .

AMENDMENT XIX
(Declared ratified Aug. 26, 1920)

The right of citizens of the United States to vote shall not be denied or abridged by the United States or by any State on account of sex.

Congress shall have power to enforce this article by appropriate legislation.

AMENDMENT XX
(Declared ratified Feb. 6, 1933)

Section 1. The terms of the President and Vice President shall end at noon on the 20th day of January, and the terms of Senators and Representatives at noon on the 3d day of January, of the years in which such terms would have ended if this article had not been ratified; and the terms of their successors shall then begin.

Section 2. The Congress shall assemble at least once in every year, and such meeting shall begin at noon on the 3d day of January, unless they shall by law appoint a different day.

Section 3. If, at the time fixed for the beginning of the term of the President, the President elect shall have died, the Vice President elect shall become President. If a President shall not have been chosen before the time fixed for the beginning of his term, or if the President elect shall have failed to qualify, then the Vice President elect shall act as President until a President shall have qualified; and the Congress may by law provide for the case wherein neither a President elect nor a Vice President elect shall have qualified, declaring who shall then act as President, or the manner in which one who is to act shall be selected, and such person shall act accordingly until a President or Vice President shall have qualified.

Seciton 4. The Congress may by law provide for the case of the death of any of the persons from whom the House of Representatives may choose a President whenever the right of choice shall have devolved upon them, and for the case of the death of any of the persons from whom the Senate may choose a Vice President whenever the right of choice shall have devolved upon them. . . .

AMENDMENT XXII
(Declared ratified Feb. 26, 1951)

Section 1. No person shall be elected to the office of the President more than twice, and no person who has held the office of President, or acted as President, for more than two years of a term to which some other person was elected President shall be elected to the office of the President more than once. But this Article shall not apply to any person holding the office of President when this Article was proposed by the Congress, and shall not prevent any person who may be holding the office of President, or acting as President, during the term within which this Article becomes operative from holding the office of President or acting as President during the remainder of such term. . . .

AMENDMENT XXIII
(Declared ratified March 29, 1961)

Section 1. The District constituting the seat of Government of the United States shall appoint in such manner as the Congress may direct:

A number of electors of President and Vice President equal to the whole number of Senators and Representatives in Congress to which the District would be entitled if it were a State, but in no event more than the least populous State; they shall be considered, for the purposes of the election of President and Vice President, to be electors appointed by a State; and they shall meet in the District and perform such duties as provided by the twelfth article of amendment.

Section 2. The Congress shall have power to enforce this article by appropriate legislation.

AMENDMENT XXIV
(Declared ratified Jan. 23. 1964)

Section 1. The right of citizens of the United States to vote in any primary or other election for President or Vice President, for electors for President or Vice President, or for Senator or Representative in Congress, shall not be denied or abridged by the United States or any State by reason of failure to pay any poll tax or other tax.

Section 2. The Congress shall have the power to enforce this article by appropriate legislation.

AMENDMENT XXV
(Declared ratified Feb. 10, 1967)

Section 1. In case of the removal of the President from office or of his death or resignation, the Vice President shall become President.

Section 2.   Whenever there is a vacancy in the office of the Vice President, the President shall nominate a Vice President who shall take office upon confirmation by a majority vote of both houses of Congress.

Section 3.   Whenever the President transmits to the President pro tempore of the Senate and the Speaker of the House of Representatives his written declaration that he is unable to discharge the powers and duties of his office, and until he transmits to them a written declaration to the contrary, such powers and duties shall be discharged by the Vice President as Acting President.

Section 4.   Whenever the Vice President and a majority of either the principal officers of the Executive departments or of such other body as Congress may by law provide transmit to the President pro tempore of the Senate and the Speaker of the House of Representatives their written declaration that the President is unable to discharge the powers and duties of his office, the Vice President shall immediately assume the powers and duties of the office as Acting President.

Thereafter, when the President transmits to the President pro tempore of the Senate and the Speaker of the House of Representatives his written declaration that no inability exists, he shall resume the powers and duties of his office unless the Vice President and a majority of either the principal officers of the executive departments or of such other body as Congress may by law provide transmits within four days to the President pro tempore of the Senate and the Speaker of the House of Representatives their written declaration that the President is unable to discharge the powers and duties of his office. Thereupon Congress shall decide the issue, assembling within forty-eight hours for that purpose if not in session. If the Congress, within twenty-one days after receipt of the latter written declaration, or, if Congress is not in session, within twenty-one days after Congress is required to assemble, determines by two-thirds vote of both houses that the President is unable to discharge the powers and duties of his office, the Vice President shall continue to discharge the same as as Acting President; otherwise, the President shall resume the powers and duties of his office.

Appendix H · Federal Law Relating to Presidential Election Procedures

UNITED STATES CODE, 1976 EDITION

TITLE 3—THE PRESIDENT

Chapter 1—Presidential Elections and Vacancies (Excerpts)

§1. Time of appointing electors.

The electors of President and Vice President shall be appointed, in each State, on the Tuesday next after the first Monday in November, in every fourth year succeeding every election of a President and Vice President.

§4. Vacancies in electoral college.

Each State may, by law, provide for the filling of any vacancies which may occur in its college of electors when such college meets to give its electoral vote.

§7. Meeting and vote of electors.

The electors of President and Vice President of each State shall meet and give their votes on the first Monday after the second Wednesday in December next following their appointment at such place in each State as the legislature of such State shall direct.

§9. Certificates of votes for President and Vice President.

The electors shall make and sign six certificates of all the votes given by them, each of which certificates shall contain two distinct lists, one of the votes for President and the other of the votes for Vice President, and shall annex to each of the certificates one of the lists of the electors which shall have been furnished to them by direction of the executive of the State.

§11. Disposition of certificates.

The electors shall dispose of the certificates so made by them and the lists attached thereto in the following manner:

First.   They shall forthwith forward by registered mail one of the same to the President of the Senate at the seat of government.

Second.   Two of the same shall be delivered to the secretary of state of the State, one of which shall be held subject to the order of the President of the Senate, the other to be preserved by him for one year and shall be a part of the public records of his office and shall be open to public inspection.

Third.   On the day thereafter they shall forward by registered mail two of such certificates and lists to the Administrator of General Services at the seat of government,

270

one of which shall be held subject to the order of the President of the Senate. The other shall be preserved by the Administrator of General Services for one year and shall be a part of the public records of his office and shall be open to public inspection.

Fourth.   They shall forthwith cause the other of the certificates and lists to be delivered to the judge of the district in which the electors shall have assembled.

§15. Counting electoral votes in Congress.

Congress shall be in session on the sixth day of January succeeding every meeting of the electors. The Senate and House of Representatives shall meet in the Hall of the House of Representatives at the hour of 1 o'clock in the afternoon on that day, and the President of the Senate shall be their presiding officer. Two tellers shall be previously appointed on the part of the Senate and two on the part of the House of Representatives, to whom shall be handed, as they are opened by the President of the Senate, all the certificates and papers purporting to be certificates of the electoral votes, which certificates and papers shall be opened, presented, and acted upon in the alphabetical order of the States, beginning with the letter A; and said tellers, having then read the same in the presence and hearing of the two Houses, shall make a list of the votes as they shall appear from the said certificates; and the votes having been ascertained and counted according to the rules in this subchapter provided, the result of the same shall be delivered to the President of the Senate, who shall thereupon announce the state of the vote, which announcement shall be deemed a sufficient declaration of the persons, if any, elected President and Vice President of the United States, and, together with a list of the votes, be entered on the Journals of the two Houses. Upon such reading of any such certificate or paper, the President of the Senate shall call for objections, if any. Every objection shall be made in writing, and shall state clearly and concisely, and without argument, the ground thereof, and shall be signed by at least one Senator and one Member of the House of Representatives before the same shall be received. When all objections so made to any vote or paper from a State shall have been received and read, the Senate shall thereupon withdraw, and such objections shall be submitted to the Senate for its decision; and the Speaker of the House of Representatives shall, in like manner, submit such objections to the House of Representatives for its decision; and no electoral vote or votes from any State which shall have been regularly given by electors whose appointment has been lawfully certified to according to section 6* of this title from which but one return has been received shall be rejected, but the two Houses concurrently may reject the vote or votes when they agree that such vote or votes have not been so regularly given by electors whose appointment has been so certified. If more than one return or paper purporting to be a return from a State shall have been received by the President of the Senate, those votes, and those only, shall be counted which shall have been regularly given by the electors who are shown by the determination mentioned in section 5† of this title to have been appointed, if the determination in said section provided for shall have been made, or by such successors or substitutes, in case of a vacancy in the board of electors so ascertained, as have been appointed to fill such vacancy in the mode provided by the laws of the State; but in case there shall arise the question which of two or more of such State authorities determining what electors have been appointed, as mentioned in section 5 of this title, is the lawful tribunal of such State, the votes regularly given of those electors, and those only, of such State shall be

* Section 6 provides for certification of votes by electors by state Governors.

† Section 5 provides that if state law specifies a method for resolving disputes concerning the vote for Presidential electors, Congress must respect any determination so made by a state.

counted whose title as electors the two Houses, acting separately, shall concurrently decide is supported by the decision of such State so authorized by its law; and in such case of more than one return or paper purporting to be a return from a State, if there shall have been no such determination of the question in the State aforesaid, then those votes, and those only, shall be counted which the two Houses shall concurrently decide were cast by lawful electors appointed in accordance with the laws of the State, unless the two Houses, acting separately, shall concurrently decide such votes not to be the lawful votes of the legally appointed electors of such State. But if the two Houses shall disagree in respect of the counting of such votes, then, and in that case, the votes of the electors whose appointment shall have been certified by the executive of the State, under the seal thereof, shall be counted. When the two Houses have voted, they shall immediately again meet, and the presiding officer shall then announce the decision of the questions submitted. No votes or papers from any other State shall be acted upon until the objections previously made to the votes or papers from any State shall have been finally disposed of.

§16. Same; seats for officers and Members of two Houses in joint meeting.

At such joint meeting of the two Houses seats shall be provided as follows: For the President of the Senate, the Speaker's chair; for the Speaker, immediately upon his left; for the Senators, in the body of the Hall upon the right of the presiding officer; for the Representatives, in the body of the Hall not provided for the Senators; for the tellers, Secretary of the Senate, and Clerk of the House of Representatives, at the Clerk's desk; for the other officers of the two Houses in front of the Clerk's desk and upon each side of the Speaker's platform. Such joint meeting shall not be dissolved until the count of electoral votes shall be completed and the result declared; and no recess shall be taken unless a question shall have arisen in regard to counting any such votes, or otherwise under this subchapter, in which case it shall be competent for either House, acting separately, in the manner hereinbefore provided, to direct a recess of such House not beyond the next calendar day, Sunday excepted, at the hour of 10 0'clock in the forenoon. But if the counting of the electoral votes and the declaration of the result shall not have been completed before the fifth calendar day next after such first meeting of the two Houses, no further or other recess shall be taken by either House.

§17. Same; limit of debate in each House.

When the two Houses separate to decide upon an objection that may have been made to the counting of any electoral vote or votes from any State, or other question arising in the matter, each Senator and Representative may speak to such objection or question five minutes, and not more than once; but after such debate shall have lasted two hours it shall be the duty of the presiding officer of each House to put the main question without further debate.

§18. Same; parliamentary procedure at joint meeting.

While the two Houses shall be in meeting as provided in this chapter, the President of the Senate shall have power to preserve order; and no debate shall be allowed and no question shall be put by the presiding officer except to either House on a motion to withdraw.

Appendix I • Rules for Election of a President in the House of Representatives

The following rules* were adopted by the House of Representatives on February 7, 1825, for the election of a president after the failure of the electoral college to produce a majority for any candidate following the presidential election of 1824. No subsequent election has ever gone to the House for decision. These rules would be the governing precedent if the House should again be called upon to elect a president, though the House might alter the rules at any time.

1. In the event of its appearing, on opening all the certificates, and counting the votes given by the electors of the several States for President, that no person has a majority of the votes of the whole number of electors appointed, the same shall be entered on the Journals of this House.

2. The roll of the House shall then be called by States; and, on its appearing that a Member or Members from two-thirds of the States are present, the House shall immediately proceed, by ballot, to choose a President from the persons having the highest numbers, not exceeding three, on the list of those voted for as President; and, in case neither or those persons shall receive the votes of a majority of all the States on the first ballot, the House shall continue to ballot for a President, without interruption by other business, until a President be chosen.

3. The doors of the Hall shall be closed during the balloting, except against the Members of the Senate, stenographers, and the officers of the House.

4. From the commencement of the balloting until an election is made no proposition to adjourn shall be received, unless on the motion of one State, seconded by another State, and the question shall be decided by States. The same rule shall be observed in regard to any motion to change the usual hour for the meeting of the House.

5. In balloting the following mode shall be observed, to wit:

The Representatives of each State shall be arranged and seated together, beginning with the seats at the right hand of the Speaker's chair, with the Members from the State of Maine; thence, proceeding with the Members from the States, in the order the States are usually named for receiving petitions,† around the Hall of the House, until all are seated.

---

* Hinds' *Precedents of the House of Representatives*, vol. III, pp. 292–93 (Washington, D.C., 1907).

† Petitions are no longer introduced in this way. This old order of calling the states began with Maine and proceeded the original thirteen states and then through the remaining states in the order of their admission to the Union.

A ballot box shall be provided for each State.

The Representatives of each State shall, in the first instance, ballot among themselves, in order to ascertain the vote of their State; and they may, if necessary, appoint tellers of their ballots.

After the vote of each State is ascertained, duplicates thereof shall be made out; and in case any one of the persons from whom the choice is to be made shall receive a majority of the votes given, on any one balloting by the Representatives of a State, the name of that person shall be written on each of the duplicates; and in case the votes so given shall be divided so that neither of said persons shall have a majority of the whole number of votes given by such State, on any one balloting, then the word "divided" shall be written on each duplicate.

After the delegation from each State shall have ascertained the vote of their State, the Clerk shall name the States in the order they are usually named for receiving petitions; and as the name of each is called the Sergeant-at-Arms shall present to the delegation of each two ballot boxes, in each of which shall be deposited, by some Representative of the State, one of the duplicates made as aforesaid of the vote of said State, in the presence and subject to the examination of all the Members from said State then present; and where there is more than one Representative from a State, the duplicates shall not both be deposited by the same person.

When the votes of the States are thus all taken in, the Sergeant-at-Arms shall carry one of said ballot boxes to one table and the other to a separate and distinct table.

One person from each State represented in the balloting shall be appointed by the Representatives to tell off said ballots; but, in case the Representatives fail to appoint a teller, the Speaker shall appoint.

The said tellers shall divide themselves into two sets, as nearly equal in number as can be, and one of the said sets of tellers shall proceed to count the votes in one of said boxes, and the other set the votes in the other box.

When the votes are counted by the different sets of tellers, the result shall be reported to the House; and if the reports agree, the same shall be accepted as the true votes of the States; but if the reports disagree, the States shall proceed, in the same manner as before, to a new ballot.

6. All questions arising after the balloting commences, requiring the decision of the House, which shall be decided by the House, voting per capita, to be incidental to the power of choosing a President, shall be decided by States without debate; and in case of an equal division of the votes of States, the question shall be lost.

7. When either of the persons from whom the choice is to be made shall have received a majority of all the States, the Speaker shall declare the same, and that that person is elected President of the United States.

8. The result shall be immediately communicated to the Senate by message, and a committee of three persons shall be appointed to inform the President of the United States and the President-elect of said election.

On February 9, 1825, the election of John Quincy Adams took place in accordance with these rules.

Appendix J • State Laws on Ballots and Elector Nominations

:

TYPE OF GENERAL ELECTION BALLOT USED BY THE STATES FOR CHOOSING PRESIDENTIAL ELECTORS

Short ballot, with names of electors excluded (38 states): Alabama, Arkansas, California, Colorado, Connecticut, Delaware, Florida, Georgia, Hawaii, Illinois, Indiana, Iowa, Kentucky, Maine, Maryland, Massachusetts, Michigan, Minnesota, Missouri, Montana, Nebraska, Nevada, New Hampshire, New Jersey, New Mexico, New York (where voting machines or short ballots are authorized), North Carolina, Ohio, Oregon, Pennsylvania, Rhode Island (on voting machines), Texas, Utah, Vermont, Washington, West Virginia, Wisconsin, Wyoming, and the District of Columbia. The laws of these states contain a provision to the effect that a vote cast for president and vice president is deemed to be a vote cast for the electors of the party that the candidates represent.

Long ballot, with the names of both the presidential candidates and the electors (11 states): Alaska, Arizona, Idaho, Kansas, Louisiana, North Dakota, Oklahoma, South Carolina (if requested in certification), South Dakota, Tennessee, and Virginia. In addition, New York uses the system in areas without voting machines or where short ballots are not authorized.

Long ballot, showing the names of presidential electors and their party designation but no names of presidential candidates (one state): Mississippi (if electors are pledged, an indication of whom they favor may appear on the ballot).

STATE LAW REQUIREMENTS ON THE METHOD OF NOMINATING CANDIDATES FOR PRESIDENTIAL ELECTOR

By state party conventions (34 states): Alaska, Arkansas, Colorado, Connecticut, Delaware, Hawaii, Idaho, Illinois, Indiana, Iowa, Kansas, Maine, Maryland, Michigan, Minnesota, Montana, Nebraska, Nevada, New Hampshire, New Mexico, North Carolina, North Dakota, Ohio, Oklahoma, Rhode Island, South Dakota, Texas, Utah, Vermont, Virginia, Washington, West Virginia, Wisconsin, Wyoming.

By state party committees (10 states): Alabama, California, Georgia, Massachusetts, Missouri, New Jersey, New York, Oregon, South Carolina, Tennessee: also the District of Columbia by party executive committee.

Sources: Congressional Quarterly Weekly Report, Oct. 25, 1980, p. 3184; *Nomination and Election of the President and Vice President of the United States,* by Thomas M. Durbin and Michael V. Seitzinger (U.S. Government Printing Office, Washington, 1980) and from secretaries of state.

By method to be stipulated by state party committees (2 states): Louisiana and Kentucky.

By governor on recommendation of state party committee (one state): Florida.

By primary election (one state): Arizona.

By mixed convention-primary system (one state): Mississippi. Under that state's law, each party's convention has the option of designating directly the elector nominees for the general election ballot or of requesting a primary between an unpledged elector slate and a slate pledged to the party's national nominee. A request of ten percent of the convention delegates necessitates a primary.

By the party's presidential nominee (one state): Pennsylvania.

Appendix K • Presidential Election Documents

I—LEGISLATIVE ELECTION TALLY SHEET

The official tally sheet showing the votes cast by members of the South Carolina Senate and House when they chose the presidential electors directly, in 1812.

32 Senators Voted
104 Members of the H. of Representa-
-tatives Voted

786

by majority .

Electors of President and Vice-President of the United States.

Joseph Gist.	*132* Votes
John Wilson.	*135* ... "
John Mc'Morries.	*133* .. "
William Strother.	*132* ... "
William Zimmerman.	*134* .... "
Joseph Bellinger.....	*129* .-- "
Langdon Cheves.....	*131* .. "
Paul Hamilton.	*133* .... "
Samuel Mays. , ...	*133* .... "
William Rouse.	*117* ..-.. "

II—EARLY ELECTOR TICKETS

(a) The ticket for Adams electors in Virginia in 1824. Along with the other anticaucus candidates in that year, Adams had no specific vice-presidential running mate. Thus voters were told only that the Adams electors would support "some tried and approved Patriot" for vice president.

(b) The ticket for Breckinridge and Lane in Virginia in 1860. Though the names of the elector candidates are given by districts, they were all elected at large in the state under the general ticket system.

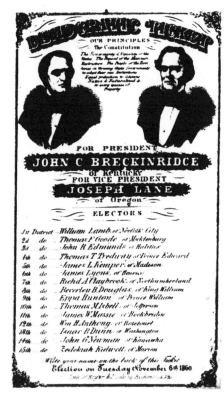

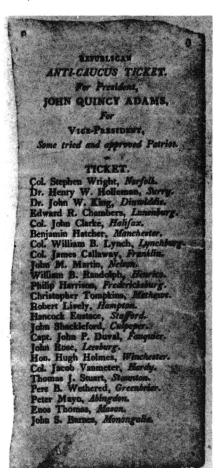

(c) The ticket for Grant and Wilson in Massachusetts, along with other Republican candidates, in 1872. Electors were all elected by general ticket, despite the individual district designations.

GRANT AND WILSON.

FOR ELECTORS OF PRESIDENT AND VICE PRESIDENT,
AT LARGE.
EBENEZER R. HOAR, of Concord,   **JOHN M. FORBES,** of Milton.
BY DISTRICTS,
1—**WILLIAM T. DAVIS,** of Plymouth.
2—**HARRISON TWEED,** of Taunton.
3—**ALVAN SIMONDS,** of Boston.
4—**EDWARD H. DUNN,** of Boston,
5—**AMOS F. BREED,** of Lynn,
6—**LUTHER DAY,** of Haverhill,
7—**JOHN C. HOADLEY,** of Lawrence,
8—**AARON C. MAYHEW,** of Milford,
9—**STEPHEN SALISBURY,** of Worcester,
10—**LEVI STOCKBRIDGE,** of Amherst,
11—**HENRY ALEXANDER, Jr.,** of Springfield.

FOR GOVERNOR,
WILLIAM B. WASHBURN,
OF GREENFIELD.

For Lieutenant-Governor,
THOMAS TALBOT,
OF BILLERICA.

FOR SECRETARY OF THE COMMONWEALTH.
OLIVER WARNER, of Northampton.
FOR TREASURER AND RECEIVER-GENERAL,
CHARLES ADAMS, Jr., of North Brookfield.
FOR AUDITOR.
CHARLES ENDICOTT, of Canton.
FOR ATTORNEY-GENERAL.
CHARLES R. TRAIN, of Boston.
FOR COUNCILLOR.—SIXTH DISTRICT.
JONATHAN B. WINN, of Woburn.

FOR SENATOR.—SEVENTH DISTRICT.
JEREMIAH CLARK, of Lowell.

FOR REPRESENTATIVE IN FORTY-THIRD CONGRESS.
EBENEZER R. HOAR, of Concord.
FOR REPRESENTATIVE IN FORTY-SECOND CONGRESS.
CONSTANTINE C. ESTY, of Framingham.

FOR COUNTY COMMISSIONER.
LEONARD HUNTRESS, of Tewksbury.

FOR REPRESENTATIVE IN THE GENERAL COURT.—DISTRICT NO. 28,
EDWARD F. WATSON.

III—MODERN BALLOT ARRANGEMENTS

(a) The New York voting machine diagram for 1964, typical of the increasingly popular short ballot, on which no names of electors appear on the ballots at all.

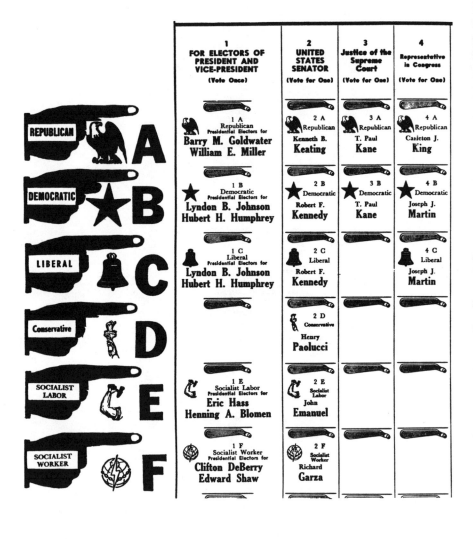

(b) The Hawaiian ballot for 1960, a short-ballot type in which even the words "Presidential electors for . . ." have been dropped. Note that voter instructions are in both English and Hawaiian.

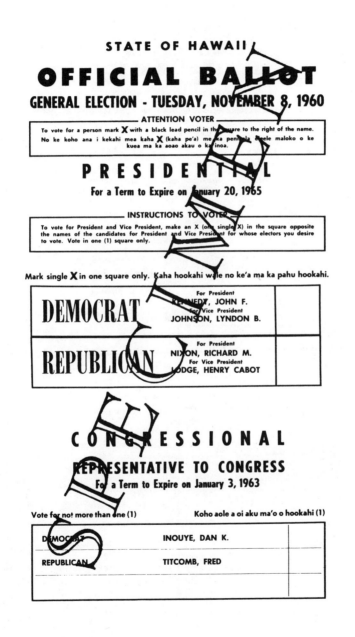

(c) The Kansas ballot for 1960, showing the form by which elector names are listed on the ballot with an indication of the presidential candidate to whom they are pledged. The voter, in effect, is obliged to vote for an entire elector slate by the single-box arrangement (unless he wants to go to the trouble of writing in another complete elector slate).

State of Kansas
GENERAL BALLOT
FIRST DIVISION
NATIONAL AND STATE TICKET

List of Candidates Nominated to be Voted for in the County of Shawnee
CITY OF TOPEKA
NOVEMBER 8, 1960

NATIONAL TICKET

If you wish to vote for the group of electors nominated by one of the political parties place a cross × in the square opposite the names of the candidates of that party for president and vice-president.

If you do not wish to vote for the group of electors nominated by any of the political parties you may write in the following blank spaces the names of all the electors for whom you wish to vote, placing a cross × in the square at the right of each.

For President and Vice-President

DECKER AND MUNN   Prohibition ☐

Presidential Electors,

RAYMOND BALTY, Burr Oak
MERLE M. FAWLEY, Milford
ADRIAN G. FIELDS, Bucklin
SHELDON G. JACKSON, Haviland
WILBUR ST. JOHN POMEROY, Emporia
STEWART REED, Emporia
ALBERT E. SMITH, McPherson
DALE YOCUM, Overland Park

For President and Vice-President

KENNEDY AND JOHNSON   Democratic ☐

Presidential Electors,

EDITH BECKMAN, Hoxie
J. DONALD COFFIN, Council Grove
REA CRESS, Junction City
MRS. MARIE HARDING, Ottawa
JOHN D. HENDERSON, Topeka
KARL C. PARKHURST, Wichita
JOHN B. SANDERS, Tonganoxie
ROBERT L. SHUMWAY, El Dorado

For President and Vice-President

NIXON AND LODGE   Republican ☐

Presidential Electors,

DONALD O. CONCANNON, Hugoton
HARRY R. HORNER, Wichita
R. E. JACOBS, Lenora
HENRY B. JAMESON, Abilene
SADIE JURNEY, Kingman
HENRY OTTO, Manhattan
WILLIAM H. VERNON, Larned
EMMETT E. WILSON, Independence

For Presidential Electors

☐
☐
☐
☐
☐
☐
☐
☐

To vote for a person, mark a cross × in the square at the right of the party name or political designation.

For Governor		Vote for One
J. J. STEELE, Coffeyville	Prohibition	☐
JOHN ANDERSON, JR., Olathe	Republican	☐
GEORGE DOCKING, Lawrence	Democrat	☐
		☐

For Lieutenant Governor		Vote for One
SAM WALKER, Junction City	Prohibition	☐
HAROLD H. CHASE, Salina	Republican	☐
JACK GLAVES, Wichita	Democrat	☐
		☐

For Secretary of State		Vote for One
K. L. SMITH, Wichita	Democrat	☐
MARIE HADIN, Leonardville	Prohibition	☐
PAUL R. SHANAHAN, Salina	Republican	☐
		☐

For State Auditor		Vote for One
CLAY E. HEDRICK, Newton	Republican	☐
WILLIAM A. BELL, Franklin	Democrat	☐
ROLLAND FISHER, Kansas City	Prohibition	☐
		☐

For State Treasurer		Vote for One
WALTER H. PEERY, Topeka	Republican	☐
NATHAN De YOUNG, Manhattan	Prohibition	☐
GEORGE HART, Wichita	Democrat	☐
		☐

For Attorney General		Vote for One
DALE A. SPIEGEL, Emporia	Democrat	☐
WILLIAM M. FERGUSON, Wellington	Republican	☐
		☐

For State Superintendent of Public Instruction		Vote for One
A. F. THROCKMORTON, Wichita	Republican	☐

(d) The Vermont ballot for 1960, an example of the ballot form in which the voter has an option of voting a straight ticket for one party's electors or of splitting his votes.

SAMPLE BALLOT

Electors of President and Vice-President of the United States

To vote a straight party ticket, make a cross (X) in the square at the head of the party column of your choice.
If you desire to vote for a person whose name is not on the ballot, fill in the name of the candidate of your choice in the blank
space provided therefor.
If you do not wish to vote for every person in a party column, make a cross (X) opposite the name of each candidate of your
choice; or you may make a cross (X) in the square at the head of the party column of your choice which shall count as a vote
for every name in that column, except for any name through which you may draw a line, and except for any name representing a candidate for an office to fill which you have otherwise voted in the manner heretofore prescribed.

REPUBLICAN PARTY	DEMOCRATIC PARTY
For President	**For President**
RICHARD M. NIXON of California	JOHN F. KENNEDY of Massachusetts
For Vice-President	**For Vice-President**
HENRY CABOT LODGE of Massachusetts	LYNDON B. JOHNSON of Texas
☐	☐
For Electors of President and Vice-President of the United States **Vote for THREE**	For Electors of President and Vice-President of the United States **Vote for THREE**
DEANE C. DAVIS, Republican, Montpelier	FREDERICK J. FAYETTE Democratic, South Burlington
JOSEPH B. JOHNSON, Republican, Springfield	ROBERT W. LARROW, Democratic, Burlington
MRS. MORTIMER R. PROCTOR Republican, Proctor	WILLIAM J. RYAN, Democratic, Montpelier

(e) The Alabama voting machine and paper ballot diagram for 1960—the only one in the U.S. on which the names of electors are given without the names of the presidential and vice presidential candidates for whom they intend to vote. For review of the

	1ST TURN SWITCH RIGHT TO CLOSE CURTAINS	WARNING—YOUR ☒ MARKS MUST BE SHOWING FOR VOTE TO REGISTER
	2ND MARK YOUR BALLOT AND LEAVE MARKS SHOWING →	3RD TURN SWITCH LEFT

	GENERAL ELECTION JEFFERSON COUNTY	GENERAL ELECTION JEFFERSON COUNTY
	DEMOCRATIC PARTY	INDEPENDENT AFRO-AMERICAN UNITY PARTY
	Column 1	Column 2

For Presidential Electors

VOTE FOR ELEVEN

Column 1	Column 2
C. G. ALLEN ☐	GROVER C. ALLEN ☐
DAVE ARCHER ☐	MRS. MARIE W. BAILEY ☐
C. L. (LEONARD) BEARD ☐	GROVER BANKS ☐
EDMUND BLAIR ☐	JAMES H. HOLLIE ☐
J. E. BRANTLEY ☐	EDDIE JONES ☐
(GOV.) FRANK M. DIXON ☐	JAMES KERSH ☐
KARL HARRISON ☐	WILL MIKE ☐
BRUCE HENDERSON ☐	ISAAC NICHOLSON ☐
C. E., JR. HORNSBY ☐	ERNEST THOMAS TAYLOR ☐
W. W., JR. MALONE ☐	JASPER J. THOMAS ☐
FRANK MIZELL ☐	JAMES C. WILLIAMS ☐

For Tax Assessor

| L. A. WHETSTONE ☐ | |

difficulties that arose from ascertaining a popular vote total from this state in 1960, see pp. 66–68. In 1966 the Alabama Democratic party discontinued its use of the slogan "White Supremacy—For the Right."

GENERAL ELECTION JEFFERSON COUNTY	GENERAL ELECTION JEFFERSON COUNTY	GENERAL ELECTION JEFFERSON COUNTY
NATIONAL STATES RIGHTS PARTY Column 3	PROHIBITION PARTY Column 4	REPUBLICAN PARTY Column 5
GEORGE E. ALLEN ☐	L. E. BARTON ☐	ROBERT S. CARTLEDGE ☐
ANNETTE M. BARTEE ☐	WILLIAM E. BROWN ☐	CHARLES H., JR. CHAPMAN ☐
LODWICK H. BARTEE ☐	L. J. CHAMBLISS ☐	J. N. DENNIS ☐
LEE J. CROWDER ☐	LEONA B. FRAME ☐	CECIL DURHAM ☐
THERMAN De LEE ☐	JOE FROST ☐	W. H. GILLESPIE ☐
MRS. LILA EVANS ☐	KATHRYNE E. GARDNER ☐	PERRY O. HOOPER ☐
WILLIE BAZZELL GARRETT ☐	O. A. GARDNER ☐	W. J. KENNAMER ☐
JOHN DOUGLAS KNOWLES ☐	A. D. PECK ☐	TOM McNARON ☐
SANFORD D. RUDD ☐	PHOEBE SHOEMAKER ☐	MRS. JOHN SIMPSON ☐
JACK ANDREW TOMLINSON ☐	C. B. STEWART ☐	T. B. THOMPSON ☐
ERNEST WILSON ☐	R. DREW WOLCOTT ☐	GEORGE WITCHER ☐

IV—OFFICIAL PRESIDENTIAL ELECTOR DOCUMENTS

(a) A Certificate of Ascertainment of the election of presidential electors, from Ohio in 1964. The electors who received 2,498,331 votes were the Democrats pledged to Johnson and Humphrey; the electors who received 1,470,865 votes were the Republican electors pledged to Goldwater and Miller. Signatures are those of Governor James A. Rhodes and Secretary of State Ted W. Brown.

JAMES A. RHODES
Governor of said State

To all to whom these Presents shall come, Greeting:

Certificate of Ascertainment

Pursuant to the act of Congress approved June twenty-fifth, 1948, and amended October 31, 1951, entitled "An act to fix the day for the meeting of the Electors of President and Vice-President, and to provide for and regulate the counting of the votes for President and Vice-President and the decision of questions arising thereon," I, JAMES A. RHODES, Governor of the State of Ohio, do hereby certify that at the election held in the several voting precincts of the State of Ohio, on the Third day of November, A. D. 1964, the following named persons were voted for, for the office of Elector of President and Vice-President of the United States and that each received the number of votes set opposite his name:

Vincent H. Beckman	2,498,331	Mark McElroy	2,498,331	Letha C. Aatry	1,470,865	Lloyd C. Moreland	1,470,865
William M. Cafaro	2,498,331	Anthony M. Rogers	2,498,331	Loren M. Berry	1,470,865	H. Richard P. Niehoff	1,470,865
William L. Coleman	2,498,331	Herman J. Rosselott	2,498,331	Albert S. Close	1,470,865	Roy Odenkirk	1,470,865
Carlos A. Cordova	2,498,331	James W. Shocknessy	2,498,331	William H. Deddens	1,470,865	Jessie Semple O'Donnell	1,470,865
Michael V. DiSalle	2,498,331	Raymond R. Spitler	2,498,331	John K. DeYarmon	1,470,865	Judy Osbersen	1,470,865
John J. Gilligan	2,498,331	William J. Timmins, Jr.	2,498,331	Homer M. Edwards	1,470,865	Walter R. Oxley	1,470,865
George A. Green	2,498,331	Joseph A. Ujhelys	2,498,331	Harley Gardell	1,470,865	Catharine Pennell	1,470,865
Greg Holbrock	2,498,331	Frank A. Vannelle	2,498,331	Redmond Greer	1,470,865	Leonard G. Richter	1,470,865
Dorothy E. Holden	2,498,331	Robert C. Weaver	2,498,331	Philip S. Hamilton	1,470,865	Ferald Ritchie	1,470,865
Helen B. Karpinski	2,498,331	William H. H. Wertz	2,498,331	Fred L. Hoffman	1,470,865	Windle Rouss	1,470,865
John P. Kelly	2,498,331	Milton J. Weston	2,498,331	Albert H. James	1,470,865	William Schneider	1,470,865
Carl W. Lehman	2,498,331	Clyde Wharton	2,498,331	Vincent B. Linn	1,470,865	John A. Skipton	1,470,865
E. E. Leonard	2,498,331	Stephen M. Young	2,498,331	Joseph E. L. MacAdam	1,470,865	Everett E. Taylor	1,470,865

I further certify that at a canvass of the official returns of said election, duly made according to law on the 1st day of December, A. D. 1964, at the office of the Secretary of State of Ohio, by said Secretary of State, it was duly ascertained that the following named persons received the highest number of votes cast at said election for said office of Elector of President and Vice-President of the United States, and were duly declared to have been elected to such office, and that they have been duly certified, commissioned and appointed as such, viz:

VINCENT H. BECKMAN   GREG HOLBROCK   MARK McELROY   JOSEPH A. UJHELYI
WILLIAM M. CAFARO   DOROTHY E. HOLDEN ANTHONY M. ROGERS   FRANK A. VANNELLE
WILLIAM L. COLEMAN   HELEN B. KARPINSKI HERMAN J. ROSSELOTT   ROBERT C. WEAVER
CARLOS A. CORDOVA   JOHN P. KELLY   JAMES W. SHOCKNESSY   WILLIAM H. H. WERTZ
MICHAEL V. DiSALLE   CARL W. LEHMAN   RAYMOND R. SPITLER   MILTON J. WESTON
JOHN J. GILLIGAN   E. E. LEONARD   WILLIAM J. TIMMINS, JR. CLYDE WHARTON
GEORGE A. GREEN   STEPHEN M. YOUNG

In Testimony Whereof, I have hereunto subscribed my name, and caused to be affixed the Great Seal of the State of Ohio, at Columbus, the _____ day of December in the year of our Lord one thousand nine hundred and sixty-four and in the one hundred and eighty-ninth year of the independence of the United States of America.

Governor.

By the Governor:

Secretary of State.

(b) Official ballots cast by presidential electors: Ohio in 1936; Ohio, New York, and California in 1948.

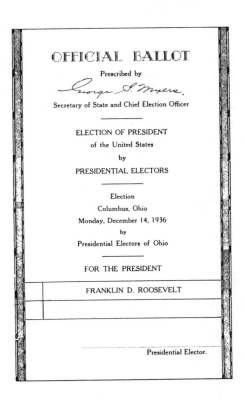

Electors' Certificate of Their Votes

State of Ohio, ss.

We, the undersigned, Electors of President and Vice-President of the United States of America, for the respective terms of four years, beginning on the Fourth day of March, in the year of our Lord one thousand nine hundred and____Twenty Nine____, being Electors duly and legally appointed and qualified by and for the State of Ohio, as appears by the annexed list of Electors, made, certified, and delivered to us by the Executive of the State, having met and convened at the State House, in the City of Columbus, in the State of Ohio, in pursuance of the direction of the Legislature of said State, on the First Wednesday, being the____2nd____ day of January, in the year of our Lord one thousand nine hundred and____Twenty Nine____;

Do Hereby Certify, That, being so assembled and duly organized, we proceeded to vote by ballot, and balloted first for such President, and then for such Vice-President, by distinct ballots;

And We Further Certify, That the following are two distinct lists; one, of the votes cast for President, and the other, of the votes for Vice-President, so cast as aforesaid.

LIST OF ALL PERSONS VOTED FOR AS PRESIDENT, WITH THE NUMBER OF VOTES FOR EACH

NAMES OF PERSONS VOTED FOR	NUMBER OF VOTES
HERBERT C. HOOVER	24

LIST OF ALL PERSONS VOTED FOR AS VICE-PRESIDENT, WITH THE NUMBER OF VOTES FOR EACH

NAMES OF PERSONS VOTED FOR	NUMBER OF VOTES
CHARLES C. CURTIS	24

In Witness Whereof, We have hereunto set our hands, at the State House, in the City of Columbus, in the State of Ohio, on the First Wednesday, being the____2nd____day of January, in the year of our Lord, one thousand nine hundred and____Twenty Nine____

Appendix L • Proposed
Constitutional Amendments

Text of the Lodge-Gossett plan for proportional division of each state's electoral votes to reflect the popular vote division, in the form that it passed the Senate (but was rejected by the House) in 1950. The major sponsors were Senator Henry Cabot Lodge, Republican of Massachusetts, and Representative Ed Gosset, Democrat of Texas. As originally proposed, the plan had stipulated no minimum percentage of the electoral vote for winning election. But the plan was amended in the Senate to require that the winner receive at least forty percent of the electoral vote, with contingent election in Congress if no candidate won 40 percent or more. Proportional plans introduced by other senators in subsequent years were essentially the same as this plan.

ARTICLE —

Section 1. The executive power shall be vested in a President of the United States of America. He shall hold his office during the term of 4 years, and together with the Vice President, chosen for the same term, be elected as provided in this Constitution.

The electoral college system of electing the President and Vice President of the United States is hereby abolished. The President and Vice President shall be elected by the people of the several States. The electors in each State shall have the qualifications requisite for electors of the most numerous branch of the State legislature. Congress shall determine the time of such election, which shall be the same throughout the United States. Until otherwise determined by the Congress such election shall be held on the Tuesday next after the first Monday in November of the year preceding the year in which the regular term of the President is to begin. Each State shall be entitled to a number of electoral votes equal to the whole number of Senators and Representatives to which such State may be entitled in the Congress.

Within 45 days after such election, or at such time as the Congress shall direct, the official custodian of the election returns of each State shall make distinct lists of all persons for whom votes were cast for President and the number of votes for each, and the total vote of the electors of the State for all persons for President, which lists he shall sign and certify and transmit sealed to the seat of the Government of the United States, directed to the President of the Senate. On the 6th day of January following the election, unless the Congress by law appoints a different day not earlier than the 4th day of January and not later than the 10th day of January, the President of the Senate shall in the presence of the Senate and House of Representatives open all certificates and the votes shall then be counted. Each person for whom votes were cast for President in each State shall be credited with such proportion of the electoral votes thereof as he received of the total vote of the electors therein for President. In making the computations fractional numbers less than one one-thousandth shall be disregarded. The person having the greatest number of electoral votes for President shall be President if such number be at least 40 percent of the whole number of electoral votes. If no person have at least 40 percent of the whole number of electoral votes, then from the persons having the two highest numbers of electoral votes for President the Senate and the House of Representatives sitting in joint session shall choose immediately by ballot the President. A majority of the votes of the combined authorized membership of the Senate and the House of Representatives shall be necessary for a choice.

The Vice President shall be likewise elected at the same time and in the same manner and subject to the same provisions as the President, but no person constitutionally ineligible for the office of President shall be eligible to that of Vice President of the United States.

The Congress may by law provide for the case of the death of any of the persons from whom the Senate and the House of Representatives may choose a President whenever the right of choice shall have devolved upon them, and for the case of the death of any of the persons from whom the Senate and the House of Representatives may choose a Vice President whenever the right of choice shall have devolved upon them.

Section 2. Paragraphs 1, 2, and 3 of section 1, article II, of the Constitution, the twelfth article of amendment to the Constitution, and section 4 of the twentieth article of amendment to the Constitution, are hereby repealed.

Section 3. This article shall take effect on the 10th day of February following its ratification.

Section 4. This article shall be inoperative unless it shall have been ratified as an amendment to the Constitution by the legislatures of three-fourths of the States within 7 years from the date of its submission to the States by the Congress.

II—THE DISTRICT PLAN

Text of the district plan for electing presidential electors, in the form in which it was proposed by its chief Senate sponsor, Karl Mundt, Republican of South Dakota, in 1965 and 1967.

ARTICLE —

Section 1. Each State shall choose a number of electors of President and Vice President equal to the whole number of Senators and Representatives to which the State may be entitled in the Congress; but no Senator or Representative, or person holding an office of trust or profit under the United States, shall be chosen an elector.

The electors to which a State is entitled by virtue of its Senators shall be elected by the people thereof, and the electors to which it is entitled by virtue of its Representatives shall be elected by the people within single-elector districts established by the legislature thereof; such districts to be composed of compact and contiguous territory, containing as nearly as practicable the number of persons which entitled the State to one Representative in the Congress; and such districts when formed shall not be altered until another census has been taken. Before being chosen elector, each candidate for the office shall officially declare the persons for whom he will vote for President and Vice President, which declaration shall be binding on any successor. In choosing electors of President and Vice President the voters in each State shall have the qualifications requisite for electors of the most numerous branch of the State legislature, except that the legislature of any State may prescribe lesser qualifications with respect to residence therein.

The electors shall meet in their respective States, fill any vacancies in their number as directed by the State legislature, and vote by signed ballot for President and Vice President, one of whom, at least, shall not be an inhabitant of the same State with themselves; they shall name in their ballots the person voted for as President, and in distinct ballots the person voted for as Vice President; and they shall make distinct lists of all persons voted for as President, and of all persons voted for as Vice President, and of the number of votes for each, excluding therefrom any votes for persons other than those named by an elector before he was chosen, unless one or both of the persons so named be deceased, which lists they shall sign and certify, and transmit sealed to the seat of government of the United States, directed to the President of the Senate; the President of the Senate shall, in the presence of the Senate and the House of Representatives, open all the certificates and the votes shall then be counted; the person having the greatest number of votes for President shall be the President, if such number be a majority of the whole number of electors chosen; and the person having the greatest number of votes for Vice President shall be the Vice President, if such a number be a majority of the whole number of electors chosen.

If no person voted for as President has a majority of the whole number of electors, then from the persons having the three highest numbers on the lists of persons voted for as President, the Senate and the House of Representatives, assembled and voting as individual Members of one body, shall choose immediately, by ballot, the President; a quorum for such purpose shall be three-fourths of the whole number of the Senators and Representatives, and a majority of the whole number shall be necessary to a choice; if additional ballots be necessary, the choice on the fifth ballot shall be between the two persons having the highest number of votes on the fourth ballot.

If no person voted for as Vice President has a majority of the whole number of electors, then the Vice President shall be chosen from the persons having the three highest numbers on the lists of persons voted for as Vice President in the same manner as herein provided for choosing the President. But no person constitutionally ineligible to the office of President shall be eligible to that of Vice President of the United States.

Section 2.   The Congress may by law provide for the case of the death of any of the persons from whom the Senate and the House of Representatives may choose a President or a Vice President whenever the right of choice shall have devolved upon them.

Section 3.   This article supersedes the second and fourth paragraphs of section 1, article II, of the Constitution, the twelfth article of amendment to the Constitution and section 4 of the twentieth article of amendment to the Constitution. Except as herein expressly provided, this article does not supersede the twenty-third article of amendment.

Section 4.   Electors appointed pursuant to the twenty-third article of amendment to this Constitution shall be elected by the people of such district in such manner as the Congress may direct. Before being chosen as such elector, each candidate shall officially declare the persons for whom he will vote for President and Vice President which declaration shall be binding on any successor. Such electors shall meet in the district and perform the duties provided in section 1 of this article.

Section 5.   This article shall take effect on the 1st day of July following its ratification.

III—DIRECT POPULAR VOTE

Following are the texts of the two major direct vote plans of 1969–70—House Joint Resolution 681, which passed the House of Representatives on September 18, 1969, by a vote of 338–70, and Senate Joint Resolution 1, which died in the Senate in late 1970.

House Joint Resolution 681

ARTICLE —

Section 1. The people of the several States and the District constituting the seat of government of the United States shall elect the President and Vice President. Each elector shall cast a single vote for two persons who shall have consented to the joining of their names as candidates for the offices of President and Vice President. No candidate shall consent to the joinder of his name with that of more than one other person.

Section 2. The electors of President and Vice President in each State shall have the qualifications requisite for electors of the most numerous branch of the State legislature, except that for electors of President and Vice President, the legislature of any State may prescribe less restrictive residence qualifications and for electors of President and Vice President the Congress may establish uniform residence qualifications.

Section 3. The pair of persons having the greatest number of votes for President and Vice President shall be elected, if such number be at least 40 per centum of the whole number of votes cast for such offices. If no pair of persons has such number, a runoff election shall be held in which the choice of President and Vice President shall be made from the two pairs of persons who received the highest numbers of votes.

Section 4. The times, places, and manner of holding such elections and entitlement to inclusion on the ballot shall be prescribed in each State by the legislature thereof; but the Congress may at any time by law make or alter such regulations. The days for such elections shall be determined by Congress and shall be uniform throughout the United States. The Congress shall prescribe by law the time, place, and manner in which the results of such elections shall be ascertained and declared.

Section 5. The Congress may by law provide for the case of the death or withdrawal of any candidate for President or Vice President before a President and Vice President have been elected, and for the case of the death of both the President-elect and Vice-President-elect.

Section 6. The Congress shall have power to enforce this article by appropriate legislation.

Section 7. This article shall take effect one year after the 21st day of January following ratification.

Senate Joint Resolution 1

ARTICLE —

Section 1. The people of the several States and the District constituting the seat of Government of the United States shall be the electors of the President and Vice President. In such elections, each elector shall cast a single vote for two persons who shall have consented to the joining of their names on the ballot for the offices of President and Vice President. No persons shall consent to their name being joined with that of more than one other person.

Section 2. The electors in each State shall have the qualifications requisite for the electors of Members of the Congress from that State, except that any State may adopt less restrictive residence requirements for voting for President and Vice President than for Members of Congress and Congress may adopt uniform residence and age requirements for voting in such elections. The Congress shall prescribe the qualifications for electors from the District of Columbia.

Section 3. The persons joined as candidates for President and Vice President, having the greatest number of votes shall be declared elected President and Vice President, if such number be at least 40 per centum of the total number votes certified. If none of the persons joined as candidates for President and Vice President shall have at least 40 per centum of the total number of votes certified, a runoff election shall be held between the two pairs of persons joined as candidates for President and Vice President who received the highest number of votes certified.

Section 4. The days for such elections shall be determined by Congress and shall be the same throughout the United States. The times, places, and manner of holding such elections and entitlement to inclusion on the ballot shall be prescribed in each State by the legislature thereof; but the Congress may at any time by law make or alter such regulations. The times, places, and manner of holding such elections and entitlement to inclusion on the ballot shall be prescribed by the Congress for such elections in the District of Columbia.

Section 5. The Congress shall prescribe by law the time, place, and manner in which the results of such elections shall be ascertained and declared.

Section 6. If, at the time fixed for declaring the results of such elections, the presidential candidate who would have been entitled to election as President shall have died, the vice-presidential candidate entitled to election as Vice President shall be declared elected President.

The Congress may by law provide for the case of the death or withdrawal of any candidate or candidates for President and Vice President and for the case of the death of both the President-elect and Vice-President-elect and, further the Congress may by law provide for the case of a tie.

Section 7. The Congress shall have power to enforce this article by appropriate legislation.

Section 8. This article shall take effect on the 1st day of May following its ratification.

Appendix M • Allocation of Electoral Votes under Alternative Systems

Proportional System—1864–1976
(Figures in parentheses show vote actually cast under existing unit vote system.)

Year	Republican	Democratic	Other
1864	129.8 (212)	103.2 (21)	— —
1868	156.1 (214)	132.9 (80)	— —
1872	205.0 (286)	159.1 (63)	1.9 —
1876	177.1 (185)	188.1 (184)	3.8 —
1880	175.1 (214)	181.9 (155)	12.0 —
1884	189.7 (182)	200.5 (219)	10.8 —
1888	185.8 (233)	202.9 (168)	12.3 —
1892	186.2 (145)	202.7 (277)	55.1 (22)
1896	215.3 (271)	221.3 (176)	10.4 —
1900	217.3 (292)	217.2 (155)	12.5 —
1904	268.5 (336)	179.0 (140)	28.5 —
1908	230.8 (321)	226.9 (162)	25.3 —
1912	113.9 (8)	246.7 (435)	170.4 (88)
1916	222.1 (254)	284.3 (277)	24.6 —
1920	299.9 (404)	212.6 (127)	18.5 —
1924	258.8 (382)	191.4 (136)	80.8 (13)
1928	291.9 (444)	231.6 (87)	7.5 —
1932	189.6 (59)	327.6 (472)	13.8 —
1936	175.6 (8)	340.3 (523)	15.1 —
1940	214.6 (82)	310.0 (449)	6.4 —
1944	223.8 (99)	294.7 (432)	12.5 —
1948	221.4 (189)	258.0 (303)	51.6 (39)
1952	288.5 (442)	239.8 (89)	2.7 —
1956	296.7 (457)	227.2 (73)	7.1 (1)
1960	266.1 (219)	265.6 (303)	5.3 (15)
1964	213.6 (52)	320.0 (486)	3.9 —
1968	231.5 (301)	225.4 (191)	79.5 (46)
1972	330.5 (520)	197.5 (17)	10.0 (1)
1976	258.0 (240)	269.7 (297)	10.2 (1)

Sources: 1864–1956: Legislative Reference Service, Library of Congress; 1960–64:

Congressional Quarterly Service; 1968: Legislative Reference Service, Library of Congress, in U.S., Congress, House, House Judiciary Committee, *Hearings on Electoral College Reform*, 91st Cong., 1st sess., Feb. and Mar. 1969, p. 973; 1972: data supplied by the Library of Congress, Congressional Research Service especially for this book; 1976: Government Division, The Library of Congress.

District System—1952-76
(Figures for previous years unavailable. Figures in parentheses
show vote under existing unit vote system.)

Year	Republican		Democratic		Other	
1952	375	(442)	156	(89)	—	—
1956	411	(457)	120	(73)	—	(1)
1960	278	(219)	245	(303)	14*	(15)
1964	72	(52)	466	(486)	—	—
1968	289	(301)	192	(191)	57	(46)
1972	474	(520)	64	(17)	—	(1)
1976	269	(240)	269	(297)	—	(1)

* 1960 votes won by unpledged electoral slates.

Note: Caution must be exercised in interpreting the possible outcome of alternative electoral count systems in past elections since the campaigns might well have been conducted differently as the presidential candidates and their managers sought to exploit the differing types of electoral bases that would have been involved.

Sources: 1952–64: Congressional Quarterly Service; 1968: Legislative Reference Service, Library of Congress, in U.S., Congress, House, House Judiciary Committee, *Hearings on Electoral College Reform*, 91st Cong., 1st sess., Feb. and Mar. 1979, p. 973; 1972: data supplied by the Library of Congress, Congressional Research Service especially for this book; 1976: calculated from data in *Congressional Quarterly Weekly Report*, Apr. 22, 1978, p. 971.

Appendix N • National Polls
on Instituting
Direct Popular Vote

I. THE GALLUP POLL

Following are excerpts from the Gallup Poll released on February 10, 1977:

Public to Congress—Retire the Electoral College
(By George Gallup)

PRINCETON, N.J.—With the battle to abandon the electoral college once again joined in Congress, the American people have added their voice to the debate—by a five-to-one margin the public favors a constitutional amendment that would eliminate the electoral college.

In Gallup surveys since 1948 the public has favored changing the present system and since 1966 has expressed a desire to switch to the direct popular election of the President. In the latest survey, three persons in four, 75 per cent, approve amending the Constitution to provide for direct election. Only about one in seven, 14 per cent, opposes such a change and the balance are undecided. . . .

This question has been asked since 1966 to determine attitudes toward the change:
"Would you approve or disapprove of an amendment to the Constitution which would do away with the electoral college and base the election of a President on the total vote cast throughout the nation?"
Here is the trend and the latest results:

Approve or Disapprove of Eliminating Electoral College
(In percent)

	Approve	Disapprove	No opinion
Latest	75	14	11
November 1968	81	12	7
October 1967	65	22	13
January 1967	58	22	20
January 1966	63	20	17

And here are the latest results by demographic groups (in percent):

	Approve	Disapprove	No opinion
National	75	14	11
Men	78	14	8
Women	72	15	13
Whites	79	13	8
Nonwhites	48	25	27
College	80	16	4
High school	74	14	12
Grade school	66	11	23
Under 30 years old	74	18	8
30–49 years	75	14	11
50 years and older ..	76	12	12
East	76	16	8
Midwest	82	12	6
South	67	17	16
West	75	13	12
Republicans	79	13	8
Democrats	71	17	12
Independents	82	11	7

II. THE HARRIS SURVEY

Following are excerpts from the Harris Survey released on May 30, 1977:

Abolish the Electoral College   (By Louis Harris)

An overwhelming majority of the American people favors President Carter's plan to do away with the electoral college in presidential elections. . . .

Here is where the public stands on the key election reforms: An overwhelming 74–13 per cent majority favors "passing a constitutional amendment to abolish the electoral college and have the President and Vice President elected by popular vote." As far as public opinion is concerned, the opponents of the electoral college system have won their battle.

The Harris Survey asked the cross section: "President Carter has asked that some majority changes be made in the federal election law. Let me read you some of the changes he wants to make and tell me if you favor or oppose each."

Proposed Federal Election Law Changes
(In percent)

	Favor	Oppose	Not sure
Passing a constitutional amendment to abolish the electoral college and have the President and Vice President elected by popular vote ...	74	13	13

The response to the question put in the Harris Survey, "Do you favor or oppose passing a constitutional amendment to abolish the electoral college and have the President and Vice President elected by popular vote" were as follows:

(In percent)

	Favor	Oppose	Not sure	Favor (omitting "not sure")
Region:				
East	77	10	13	89
Midwest	75	16	9	82
South	65	16	19	80
West	81	10	9	90
Area:				
Cities	71	14	16	83
Suburbs	76	15	9	84
Towns	75	11	14	87
Rural	73	12	15	86
Age:				
18 to 29	73	13	14	85
30 to 49	79	11	11	88
50 and over	69	16	15	81
Education:				
8th grade	53	13	34	80
High school	73	14	13	84
College	81	13	7	86
Type of work:				
Professional	80	14	6	85
Executive	75	17	8	81
Skilled labor	75	10	15	88
White collar	76	16	8	83
Union member	78	12	10	87
Sex:				
Men	76	14	10	84
Women	71	12	16	86
Race:				
Black	51	12	37	81
White	76	14	10	84
Income:				
Under $5,000	60	10	30	85
$5,000 to $9,999	70	15	15	82
$10,000 to $14,999	77	12	11	87
$15,000 and over	81	13	6	86

	Favor	Oppose	Not sure	Favor (omitting "not sure")
Political philosophy:				
Conservative	71	18	11	80
Middle of road	78	10	12	88
Liberal	78	12	10	86
Political party:				
Democrat	74	12	15	86
Republican	69	22	9	76
Independent	81	9	9	90
Voted:				
Ford	74	20	6	79
Carter	77	11	12	87
Religion:				
Catholic	82	9	9	91
Protestant	73	16	11	88
Jewish	88	9	3	81

A Selected Bibliography

PART A: MAJOR SENATE DOCUMENTS ON THE ELECTORAL COLLEGE

U.S., Congress, Senate, Judiciary Committee, *Hearings on the Electoral College and Direct Election*, 95th Cong., 1st sess., January 27, February 1, 2, 7, and 10, 1977 (cited as the February 1977 Senate *Hearings*).

U.S., Congress, Senate, Judiciary Committee, Subcommittee on the Constitution, *Hearings on the Electoral College and Direct Election*, 95th Cong., 1st sess., July 20, 22, 28, and August 2, 1977 (cited as the July 1977 Senate *Hearings*).

U.S. Congress, Senate, Judiciary Committee, *Direct Popular Election of the President and Vice President of the United States*, December 1977 (cited as the December 1977 Senate *Report*).

U.S., Congress, Senate, Judiciary Committee, Subcommittee on the Constitution, *Hearings on Direct Popular Election of the President and Vice President of the United States*, 96th Cong., 1st sess., March 27 and 30 and April 3 and 9, 1979 (cited as the 1979 Senate *Hearings*).

U.S., Congress, Senate, Judiciary Committee, *Direct Popular Election of the President and Vice President of the United States*, 1979 (cited as the 1979 Senate *Report*).

PART B: RECENT RESEARCH ON THE ELECTORAL COLLEGE

Affuso: see Brams and Affuso.

Best, Judith. *The Case Against Direct Election of the President*. Ithaca: Cornell University Press, 1975. Chapters 1 and 7 of this book can also be found in the July 1977 Senate *Hearings*, pp. 65–113. Chapter 3 of this book can be found in the 1979 Senate *Hearings*, pp. 264–305.

———. "The Case For the Electoral College." Paper delivered at the Annual Meeting of the American Political Science Association, September 1–4, 1977, Washington, D.C. Also in the July 1977 Senate *Hearings*, pp. 56–64.

Blair, Douglas H. "Electoral College Reform and the Distribution of Voting Power." The Wharton School Department of Economics, Discussion Paper no. 362. Reprinted in the February 1977 Senate *Hearings*, pp. 503–14.

Brams, Steven J. *Game Theory and Politics*. New York: The Free Press, 1975, esp. pp. 191–92 and 243–78.

———. "How the Presidential Candidates Run the Final Stretch." In February 1977 Senate *Hearings*, pp. 538–40.

———. "Bias in the Electoral College." In February. 1977 Senate *Hearings*, pp. 540–42.

———. *The Presidential Election Game*. New Haven: Yale University Press, 1978, esp. chap. 3, "The General Election: How to Run the Final Stretch." This section can also be found in the 1979 Senate *Hearings*, pp. 477–531.

————. "Resource Allocation in the 1976 Campaign." In the 1979 Senate *Hearings*, pp. 455–62.

Brams, Steven J., and Paul J. Affuso. "Power and Size: A New Paradox." *Theory and Decision* 7 (1976): 29–56.

Brams, Steven J., and Morton D. Davis. "Resource-allocation Models in Presidential Campaigning: Implications for Democratic Representation." *Annals of New York Academy of Sciences* 219 (1973): 105–23.

————. "The 3/2s Rule in Presidential Campaigning." *American Political Science Review* 68 (March 1974): 113–34. Reprinted in February 1977 Senate *Hearings*, pp. 515–37.

Brams, Steven J., and Peter C. Fishburn. "Approval Voting." Paper delivered at the Annual Meeting of the American Political Science Association, September 1–4, 1977, Washington, D.C. Also in *The American Political Science Review* 73 (September 1978), 831–47.

Brams, Steven J., and Mark Lake. "Power and Satisfaction in a Representative Democracy." Paper prepared for delivery at the Conference on Game Theory and Political Science, July 10–17, 1977, Hyannis, Massachusetts. Also in *Game Theory and Political Science*, edited by Peter C. Ordeshook. New York: New York University Press, 1978.

Braun: see Longley and Braun.

Colantoni, Claude S., Terrance J. Levesque, and Peter C. Ordeshook. "Campaign Resource Allocations Under the Electoral College." *American Political Science Review* 69 (March 1975): 141–54. "Comment" by Brams and Davis, pp. 155–56. "Rejoinder" by Colantini, Levesque and Ordeshook, pp. 157–61.

Cronin, Thomas. "Choosing a President." *The Center Magazine*, September/October 1978, pp. 5–15.

————. "The Direct Vote and the Electoral College: The Case for Messing Things Up!" Paper delivered at the Center for the Study of Democratic Institutions, June 26, 1978, Santa Barbara, California. Also in *Presidential Studies Quarterly* 9 (Spring 1979): 144–163.

Davis: see Brams and Davis.

Diamond, Martin. *The Electoral College and the American Idea of Democracy*. Washington, D.C.: American Enterprise Institute for Public Policy Research, 1977. Reprinted in the July 1977 Senate *Hearings*, pp. 161–85.

Dickens: see Spilerman and Dickens.

Fishburn: see Brams and Fishburn.

Goetz, Charles J. "Further Thoughts on the Measurement of Power in the Electoral College." Paper delivered at the Annual Meeting of the Public Choice Society, May 4, 1972.

————. "An Equilibrium-Displacement Measurement of Voting Power in the Electoral College." Paper delivered at the Annual Meeting of the American Political Science Association, 4–8 September 1973, New Orleans.

Hinich, Melvin J., and Peter C. Ordeshook. "The Electoral College: A Spatial Analysis." Paper delivered at the Annual Meeting of the Midwest Political Science Association, May 1973, Chicago. Also in *Political Methodology* 1 (Summer 1974): 1–29.

Hinich, Melvin J., Richard Michelsen, and Peter Ordeshook. "The Electoral College vs. a Direct Vote: Policy Bias, Indeterminate Outcomes and Reversals." *Journal on Mathematical Sociology* 4 (1975): 3–35.

Keech, William R. "Background Paper." In *Winner Take All: Report of the Twentieth*

Century Fund Task Force on Reform of the Presidential Election Process, New York: Holmes and Meier Publishers, 1978.

Lake: see Brams and Lake.

Levesque: see Colantoni, Levesque, and Ordeshook.

Longley, Lawrence D. "The Electoral College." *Current History* 67 (August 1974): 64–69 and ff.

———. "Prepared Statement of Lawrence D. Longley." February 1, 1977, Senate *Hearings*, pp. 88–105.

———. "The Case Against the Electoral College." Paper delivered at the Annual Meeting of the American Political Science Association, September 1–4, 1977, Washington, D.C.

———. "Electoral College Reform: Problems, Politics, and Prospects." In *Paths to Political Reform*, edited by William J. Crotty. Lexington, Mass.: D.C. Heath-Lexington for the Policy Studies Organization, 1980.

———. "Minorities and the 1980 Electoral College." Paper delivered at the Annual Meeting of the American Political Science Association, August 28–31, 1980, Washington, D.C.

Longley, Lawrence D., and Alan G. Braun. *The Politics of Electoral College Reform*. 2nd ed. New Haven: Yale University Press, 1975.

Longley, Lawrence D., and John H. Yunker. "Who is Really Advantaged by the Electoral College—and Who Just Thinks He Is?" Paper delivered at the Annual Meeting of the American Political Science Association, September 7–11, 1971, Chicago.

———. "The Changing Biases of the Electoral College." Paper delivered at the Annual Meeting of the American Political Science Association, September 4–8, 1973, New Orleans. Also in U.S., Congress, Senate, Judiciary Committee, Subcommittee on Constitutional Amendments, *Hearings on Electoral Reform*. 93rd Cong., 1st sess., September 26 and 27, 1973, pp. 187–212.

Longley: See also Yunker and Longley (1973 and 1976).

Merrill, Samuel, III. "Citizen Voting Power Under the Electoral College: A Stochastic Model Based on State Voting Patterns." *SIAM Journal on Applied Mathematics* 34 (March 1978): 376–90.

———. "Empirical Estimates for the Likelihood of a Divided Verdict in a Presidential Election." *Public Choice* 33 (no. 2, 1978): 127–33.

Michelsen, R., and P. C. Ordeshook. "The Electoral College and the Probability of Reversals." In *Modeling and Simulations*. Pittsburgh: University of Pittsburgh Press, forthcoming.

Michelsen: see Hinich, Michelsen, and Ordeshook.

Nelson, Michael C. "Partisan Bias in the Electoral College." *The Journal of Politics* 27 (November 1974): 1033–48.

Niemi, Richard, and William H. Riker. "The Choice of Voting Systems." *Scientific American* 234 (June 1976): 21–27.

Ordeshook: see Colantoni, Levesque, and Ordeshook; Hinich, Michelsen, and Ordeshook; and Michelsen and Ordeshook.

Owen, Guillermo. "Evaluation of a Presidential Election Game." *American Political Science Review* 69 (September 1975): 947–53. Also, "Communication" by Chester Spatt, "Evaluation of a Presidential Election Game." *APSR* 70 (December 1976): 1221–23, and "Rejoiner" by Guillermo Owen, *APSR* 70 (December 1976): 1223–24. The Spatt and Owen exchange is reprinted in the February 1977 Senate *Hearings*, pp. 549–53.

——. "Multilinear Extensions and the Banzhaf Value." *Naval Research Logistics Quarterly* 22 (December 1975): 741–50.

Parris: see Sayre and Parris.

Power, Max S. "A Theoretical Analysis of the Electoral College and Proposed Reforms." Ph.D. Dissertation, Yale University, 1971.

——. "The Logic and Illogic of the Case for Direct Popular Election of the President." Paper delivered at the Western Political Science Association Meeting, April 8–10, 1971, Albuquerque, New Mexico.

——. "Logic and Legitimacy: On Understanding the Electoral College Controversy." In *Perspectives on Presidential Selection*, edited by Donald R. Matthews. Washington, D.C.: The Brookings Institution, 1973.

Sayre, Wallace S., and Judith H. Parris. *Voting for President: The Electoral College and the American Political System*. Washington, D.C.: The Brookings Institution, 1970.

Sindler, Allan. "Basic Change Aborted: The Failure to Secure Direct Popular Election of the President, 1969–70." In *Policy and Politics in America*, edited by Allan Sindler. Boston: Little, Brown and Company, 1973.

Smolka, Richard G. "Possible Consequences of Direct Election of the President." *State Government* 50 (Summer 1977): 134–40. Reprinted in 1979 Senate *Hearings*, pp. 629–36.

Spatt: See Owen entry.

Spilerman, Seymour, and David Dickens. "Who Will Gain and Who Will Lose Influence Under Different Electoral Rules." Discussion paper, Institute for Research on Poverty, University of Wisconsin, Madison, December 1972. Also in *American Journal of Sociology* 80 (September 1974): 443–77. Reprinted in February 1977 Senate *Hearings*, pp. 554–91.

Sterling, Carleton W. "The Political Implications of Alternative Systems of Electing the President of the United States." Ph.D. dissertation, University of Chicago, 1970.

——. "The Failure of Bloc Voting in the Electoral College to Benefit Urban Liberal and Ethnic Groups." Paper delivered at the Annual Meeting of the American Political Science Association, September 1970, Los Angeles.

——. "The Electoral College: The Representation of Non-Voters." Manuscript.

——. "The Electoral College and the Impact of Popular Vote Distrition." *American Politics Quarterly* 12 (April 1974): 179–204.

——. "Biases of the Electoral College Evaluated Through Mathematical Models." Manuscript.

——. "A Geometric Analysis of Electoral College Misrepresentation." In July 1977 Senate *Hearings*, pp. 409–32.

——. "The Electoral College Biases Revealed, The Conventional Wisdom and Game Theory Models Notwithstanding." In July 1977 Senate *Hearings*, pp. 432–54. Also in *The Western Political Quarterly* 31 (June 1978): 159–77.

Straffin, Philip, Jr. "Homogeneity, Independence and Power Indices." *Public Choice* 30 (Summer 1977): 107–18.

Uslaner, Eric M. "Pivotal States in the Electoral College: An Empirical Investigation." *Annals of New York Academy of Science* 219 (1973): 61–76.

——. "Spatial Models of the Electoral College: Distribution Assumptions and Biases of the System." Paper delivered at the Annual Meeting of the American Political Science Association, August 29–September 2, 1974, Chicago. Also in *Political Methodology* (Summer, 1976): 335–81.

Young, H. P. "The Allocation of Funds in Lobbying and Campaigning." *Behavioral Science*, in press.

Yunker, John H. "Prepared Statement of John Yunker." February 1977 Senate *Hearings*, pp. 498–500.

Yunker, John H., and Lawrence D. Longley. "The Biases of the Electoral College: Who is Really Advantaged?" In *Perspectives on Presidential Selection*, edited by Donald R. Matthews. Washington, D.C.: The Brookings Institution, 1973.

———. *The Electoral College: Its Biases Newly Measured for the 1960s and 1970s*. Sage Professional Papers in American Politics. Beverly Hills, Calif.: Sage Publishers, 1976.

Yunker: See also Longley and Yunker.

Zeidenstein, Harvey. *Direct Election of the President*. Lexington, Mass.: Heath-Lexington Books, 1973.

PART C: SELECTED MATERIALS FOR AND AGAINST THE ELECTORAL COLLEGE

1. Works Generally Supporting the Abolition of the Electoral College

Broder, David S. "Admirable Case, Wrong Defendant." *Washington Post*, March 21, 1979. Also in the 1979 Senate *Hearings*, pp. 57–58.

"Demolish the College." Editorial, *Washington Post*, February 1, 1977. Also in the February 1977 Senate *Hearings*, p. 114, and in the July 1977 Senate *Hearings*, pp. 493–94.

Feerick, John D. "The Electoral College and the Election of 1976." *Journal of the American Bar Association* 63 (June 1977): 757–75. Also in the July 1977 Senate *Hearings*, pp. 360-363.

———. "Electoral College Archaic, Dangerous: Democracy Demands Popular Vote." Syndicated column, January 21, 1977. Also in the July 1977 Senate *Hearings*, pp. 490–92.

Lewis, Anthony. "Again: Why Keep the Electoral College?" *New York Times*, November 7, 1976.

Longley, Lawrence D. "Electoral College Should Be Abolished." *Minneapolis Tribune*, December 12, 1976.

Peirce, Neal R. "Electoral College: Its Time Has Run Out." *Washington Post*, December 3, 1976. Also in the July 1977 Senate *Hearings*, pp. 485–86.

Wicker, Tom. "An Old Idea Still Needed." *New York Times*, November 16, 1976. Also in the July 1977 Senate *Hearings*, p. 480.

———. "One Person, One Vote." *New York Times*, March 27, 1977.

———. "Black Voting Power." *New York Times*, September 16, 1977.

See also the various statements contained in the February 1977 Senate *Hearings*, especially those by Senators Humphrey and Dole; Longley, Yunker, and Braun; Justin Stanley and John Feerick of the American Bar Association; Gus Tyler of the ILGWU; and Clark MacGregor of the U.S. Chamber of Commerce. Additional statements supporting the abolishment of the electoral college can also be found in the reopened July 1977 *Hearings*, especially those by Paul A. Freund, Richard M. Scammon, Lance Tarrance, Douglas L. Bailey, and Senator Robert Dole. The July 1977 Senate *Hearings* contains an extensive selection of newspaper and magazine editorials and articles favoring electoral college reform, pp. 471–503.

Further testimony in favor of abolishing the electoral college can be found in the 1979 Senate *Hearings*, especially by John D. Feerick, Doug Bailey, and James A. Michener.

An excellent summary of the case for the abolishment of the electoral college will be found in the December 1977 Senate *Report*, pp. 1–23. This report includes discussions of the defects and deficiencies of the present electoral college system; the opponents' arguments and some counterpoints; the effects of direct election on the two-party system, federalism, and direct election; the impact of direct election on the smaller states; its consequences in terms of voter fraud, vote recounts, and possible run offs; and social and minority group voting power under electoral college and direct electoral systems.

2.   *Works Generally Supporting the Retention of the Electoral College*

"A Bad Idea Whose Time Has Come." Editorial, *New Republic*, May 7, 1977. Also in the July 1977 Senate *Hearings*, pp. 525–28.

American Enterprise Institute. *Direct Election of the President*. Washington, D.C.: The American Enterprise Institute for Public Policy Research, 1977. Reprinted in the July 1977 Senate *Hearings*, pp. 384–97.

"Busybody 'Reform.' " Editorial, *Wall Street Journal*, March 28, 1977. Also in the July 1977 Senate *Hearings*, pp. 511–12.

Diamond, Martin. "Testimony in Support of the Electoral College." Reprint no. 76. Washington, D.C.: The American Enterprise Institute for Public Policy Research, 1977.

"Election Reform." Editorial, *New Republic*, June 25, 1977. Also in the July 1977 Senate *Hearings*, pp. 534–35.

"Electoral College Reform." Editorial, *New York Times*, November 16, 1976.

Kilpatrick, James J. "Yes, an 18th Century Idea." Syndicated column, *Washington Star*, August 11, 1977. Also in July 1977 Senate *Hearings*, pp. 536–37.

Hunt, Albert R. "Don't 'Fix' the Electoral College." *Wall Street Journal*, July 5, 1979.

"Making the Vote and Voting More Popular." Editorial, *New York Times*, March 23, 1977. Also in the July 1977 Senate *Hearings*, pp. 510–11.

"Old Reform, New Risks." Editorial, *New York Times*, February 6, 1977. Also in the February 1977 Senate *Hearings*, p. 357, and the July 1977 Senate *Hearings*, pp. 506–07.

Perkins, Paul M. "What's Good About the Electoral College." *Washington Monthly*, April 1977, pp. 40–41. Also in the 1979 Senate *Hearings*, pp. 658–59.

"The 'Plebiscitary Presidency." Editorial, *Washington Star*, April 6, 1979.

Ranney, Austin. "Keep the Electoral College." *Baltimore Sun*, April 28, 1977. Also in the 1979 Senate *Hearings*, pp. 655–56.

" 'Reforming' the Electoral College." Editorial, *Wall Street Journal*, January 6, 1977. Also in the July 1977 Senate *Hearings*, pp. 505–06.

Schlesinger, Arthur M. "The Elector College Conundrum." *Wall Street Journal*, April 4, 1977. Also in the July 1977 Senate *Hearings*, pp. 514–16.

"Senator Bayh's Nightmare." Editorial, *Washington Star*, November 18, 1976.

Wildavsky, Aaron. "The Plebiscitary Presidency: Direct Election as Class Legislation." *Commonsense* 2 (Winter 1979): 1–10. Also in the 1979 Senate *Hearings*, pp. 533–42.

Will, George F. "Don't Fool With the Electoral College." *Newsweek*, April 4, 1977, p. 96. Also in the July 1977 Senate *Hearings*, pp. 509–10, and in the 1979 Senate *Hearings*, pp. 231–32.

———. "Constitutional Numbers Games." *Washington Post*, August 18, 1975. Also in the July 1977 Senate *Hearings*, pp. 519–20.

Williams, Eddie N. "Would Popular Election Dilute the Black Vote?" *Washington Post*, April 14, 1977. Also in the July 1977 Senate *Hearings*, pp. 518–19, and in the 1979 Senate *Hearings*, p. 628.

See also the various statements contained in the February 1977 Senate *Hearings* and in the reopened July 1977 Senate *Hearings*, especially those by Austin Ranney, Aaron Wildavsky, Martin Diamond, Herbert Storing, Judith Best, and Eddie Williams. The July 1977 Senate *Hearings* contains an extensive selection of newspaper and magazine editorials opposing electoral college reform, pp. 505–37.

Further testimony in favor of retaining the electoral college can be found in the 1979 Senate *Hearings*, especially by Harry Bailey, Walter Berns, Judith Best, Vernon Jordan, Jeane Kirkpatrick, Howard M. Squadron, Theodore White, and George Will.

A comprehensive summary of the case against the abolishment of the electoral college will be found in the December 1977 Senate *Report*, "Minority Views of Messrs. Eastland, Allen, Thurmond, Scott, Laxalt, Hatch, and Wallop on S.J. Res. 1," pp. 24–32.

"In summary, we believe that the proposal should be rejected for the following reasons:
It would cripple the party system and encourage splinter parties;
It would undermine the federal system;
It would alter the delicate balance underlying separation of powers;
It would encourage electoral fraud;
It could lead to interminable recounts and challenges;
It would necessitate national control of every aspect of the electoral process;
It would give undue weight to numbers, thereby reducing the influence of small states;
It would encourage candidates for President to represent narrow geographical, ideological, and ethnic bases of support;
It would encourage simplistic media-oriented campaigns and bring about drastic changes in the strategy and tactics used in campaigns for the Presidency; and,
It would increase the power of big city political bosses."

Notes

CHAPTER ONE

1. For a fuller discussion of the 1976 election and possible electoral vote outcomes, see pp. 80–84.

2. The terms "colleges of electors" and "electoral college" appeared first in congressional debates around 1800. They were first incorporated in legislation in 1845. J. Hampden Dougherty, *The Electoral System of the United States* (New York, 1906), p. 74.

3. Ibid., pp. 253–54.

4. Joseph E. Kallenbach, quoted in *Congressional Record*, 1949, p. 4449.

5. An opinion attributed to delegate Abraham Baldwin of Georgia, cited by Lucius Wilmerding, *The Electoral College* (New Brunswick, N.J., 1958), p. 4.

6. Senate Report No. 22, 19th Cong., 1st sess., Jan. 19, 1826, p. 4. Benton, author of the report, was referring specifically to the discretion given presidential electors to vote for whomever they please.

7. *Gray v. Sanders*, 372 U.S. 368 (1963).

8. American Bar Association, *Electing the President: A Report of the Commission on Electoral College Reform* (Chicago: A.B.A., 1967). This report is reprinted in most of the congressional hearings of 1967 to 1970.

9. Edward S. Corwin, *The President, Office and Powers* (New York, 1957), p. 67.

10. For further background see: Clinton Rossiter, *1787—The Grand Convention* (New York, 1966), pp. 23–40; John Bach McMaster, *A History of the People of the United States from the Revolution to the Civil War*, 8 vols. (New York, 1893–1924), I, pp. 1–102; William Anderson, "Federalism—Now and Then," *State Government*, May 1943, pp. 107–12.

11. *American Museum*, Jan. 1787, quoted by McMaster, op. cit., p. 26.

12. Rossiter *The American Presidency* (New York, 1956), pp. 4–25.

13. Ibid., p.3.

CHAPTER TWO

1. Max Farrand, ed., *The Records of the Federal Constitutional Convention of 1787*, 4 vols. (New Haven, 1911, 1937; referred to hereafter as Farrand, II, p. 501.

2. John P. Roche, "The Founding Fathers: A Reform Caucus in Action," *American Political Science Review*, Dec. 1961, p. 810.

3. Letter to George Washington, Nov. 24, 1786, cited by Charles C. Thach, *The Creation of the Presidency, 1775–1789* (Baltimore, 1922), p. 29.

4. *Rights of Man* (Everyman ed.), p. 207, cited by Thach, op. cit., p. 30.

5. Letter to his father, Nov. 1786, *Madison's Works* (Cong. ed.), I, p. 253, cited by Thach, op. cit., p. 19.

6. Farrand, op. cit., II, p. 35.

7. Letter to Carrington, Aug. 4, 1787, *Jefferson's Writings* (Ford ed.), IV, p. 424, cited by Thach, op. cit., p. 71. Jefferson was the United States minister to France at the time of the Constitutional Convention, and thus did not serve as a delegate.

8. Thach, op. cit., pp. 36–37. The chief authors of the New York Constitution were John Jay, Robert Livingston, and Gouverneur Morris. Morris left New York following his 1779 defeat for reelection to the Continental Congress and settled in Philadelphia. He was designated as one of the Pennsylvania delegates to the Constitutional Convention. Subsequently, he served as a U.S. minister in Europe and resettled in New York, serving as a U.S. senator from that state from 1800 to 1803.

9. Farrand, op. cit., I, pp. 52, 65, 97.

10. Ibid., I, pp. 65–66, 85.

11. Ibid., I, p. 97; II, p. 29. The June 4 vote was 7–3, the July 17 vote, 10–0.

12. Ibid., II, p. 171. The title "President" appears to have been proposed to the convention by Charles Pinckney of South Carolina, to whom it may have been suggested by the title at that date of the chief magistrate of Delaware. See Thach, op. cit., p. 109.

13. Thach, op. cit., pp. 166–67.

14. Farrand, op. cit., I, p. 68; II, p. 55.

15. Ibid., I, p. 69; II, p. 33.

16. Ibid., I, p. 292; II, p. 35.

17. A summary of other Convention voting on the length of term and reeligibility: *Under proposals for election of the President by the national legislature:* Proposals for a seven-year term with reeligibility unspecified were approved by the convention June 1 on a 5–4 vote, with one state divided, and June 2 by an 8–2 vote (Farrand, op. cit., I, pp. 69, 77). The convention June 2 voted 7–2, with one state divided, to limit the executive to a single seven-year term (ibid., I, p. 88). On July 16, the convention voted 6–4 to permit the chief executive to seek reelection (ibid., II, p. 35). Proposals to make him ineligible for reelection but extend his term up to 8, 11, 15, or even 20 years were considered July 24 (ibid., II, p. 102). The convention July 26 voted to return to the seven-year term with a one-term limit, by a vote of 7–3 (ibid., II, p. 120). The report of the Committee of Detail, submitted August 6, contained an identical provision.

Under proposals for election by intermediate electors: Under an early version of this plan, the convention voted 8–2 on July 19 to make the chief executive eligible for reelection, and voted to reduce the term from seven to six years (ibid., II, pp. 58–59). The final plan, submitted by the Committee of Eleven on September 4, provided for a four-year term and indefinite reeligibility. The convention September 6 voted 3–8 to reject a motion to extend the term to seven years, and 2–9 against a motion to extend it to six years. The four-year provision was approved by a 10–1 vote (ibid., II, p. 525). The provision for indefinite reeligibility was not challenged during this final stage of the debate.

18. Clinton Rossiter, *1787—The Grand Convention* (New York, 1966), pp. 222–23.

19. Farrand, op. cit., I, p. 242.

20. Three states were opposed and one divided. The vote could not be characterized completely as a large- versus small-state decision, since New York joined Delaware and New Jersey in voting to use the New Jersey Plan as the basis for further debate.

21. Roche, loc. cit., p. 808.

22. Farrand, op. cit., I, pp. 343, 447–48, 483.

23. Ibid., II, p. 15. Voting in favor were Connecticut, New Jersey, Delaware, Virginia, and North Carolina. Opposed were Pennsylvania, South Carolina, Maryland, and Georgia. Massachusetts was divided. New York did not vote, since two of its three delegates (Robert Yates and John Lansing, Jr.), both of whom were strongly antinationalist and out of sympathy with the effort to write a strong constitution, had departed Philadelphia early in July. Alexander Hamilton, the third member of the New York delegation, attended sporadically but could not cast a vote for the state.

24. Ibid., II, pp. 30, 111, 401, 403.

25. Ibid., II, p. 404. Both votes occurred Aug. 24.

26. Ibid., II, p. 513.

27. Jonathan Elliott, *The Debates in the Several State Conventions on the Adoption of the Federal Constitution*, 2nd ed. (Washington, D.C. 1836), II, pp. 495, 464. See also John P. Feerick, "The Electoral College: Why It Was Created," *American Bar Association Journal*, Mar. 1968, p. 254.

28. Farrand, op. cit., II, pp. 201-04.

29. Ibid., II, pp. 201, 204, 208.

30. Ibid., II, pp. 206, 216. Scraps of memoranda of the members of the Committee of Detail indicated they had considered such voter qualifications as "possession of real property," "inrolment in the militia," and "freeholders." Ibid., II, pp. 140, 151.

31. Ibid., I, p. 81; II, p. 404.

32. Ibid., II, pp. 57, 111.

33. The proposal for election by state governors was advanced by Elbridge Gerry of Massachusetts and rejected by the convention, 9 states opposed and one divided (Farrand, op. cit., I, pp. 175-76). Gerry subsequently proposed that state governors appoint the president with the advice of the governors' councils, but if the state had no council (all but New York did at the time), then by the state legislature. The motion never came to a vote (ibid., II, p. 109). A proposal for electing the president by fifteen members of Congress chosen by lot was advanced, perhaps ironically, by Wilson of Pennsylvania, otherwise a strong backer of direct election by the people. Wilson commented candidly that his proposal for choice by fifteen congressmen was "not a digested idea and might be open to strong objections." It was not brought to a vote (ibid., II, p. 103). Other hybrid plans included a proposal by Oliver Ellsworth of Connecticut that the president be chosen by Congress unless the incumbent had been in office for a whole term and would be eligible for reelection, in which case electors selected by the state legislatures would choose. The proposal was rejected, 4 states to 7 (ibid., II, pp. 108, 112). John Dickinson of Delaware suggested that each state be allowed to choose its best citizen, and of the thirteen men so designated, the president would be chosen by Congress or electors appointed by Congress. The proposal never came to a vote (ibid., II, pp. 114-15).

34. Ibid., I, p. 65.

35. Ibid., II, pp. 29, 34, 175, 500.

36. Ibid., I, p. 81; II, pp. 33, 101, 120, 185, 404, 511.

37. Ibid., I, pp. 68-69; II, pp. 29, 52-53, 111, 403.

38. Ibid., II, pp. 29-31; 57, 114.

39. Ibid., II, pp. 30-31.

40. Ibid., II, pp. 32, 402.

41. Under the Maryland plan, the state senate was chosen by an electoral college of forty members—two from each county, plus one additional from Baltimore City and one additional from Annapolis. The electors were charged with selecting persons "of the most approved wisdom, experience and virtue." The electors were required to choose nine of the fifteen-member senate from the Western Shore of Maryland and six from the Eastern Shore. They could choose persons from their own number as senators, or any number from any given county, as long as the 9-6 ratio was preserved. Within a generation, one Maryland historian records, the state senate was not only "free from the gusts of popular passions" (a phrase Alexander Hamilton used in defending the institution), but also "not open to decent ventilation" (a phrase used by the Jeffersonian Democrats in attacking it). Matthew Page Andrews, *History of Maryland* (Garden City, N.Y., 1929), pp. 330-31.

42. Farrand, op. cit., II, p. 500.

43. Ibid., I, p. 81; II, pp. 33, 58, 64, 95.

44. Roche, loc. cit., p. 810.

45. Farrand, op. cit., II, p. 525.

46. Ibid., II, p. 537.

47. Ibid., II, p. 511.

48. Ibid., II, p. 501.

49. Ibid., II, p. 521.

50. In debate on this section, a motion was made that the electors meet at the seat of the national government, but only one state (North Carolina) voted for it. Ibid., II, p. 525.

51. The word "appointed" did not appear in the Committee of Eleven draft. It was inserted on the motion of Dickinson of Delaware "to remove ambiguity"—and, as experience would demonstrate in the early years, to make it easier to achieve a majority if some states failed to appoint electors. Dickinson's motion was approved by an 8-2 vote. Ibid., II, p. 515.

52. Ibid., II, pp. 513-14.

53. A more perspicacious observer was Baldwin of Georgia, who thought the Senate would "be less and less likely to have the eventual appointment" because of "the increasing intercourse among the people of the states," making candidates well known to all. Ibid., II, p. 501.

54. Ibid., II, pp. 512-13.

55. Ibid., II, pp. 522-23, 527.

56. Ibid., II, p. 527. Williamson's first proposal was actually for choice of "the legislature," apparently meaning both houses. Sherman suggested the modification to choice by the House, which was approved.

57. Ibid., II, p. 536.

58. Ibid., II, pp. 514–15.

59. Ibid., II, p. 526.

60. Ibid., II, p. 526.

61. Ibid., II, p. 535.

62. *Congressional Quarterly 1965 Almanac* (Washington D.C., 1966), pp. 573-81; John D. Feerick, *From Failing Hands: The Story of Presidential Succession* (New York, 1965).

63. The major opposition arguments—such as they were—did not appear until the convention in Virginia, the tenth of the thirteen original states to ratify. It was claimed that foreign states might interfere in presidential elections or that the president would conspire with Congress to stay in office for life or that he would become a despot. One of the more cogent arguments was that if an election were thrown into the House, the majority could consist of 15 representatives constituting a majority of the delegations of seven states—outvoting 50 other representatives from the other six states. George Mason contended that the elector system "was a mere deception—a mere *ignis fatuus* on the American people—and thrown out to make them believe they were to choose" the president. "The people will, in reality, have no hand in the election," Mason said. Elliott, op. cit., III, pp. 492-93.

64. Ibid., II, p. 511.

65. *The Federalist*, Jacob E. Cooke, ed. (Middletown, Conn., 1961), pp. 457-58.

66. Elliott, op. cit., III, pp. 487, 494.

67. Cooke, op. cit., p. 252.

68. Elliott, op. cit., II, p. 512.

69. Cooke, op. cit., pp. 458, 460.

70. Ibid., pp. 311, 458–59.

71. Elliott, op. cit., III, pp. 486, 488. Monroe opposed ratification.

72. Cooke, op. cit., pp. 458–59.

73. Carl Becker, "The Will of the People," *Yale Review*, March 1945, p. 389.

74. Roche, loc. cit., p. 811.

75. Letter to George Hay, Aug. 23, 1823, cited in Farrand, op. cit., III, p. 458.

CHAPTER THREE

1. John Bach McMaster, *A History of the People of the United States from the Revolution to the Civil War*, 8 vols. (New York, 1893–1924), I pp. 538–40.

2. Edward Stanwood, *A History of the Presidency from 1788 to 1897* (Boston, 1898); p. 20. North Carolina and Rhode Island refused to ratify until Congress proposed a series of twelve amendments, ten of which were adopted—the "Bill of Rights." Neither participated in the first election.

3. Ibid., pp. 22–23.

4. Ibid., p. 26.

5. Ibid., p. 27.

6. In debate on the president's power to remove federal officers. *Annals of Congress*, I, pp. 550, 554. Elbridge Gerry of Massachusetts took a different view. Ibid., I, p. 557.

7. Stanwood, op. cit., p. 48.

8. Ibid., p. 51.

9. Ibid., p. 52.

10. Issue of Feb. 15, 1798, cited by Charles A. O'Neil, *The American Electoral System* (New York, 1887), p. 66.

11. Stanwood, op. cit., pp. 54–57; O'Neil, op. cit., p. 83.

12. Jefferson, *Works*, I, p. 381, cited by Lucius Wilmerding, *The Electoral College* (New Brunswick, N.J., 1958), p. 32. Burr had contributed to the Republican cause by helping to persuade George Clinton to come out of retirement and head up a "blue ribbon" ticket of Republican candidates for the state Assembly (which chose the presidential electors). Under Clinton the Republicans scored an upset victory.

13. Letter of Jan. 12, 1800, cited by J. Hampden Dougherty, *The Electoral System of the United States* (New York, 1906), p. 286.

14. Cited by O'Neil, op. cit., pp. 71, 261–62.

15. Issue of Nov. 4, 1800.

16. O'Neil, op. cit., p. 73.

17. Ibid., pp. 74–75.

18. Stanwood, op. cit., p. 59.

19. Ibid., p. 63. A slight exception to the southern sweep was the victory of 4 Federalist electors in North Carolina (out of the state's total of 12).

20. Ibid., p. 70. The 1792 law provided that whenever the offices of president and vice president both became vacant, a special election should be held. Paragraph 6 of article II, section 1 of the Constitution provided that Congress might appoint an officer to act as president "until . . . a President shall be elected." The original proposal for this section of the Constitution, as considered by the convention on September 7, 1787, had read, "until the time of electing a President shall arrive." Madison had objected that this "would prevent a supply of the vacancy by an intermediate election of the President," and moved to substitute the wording, "until . . . a President shall be elected." (Max Farrand, ed., *The Records of the Federal Constitutional Convention of 1787*, 4 vols. [New Haven, 1911, 1937], II, p. 535.) Until 1947, presidential succession laws permitted a special election in the event of a dual vacancy. See John D. Feerick, *From Failing Hands: The Story of Presidential Succession* (New York, 1965), pp. 146, 209.

21. Samuel Eliot Morison and Henry Steele Commager, *The Growth of the American Republic* (New York, 1950), I, p. 381.

22. Cited by Stanwood, op. cit., p. 70, and Wilmerding, op. cit., p. 32.

23. Sidney Hyman, *The American President* (New York, 1954), p. 128.

24. O'Neil, op. cit., pp. 87–88.

25. Cited by O'Neil, op. cit., p. 72.

26. Cited by Stanwood, op. cit., p. 72.

27. For state-by-state balloting chart, see Stanwood, op. cit., p. 72.

28. Eugene H. Roseboom, *A History of Presidential Elections* (New York, 1959), p. 46; *Annals*, XIII, p. 158.

29. See Wilmerding, op. cit., p. 36.

30. Herman V. Ames, "The Proposed Amendments to the Constitution of the United States During the First Century of Its History," *Annual Report of the American Historical Association for 1896* (Washington, D.C., 1897), pp. 77–78.

31. The Senate vote was 15–8 in favor Ames, op. cit., p. 78.

32. Farrand, op. cit., III, pp. 393–95.

33. Cited by Stanwood, op. cit., pp. 79–80.

34. Ames, op. cit., p. 78.

35. *Annals*, XIII, pp. 155, 194–95.

36. *Annals*, XIII, pp. 87, 128.

37. Ames, op. cit., p. 79.

38. Senate Report 22, 19th Cong. 1st sess., Jan. 19, 1826, p. 2.

39. *Annals* XXXI, p. 180.

40. *Annals* XXXI, pp. 182–83; see also Stanwood, op. cit., p. 103.

41. Wilmerding, op. cit., p. 46.

42. Ibid., p. 58.

43. Letter to George Hay, Aug. 23, 1823, printed in Farrand op. cit., III, p. 459.
44. Wilmerding, op. cit., pp. 45–46.
45. 1826 Senate Report, p. 17. See also comment by Jefferson, in Wilmerding, op. cit., p. 46.
46. Wilmerding, op. cit., p. 59.

CHAPTER FOUR

1. Eugene H. Roseboom, *A History of Presidential Elections* (New York, 1959), p. 82; Edward Stanwood, *A History of the Presidency from 1788 to 1897* (Boston, 1898), pp. 127–31.
2. Stanwood, op. cit., pp. 135–36.
3. Ibid., p. 139; Roseboom, op. cit., p. 84.
4. Cited by Roseboom, op. cit., p. 88. See also Stanwood, op. cit., pp. 138–39.
5. Cited by Samuel Eliot Morison and Henry Steele Commager, *The Growth of the American Republic* (New York, 1950), I, p. 464.
6. Richard C. Baker, "On Becoming President by One Vote," *American Bar Association Journal*, May 1962, p. 455; Roseboom, op. cit., p. 86. For text of rules under which the House operated in choosing a president, see Appendix I.
7. Cited by Charles A. O'Neil, *The American Electoral System* (New York, 1887), p. 124.
8. Stanwood, op. cit., p. 393. See also, concerning the election of 1876, the discussion in William R. Keech, "Background Paper," in *Winner Take All: Report of the Twentieth Century Fund Task Force on Reform of the Presidential Election Process* (New York, 1978), chap. III: "Comparing the Alternatives: Does the 'Right' Candidate Win?".
9. See Stanwood, op. cit., p. 383.
10. Roseboom, op. cit., pp. 242–43.
11. Ibid, pp. 243–45.
12. Stanwood, op. cit., p. 381; Roseboom, op. cit. p. 245.
13. Cited by J. Hampden Dougherty, *The Electoral System of the United States* (New York 1906), p. 108.
14. Ibid., pp. 109–10, 126–35.
15. Ibid, pp. 110–16.
16. Roseboom, op. cit., p. 247.
17. Stanwood, op. cit., pp. 390–91.
18. Roseboom, op. cit., p. 249.
19. Ibid., pp. 248–49.
20. Cited by Sidney Hyman, *The American President* (New York, 1954), pp. 29–30.
21. Stanwood, op. cit., pp. 457–83.
22. Ibid., pp. 447–49.
23. Roseboom, op. cit., p. 387.
24. For more detailed background on the 1948 campaign, see Congressional Quarterly, *Congress and the Nation* (Washington, D.C., 1965), pp. 5–8; also Jules Abels, *Out of the Jaws of Victory* (New York, 1959).
25. Richard M. Scammon, "How Barkley Became President," *Northern Virginia Sun*, Mar. 7, 1960.
26. For further background on the 1960 campaign, see Theodore H. White, *The Making of the President, 1960*, (New York, 1961); also *Congress and the Nation* as cited, pp. 32-39, and Lawrence D. Longley and Alan G. Braun, *The Politics of Electoral College Reform*, (New Haven, 1975), chapter 1. The congressional apportionment in effect in 1960—and consequently the electoral vote apportionment—was based on the 1950 census. As a result, the president chosen in 1960 to serve from 1961 to 1965 was selected by an electoral college apportioned according to population distributions ten years old.
27. The commonly accepted practice in determining popular votes for president is to credit the candidate with the number of votes received by the highest-polling elector pledged to him in the state.

28. *Congressional Quarterly Weekly Report*, Feb. 17, 1961, pp. 285–88. See also U.S., Congress, Senate, Committee on the Judiciary, Subcommittee on Constitutional Amendments, *Hearings, Nomination and Election of President and Vice President and Qualifications for Voting* 87th Cong. 1st sess. 1961, pp. 391–99. Hereafter cited as 1961 Senate *Hearings*.

29. *Chicago Tribune*, Nov. 14, 1960.

30. *New York Herald Tribune*, July 14, 1961.

31. *New York Times*, Mar. 4, 1962.

32. Ibid., Dec. 11, 1960.

33. *Washington Evening Star*, Dec. 12, 1960.

34. Associated Press dispatch, Dec. 12, 1960.

35. 1961 Senate *Hearings*, p. 622.

36. For Irwin's testimony, which includes copies of his correspondence with other Republican electors and southern unpledged elector leaders, see 1961 Senate *Hearings*, pp. 562–655. One result of Henry Irwin's action was that Oklahoma, in 1961, passed the nation's most stringent law binding electors to oaths to support their party's nominees or face penalties up to a fine of one thousand dollars. Such laws, however, are probably unconstitutional on the grounds that the Constitution provides for electors *voting*, which implies a freedom of action. See James C. Kirby, Jr., "Limitations on the Power of State Legislatures over Presidential Elections," *Law and Contemporary Problems*, Spring 1962, pp. 495–509.

37. The unpledged electors from Alabama and Mississippi had voted for Thurmond for vice president, while the bolting Republican elector from Oklahoma, Henry D. Irwin, had cast his vice presidential vote for Goldwater. *See the Congressional Record*, Jan. 6, 1961, p.291. For a journalistic account of the joint session, see *New York Times*, Jan. 7, 1961.

38. The following discussion draws upon material originally published in Longley and Braun, op. cit., pp. 7–17, and Neal R. Peirce, *The Deep South States of America* (New York, 1974), pp. 253–55.

39. This and the following three paragraphs are based on interviews and materials originally published in Peirce, op. cit., pp. 254–55.

40. Senator Birch Bayh, quoted in "The Electoral College," *Congressional Quarterly Guide to Current American Government*, (Spring 1970), p. 144.

41. "Wallace Candidacy Raises Fears of Electoral Stalemate," *Congressional Quarterly Weekly Report*, July 19, 1968, p. 1818.

42. League of Women Voters of the United States, *Who Should Elect the President?* (Washington, D.C. 1969).

43. As we note elsewhere, Wallace's electoral vote total was later increased by one and Nixon's decreased by a like amount, by the actions of an individual Nixon elector.

44. An electoral college majority in 1968 was 270 votes out of a total of 538, while in 1960 it was 269 votes out of a total of 537. The reason for this change was that the total electoral college vote rose temporarily to 537 for the 1960 election to accommodate the new states of Alaska and Hawaii, while in 1968 the total electoral college vote had increased permanently to 538 electoral votes when the 23rd amendment gave the District of Columbia 3 electoral votes.

45. 30,631 votes in New Jersey, 10,245 in Missouri, and 12,158 in New Hampshire. Based on "Final 1968 Presidential Election Results as reported to *Congressional Quarterly* by the Governmental Affairs Institution," in Congressional Quarterly, *Politics in America*, 3rd ed. (Washington, D.C., 1969), p. 127. This analysis is, of course, based solely on the actual November election results. If one takes into account the later action of Nixon elector Dr. Lloyd W. Bailey in voting for Wallace, different results are found since only 32 rather than 33 electoral votes would have to shift. In this case, a shift of 41,971 votes from Nixon to Humphrey in New Jersey (30,631), Missouri (10,245), and Alaska (1,095) could have deadlocked the election.

46. Bailey's action gave rise to debate by both houses of Congress on January 6, 1969, over a challenge to his vote by Senator Edmund Muskie (D. Maine) and Representative James G. O'Hara (D., Mich.), which was finally defeated. For a more detailed discussion, see chap. 7; also Congressional Quarterly, *Guide to Congress*, 2nd (Washington, D.C., 1976), pp. 240–41; and Congressional Quarterly *Guide to U.S. Elections* (Washington, D.C., 1975), pp. 211–12.

47. Judson L. James, *American Political Parties: Potential and Performance* (New York, 1969), p. 52.

48. James A. Michener, *Presidential Lottery: The Reckless Gamble in Our Electoral System* (New York, 1969), pp. 16 and 56. Another plan, widely reported during the months of the election had been advanced by Gary Orfield, an assistant professor of government at the University of Virginia, in an article in the *Washington Post* of July 7, 1968. The Orfield proposal, quickly adopted by then Representative, later Senator, Charles E. Goodell (R., N.Y.) and Representative Morris K. Udall (D., Ariz.), would have the leaders of both parties pledge that if the 1968 election resulted in an electoral college deadlock, they would provide sufficient House votes to elect whomever had been the popular vote winner. This plan, of course, could have been as easily implemented in the electoral college as in the House of Representatives. "Wallace Candidacy Raises Fears of Electoral Stalemate," as cited, p. 1820.

49. This potential tension actually appeared in a rather subtle form in the campaign statements of the two candidates about the possibility of electoral college deadlock. Humphrey stressed the need to follow the prescribed constitutional contingent procedure, while Nixon stated his belief that "whoever wins the popular vote should be the next President of the United States." Quoted in "The Electoral College," *Congressional Quarterly Guide to Current American Government*, (Spring 1970), p. 144.

50. Among the nastiest rumors of the 1968 election was that if electoral college deadlock appeared immanent and if the new House appeared likely to elect Nixon, outgoing president Johnson might reconvene the old Congress for the purpose of moving the meeting time of the new Congress back beyond January 6 so that the old, Democratic Congress could choose the new president. This rumor never had any substance but illustrates both the suspicious generated by threatened deadlock and the frightening possibilities under the contingent proceedings.

51. "House Membership in the 91st Congress, 1st Session," *Congressional Quarterly Weekly Report*, Jan. 3, 1969, pp. 38–39.

52. Much of this material is adapted from Longley and Braun, op. cit., pp. 15–17.

53. "Wallace Candidacy Raises Fears of Electoral Stalemate," as cited, pp. 1821–22.

54. "House Candidates Pledges," *Congressional Quarterly Weekly Report*, Oct. 25, 1968, p. 2956. The pledges were made as a result of widespread speculation that the election might go to the House and that in that case representatives would vote for the nominee of thier party. For Democrats in districts that were expected to go to Nixon or Wallace, this was potentially a detrimental campaign issue. In order to protect themselves, candidates pledged to follow the mandate of their districts and to vote in the House for the winner of their districts, regardless of party affiliation.

55. Compiled from National Municipal League, *Apportionment in the Nineteen Sixties* (New York, 1967), pages unnumbered, and Luman H. Long, ed. *World Almanac, 1969* (New York, 1968), pp. 907–08.

56. National Municipal League, *Apportionment in the Nineteen Sixties*, and Long, *World Almanac, 1969*, pp. 907–08.

57. This incomplete analysis of possible voting alignments in the House highlights another aspect of the inequality of the contingent election scheme. One man representing the 285,278 citizens of Nevada, would cast one-fiftieth of the vote for president. At the same time, had the Illinois, Maryland, Montana, and Oregon delegations voted along party lines, they would have been divided and would have lost their vote; over 15 million people would, therefore, have been disenfranchised. This is in addition to the total and automatic disenfranchisement of the 700,000 residents of the District of Columbia.

58. The possibilities inherent in this period of uncertainty as the House moves through successive ballots was fascinatingly described in a fantasy written in early 1968 by Russell Baker of the *New York Times*, entitled *Our Next President: The Incredible Story of What Happened in the 1968 Elections* (New York, 1968). Two less realistic fictional accounts of possible events surrounding electoral college deadlock in 1968 and subsequent House contingent activities are Theodore G. Venetoulis, "1968: The Year No President Was Elected," in *The House Shall Choose* (Margate, N.J., 1968), pp. 154–77; and Sherwin Markman, *The Election* (New York, 1970). *The Election* includes a narrative of a black insurrection in California that complicates House activities.

One can carry this type of analysis on and on—for example to show how a Democratic Senate might have had to choose for vice president between Spiro Agnew and Curtis Le May for vice president if, as some September predictions suggested, the Wallace-Le May ticket ran ahead, in electoral votes, of the Humphrey-Muskie ticket, thus becoming the second ticket and thereby excluding Senator Muskie from Senate consideration.

59. Some of the following analysis of the 1976 election is adapted from material originally appearing in Lawrence D. Longley, "Electoral College Reform: Problems, Politics , and Prospects," in *Paths to Political Reform* ed. William J. Crotty (Lexington, Mass., for the Policy Studies Organization, 1980).

60. See: "Testimony of Douglas Bailey," media manager of the Ford-Dole campaign, Aug. 2, 1977, in U.S. Congress, Senate, Judiciary Committee, Subcommittee on the Constitution, *Hearings on Electoral College and Direct Election*, 95th Cong. 1st sess. July 20, 22, 28, and Aug. 2, 1977 (hereafter cited as July 1977, Senate *Hearings*), pp. 258–73, as well as the testimony at the same hearings by Senator Robert Dole, who also stressed the campaign distortions created by the electoral college (pp. 26–40). See also, "Impact of Direct Election on the Smaller States," in U.S., Congress Senate, Judiciary Committee, *Direct Popular Election of the President and Vice President of the United States*, Dec. 1977 (hereafter cited as Dec. 1977 Senate Report), pp. 14–16.

61. For a discussion of campaign resource allocation biases, see Claude S. Colantoni, J. Levesque, and Peter C. Ordeshook, "Campaign Resource Allocations Under the Electoral College," *American Political Science Review* (Mar. 1975), pp. 141–54, and the discussion concerning this article in the same issue, pp. 155–61; Steven J. Brams and Morton D. Davis, "The 3/2s Rule in Presidential Campaigning," *American Political Science Review*, Mar. 1974, pp. 113–34 (reprinted in U.S., Congress, Senate, Judiciary Committee, Subcommittee on the Constitution, *Hearings on the Electoral College and Direct Election*, 95th Cong., 1st sess., Jan. 27, Feb. 1, 2, 7, and 10, 1977 (hereafter cited as Feb. 1977, Senate *Hearings*), pp. 515–37); Stephen J. Brams, *The Presidential Election Game* (New Haven, 1978), esp. chap. 3; and "Testimony of the Honorable Hubert H. Humphrey, U.S. Senator from the State of Minnesota," Jan. 27, 1977, in Feb. 1977 Senate *Hearings*, p. 25.

62. The faithless elector of 1972 was Republican Roger Lea MacBride of Virginia who deserted Republican nominee Richard Nixon to vote for Libertarian party candidate John Hospers, head of the School of Philosophy at the University of Southern California. Roger MacBride the cocreator of the television series "The Little House on the Prairie," was also the author of an obscure book on the electoral college, *The American Electoral College* (Caldwell, Idaho 1953). His is the first known case of a writer about the electoral college creating a personal footnote in the history of the electoral college by being a faithless elector. Mr. MacBride went on to become the 1976 presidential candidate of the Libertarian party, receiving 173,019 votes in that year, including a noteworthy 5.5 percent of all votes cast for president in Alaska.

63. "Testimony of *Honorable Robert Dole, U.S. Senator from* the State of Kansas," Feb. 1977 Senate *Hearings*, pp. 36–37. A *Washington Post* editorial commenting upon this Dole statement can be found reprinted in these same *Hearings*, pp. 114–15.

64. See the Feb. 1977 Senate *Hearings*, p. 115.

65. This analysis assumes, of course, the nondefection of Republican elector Mike Padden of Washington. If he had nevertheless declined to vote for Ford, the election would have been inconclusive and would have gone to the House in January 1977.

66. Alabama, Arkansas, Connecticut, Delaware, Kentucky, Maine, Massachusetts, Michigan, Mississippi, New York, North Carolina, Tennessee, Vermont, and Wisconsin.

67. *Newsweek*, Nov. 10, 1980.

68. *The Federalist* (Modern Library 2nd ed.), p. 441.

CHAPTER FIVE

1. Carl Becker, "The Will of the People," *Yale Review*, Mar. 1945, pp. 389, 399.

2. For a comprehensive background on political conventions, see Paul T. David, Ralph M. Goldman, and Richard C. Bain, *The Politics of National Party Conventions* (Washington, D.C.,

1960). An excellent overview of the presidential selection process that includes insightful analysis of the national conventions is provided in Nelson W. Polsby and Aaron B. Wildavsky, *Presidential Politics*, 5th ed. (New York, 1980).

3. For data on congressional apportionment procedures and patterns, see Congressional Quarterly Service, *Representation and Apportionment* (Washington, D.C., 1966), pp. 51-61; also Floyd M. Riddick, *The United States Congress: Organization and Procedure* (Manassas, Va., 1948), pp. 6–10. In late August, 1978, the Senate approved and sent to the states a previously House-passed constitutional amendment providing for congressional and electoral college representation for the District of Columbia as if it were a state. Among the provisions of the amendment is language that would repeal the 23rd amendment, which limited the District of Columbia to electoral votes equal to the least number allotted to any state—in other words, three. Under the proposed amendment the District of Columbia would receive the same number of electoral votes it would be entitled to if it were a state—in all likelihood four.

This amendment, if ratified, would have the effect of temporarily increasing the size of the electoral college from 538 to 539 members because of the likely fourth electoral vote for the District of Columbia. This temporary increase would exist only until the next congressional reapportionment of seats among the states (in 1991), which would return the size of the House from 437 to its usual 435 members and the electoral college from a temporary 539 to a permanent 537 members—corresponding to 435 representatives and 102 senators. This assumes, of course, that the electoral college has not meanwhile, through some stroke of wisdom, been abolished.

4. 481 U.S. 1 (1892).

5. U.S. Congress, *Register of Debates*, II, p. 1405, cited by Lucius Wilmerding, *The Electoral College* (New Brunswick, N.J., 1958), p. 43.

6. *Ex parte Yarbrough*, 110 U.S. 651 (1884); *Burroughs and Cannon v. United States*, 290 U.S. 534 (1934).

7. See James C. Kirby, Jr., "Limitations on the Power of State Legislatures over Presidential Elections," *Law and Contemporary Problems*, Spring 1962, pp. 497–504.

8. Senate Report No. 22, 19th Cong. 1st sess. Jan. 19, 1826, (hereafter cited as 1826 Senate Report), p. 4.

9. Wilmerding, op. cit., p. 175.

10. U.S. Congress, Senate, Committee on the Judiciary, Subcommittee on Constitutional Amendments, *Hearings, Nomination and Election of President and Vice President and Qualifications for Voting*, 87th Cong. 1st sess. 1961, p. 546 (hereafter cited as 1961 Senate *Hearings*).

11. James A. Michener, *Presidential Lottery: The Reckless Gamble in Our Electoral System* (New York, 1969), p. 9.

12. Robert G. Dixon, Jr., "Electoral College Procedure," *Western Political Quarterly*, June 1950, p. 216.

13. The Congress apparently refrained from setting a specific date for two reasons: because it would be inconvenient for state legislatures that might choose the electors themselves and would need more than a single day to complete their debates and action, and because states'-rights advocates said Congress should not place unnecessary restrictions on the states. See Charles A. O'Neil, *The American Electoral System* (New York, 1887), pp. 41–43.

14. Ibid., pp. 43–44.

15. J. Hampden Dougherty, *The Electoral System of the United States* (New York, 1906), pp. 392–93.

16. Dixon, loc. cit., p. 217.

17. "The Electoral College: Operation and Effect of Proposed Amendments," memorandum prepared by the staff of the Senate Judiciary Committee, Subcommittee on Constitutional Amendments, Oct. 10, 1961, p. 16 (hereafter cited as 1961 Senate Committee Memorandum).

18. Dixon, loc. cit., p. 217. Other instances where close votes resulted in election of split elector slates: North Dakota in 1892 (1 Republican, 2 Democratic electors); Maryland in 1908 (2 Republican, 6 Democratic); Ohio in 1892 (22 Republican, 1 Democratic); West Virginia in 1916 (7 Republican, 1 Democratic); California in 1880 (5 Republican, 1 Democratic); California in 1892 (8 Democratic, 1 Republican). See Wilmerding, op. cit., p. 74.

19. O'Neil, op. cit., p. 48.

20. Wilmerding, op. cit., p. 174.

21. Cited by O'Neil, op. cit., p. 56.

22. 1826 Senate Report, p. 4.

23. Cited by Dougherty, op. cit., p. 250.

24. Ibid., p. 251.

25. Justice Jackson's inspiration obviously came from a song by Sir Joseph Porter and the chorus in act I of Gilbert and Sullivan's *Pinafore*:

> I grew so rich that I was sent
> By a pocket borough into Parliament.
> I always voted at my party's call,
> And I never thought of thinking for myself at all.

W.S. Gilbert and Arthur Sullivan, *H.M.S. Pinafore, or, The Lass That Loved a Sailor* (Boston, 1880), p. 36.

26. *Ray v. Blair*, 343 U.S. 214.

27. *Rotarian* magazine, July 1949.

28. 1826 Senate Report, p. 5.

29. Cited by Edward S. Corwin, *The President, Office and Powers* (New York, 1957), p. 41.

30. Everett S. Brown, *William Plumer's Memorandum of Proceedings in the United States Senate* (New York, 1932), p. vii, cited by Wilmerding, op. cit., p. 176.

31. John Bach McMaster, *A History of the People of the United States from the Revolution to the Civil War*, 8 vols. (New York, 1893-1924), V, pp. 74-75; A. R. Newsome, *The Presidential Election of 1824 in South Carolina* (Chapel Hill, N.C., 1939), chap. 8, cited by Wilmerding, op. cit., pp. 177–78.

32. Wilmerding, op. cit., pp. 178–79.

33. *New York Times*, Dec. 18, 1956.

34. 1961 Senate *Hearings*, pp. 445–46, 634. The television program, reprinted in the *Hearings*, was a *CBS Reports* program of Jan. 5, 1961.

35. Letter from Lowell to Leslie Stephen, quoted in Horace Elisha Scudder, *James Russell Lowell* (Boston, 1901), I, p.217.

36. 1961 Senate *Hearings* p. 446 (in transcript of *CBS Reports* program).

37. Robert L. Tienken, *Proposals to Reform Our Electoral System*, Legislative Reference Service, Library of Congress (Washington, 1966), pp. 9-11 (hereafter cited as 1966 LRS Report).

38. U.S. Congress, House, Committee on the Judiciary Subcommittee No. 5, *Hearings, Amending the Constitution with Respect to Election of President and Vice President* 81st Cong., 1st sess. 1949, p. 148 (hereafter cited as 1949 House *Hearings*).

39. The fifteen states that require electors by law to vote for their party's presidential candidate: Alaska, California, Connecticut, Colorado, Florida, Hawaii, Idaho, Maryland, Nevada, New Mexico, New York, Oklahoma, Oregon, Tennessee, Virginia, and the District of Columbia. See 1966 LRS Report, pp. 13–17.

40. *Ray v. Blair*; see also, "Presidential Electors," *Columbia Law Review* Apr. 1965, p. 696.

41. Kirby, op. cit., p. 509.

42. Before the 1964 election, substantial efforts were made to open the way for the entry of unpledged elector slates in Florida, South Carolina, Virginia, and Georgia, in addition to Alabama and Mississippi. In each case, an effort was made to get the legislature, or party committees if they had sufficient authority under state law, to authorize unpledged states. Democrats loyal to the national party were able to thwart most of these moves, however. In the case of Florida, President Kennedy reportedly made a personal telephone call to the House Speaker to prevent passage of enabling legislation for independent electors. See *Congressional Quarterly Weekly Report*, June 14, 1963, p. 969, and Sept. 13, 1963, p. 1572. Alabama Governor George C. Wallace announced on July 4, 1964, that he had "definite, concrete plans" to run for president in sixteen states: Alabama, Arkansas, Florida, Georgia, Illinois, Indiana, Kentucky, Louisiana, Mississippi, Missouri, New York, North Carolina, South Carolina, Tennessee, Virginia, and Wisconsin. But he withdrew July 19, four

days after Goldwater's nomination. See *Congressional quarterly Weekly Report* July 17, 1964, p. 1499, and July 24, 1964, p. 1547. For further background on the 1960 effort, see *Congressional Quarterly Weekly Report*, Apr. 1, 1960, p. 569; 1961 Senate *Hearings*, pp. 562 ff., especially pp. 622–25, showing plans to mobilize independent electors for subsequent elections.

43. Rufus King in 1824. See *Annals of Congress*, 18th Cong. 1st sess. I, p. 355.

44. Dougherty, op. cit., p. 226.

45. See U.S. Code, Title 3, chap. 1, for statutory provisions regarding the meeting of electors, reprinted in Appendix H, below.

46. Dixon, loc. cit., pp. 218–219.

47. *Ann Arbor News*, Dec. 14, 1948, cited in *Congressional Record* Apr. 13. 1949, p. 4449.

48. Dixon, loc. cit., p. 220.

49. Cited by Dixon, loc. cit., p. 221. Using the 1948 Ohio electoral college as an example, Dixon listed the array of political paraphernalia sometimes involved in electoral college proceedings: (1) opening of session with secretary of state presiding; (2) calling of roll to ascertain if quorum is present; (3) prayer; (4) election of temporary chairman; (5) calling of the official roll and swearing in of members (the point at which vacancies are filled, if necessary); (6) oral statement by governor of electors' duties; (7) appointment of four committees—rules and order of business, permanent organization, mileage and per diem, resolutions; (8) recess for lunch; (9) reconvening, report of committee on permanent organization, election of permanent chairman and of the secretary of state as ex *officio* secretary of the college; (10) address by the permanent chairman; (11) reports of committees on rules and order of business, on mileage and per diem, and on resolutions; (12) casting and counting of ballots for president and vice president of the United States; (13) signing of the requisite certificates of votes and provision for their disposition; (14) authorization for printing the proceedings of the college; (15) reading of a letter regarding a dinner planned in Washington for members of all the electoral colleges in the various states, to take place on the eve of the inauguration; (16) adjournment. (pp. 219–20).

50. See Lawrence D. Longley, "Why the Electoral College Should Be Abolished," (Speech to the 1976 Electoral College, Madison, Wisconsin, December 13, 1976).

51. Dixon, loc. cit., pp. 220–21.

52. James Cheetham to Thomas Jefferson, Dec. 10, 1801, in *Proceedings of the Massachusetts Historical Society*, 3rd series, I, p. 47; cited by Wilmerding, op. cit., p. 183.

53. William Purcell, cited by Dougherty, op. cit., p. 253.

54. See U.S. Code, Title 3, chap. 1, in Appendix H, below; also Dixon, loc. cit., p. 222.

55. David A. McKnight, *The Electoral System of the United States* (Philadelphia, 1878), p. 15.

56. Dougherty, op. cit., p. 51–57; pp. 86–87; 1949 House Hearings, p. 15.

57. The congressional debates on the challenge to Dr. Bailey's electoral vote are summarized in *Congressional Quarterly Weekly Report*, Jan. 10, 1969, pp. 54–55. The House and Senate roll call votes can be found in ibid., p. 79. A useful summary discussion of these events can be found in Congressional Quarterly, *Guide to Congress* 2nd ed. (Washington, D.C. 1976), pp. 8–9.

58. Letter to George Hay, Aug. 17, 1823, in Paul L. Ford ed., *The Works of Thomas Jefferson* (New York, 1905), XII, p. 303.

59. Cited by John B. Andrews, "Should the President Be Elected by Direct Popular Vote? Yes!," *Forum*, Oct. 1949, p. 231.

60. Cited by Dougherty, op. cit., pp. 23–24.

61. Paul J. Piccard, "The Resolution of Electoral Deadlocks by the House of Representatives," in *Selecting the President: The 27th Discussion and Debate Manual* (1953–54), vol. I, reprinted in 1961 Senate *Hearings*, pp. 826–43. See also the excellent summary discussion of the power of Congress to elect the president, in the Congressional Quarterly's *Guide to Congress*, loc. cit., pp. 5–7.

62. Sidney Hyman, *The American President* (New York, 1954), p. 145; Wilmerding, op. cit., p. 209.

63. Edward Stanwood, *A History of the Presidency from 1788 to 1897* (Boston, 1898), pp. 187–88.

64. John D. Feerick, *From Failing Hands: The Story of Presidential Succession* (New York, 1965), pp. 271–72, 324–25.

65. Ibid., pp. 161, 271.

66. Ibid., pp. 271–72.

67. Corwin, op. cit., pp. 339–40; Stanwood, op. cit., pp. 353–54.

68. Feerick, op. cit., p. 274. The 1873 precedent, in which Congress refused to count the Greeley votes, would not be binding, because Greeley was already dead when the electors cast their votes.

69. For further background, see *Congressional quarterly Weekly Report*, Nov. 18, 1960, p. 1901.

70. In an attempt to show that voters in population-heavy states have inordinate power in the presidential election, the Committee on Electoral College Reform of the American Good Government Society and Senator Karl Mundt at one point advanced a most curious method of computing "votes" as opposed to "voters." In the 1960 election, for instance, they claimed that 7,290,823 voters in New York State actually cast an astronomical 328,000,000 "votes" for president since each voter chose 45 presidential electors. But the voters of Alaska, 60,762 in number, are claimed to have cast only 182,286 votes, since each voter chose only three presidential electors. This remarkable way of counting may be an interesting mathematical game, but it is no substitute for serious analysis. The method overlooks the fundamental—and important—fact that the number of voters per electoral vote is actually much less in Alaska (where there were 20,254 voters for each electoral vote) than in New York (where there were 162,018 voters per electoral vote), a situation that arises, of course, form the "extra" votes corresponding to the senators, which effectively gives individual voters in smaller states greater proportionate power than their counterparts in more populous states. Therefore, the fact that New Yorkers in 1960 voted for 45 electors, while Alaskans voted for only 3, is more than overbalanced by the relevant fact of the population disparity between the two states.

71. In the nineteenth century a few states followed the practice of averaging the number of votes received by the various members of an electoral slate, rather than taking the highest electoral vote. The practice has since been discontinued. The only difficulty in the prevailing method arises in rare instances, like that of Alabama in 1960, when the members of the same electoral slate in a particular state favor different candidates. See pp. 68–71 above.

72. Figures presented by former representative Clarence F. Lea of California in 1949 House *Hearings*, p. 28.

73. See plaintiff's complaint in *Delaware v. New York*, a legal challenge to the general ticket system filed in the U.S. Supreme Court in 1966; quoted in *Congressional Quarterly Weekly Report*, Aug. 19, 1966, p. 1812.

74. Dougherty, op. cit., p. 73.

75. Reprinted from 1961 Senate *Hearings*, p. 670.

76. See 1961 Senate Committee Memorandum; also fact sheet on voting participation, *Congressional Quarterly Weekly Report*, Sept. 18, 1964, p. 2181.

77. Adapted from material presented by C. S. Potts, Dean Emeritus, Southern Methodist University, 1949 House *Hearings*, p. 181.

78. For further discussions of partisan biases in the electoral college, see Michael C. Nelson, "Partisan Bias in the Electoral College, *Journal of Politics*, Nov. 1974, pp. 1033–48, and Carleton W. Sterling, "The Electoral College Biases Revealed, The Conventional Wisdom and Game Theory Models Notwithstanding," *Western Political Quarterly*, June 1978, pp. 159–77; see also the other literature cited in the Selected Bibliography, Part B.

79. The following discussion is based on Lawrence D. Longley, "Electoral College Reform: Problems, Politics, and Prospects," in *Paths to Political Reform*, William J. Crotty (Lexington, Mass., for the Policy Studies Organization 1980) and draws upon research reported on in John H. Yunker and Lawrence D. Longley, "The Biases of the Electoral College: Who is Really Advantaged?" in *Perspectives on Presidential Selection*, ed. Donald R. Mathews (Washington D.C., 1973), and later research presented in John H. Yunker and Lawrence D. Longley, *The Electoral College: Its Biases*

Newly Measured for the 1960s and 1970s, Sage Professional Papers in American Politics (Beverly Hills Calif. 1976). This latter work contains the most complete and current statement of the methodology followed here.

80. See the works cited in the Selected Bibliography, Part B. See also Lawrence D. Longley and Alan G. Braun, *The Politics of Electoral College Reform*, 2nd ed., (New Haven, 1975), pp. 121–28, Yunker and Longley, 1973, op. cit., pp. 190–95; Lawrence D. Longley and John H. Yunker, "The Changing Biases of the Electoral College" (Paper delivered at the Annual Meeting of the American Political Science Association, New Orleans, September 4–8, 1973), in U.S. Congress, Senate, Judiciary Committee, Subcommittee on Constitutional Amendments, *Hearings on Electoral College Reform*, 93rd Cong. 1st sess. Sept. 26 and 27, 1973, pp. 207–10; and Yunker and Longley, 1976, op. cit., pp. 31–44. This literature is subject to a very thoughtful and complete critique in William R. Keech, "Background Paper," in *Winner Take All: Report of the Twentieth Century Fund Task Force on Reform of the Presidential Election Process*, (New York, 1978), chap. II: "Comparing the Alternatives: The Effect on Voter Equality."

81. Longley and Braun, op. cit., p. 115; Yunker and Longley, 1973, op. cit. p. 182; Longley and Yunker, op. cit. pp. 189–200; Yunker and Longley, 1976, op. cit., pp. 9–21.

82. Longley and Yunker, op. cit., p. 193; Yunker and Longley 1976, op. cit., p. 13.

83. Suburban residents are defined as residents in urban areas contained within Standard Metropolitan Statistical Area (SMSA) regions, minus central city areas inside SMSA's. In effect, we are looking at the urban fringe within SMSA's. Appreciation is expressed to John H. Yunker of the University of Minnesota for this analysis.

84. The voting advantage of suburban residents in the electoral college is due to the fact that 49.5 percent of the nation's suburban population is contained in the six largest (and greatly advantaged) states, while only 40.8 percent of the nation's population as a whole is located in these six states.

85. Much of the following discussion was originally prepared by John H. Yunker of the University of Minnesota for the Senate Judiciary Committee, and can be found on pp. 498–500 of U.S., Congress, Senate, Judiciary Committee, Subcommittee on the Constitution, *Hearings on the Electoral College and Direct Election*, 95th Cong., 1st sess., Jan. 27, Feb. 1, 2, 7, and 10, 1977. Appreciation is expressed to John H. Yunker for permission to use this analysis in this book. For further discussion of the controversy concerning the voting power of blacks under the electoral college and direct election system, see the Dec. 1977 Senate Report, especially "Racial and Minority Group Voting Power Under Electoral College and Direct Election Systems," pp. 20–23, and Lawrence D. Longley, "Minorities and the 1980 Electoral College" (Paper delivered at the Annual Meeting of the American Political Science Association, Washington, D.C., August 28–31, 1980).

CHAPTER SIX

1. *New York Times*, Mar. 12, 1950.

2. Computed from Herman V. Ames, "Proposed Amendments to the Constitution of the United States During the First Century of Its History," *Annual Report of the American Historical Association for 1896* (Washington, D.C., 1897).

3. Count since 1889 based on various compilations by the Legislative Reference Service of the Library of Congress and Congressional Quarterly Service. Between 1889 and 1946, 109 amendments on presidential election were offered; between 1947 and 1963, 151 amendments; between 1964 and 1968, 29 amendments.

4. *Annals of Congress*, XLI, p. 170.

5. *Congressional Record*, 1950, p. 883.

6. Max Farrand, ed., *The Records of the Federal Constitutional Convention of 1787*, 4 vols. (New Haven, 1911, 1937), III, p. 459. One hesitates to contradict the "father of the Constitution," but the debates of the Constitutional Convention contain only one fleeting reference to a district system (see p. 23, above), and the question was not raised in the subsequent ratifying conventions.

7. Ames, op. cit., p. 81.

8. Cited by Ames, op. cit., pp. 81–82.

9. Ibid., pp. 83–84.

10. Cited by J. Hampden Dougherty, *The Electoral System of the United States* (New York, 1906), pp. 327, 333. On other occasions, however, Van Buren supported the district plan.

11. Senate Report No. 22, 19th Cong. 1st sess., Jan. 19, 1826, pp. 3, 7–8. Benton reportedly inserted the national runoff in place of a contingent election in Congress on the urging of Andrew Jackson.

12. Giles & Seaton's *Debates*, p. 693, cited by Ames, op. cit., p. 91.

13. U.S., Congress, House, *Journal*, 22nd Cong., 1st sess., Dec. 8, 1829, p. 15.

14. Ames, op. cit., p. 91.

15. Cited by Dougherty, op. cit., pp. 345–46, and Ames, op. cit., p. 93.

16. Cited by Dougherty, op. cit., p. 348.

17. In 1956, Coudert introduced a separate amendment to abolish the office of elector while retaining other provisions of the district plan. But he made no special effort on its behalf.

18. Among those supporting the Mundt-Coudert bill in 1955 Senate hearings was Leander H. Perez, district attorney of Plaquemines–St. Bernard District, La., one of the nation's foremost white supremacy advocates. U.S., Congress, Senate, Committee on the Judiciary, *Hearings, Nomination and Election of President and Vice President*, 84th Cong., 1st sess., 1955, p. 122. But from time to time, the district system was advocated by men of more moderate political philosophy, including Senators Thurston B. Morton of Kentucky and Hugh Scott of Pennsylvania.

19. *Congressional Record*, 1956, pp. 5352–53.

20. Ibid., pp. 5150, 5253, 5539–40, 5548.

21. Ibid., p. 5555.

22. U.S., Congress, Senate, Committee on the Judiciary, Subcommittee on Constitutional Amendments, *Hearings, Nomination and Election of President and Vice President and Qualifications for Voting*, 87th Cong., 1st sess., 1961, pp. 52, 172, 332–33 (hereafter cited as 1961 Senate *Hearings*).

23. Ibid., pp. 519, 676.

24. *The Electoral College*, a memorandum (Washington, D.C., 1961).

25. Letter to James Monroe, Jan. 12, 1800, cited by Lucius Wilmerding, *The Electoral College* (New Brunswick, N.J., 1958), p. 145. Wilmerding disagrees with Jefferson's contention, however, claiming that the disfranchised votes for both candidates would more likely balance out on a multidistrict system than when the states are the smallest unit.

26. District system vote calculations by Congressional Quarterly Service and the sources cited in Appendix M. For comparison with the disparity between the popular and electoral vote under the existing unit vote system, see Appendix D. For actual district system results, see Appendix M.

27. Testimony of Feb. 28, 1966.

28. Lawrence D. Longley and John H. Yunker, "The Changing Biases of the Electoral College" (Paper delivered at the Annual Meeting of the American Political Science Association, New Orleans, September 4–8, 1973), in U.S., Congress, Senate, Judiciary Committee, Subcommittee on Constitutional Amendments, *Hearings on Electoral College Reform*, 93rd Cong., 1st sess., Sept. 26 and 27, 1973, pp. 204 and 209; and John H. Yunker and Lawrence D. Longley, *The Electoral College: Its Biases Newly Measured for the 1960s and 1970s*, Sage Professional Papers in American Politics, (Beverly Hills, Calif., 1976), pp. 30 and 40. The district plan is subject to detailed analysis and assessment, and arguments pro and con are summarized in Lawrence D. Longley and Alan G. Braun, *The Politics of Electoral College Reform*, 2nd ed. (New Haven, 1975), pp. 57–64 and 79–81.

29. The dangers of the contingency election procedure generally are not dealt with by this plan—except that, in all probability, an electoral college deadlock would be made greater since the multiplier effect of the electoral college would be absent. The proportional plan is subject to detailed analysis and assessment, and arguments pro and con are summarized, in Longley and Braun, op. cit., pp. 49–57 and 78–79.

30. Ames, op. cit., pp. 95–98.

31. Cited by Ames, op. cit., p. 97.

32. The proportional vote for each state is determined by multiplying the number of popular votes a candidate has received by the state's electoral vote allotment and then dividing the sum derived by the total popular vote of the state. Fractional votes of less than one-thousandth are disregarded. An example, showing the proportional division of Alaska's three electoral votes in the election of 1960:

For Nixon: 30,953 votes; for Kennedy: 29,809 votes; total: 69,762.

Nixon proportion: 30,953 × 3 electoral votes = 92,859; 92,859 divided by total popular vote of 60,762 = 1.5282.

Kennedy proportion: 29,809 × 3 electoral votes = 89,427; 89,427 divided by total popular vote of 60,762 = 1.4717.

With fractions of less than one-thousandth disregarded, the electoral vote of the state is thus Nixon 1.528; Kennedy 1.471.

33. Cited by Dougherty, op. cit., pp. 352–53.

34. Ibid., pp. 357–58.

35. The proposal was defeated. See p. 158.

36. *Congressional Record*, 1950, p. 884. To allay fears that splinter parties might be encouraged, the Senate accepted an amendment by Scott Lucas of Illinois to require that a candidate receive at least 40 percent of the proportionalized electoral vote to be elected, with the choice of a president going to a joint session of Congress, in which each senator and representative would have a single vote, when 40 percent was not achieved.

37. *Congressional Record*, 1950, pp. 1064–65.

38. Ibid., p. 1269.

39. Ibid., p. 886.

40. Ibid., p. 1066.

41. Wright Patman, "Should the United States Abolish the Electoral College? No!" *Rotarian*, July 1949.

42. *Congressional Record*, 1950, p. 886.

43. Ibid., p. 880. Lodge personally favored the direct vote but felt it could not pass because of small-state opposition. See pp. 163–64.

44. *Congressional Record*, 1950, p. 1278; individual votes also recorded in Congressional Quarterly, *Congress and the Nation* (Washington, D.C., 1965), p. 51a.

45. *Congressional Record*, 1950, p. 10416.

46. Ibid., p. 10417.

47. Ibid., p. 10425.

48. Ibid., p. 10427; *Congress and the Nation*, as cited, p. 54a.

49. U.S., Congress, House, Committee on the Judiciary, *Hearings, Amending the Constitution With Respect to Election of President and Vice President*, 82nd Cong., 1st sess., 1951, pp. 305–08 (hereafter cited as 1951 House *Hearings*).

50. 1951 House *Hearings*, pp. 308–10.

51. For debate relevant to the district system portion of the Daniel substitute, see pp. 151–53.

52. Figures based on a study by Dr. Ruth Silva of Pennsylvania State University. The Republican electoral vote percentage would have lagged behind the Republican popular vote percentage by percentage point gaps ranging from −.004 in 1904 to −5.316 in 1924. *Congressional Record*, 1956, p. 5564.

53. *Congressional Record*, 1956, p. 5564. Douglas produced figures to show that in the 1952 presidential election the voting turnout—measured in the percentage of voting-age citizens actually casting ballots for president—was 39.1 percent in the 11 states of the Deep South, 66.4 percent in 5 border states, and 70.2 percent in the remaining 32 northern states. *Congressional Record*, 1956, p. 5550.

54. The amendment provided for election of the president in a joint session of Congress, with each member casting a single vote, in cases where the requisite percentage was not achieved. For amendment text, see *Congressional Record*, 1956, pp. 5644–46.

55. Ibid., 1956, pp. 5249–50, 5555, 5558.

56. Ibid., p. 5159.

57. Ibid., p. 5156.

58. Ibid., pp. 5673–74; *Congressional Quarterly Almanac*, 1956, p. 161.

59. 1961 Senate *Hearings*, pp. 169, 466.

60. Ibid., pp. 253–54, 365.

61. Kefauver, "The Electoral College: Old Reforms Take on a New Look," *Law and Contemporary Problems*, Spring 1962, p. 203.

62. A significant distinction between the two kinds of minor or splinter parties was made by Prof. Allan P. Sindler of Duke University in a 1962 essay, "Presidential Election Methods and Urban-Ethnic Interests," *Law and Contemporary Problems*, Spring 1962, pp. 221–24. The "guarantee" of electoral votes under a proportional system would offer no new inducement, he said, to "ideologically-oriented third parties outside the mainstream of national power politics, such as Vegetarians, Socialist Workers, Single Taxers, etc." The real problem, he suggested was in "blackmail" factional defection such as the 1948 Progressive and Dixiecrat movements, which constituted "a punitive flank attack, from opposite ideological directions, on the Democratic party." Sindler suggested that the existing unit vote system "can be exploited, and in that sense, invites exploitation, by *ad hoc*, transitory third-party activity" of the latter type.

63. 1961 Senate *Hearings*, pp. 509–10.

64. In Appendix M, the 1960 proportional plan vote is reported as 266.1 Nixon, 265.6 Kennedy, and 5.3 other. These figures are based on the arbitrary division of the Democratic electoral vote in Alabama, which was split between pledged and unpledged electors. Different figures for the proportional plan in the 1960 election are reported in Figure 1, which are based on an alternative basis of determining the Democratic vote in Alabama. The Nixon lead under the proportional plan in 1960 would be due to quirks in the distribution of the two candidates' votes. For example, in 1960, Kennedy received 50.1 percent of Illinois's popular vote. Under the existing electoral college arrangement he consequently obtained all 27 of that state's electoral votes. Under the proportional plan Kennedy would have received 13.577 electoral votes from Illinois, while Nixon would have received 13.471 electoral votes. Anthony Lewis, "The Case against Electoral Reform," *Reporter*, Dec. 8, 1960, p. 31. The proportional plan results for all the states in 1960 can be found in U.S., Congress, House, Judiciary Committee *Hearings on Electoral College Reform*, 91st Cong., 1st sess., Feb. and Mar. 1969 (hereafter cited as 1969 House *Hearings*), pp. 980–81.

65. Longley and Yunker, op. cit., pp. 201, 209; Yunker and Longley, 1976, op. cit., pp. 30, 39.

66. Testimony of Feb. 28, 1966.

67. Testimony of Mar. 8, 1966.

68. Letter from Jefferson to Gallatin, Sept. 18, 1801, in Jefferson, *Works*, IX, cited by Wilmerding, op. cit., p. 170.

69. The automatic plan is subject to detailed analysis and assessment, and arguments pro and con are summarized in Longley and Braun, op. cit., pp. 43–49, 76–78.

70. Ames, op. cit., pp. 94–95.

71. Ibid., pp. 94, 99.

72. U.S., Congress House, *Journal*, 42nd Cong. 1st sess., pp. 14–15.

73. Norris frequently spoke of the need to abolish the electoral college, but by that he meant simply instituting the automatic system. His words, however, could be used in the direct popular vote cause today. In 1923, he said, "No reason can be given why an independent people, capable of self-government, should not have the right to vote directly for the chief magistrate, who has more power than any other official in our government." Norris said the electoral college was "unnecessary, cumbersome and confusing" and could take from the voter "the right to effectively express his will." *Congressional Record*, 1923, p. 3506.

74. Ibid., 1934, pp. 8944-45, 9127. On reconsideration the day after its initial defeat, the Norris amendment was again defeated, this time 52–29.

75. Ibid., 1950, pp. 1277–78.

76. Ibid., 1956, p. 5574.

77. The Kennedy amendment provided for contigent election by joint session of Congress, with each member having a single vote and a plurality sufficient to elect, if no candidate won an electoral vote winners. For text, see 1961 Senate *Hearings*, pp. 371–72.

78. 1961 Senate *Hearings*, pp. 258–59, 337, 363.

79. *Congressional Quarterly Weekly Report*, Feb. 5, 1965, pp. 171, 211.

80. Ibid., Jan. 28, 1966, p. 307; Mar. 11, 1966, pp. 557–58; Mar. 18, 1966, p. 603.

81. Testimony of Donald H. Scott, chairman of the Chamber Study Group on Electoral College Reform, March 9, 1966.

82. *Congressional Record*, 1966, p. 3764 (daily ed.).

83. Technically, Lacock's motion was to recommit the district amendment with instructions to the Senate committee to report an amendment providing for direct election of the president and vice president by the eligible voters of each state. Before the vote, Lacock modified his motion to require only a committee investigation of the direct vote. *Annals of Congress*, XXIX, p. 220.

84. Ibid., pp. 223–26.

85. U.S. Congress, House *Journal*, Jan. 3, 1826, p. 115.

86. Ames, op. cit., p. 88.

87. U.S., Congress, House *Journal*, Dec. 8, 1829, p. 15.

88. In 1838 and 1842, however, Representative Joseph R. Underwood of Kentucky suggested that the state legislatures nominate presidential candidates, with the final choice in a direct national election. Ames, op. cit., p. 99.

89. Ames, op. cit., pp. 88–89; Dougherty, op. cit., pp. 342–44.

90. *Congressional Record*, 1956, pp. 5137–38.

91. Ibid., 1950, p. 1273.

92. Ibid., pp. 1269–70. Taft had reservations about giving up the state unit vote system, however, and said he would not favor direct vote "unless such a course seemed to be the only solution."

93. *Congressional Record*, 1953, p. 1726.

94. Ibid., 1950, p. 5138.

95. Ibid., 1947, p. 1962.

96. Ibid., 1950, pp. 1276–77.

97. Ibid., 1956, pp. 5159, 5245, 5637, 5657; *Congressional Quarterly Almanac*, 1956, p. 161.

98. *Congressional Record*, 1956, p. 5162.

99. 1961 Senate *Hearings*, pp. 31, 501.

100. Ibid., p. 140, 326, 330.

101. Ibid., p. 114.

102. *Congressional Record*, 1961, p. 350.

103. 1961 Senate *Hearings*, p. 425. A similar provision was included in a direct vote amendment introduced by Senator Everett McKinley Dirksen in 1967, with the assistance of the American Bar Association. For fuller discussion of procedures in calling state ratifying conventions, see 1961 Senate *Hearings*, p. 939.

104. *Congressional Quarterly Weekly Report*, May 20, 1966, p. 1042.

105. Ibid.

106. Ibid., Aug. 19, 1966, pp. 1811–15.

107. Ibid., Jan. 6, 1967, p. 28.

108. For complete state-by-state table, see ibid., Dec. 16, 1966, p. 3030.

109. Before the 1967–68 Senate hearings went to press, an advance copy of the entire Banzhaf article was made available and was reprinted on pp. 904–47 of these hearings.

110. The Banzhaf article was later reprinted in 1969 House *Hearings*, pp. 309–52; and Judiciary Committee, Subcommittee on Constitutional Amendments, Senate, *Hearings on Electing the President*, 91st Cong., 1st sess., Jan., Mar., Apr., and May, 1969, pp. 823–66. The original tables themselves were reprinted even more widely including in various Senate and House committee reports from 1969 on and in the appendixes of several books of this period. Throughout this time, Mr. Banzhaf's findings served as grist for the polemic arguments of both sides, some using his data to show the inequities of the present electoral college and most alternative plans and others using his data to prove the necessity of retaining a defense for the large states or for other favored groups.

111. See chapter 5, section entitled "The Biases of the Electoral College"; Lawrence D. Longley and John H. Yunker, "Who Is Really Advantaged by the Electoral College—and Who Just Thinks

He Is?'' (Paper delivered at the Annual Meeting of the American Political Science Association, Chicago, September 7–11, 1971); John H. Yunker and Lawrence D. Longley, ''The Biases of the Electoral College: Who Is Really Advantaged?'' in *Perspectives on Presidential Selection*, ed. Donald R. Matthews (Washington, D.C., 1973); Longley and Yunker, 1973, op. cit; and Yunker and Longley, 1976, op. cit.

112. Arthur M. Schlesinger, Jr., ''If You Abolish the Electoral College, Why Not the Senate, Too,'' *Los Angeles Times*, Apr. 10, 1977.

113. Hybrids and other miscellaneous plans are subject to detailed analysis and assessment, and arguments pro and con are summarized, in Longley and Braun, op. cit., pp. 69–73 and 81–82.

114. Ames, op. cit., pp. 100–01; cited by Charles A. O'Neil, *The American Electoral System* (New York, 1887), pp. 257–58.

115. Ames, op. cit., p. 101.

116. Ibid., p. 103.

117. Ibid., p. 104.

118. Ibid., p. 102.

119. Ibid., p. 100.

120. Ibid., pp. 105, 234–35.

121. *Congressional Record*, 1956, p. 5365. For full discussion, see Ralph M. Goldman, ''Hubert Humphrey's S.J. 152: A New Proposal for Electoral College Reform,'' *Midwest Journal of Political Science*, Feb. 1958, p. 89.

122. *Congressional Quarterly Weekly Report*, Feb. 17, 1961, p. 288.

123. The national bonus plan would also do away with electors, with electoral votes being automatically determined. The task force plan also provides for a runoff election in the unlikely instance that no candidate receives a majority of electoral votes. This runoff would be between the top two candidates in electoral votes and would once again be in terms of the traditional electoral votes plus a winner-take-all pool of 102 bonus votes. Task Force member Neal Peirce dissented from the report in this regard, calling instead for a simple direct election runoff should one be necessary. All were in agreement that any runoff was quite unlikely ever to be necessary because of the effect of the bonus 102 electoral votes. Even more importantly, all agreed that this plan would virtually ensure the electoral college's election of the popular vote leader. See: *Winner Take All: Report of the Twentieth Century Fund Task Force on Reform of the Presidential Election Process* (New York, 1978); Neal Peirce, ''A Plan to Break Electoral College Logjam,'' *Minneapolis Tribune*, Mar. 19, 1978, and in many other newspapers nationally as a syndicated column; *Congressional Quarterly Weekly Report*, Mar. 25, 1978, p. 753; and Thomas E. Cronin, ''Instead, 640 Electors,'' *New York Times*, May 1, 1978, ''The Direct Vote and the Electoral College: The Case for Messing Things Up,'' paper prepared for delivery at the Center for the Study of Democratic Institutions, Santa Barbara, Calif. June 26, 1978, and ''Choosing a President,'' *The Center Magazine*, Sept.–Oct. 1978, pp. 5–15.

124. Ames, op. cit., pp. 105–11.

125. *Congressional Record*, Sept. 18, 1969, p. H 8108.

126. Farrand, op. cit., III, pp. 166–67.

CHAPTER SEVEN

1. Chamber of Commerce of the United States, *Electoral College Reform* (Washington D.C., 1963). Chamber of Commerce of the United States, *Referendum No. 98 on: Electoral College Reform* (Washington, D.C., 1965); this document is reprinted in most of the congressional hearings of 1967 to 1970.

2. American Bar Association *Electing the President: A Report of the Commission on Electoral College Reform* (Chicago, 1967). This report is reprinted in most of the congressional hearings of 1967 to 1970. The members of the ABA Commission were: Robert G. Storey, Texas lawyer; Henry Bellmon, Oklahoma governor; Paul Freund, Harvard University law professor; E. Smythe Gambrell, Georgia lawyer; Ed Gossett, former representative from Texas; William T. Gossett, Michigan lawyer and president of the ABA; William J. Jameson, Montana lawyer; Kenneth B.

Keating, former senator from New York; Otto Kerner, Illinois governor; James C. Kirby, Jr., Northwestern University law professor; James M. Nabrit, Jr., president of Howard University; Herman Phleger, California lawyer; C. Herman Pritchett, University of California political scientist; Walter P. Reuther, United Auto Workers president and Whitney North Seymour, New York lawyer.

3. The material in this and the following section is drawn from Lawrence D. Longley and Alan G. Braun, *The Politics of Electoral College Reform*, 2nd ed., (New Haven, 1975), chap. 5, "Direct Vote: A Goal Nearly Reached." For valuable background information and specifics on the material in this section, appreciation is expressed to the members of the House Judiciary Committee who completed a mail questionnaire, as well as to the following persons who were interviewed in Washington, D.C.: Donald Channell, director of the Washington Office of the ABA; Bess Dick, staff director, House Judiciary Committee; Joseph J. Fanelli, manager of Public Affairs Department of Chamber of Commerce of the United States; Representative Clark MacGregor (R. Minn.); and Benjamin L. Zelenko, general counsel of House Judiciary Committee (telephone interview).

4. See, for example, Alexander Bickel, "Wait a Minute!"; "The Talk of the Town," *New Yorker*, Feb. 8, 1969, pp. 25–26; Gaylord Nelson, "How Not to Elect a President," *Playboy* (Sept. 1969), pp. 141 ff.; William T. Gossett, "Electing the President: New Hope for an Old Ideal", "Electing the President," *National Civic Review*, (June 1969), pp. 241–47; and "Direct Popular Election."; John D. Feerick, "The Electoral College: Why It Was Created," *ABA Journal*, (Mar. 1968, pp. 249 ff.; "The Electoral College—Its Defects and Dangers"; and "The Electoral College: Why It Ought to Be Abolished.", Ed Gossett, "Will We Elect the President We Vote for in 1968," *Reader's Digest* Nov. 1967, pp. 211–18; Paul Freund, "Direct Election of the President.

The most elegantly stated claim by Professor Bickel for the present system was: "It simply happens that the electoral college can satisfy, at once, the symbolic aspirations and remote hopes of the small states, and the present, practical needs of the large ones. Not many human instituiions work out quite as artistically as that." "Wait a Minute!," p. 13. Professor Bickel's major articles in the *New Republic* included: "Case for the Electoral College," "Wait a Minute!"; "Misreading Democracy," Sept. 27, 1969, pp. 9–10; and "Direct Election of the President;" as well as a lengthy piece in *Commentary*, "Is Electoral Reform the Answer?", Dec. 1968, pp. 41–51, later published as a brief book, *New Age of Political Reform*. A revised version of this last volume was published in 1971 under the title *Reform and Continuity*.

5. U.S., Congress, Senate, Judiciary Committee, Subcommittee on Constitutional Amendments, *Hearings on Electing the President*, 91st Cong., 1st sess., Jan., Mar., Apr., and May, 1969; and U.S., Congess, House Judiciary Committee, *Hearings on Electoral College Reform*, 91st Cong., 1st sess., Feb. and Mar. 1969 (hereafter cited as 1969 House *Hearings*).

6. The text of President Nixon's statement can be found in the *Congressional Quarterly Weekly Report*, Feb. 28, 1969, p. 323. A summary of congressional reaction can be found in ibid., p. 308.

7. In contrast the comparable Senate hearings were held by an eleven-man subcommittee of the Senate Judiciary Committee, the Subcommittee on Constitutional Amendments. Although chaired by Senator Bayh, a direct vote advocate, this subcommittee proved to be hostile to the direct vote and only subsequent action by the full Judiciary Committee, ironically chaired by direct vote opponent Senator James O. Eastland, saved the direct vote plan.

8. Within the preceding month, both House Judiciary Committee Chairman Emanuel Celler and ranking minority member William M. McCulloch had publicly endorsed the direct vote plan.

9. The latter point was made in a Washington interview with Donald Channell, director, Washington Office, ABA, on September 14, 1970.

10. Representative Charles E. Wiggins (R., Calif.), response to questionnaire. (see n. 3, above). Much the same point was also made in a questionnaire response by Representative Tom Railsback (R., Ill.), in a Washington interview with Representative Clark MacGregor (R. Minn.), and in a telephone interview with Benjamin L. Zelenko, general counsel of the committee, on October 30, 1970. The Banzhaf findings subsequently made their way into the editorial columns of the *New York Times*. In an editorial of May 11, 1969, that newspaper observed: "Computer studies on the power of individual voters to affect Presidential elections recently confirmed what politicians have intuitively known. Voters in states like California and New York have more than twice as much chance to influence the outcome of Presidential elections as voters in smaller states. More voters

go to the polls in the larger states, but they are able to influence the casting of many more electoral votes."

11. 1969 House *Hearings*, p. 2.

12. U.S., Congress, House, House Judiciary Committee, *Direct Popular Election of the President: Report on H. J. Res. 681*, 91st Cong., 1st sess., May 16, 1969 (hereafter cited as May 1969 House *Report*).

13. David B. Truman, *The Governmental Process: Political Interests and Public Opinion* (New York, 1951), p. 265.

14. U.S., Congress, House, House Rules Committee, *Hearings on Proposing an Amendment to the Constitution of the United States Relating to the Election of the President and the Vice President*, 91st Cong., 1st sess., June and July 1969. During House floor debate, Representative William McCulloch similarly observed: "Although a good majority of the Republican members of the committee favored some reform other than the direct plan at the start of those hearings, 12 of the 15 Republican members were persuaded by the merits of the direct plan by the time the hearings had concluded . . . During those hearings we learned that the direct plan was supported by the ABA, the U.S. Chamber of Commerce, the National Federation of Independent Business, and the AFL-CIO." *Congressional Record*, Sept. 10, 1969, p. H7751.

15. Those opposed were three Republicans, Representatives David W. Dennis (Ind.), Edward Hutchinson (Mich.), and Richard H. Poff (Va.), and three southern Democrats, Representatives John Dowdy (Tex.), Walter W. Flowers (Ala.), and James R. Mann (S.C.).

16. May 1969 House *Report*.

17. Editorial, *New York Times*, June 2, 1969.

18. *Congressional Record*, Sept. 10, 1969, p. H7747.

19. Quoted in *New York Times*, Sept. 11, 1969.

20. Quoted in Longley and Braun, op. cit., p. 127.

21. The Dowdy-Dennis-Poff substitute amendment lost on a teller vote of 159 to 192, and Representative Poff (but not Dowdy or Dennis) voted for House Joint Resolution 681 on final passage.

22. It is ironic that the House of Representatives should at first in eliminating its own unique powers and responsibilities for presidential selection in the case of electoral college deadlock.

23. Both House roll call votes can be found in *Congressional Quarterly Weekly Report*, Sept. 26, 1969, p. 1830. The final House vote on passage of H.J.R. 681 was widely and erroneously reported at the time in wire service reports, as well as in the daily edition of the *Congressional Record*, to be 339 to 70. The actual roll call, as printed in the later bound *Congressional Record* and in the *Congressional Quarterly*, however, shows the correct affirmative vote to be 338.

24. Longley and Braun, op. cit. pp. 150–53.

25. "News of the Week in Review," *New York Times*, Sept. 21, 1969. It was also noted that the appointment of Senator Robert P. Griffin (R., Mich.) to the Senate Judiciary Committee on September 19 might provide a crucially needed new vote for direct vote in that committee.

26. *New York Times*, Sept. 21, 1969.

27. Max Lerner syndicated column, Sept. 25, 1969. Max Lerner also expressed concern about the psychological loss of the electoral college, which provides a "sense of identity. By being part of the big-state vote in the popular states, the historic American minorities—Catholics, Jews, Negroes—have had some sort of psychological equalization for their minority position." Syndicated column, Sept. 24, 1969.

28. See, for example, *New York Times*, editorial of Sept. 21, 1969.

29. The complete text of President Nixon's statement can be found in the *Congressional Quarterly Weekly Report*, Oct. 3, 1969, p. 1880.

30. *New York Times*, Oct. 1, 1969.

31. *New York Times*, Oct. 7, 1969.

32. For valuable background information and specifies on this material, appreciation is expressed to the sixty-eight United States senators (thirty-six Democrats and thirty-two Republicans) who responded to requests during the summer of 1970 for information about their position on electoral reform, as well as to the following persons who were interviewed in Washington during 1970: Doug Bennet, Jr., administrative assistant to Senator Eagleton; Jason Berman, staff director,

Subcommittee on Constitutional Amendments; Judy Campbell, League of Women Voters of the United States, Legislative Action Committee; Donald Channell, director of the Washington Office of the ABA; David Clanton, legislative assistant to Senator Griffin; Myron P. Curzan, member of Washington law firm of Arnold and Porter; Ken Davis, legislative assistant to Senator Scott; Joseph J. Fanelli, manager of Public Affairs Department of Chamber of Commerce of the United States; Charles Ferris, staff member, Democratic Policy Committee, Jack Lewis, legislative assistant to Senator Spong; David Osterhort, legislative assistant to Senator Nelson; Neal R. Peirce, associate editor of the *National Journal*; Richard Scammon, director of Elections Research Center; Robert Smith, chief counsel of the Subcommittee on Revision and Codification of the Senate Judiciary Committee; and Dorothy Stimpson, staff director, Legislative Action Committee of the League of Women Voters of the United States.

33. *New York Times*, Feb. 4, 1970.

34. U.S., Congress, Senate, Senate Judiciary Committee, *Supplemental Hearings on Electoral Reform*, 91st Cong., 2d sess., Apr. 1970 (hereafter cited as 1970 Senate *Supplemental Hearings*). It was reported that these hearings, and the witnesses for them, had been secretly arranged in advance by Senator Sam Ervin, Jr. (D., N.C.) and Senator Roman Hruska (R., Nebr.), both staunch opponents of direct vote.

35. *New York Times*, Apr. 16, 1970.

36. See 1970 Senate *Supplemental Hearings*.

37. *New York Times*, Apr. 19, 1970.

38. Those who voted for the proportional plan were Senators James O. Eastland (D., Miss.), John L. McClellan (D., Ark.), Sam J. Ervin, Jr. (D., N.C.), Robert C. Byrd (D., W.Va.), Roman L. Hruska (R., Nebr.), Hiram L. Fong (R., Hawaii), Hugh Scott (R., Pa.), and Strom Thurmond (R., S.C.). Those opposed to the proportional plan (and thus in favor of the direct vote plan) were Senators Thomas J. Dodd (D., Conn.), Philip A. Hart (D., Mich.), Edward M. Kennedy (D., Mass.), Birch Bayh (D., Ind.), Quentin N. Burdick (D., N.Dak.), Joseph D. Tydings (D., Md.), Robert D. Griffin (R., Mich.), Marlow W. Cook (R., Ky.), and Charles McC. Mathias, Jr. (R., Md.). On the final vote on passage of the direct vote plan, these latter nine senators were joined by Senators Byrd and Scott who had previously voted for the proportional plan, resulting in eleven votes for S.J.R. 1.

39. *New York Times*, Apr. 26, 1970.

40. Senate Joint Resolution 1 as approved by the Senate Judiciary Committee different from the House-passed H.J.R. 681 in only one significant respect—the date when the proposed constitutional amendment would become effective after ratification by the states. While the House measure provided for a January 21 date, and the Senate bill for April 15, Senator Bayh noted that he had an agreement from the House leadership to accept the later date. *New York Times*, Apr. 24, 1970.

41. Washington interviews with Jason Berman, Sept. 17, 1970; and Malcolm Hawk, Sept. 16, 1970. The benefits of delay to direct vote opponents were clear to all concerned. The reason for such delay on the part of the minority is thus easily understood; however, the delays on the part of the committee majority are less comprehensible.

42. Telephone interview with Benjamin L. Zelenko, Oct. 30, 1970. One of the chief Senate aides working for direct vote concluded that the delay in obtaining a committee vote and the delay in getting the bill to the floor were probably, in retrospect, what hurt electoral reform the most. Washington interview with Jason Berman, Nov. 13, 1970.

43. During the intervening months, one significant external event had occurred, somewhat boosting electoral reform's chances. This was the June 2 narrow victory of George Wallace in the Alabama gubernatorial primary, which, in addition to giving him a base for the 1972 presidential election, revived speculation about the possibilities of an electoral college deadlock resulting from a three-way 1972 contest. Some news reports went as far as to suggest that the renewed Wallace threat might lead President Nixon to push electoral reform in the Senate and, subsequently, in the states. See, for example, *New York Times*, June 4, 1970.

44. U.S., Congress, Senate, Senate Judiciary Committee, *Direct Popular Election of the President: Report on Senate Joint Resolution 1* 91st Cong., 2nd sess., Aug. 14, 1970.

45. Ibid., pp. 24–55, esp. pp. 24 and 51.

46. The League of Women Voters of the United States announced its support for direct election on January 15, 1970, following a poll showing 78 percent of its 160,000 members favoring the recently passed H.J.R. 681.

47. Washington interview with Joseph J. Fanelli, manager of Public Affairs Department of the Chamber of Commerce of the United States, Sept. 14, 1970.

48. See New York Times, July 12, 1970, and Congressional Quarterly Weekly Report, May 15, 1970, p. 1314.

49. Washington interviews with Joseph J. Fanelli, Sept. 14, 1970, and Nov. 12, 1970. See also New York Times, Sept. 10, 1970.

50. A Rowland Evans and Robert Novak nationally syndicated column of April 7 reported that the Nixon administration had seemed to have lost all interest in electoral reform due to a view that direct vote might hurt Nixon's reelection prospects. A public repudiation of the 1969 endorsement, however, would be politically awkward; therefore, the administration strategy was one of "non-response," together with a private hope that the direct vote plan would be defeated in the Senate.

51. Interestingly enough, this criticism of Congress for not acting faster on a matter on which he himself had been so long ambivalent, was contained in a statement entitled "A Call for Cooperation."

52. Washington interview with David Osterhort, Sept. 15, 1970; Washington interview with Doug Bennet, Jr., Sept. 16, 1970.

53. "Hardy College Spirit: Senate Debate," Newsweek, Sept. 21, 1970, p. 42.

54. Fanelli interview, Sept. 14, 1970.

55. Hawk interview, Sept. 16, 1970. This general conclusion was also reached in Washington interviews with Berman, Sept. 17, 1970; Dan Leach, Sept. 15, 1970; and Dorothy Stimpson, Sept. 14, 1970.

56. Bayh, quoted in New York Times editorial, Sept. 10, 1970.

57. Congressional Quarterly Weekly Report, Sept. 11, 1970. p. 2212.

58. Ibid.

59. Comment on the floor of the U.S. Senate, Sept. 17,1970. An inspection of the Congressional Record of that day fails to find that observation remaining in the edited record.

60. See New York Times, Sept. 14, 1970.

61. Bennet interview, Sept. 16,1970.

62. The preceding discussion of the nature of this issue is drawn from interviews with Bennet, Sept. 16, 1970; Berman, Sept. 17, 1970; Fanelli, Sept. 14, 1970; and Hawk, Sept. 16, 1970.

63. New York Times, Sept. 10, 1970. This assessment so heartened direct vote opponent Senator Strom Thurmond that he reportedly began to feel that a filibuster might not be necessary.

64. New York Times, Sept. 14, 1970. This article was resented by direct vote supporters who objected to its air of finality. One key legislative aide opposed to direct vote stresses the importance of this and other articles in the New York Times at this time: "I feel they signaled the death knell for S.J. Res. 1 and were perceived as such by several wavering Senators." Personal letter from Malcolm Hawk, legislative assistant to Senator Roman Hruska, July1, 1971.

65. This senator was Eugene J. McCarthy (D., Minn.) who, on September 15, cosigned a letter with Senator Sam J. Ervin, Jr. (D., N.C.) strongly opposing direct vote, which was then sent to all members of the Senate. In spite of what was described by an Ervin aide as "a sexy angle," Senator McCarthy's position failed to sway any other senators. The quoted statement was made by Professor Charles Black of Yale Law School, and was quoted approvingly by Senators Ervin and McCarthy in their letter.

66. Osterhort interview, Sept. 15, 1970.

67. Mr. Mode was chief counsel of the Subcommittee on Constitutional Amendments.

68. Interviews with Berman, Sept. 17, 1970; Fanelli, Sept. 18, 1970; and Hawk, Sept. 16, 1970. During this time, the Bayh and Mansfield staff worked essentially independently on such important matters as counting votes, with, as one key aide put it, Mansfield clearly playing the role of majority leader, as opposed to proponent of the bill. Berman interview, Sept. 17, 1970.

69. New York Times, Sept. 15, 1970.

70. Ibid.

71. Leach interview, Sept. 15, 1970. Such a cloture vote would also move the Senate along toward adjournment.

72. Berman interview, Sept. 17, 1970; Hawk interview, Sept. 16, 1970.

73. This observation, and much of the preceding paragraph, is drawn from a Washington interview with Robert Smith, Sept. 16, 1970. Mr. Smith served, in effect, as a member of Senator Ervin's staff.

74. This observation, and much of the preceding paragraph, is drawn from the Hawk interview, Sept. 16, 1970.

75. Dan Leach, of Senator Mansfield's staff, discussed, in an interview held on the morning of September 15, 1970, the meeting of southern direct vote opponents currently in progress.

76. *Congressional Record* (daily ed.), Sept. 15, 1970, p. S15477.

77. This cloture petition had 5 signatures more than needed, for a total of 21: 14 Democrats and 7 Republicans.

78. One key lobbyist working for direct vote criticized Mansfield's decision to push for cloture on September 15, because this move may have been unfortunately premature. Apparently, this lobbyist would have preferred to have seen the attempts to work out a unanimous consent agreement continued and the cloture motion held back a little. These goals, of course, would have been comparable with those of Senator Bayh, but somewhat incompatible with the goals of the majority leader. They were also, in the light of the southern caucus decision of September 15, quite impossible. Telephone interview with Fanelli, Sept. 18, 1970.

79. *New York Times* editorial, Sept. 18, 1970; ibid., Sept. 19, 1970; column by Tom Wicker, ibid., Sept. 17, 1970.

80. *Congressional Quarterly Weekly Report*, Sept. 18, 1970, p. 2239; and Associated Press report, Sept. 18, 1970.

81. Berman interview, Sept. 17, 1970.

82. See, for example, Lewis A. Froman, Jr., *The Congressional Process: Strategies, Rules, and Procedures* (Boston, 1967).

83. Since it was an election year, adjournment or recess by October 15 was necessary to allow senators up for reelection some time to make an appearance in their states. The question was not really whether there would be adjournment by October 15, but whether it would be necessary to come back for a lame-duck congressional session after the election in November. It was.

84. *New York Times*, Sept. 26, 1970; editorial in ibid., Sept. 29, 1970; ibid., Sept. 26, 1970.

85. Ibid., Sept. 30, 1970.

86. Ibid.

87. Washington interviews with Berman, Nov. 13, 1970, and Fanelli, Nov. 12, 1970, and news story in *Milwaukee Sentinel*, Oct. 6, 1971.

88. The roll call vote on the first cloture vote can be found in *Congressional Quarterly Weekly Report*, Sept. 18, 1970, p. 2239. The roll call vote on the second cloture vote can be found in *Congressional Quarterly Weekly Report*, Oct. 2, 1970, p. 2296.

89. Longley and Braun, op. cit., pp. 172–75.

90. U.S., Congress, Senate, Judiciary Committee, Subcommittee on Constitutional Amendments, *Hearings on Electoral Reform*, 93rd Cong., 1st sess., Sept. 26 and 27, 1973.

91. The interpretative summary of 1977–79 congressional activities concerning electoral college reform that follows is drawn from numerous personal and confidential conversations, correspondence, and interviews with senators and senatorial staff personnel between 1977 and 1979. An earlier version of the material dealing with 1977 and 1978 events was published in Lawrence D. Longley, "Electoral College Reform: Problems, Politics, and Prospects," in *Paths to Political Reform*, ed. William J. Crotty, (Lexington, Mass., for the Policy Studies Organization, 1980).

92. The hearings were only formally by the entire committee since subcommittee members had not yet been officially determined and were actually organized by the staff of the Subcommittee on Constitutional Amendments and chaired by its longtime chairman, Senator Birch Bayh, Ind.).

93. U.S., Congress, Senate, Judiciary Committee, *Hearings on the Electoral College and Direct Election*, 95th Cong., 1st sess., Jan. 27, Feb. 1, 2, 7, and 10, 1977. All 1977 and 1978 congressional

activity was in the Senate since the House appeared to feel disinclined to expend any energy on the issue until the Senate had shown it could act—unlike 1970.

94. See, for example, "Carter Proposes End of Electoral College in Presidential Vote," *New York Times*, Mar. 23, 1977, where Warren Weaver, Jr. reports: "The President's full endorsement of direct popular election came as a modest surprise. His recent public and private statements indicated that he would support elimination of the electors, and retain in some modified form the electoral vote machinery that distorts the one man-one vote principle in all national elections." The text of president Carter's statement concerning the electoral college can be found in U.S., Congress, Senate, Judiciary Committee, Subcommittee on the Constitution, *Hearings on the Electoral College and Direct Election*, 95th Cong., 1st sess., July 20, 22, 28, and Aug. 2, 1977 (hereafter cited as July 1977 Senate *Hearings*), p. 2.

95. The text of this famous (and possibly unique) letter can be found in the July 1977 Senate *Hearings*, p. 10.

96. See also "Impact of direct election on the smaller states," in U.S., Congress, Senate, Judiciary Committee, *Direct Popular Election of the President and Vice President of the United States*, Dec. 1977, pp. 14–16.

97. Direct vote supporters found encouragement in evidence of continued public support for abolishing the electoral college. A Harris Survey released in late May reported that 74 percent of the respondents favored (and 13 percent opposed) "passing a constitutional amendment to abolish the electoral college and have the President and Vice-President elected by popular vote." Similarly, a Common Cause membership poll found 82 percent favored abolishing the electoral college (12 percent opposed, the rest uncertain). *In Common*, Spring 1977, p. 17. A slightly earlier Gallup Poll in February had found 75 percent of the respondents approved of "an amendment to the Constitution which would do away with the electoral college and base the election of a President on the total vote cast throughout the nation." Louis Harris concluded in his release of May 30, "As far as public opinion is concerned, the opponents of the electoral college system have won their battle." Except from the Feb. 10, 1977, Gallup Poll and May 30 Harris Survey releases can be found in Appendix N.

98. For keeping the direct vote plan alive: Senators Kennedy (D., Mass.), Bayh (D., Ind.), Byrd (D., Va.)—at only the last moment, Abourezk (D., S.Dak.), Biden (D., Del.), Culver (D. Iowa), Metzenbaum (D., Ohio), De Concini (D., Ariz.), and one Republican, Senator McC. Mathias, (R., Md.). Opposed to the direct vote plan were: Senator Eastland (D., Miss.), McClelland (D., Ark.), Allen (D., Ala.), Thurmond (R., S.C.), Scott (R., Va.), Laxalt (R., Nev.), Hatch (R., Utah), and Wallop (R., Wyo.).

99. See Rhodes Cook, "Bayh May Bypass Committee on Electoral College Bill," *Congressional Quarterly*, June 25, 1977.

100. These reopened Senate hearings were technically held by the Subcommittee on the Constitution, but they were in effect, a direct continuation of the February 1977 Senate hearings by the entire Senate Judiciary Committee. See note 92, above. For a discussion of the July arrangements between Senators Scott and Bayh, see the July 1977 Senate *Hearings*, pp. 1–2.

101. Very Little press coverage was given these July 1977 hearings, which did not seem to upset electoral reform supporters. The printed *Hearings* was itself not available until January 1978, five months after the hearings and four months after the final committee vote.

102. The automatic plan substitute was moved by Senator Scott (R., Va.), the proportional plan by Senator Thurmond (R., S.C.), and the district plan by Senator Allen (D., Ala.).

103. The individual votes for both the test vote in July as well as the final vote in September are given in note 98, above.

104. Two things did occur during 1978 that have the potential of affecting the electoral college as well as the politics of electoral college reform. The first was the proposal by Congress to the states of an amendment providing for congressional and electoral college representation for the District of Columbia as if it were a state. (See chap. 5, n.3., above, for details on the temporary change in the size of the House and the electoral college that would result from the ratification of this amendment.) The proposed amendment would also treat the District of Columbia as if it were a state for the purpose of ratifying future amendments to the Constitution. By thus creating 51 rati-

fying units, the amendment would also raise the three-quarters ratifying margin necessary for future amendments from 38 "states" to 39 "states." Also in 1978, the Twentieth Century Fund Task Force on Reform of the Presidential Election Process issues its final report, *Winner Take All*. In this report the task force advocated a new compromise reform plan for the electoral college that would add to the existing electoral college 102 additional "national bonus" electoral votes for that candidate who was the national popular vote plurality winner. This plan has been discussed earlier (see pp. 176–77, above); despite its promise of being a compromise proposal on which electoral college critics and defenders could agree, there was little evidence in the months following its announcement of significant support gravitating to it.

105. U.S., Congress, Senate, Senate Judiciary Committee, Subcommittee on the Constitution, *Hearings on Direct Popular Election of the President and Vice President of the United States*, 96th Cong., 1st sess., Mar. 27 and 30, and Apr. 3 and 9, 1979 (hereafter cited as the 1979 Senate *Hearings*). S.J.R. 28 is reprinted in pp. 4–7 of these *Hearings*.

106. 1979 Senate *Hearings*, p. 347. The complete testimony of Theodore White can be found in pp. 341–59 of these *Hearings*.

107. Joseph B. Gorman, "Effect of the Adoption of Direct Popular Election of the President and Vice President on the Relative Influence of the Several States in Electing the President and Vice President in 1976," unpublished memorandum, Congressional Research Service, The Library of Congress, Mar. 5, 1979. This memorandum is reprinted in the 1979 Senate *Hearings*, pp. 37–p41, and can also be found in the *Congressional Record* (daily ed.), Mar. 14, 1979, pp. S2716–17.

108. Joseph B. Gorman, memorandum to the Honorable Birch Bayh, Mar. 12, 1979, in the 1979 Senate *Hearings*, pp. 42–50. The conclusion quoted here can be found on pp. 49–50. This memorandum was also reprinted in the *Congressional Record* (daily ed.), Mar. 14, 1979, pp. S2718–19, and Mar. 15, 1979, pp. S2840–41.

109. Prepared testimony of Howard M. Squadron, 1979 Senate *Hearings*, p. 220.

110. 1979 Senate *Hearings*, p. 196. The complete testimony of Howard M. Squadron can be found in pp. 187–220 of these *Hearings*.

111. Prepared testimony of Vernon E. Jordan, Jr., 1979 Senate *Hearings*, p. 183.

112. 1979 Senate *Hearings*, p. 172. The complete testimony of Vernon E. Jordan can be found in pp. 163–86 of these *Hearings*.

113. U.S. Senate Judiciary Committee, Report on S.J.R. 28, *Direct Popular Election of the President and Vice President of the United States* (Washington, D.C., 1979. (hereafter cited as the 1979 Senate *Report*.) Besides the direct election plan, this report also discussed other frequently proposed electoral college reforms: the proportional plan (pp. 38–39), the district plan (pp. 39–40), the national bonus plan (pp. 40–41), and the automatic plan (p. 41). The report also assessed the following arguments and counterarguments about electoral reform: direct election would not weaken federalism; direct election results in reasonable majorities; direct election would require broad geographic distribution of votes: direct election would strengthen the two-party system; the impact of direct election on smaller states; direct election would serve minorities; direct election would discourage voter fraud; direct election, counts, and recounts; direct election and runoff; why the electoral college should be replaced; and why direct election should be established.

114. 1979 Senate *Report*, p. 13.

115. 1979 Senate *Report*, minority views, p. 42. The quoted statement, with which Senators Hatch, Thurmond, and Simpson agreed, was by Yale Law School professor Charles Black.

116. Warren Weaver, Jr., "Senate Rejects Proposal to End Electoral College," *New York Times*, July 11, 1979.

117. Warren Weaver, Jr., "Minorities Opposing Senate Move for Abolition of Electoral College," *New York Times*, July 4, 1979. See also Senator Bayh's remarks in the *Congressional Record* (daily ed.), July 9, 1979, p. S8804.

118. Direct plan opponent Senator Orrin Hatch (R., Utah) had himself filed 24 additional amendments described as hardy "discussion vehicles." Rhodes Cook, "Senate Nears Key Electoral College Vote," *Congressional Quarterly Weekly Report*, June 30, 1979, p. 1300.

119. Senator Harry F. Byrd (Ind., Va.) initially resisted withdrawing his balanced federal budget

amendment, but after pressure in a corner of the Senate chambers, agreed to do so on the promise of future committee hearings on his bill.

120. Senator Robert Packwood (R., Ore.) was absent.

121. The roll call vote on S.J. Res. 28, the direct vote plan, can be found in the *Congressional Record* (daily ed.), July 10, 1979, p. S9109; the *Congressional Quarterly Weekly Report*, July 14, 1979, p. 1421, and the *New York Times*, July 11, 1979.

122. Rhodes Cook, "Constitutional Amendment to Abolish Electoral College Falls Far Short in Senate," *Congressional Quarterly Weekly Report*, July 14, 1979, p. 1407.

123. *New York Times*, July 4, 1979.

124. Although the American Jewish Congress and its president, Howard M. Squadron, were central in leading the opposition to S.J. Res. 28, this intensity of feeling against the direct vote plan was somewhat localized in the New York headquarters and personalized in the interest of Mr. Squadron. The Washington-based lobbyists for the Congress were less inclined to view electoral reform as an anti-Jewish proposal. Telephone interview with Marcia Atcheson, counsel, Senate Judiciary Committee Subcommittee on the Constitution, July 11, 1979; Washington interview with Louise Milone, professional staff member, Senate Judiciary Committee Subcommittee on the Constitution, Nov. 2, 1979; and telephone interview with Sarah Ehmann, former lobbyist, American Jewish Congress, Nov. 5, 1979.

125. *Congressional Quarterly Weekly Report*, June 30, 1979, p. 1300. There was, of course, no unanimity of agreement on the historic question of whether the electoral college in fact favors large or small states. During Senate debate on S.J. Res. 28, some senators defended the electoral college on the grounds that it must favor small states because of the higher share of national electoral votes those states have than shared popular votes (the Thurmond–first Congressional Research Service argument). These electoral college defenders would often be followed by other senators who defended the electoral college on precisely the opposite grounds—that the electoral college favors large states because of the winner-take-all feature (essentially the conclusion of the second Congressional Research Service analysis—see pp. 202–03 above). *Congressional Quarterly Weekly Report*, June 30, 1979, p. 1300.

126. *New York Times*, July 11, 1979. Some had problems with the claim that inequalities favoring black or Jewish influence were built into the Constitution. As one Jewish representative from New York put it, "I'd feel a lot better if I could find a supporting quote in the Federalist Papers." *New York Times*, July 4, 1979.

127. Mike Cole, legislative director of Common Cause, was quoted as observing: "It's not an issue that all conservatives are against or all liberals are for. It's not a traditional ideological split." Stephen Markman, minority counsel to the Senate Judiciary Committee Subcommittee on the Constitution, observed: "It's a mixed coalition. It relates to one's feeling about the Constitution." Further confusing the selection were surprising splits among interest groups: the Chamber of Commerce of the United Stated *favored* direct vote, the National Association of Manufacturers *opposed* it; the American Civil Liberties Union *supported* S.J.R. 28, the American Jewish Congress and various black groups were *against* it; former Republican president Gerald Ford was *for* the bill, the Republican National Committee came out *against* it. *Congressional Quarterly Weekly Report*, June 30, 1979, p. 1295.

128. Much of the preceding analysis is adapted from the *Congressional Quarterly Weekly Report*, July 14, 1979, pp. 1407–08.

CHAPTER EIGHT

1. Clinton Rossiter, *The American Presidency* (New York, 1956), pp. 144–45.

2. Carl Becker, "The Will of the People," *Yale Review*, Mar. 1945, pp. 393–94.

3. Cited by Sidney Hyman, *The American President* (New York, 1954), pp. 155–56, see also Margaret L. Coit, *John C. Calhoun* (Boston, 1950), pp. 235–36.

4. *Congressional Quarterly Weekly Report*, April 12, 1963, p. 575.

5. U.S., Congress, House, Committee on the Judiciary, Subcommittee No. 1, *Hearings,*

Amending the Constitution with Respect to Election of President and Vice President, 81st Cong., 1st sess., 1949, p. 163 (hereafter cited as 1949 House *Hearings*).

6. Rossiter, *Parties and Politics in America* (Ithaca, N.Y., 1962), p. 8.

7. Ibid., p. 10.

8. V. O. Key, *Parties and Pressure Groups*, 5th ed. (New York, 1964), p. 209.

9. E. E. Schattschneider, *Party Government* (New York, 1960; orig. ed., 1941), p. 75.

10. Ibid., pp. 81–83.

11. Allan P. Sindler, *Political Parties in the United States* (New York, 1966), pp. 53–54.

12. Ibid, pp. 57–59.

13. *Congressional Record*, 1956, p. 5159.

14. Ibid., 1967, p. S1587 (daily ed.).

15. Testimony of Martin Diamond before the Senate Judiciary Committee, in U.S., Congress, Senate, Judiciary Committee, Subcommittee on the Constitution, *Hearings on the Electoral College and Direct Election*, 95th Cong., 1st sess., July 20, 22, 28, and Aug. 2, 1977 (hereafter cited as July 1977 Senate *Hearings*), p. 153. Professor Diamond's testimony was later reprinted: Martin Diamond, "Testimony in Support of the Electoral College," Reprint no. 76, The American Enterprise Institute for Public Policy Research, 1977.

16. *Federalist* No. 39: "The executive power will be derived from a very compound source. The immediate election (by electors) is to be made in the states in their political characters. The votes allotted to them are in a compound ratio, which considers them partly as distinct coequal societies, partly as unequal members of the same society." *The Federalist*, Jacob E. Cooke, ed., (Middletown, Conn., 1961), p. 255.

17. *Annals of Congress*, XXX, p. 309.

18. Polk's Fourth Annual Message to Congress, Dec. 5, 1848.

19. *Congressional Record*, 1956, p. 5642.

20. Ibid., pp. 5163, 5648.

21. 1949 House *Hearings*, p. 163.

22. *New York Times*, Jan. 12, 1967.

23. The primary runoff states are Alabama, Arkansas, Georgia, Florida, Louisiana, Mississippi, Oklahoma, South Carolina, and Texas. North Carolina and Virginia also provide for runoffs but only if they are requested by the second-running candidate.

24. Other nations with runoff provisions for their chief executives, according to study papers prepared for the ABA Commission on Electoral College Reform, include Costa Rica, Gabon, the Ivory Coast, and Malagasy. The only one of these that requires 40 percent rather than a majority in the first election is Costa Rica. An interesting provision of the Costa Rican Constitution is that if there is a tie, the older candidate is considered elected president.

25. Testimony of Donald E. Stokes, Department of Political Science, University of Michigan, before the U.S. Senate Judiciary Subcommittee on Constitutional Amendments, July 18, 1967. Even in southern primaries, which tend to be free-for-alls with none of the restraining influences exercised by prior official nominating conventions, a study showed that 84.2 percent of 3,105 contests resulted in a candidate's receiving a majority, and thus the nomination, in the first primary. The percentage of a first primary winners would doubtless have been much higher if the requirement had been 40 percent rather than an absolute majority. See Cortez A. M. Ewing, *Primary Elections in the South* (Norman, Okla., 1953), p. 96.

26. Cited by J. Hampden Dougherty, *The Electoral System of the United States* (New York, 1906), pp. 346–47.

27. This conclusion is based on a survey of prominent studies in the field of voter behavior by Angus Campbell, Warren E. Miller, V. O. Key, and others, reported by Ralph M. Goldman in "Hubert Humphrey's S.J. 152: A New Proposal for Electoral College Reform," *Midwest Journal of Political Science*, Feb. 1958, p. 95. Exceptions to the rule might be the unusually strong movement of Catholics to the Democratic column when John F. Kennedy ran for president, or of blacks to the Democrats when the Republicans nominated Barry Goldwater, an open opponent of civil rights legislation. These strong voter shifts, however, took place spontaneously under the special condi-

tions of those campaigns and were probably due only secondarily to open urgings of Catholic and black leaders.

28. See Alexander Bickel, "The Case for the Electoral College," *New Republic*, Jan. 28, 1967, pp. 15–16, and Neal R. Peirce, "The Case Against the Electoral College," *New Republic*, Feb. 11, 1967, pp. 12–13.

29. Testimony of Eddie N. Williams, July 1977 Senate *Hearings*, p. 245. See also Eddie N. Williams, "Would Popular Election Dilute the Black Vote?" *Washington Post*, Apr. 14, 1977: also in the July 1977 Senate *Hearings*, pp. 518–19.

30. Tom Wicker, "Black Voting Power," *New York Times*, Sept. 16, 1977. See also Lawrence D. Longley, "Minorities and the 1980 Electoral College" (Paper delivered at the annual meeting of the American Political Science Association, Washington, D.C., August 28–31, 1980).

31. Estes Kefauver, "The Electoral College: Old Reforms Take on a New Look," *Law and Contemporary Problems*, Spring 1962, pp. 188–89.

32. Tom Wicker, "In the Nation: Graduating from the Electoral College," *New York Times*, Jan. 10, 1967.

33. Figures based on U.S., Census Bureau, *Current Population Reports*, "Projections of the Population of the United States by Age and Sex, 1964 to 1985, with Extensions to 2010," Series P-25, No. 286, July 1964. The Census reports include four alternative series of projections, ranging from the most conservative estimate (321,916,000 by 2010) to the most liberal (437,578,000 by 2010). Projections in this chart are based on Census Series C, the next to the most conservative.

34. Statement of the American Good Government Society, *Congressional Record*, 1967, p. S1588 (daily ed.), in remarks of Senator Mundt. Senator Holland of Florida advanced the same argument in July 12, 1967, testimony before the Senate Judiciary Constitutional Amendments Subcommittee. According to Weather Bureau data on storms and unusual weather phenomena during the first week of November in recent years, Holland reported, voters might have been hindered from going to the polls in certain areas of three states in 1960, in nine states in 1961, in all of one state and parts of five others in 1962, in all of two states and parts of eight others in 1963, in certain areas of four states in 1964, in all of four states and parts of three others in 1965, and in all of two states and parts of ten others in 1966.

35. *Winner Take All: Report of the Twentieth Century Fund Task Force on Reform of the Presidential Election Process* (New York, 1978). For a discussion of this report and its recommendations, see pp. 176–77.

36. U.S., Congress, Senate, Committee on the Judiciary, Subcommittee on Constitutional Amendments, *Hearings, Nomination and Election of President and Vice President and Qualifications for Voting*, 87th Cong., 1st sess., 1961 (hereafter cited as 1961 Senate *Hearings*), p. 61.

37. *Washington Post*, Nov. 14, 1960.

38. *Winner Take All*, p. 12.

39. Ibid.

40. L. Kinvin Wroth, "Election Contests and the Electoral Vote," *Dickinson Law Review*, June 1961, p. 321.

41. Ibid., p. 353.

42. *Congressional Record*, 1956, p. 5648. For fuller discussion on this point, see p. 166 above.

43. Richard G. Smolka, "Possible Consequences of Direct Election of the President," *State Government*, Summer 1977, pp. 134–140.

44. 1961 Senate *Hearings*, pp. 1–2.

Index